A Methodology for Social Research

A Methodology
for Social Research

Gideon Sjoberg and Roger Nett

Harper & Row, Publishers
New York, Evanston, and London

1457984

Contents

Preface

We conceive of this work as a monograph-text. As such it should be usable in advanced courses in research methods and even for some courses in social theory. But we have sought to do more than write another survey of research methods. We have attempted to recast the research process into a markedly different, and, we hope, more useful, perspective by (1) detailing the impact of theory upon social research and (2) examining the impact of the researcher upon each step of the research process.

Much of our argument rests upon a basic reformulation of the nature of theory and theory building. We examine various unexplored aspects of the interaction between theory and research. The researcher's theoretical commitment not only influences his choice of a topic and statement of the problem but it also often affects his selection of research procedures and the specific manner in which he analyzes and disseminates his findings.

The other key aspect of our discussion rests upon the premise that the researcher is a variable in the research design. This premise, in turn, is associated with the sociology of knowledge orientation which we employ as a means to understanding the research process. It is essential that we examine how the researcher's particular sociocultural background affects his adherence to, or interpretation of, the normative order of science. Moreover, we must be ever aware of the interaction between ideal and actual norms in social research.

Our general framework permits us to redefine the parameters of the research enterprise. It allows us to incorporate the initial selection and formulation of the research problem and the dissemination of the findings as legitimate topics of concern in research methodology. Within this perspective, ethical and political decisions are necessarily viewed as integral features of the research design. Before today, these decisions generally have been considered beyond the proper scope of research methodology—but they are not. We hope the present work, by presenting an alternative orientation for understanding the research process, will encourage others to explore issues that have too long been ignored by social scientists concerned with the logic of inquiry and the utility of particular research methods.

As is the case in all social enterprises, we have not functioned in isolation during the writing of this book. We have carried on dialogues with a number of persons who were kind enough to read portions of the manuscript at different stages of its development. Ted R. Vaughan and Jo Lewis served especially as sounding boards for our various ideas, and their many useful suggestions are reflected throughout this volume. Patrick Marnane's critical acumen saved us from several embarrassing errors. Finally, Andrée F. Sjoberg deserves special thanks for her extensive editorial assistance.

Gideon Sjoberg and Roger Nett

A Methodology for Social Research

CHAPTER 1

Introduction

The scientific revolution led to, and in turn was supported by, the industrial revolution. One consequence of the resultant changes is that man has been able to gain ever greater control over his environment and his destiny. His achievements in manipulating his physical world have been no less than remarkable, and this success has encouraged efforts to utilize the scientific method to gain command of his social environment as well. The advance of industrial urbanization has, moreover, made available an expanding supply of funds and personnel for social research activities.

But the extension of scientific investigation into the social realm has been accompanied by strident criticisms from many persons who question the adequacy and essential worth of the scientific method as applied to the individual and the social group. There are those who remain unconvinced that the social researcher can ever become a "scientist." Indeed, some social researchers themselves entertain doubts as to the ultimate worth and possible success of their efforts. Even the most ardent proponents of scientific status for the social sciences concede that social scientists, judged by their ability to predict and control happenings in the world they study, fall far short of matching the achievements of the natural scientists.

But what are the facts (and the issues) regarding the reliability and validity of social research? To answer this question we must examine the assumptions that underlie the theories and research procedures of social science, and we must critically evaluate the successes and the failures of the practitioners in this field.

Goals and Basic Themes

Our purpose is to examine the logical and theoretical basis of social research—its "methodology." The term "methodology" is at times used simply to refer to the procedures or techniques involved in the collection of data. Our application of the concept is much broader. Thus, in our examination of the more widely employed research tools, the procedures involved in the selection of the units for study and in direct and indirect observation, we purposively set them within the context of the overall research process.

We feel justified in concentrating upon the more theoretical aspects of research, because these tend to be neglected in existing surveys of research methods. A wealth of books and, particularly, articles on the subject of social research are available to students and practitioners seeking guidance in the use of specific procedures.[1] But rarely are these examined in their relationship to broader logical and theoretical considerations.

We proceed on the assumption that an understanding of the theoretical bases of social research and the ability to examine one's precedures in relation to the overall research design enable the social investigator to transcend the technician's role and attain that of the research scientist, with consequent gains to the cause of science.

Besides this broad objective of focusing on theory, several specific themes—in general little marked by methodologists—pervade this work. That science is a social enterprise par excellence is one such theme. A good part of our analysis rests upon this elementary premise, the implications of which are complex and far-reaching. Once this postulate is accepted, the methodology of social research becomes a part of the sociology of research. For research procedures themselves are social norms. By examining the research process from this vantage point, we can clarify and objectify a wide variety of research methods. Moreover, this approach enables us to explore topics such as the selection of the problem to be studied and the diffusion of research findings, that are usually considered to be outside the realm of methodological analysis.

Another theme that emerges from the sociology of knowledge orientation is the constant tug of war within the scientific system between order and change. We consider the matter in some detail in our chapter on the logic of inquiry—wherein the ideas of Popper and Hanson are set side by side—and we return to this theme in succeeding chapters.[2]

Then too, the researcher himself is a variable in the research design. He

---

[1] See William J. Goode and Paul K. Hatt, *Methods in Social Research* (New York: McGraw-Hill, 1952); Claire Selltiz *et al.* (eds.), *Research Methods in Social Relations,* rev. ed. (New York: Holt, Rinehart and Winston, 1959); Matilda White Riley, *Sociological Research: 1. A Case Approach* (New York: Harcourt, Brace & World, 1963); Fred N. Kerlinger, *Foundations of Behavioral Research* (New York: Holt, Rinehart and Winston, 1964); and Bernard S. Phillips, *Social Research* (New York: Macmillan, 1966).

[2] Cf. Karl R. Popper, *The Logic of Scientific Discovery* (New York: Wiley, Science Editions, 1961); and Norwood R. Hanson, *Patterns of Discovery* (London: Cambridge, 1958).

influences the course of any research venture he undertakes, and his actions are in turn structured by the broader society in which he lives. To understand and objectify the impact of the scientist upon the research design, some version of the sociology of knowledge perspective is essential. This leads us to examine the researcher's role in cross cultural context, for the manner in which he applies his methods and analytical tools varies somewhat according to which socio-cultural system he belongs to as well as the system under study.

But even within a particular sociocultural setting, sociologists may carry out divergent and conflicting roles. The researcher must often identify with both the "scientific community" and the broader society or segments thereof. But the norms and demands of these reference groups are frequently at odds with one another. Consequently, the scientist may find himself compromising his scientific ideals in order to satisfy other demands—for example, to protect his social position or the image of the discipline itself. These compromises frequently result in modifications in the ideal research procedures, some of which may become regularized and standardized. These discrepancies between the "ideal" and the "actual" norms in research give rise to a broad range of problems having far-reaching theoretical implications for social science.

Once we recognize that the researcher himself has an impact on the research design, the question of ethics in scientific investigation can no longer be pushed aside; instead it becomes central to sociological inquiry. In this book we attempt to demonstrate that the ethical norms arising from one's commitment to the scientific community may be at odds with the ethical norms that stem from the scientist's commitment to the broader society. The scientist's solution to such dilemmas affects the structure of the overall research design: that is, the specific methods of data collection and the analysis of the data themselves.

In addition to the sociology of knowledge perspective and what it implies, we need to pay special heed to the interrelationships between theory and method. Merton, for example, has elaborated upon the interaction of theory and data, and his position is widely accepted in modern sociology. Our argument, however, goes considerably beyond that advanced by Merton.[3] For we seek to demonstrate that certain kinds of research procedures are far more compatible with particular kinds of theoretical systems than with others.

To support these contentions we must, of course, discuss the nature of theory, an area of considerable confusion within sociology. We shall attempt to clarify the meaning of theory by detailing its various dimensions—including the logic of inquiry and the role of theoretical assumptions.

Clearly, the sociologist's theoretical assumptions or premises concerning the nature of social reality or of human nature commit him to particular kinds of

[3] Robert K. Merton, *Social Theory and Social Structure*, rev. ed. (New York: Free Press, 1957), esp. chaps. 2 and 3.

procedures when he collects and analyzes his data. So too, because certain techniques are more compatible with some theoretical assumptions than with others, the scientist, simply by selecting a given set of research methods, necessarily assumes a particular theoretical stance.

The interpenetration of theory and method is heightened by two other considerations to which we shall give considerable emphasis. These are (1) the primacy of the overall research design and (2) the interrelationships among all phases of the research process. It is convenient to speak, as we do throughout this work, of analyzing one's data after these have been collected. Nevertheless, the initial plan, including the theoretical assumptions and the research design, shapes the manner in which the researcher gathers his data, and this plan in turn either determines or, more generally, sets limits to the kinds of analysis that can be employed. It follows that an emphasis upon mere technical virtuosity in research, with insufficient attention to the overall design, is apt to lead to sterile results.

But our purposes involve more than merely cataloguing the diverse problems that beset the researcher. Our objectification of the social context within which the researcher functions, as well as our disquisition upon the relationships between theory and method, has as its goal the improvement of the ideal norms or methods that govern the collection and analysis of social data. In some instances these procedures can be modified so as to make them more effective; in other instances new ideal norms must be created.

Our approach, although quite theoretical, is distinctly empirical. Most philosophers of science who have written on the methodology of social research rely upon a few theoretical works (for example, those by Parsons, Merton, and Malinowski) and usually ignore the research monographs. As Lazarsfeld rightly suggests, these philosophers spend too much of their time enjoining social researchers to emulate the normative order of the physical sciences.[4] But an adequate methodology for sociology must take cognizance not just of the theoretical writings but also of the actions of researchers in the everyday research situation—of what social researchers actually do.

Underlying Assumptions of Our Theoretical Perspective

If we are to clarify the nature of our perspective, we must describe in schematic form the methodological position of two major schools of thought, or intellectual traditions, that have long competed for support among sociologists and other social scientists. The protagonists differ both in their orientation toward

[4] Paul F. Lazarsfeld, "Philosophy of Science and Empirical Social Research," in Ernest Nagel *et al.* (eds.), *Logic, Methodology and Philosophy of Science* (Stanford, Cal.: Stanford, 1962), 466–467.

the "subject matter" of social science and in many of their research procedures.

One of these schools represents the neo-idealist tradition, the other the positivist one. Methodologists generally regard these two approaches as incompatible. Yet we question such a judgment. Certain methodological difficulties in social science can be resolved only if we draw upon the strengths of both of these theoretical perspectives.

What, in essence, are these two opposing points of view? The first, arising out of the Kantian and Hegelian idealist tradition, was dramatized in the writings of a highly creative group of German theoreticians during the latter half of the nineteenth century and the early part of the twentieth. Outstanding among these scholars were Richert, Windelband, and especially Dilthey, as well as the sociologist Max Weber, who drew upon the works of his more philosophically inclined compatriots.[5]

Although these theorists differed among themselves in significant respects, they were of one mind when they argued that the natural and the social sciences are distinctive bodies of knowledge. What is significant for our purposes about their reasoning is that they perceived of this divergence as residing essentially in the nature of the subject matter involved. From this premise that the data of the natural and the social worlds are discrete, Dilthey and Weber, among others, went on to argue that natural scientists and social scientists must therefore employ divergent methodologies and research strategies. The social scientist, for example, must take cognizance of both the historical dimension of human action and the subjective aspects of human experience. Unlike the natural scientist, the social scientist can "get inside" his subject matter.

It is out of this body of thought that Weber developed his *verstehen* sociology.[6] His argument, in broad terms, was that if social scientists are to comprehend the actions of individuals and groups they must learn to "take the role of the other" (to employ Mead's terminology). They must gain an understanding of the author's view of social reality: his symbols, attitudes, and values. Many of Weber's procedures, most notably his formulation and use of the ideal type, rest upon this particular conception of social reality.

Some American social scientists still sustain this overall theoretical perspective.[7] Other sociologists, those who work within the tradition of such symbolic interactionists as Mead and Cooley, share certain assumptions with the afore-

[5] See Carlo Antoni, *From History to Sociology*, trans. by Hayden V. White (Detroit: Wayne State University Press, 1959); H. Stuart Hughes, *Consciousness and Society* (New York: Vintage Books, Inc., Random House, 1961); and Gerhard Masur, *Prophets of Yesterday* (New York: Macmillan, 1961).

[6] See Max Weber, *The Theory of Social and Economic Organization*, trans. by A. M. Henderson and Talcott Parsons (New York: Free Press, 1964).

[7] Severyn T. Bruyn, *The Human Perspective in Sociology* (Englewood Cliffs, N.J.: Prentice-Hall, 1966).

mentioned German theoreticians. However, unlike these latter, the symbolic interactionists are concerned not with historical traditions but with the social-psychological dimension of contemporary social actions. Interestingly, writers like Mead and Dewey, who rejected the idealistic framework, were once students of Hegel; this accounts for some of the overlap between the American and the German writers.

One of the most outspoken champions of the symbolic interactionist position in recent decades has been Herbert Blumer.[8] Significantly, Blumer espouses the view that the subject matter, and consequently the methodological structure, of the natural and of the social sciences is distinctly different. Blumer stresses not only the subjective facet of human action but also the evolutionary creativeness of the "social act." For him, men are continually remaking their social and physical environment; the social order is constantly in a state of becoming. Much of Blumer's insistence upon the priority of "sensitizing concepts" over operationally defined ones follows logically from the idea of the emergent act. For he holds that scientists can not impose fixed, rigid categories upon a social world in the throes of evolution.

One major weakness of the neo-idealist orientation, most markedly displayed in the works of the German theorists such as Dilthey, is the tendency to lapse into (or even openly to espouse) "historicism."[9] In an extreme form, scholars in this tradition assume that each sociocultural system has its own laws and destiny and that in effect a social scientist can do no more than grasp the essence of each culture and its dynamics. But the historicist (or cultural relativist) position leads to a denial of the very possibility of obtaining objective knowledge and consequently of any generalizing science of society. Such a position, in our judgment, is untenable; it ignores the existence of a degree of unity among human beings and their cultures. Moreover, the idea that each culture is governed by its own laws is itself a universal that points up a basic contradiction in the historicist's thinking. Our goal is more, not less, objectivity.

Those neo-idealists who, like Max Weber, have tended to reject extreme

[8] Herbert Blumer, "Society as Symbolic Interaction," in Arnold Rose (ed.), *Human Behavior and Social Processes* (Boston: Houghton Mifflin, 1962), 20–38; and Herbert Blumer, "What is Wrong with Social Theory?" *American Sociological Review,* 19 (February, 1954), 3–10. Although we use Blumer's writings as illustrative of the symbolic interactionist position, it should be recognized that there is another group of symbolic interactionists, one that has adopted a number of elements of the positivist tradition. See, e.g., Manford H. Kuhn, "Major Trends in Symbolic Interaction Theory in the Past Twenty-five Years," *Sociological Quarterly,* 5 (Winter, 1964), 61–84. Other articles in this issue reflect Kuhn's approach.

[9] The term "historicism" is not without ambiguity. See Dwight E. Lee and Robert N. Beck, "The Meaning of 'Historicism,'" *American Historical Review,* 59 (April, 1954), 568–577; and Calvin G. Rand, "Two Meanings of Historicism in the Writings of Dilthey, Troeltsch, and Meinecke," *Journal of the History of Ideas,* 25 (October–December, 1964) 503–518.

historicism, still find themselves bound by other strictures. They have, for instance, failed to recognize that the scientific method in the natural sciences and that in the social sciences have some abstract principles in common and have generally failed to place the contributions of the positivists to the study of society in sociological perspective. In addition, those like Weber and his followers, though they assume that some objective knowledge is possible, continue to take the means for its attainment all too much for granted, and in the end they become more committed to a form of historicism than is generally recognized.[10]

In the end, we reject certain features of the neo-idealist position as it has been formulated in the literature. But we also recognize that the implications of the neo-idealist's insistence upon the divergency between the subject matter of the natural sciences and that of the social sciences has not been carefully explored. The nature of one's data affects the application of one's research methods and the reliability and validity of one's findings as well.

Aligned against those social scientists who hold that the social and the natural sciences are distinct branches of knowledge are the adherents of positivism or of the "natural science" approach. Positivism, of course, has a long and complex history.[11] There is the positivism of Comte, that of Karl Pearson, and that of the Vienna Circle and Bridgman on whom Lundberg, among others, has relied. A fourth perspective, which emerged in the past decade or so, is reflected in the works of such philosophers of science as Hempel and the sociologist Schrag.[12] The last-mentioned writers are apt to refer to themselves as logical empiricists rather than positivists.

Although we recognize the changing formulations of the positivists over time, certain ideas constantly reappear in their writings. First, the positivists assume that scientists can, almost automatically, attain objective knowledge in the study of both the social and the natural worlds. Second, they argue that the natural and social sciences share a basic methodology, that they are similar, not by virtue of their subject matter but because they employ the same logic of inquiry and similar research procedures. The application of the scientific method is everywhere the same, whether in Afghanistan, the Soviet Union, China, or the United States. Third, the positivists, unlike the writers in the neo-idealist tradition, generally think of a mechanistic natural and social order.

[10] Talcott Parsons appears to belong to this group. See his *The Structure of Social Action,* 2nd ed. (New York: Free Press, 1949), and some of his other writings as well.

[11] On the nature of positivism, see W. M. Simon, *European Positivism in the Nineteenth Century* (Ithaca, N.Y.: Cornell, 1963); A. J. Ayer (ed.), *Logical Positivism* (New York: Free Press, 1959), 3–28; and Edward H. Madden, *The Structure of Scientific Thought* (Boston: Houghton Mifflin, 1960).

[12] Carl G. Hempel, *Aspects of Scientific Explanation* (New York: Free Press 1965); and Clarence Schrag "Some Demerits of Contemporary Sociology," *Pacific Sociological Review,* 4 (Fall, 1961), 43–51.

As we observed above, we believe scientists should search for objective knowledge. Moreover, we assume that the scientific method, in its abstract principles, is unvarying regardless of the kind of data under study. However, for us these principles are of a rather different sort than those enunciated by the positivists (see Chapter 2). Then too, we recognize that fundamental differences between natural and social data affect the way in which the broader principles are applied and that specific research methods and analytic procedures must be adapted to fit the differing kinds of data. Although some positivists admit this at least implicitly, they have neglected to examine the manner in which the scientist necessarily modifies his research procedures when he studies social phenomena.

The social scientist must cope with a far greater range of variables than the natural scientist. Furthermore, the relationships among the variables in the social order are not as "stable" over time and space as those in the natural one. And what is especially significant for us, the social scientist's relationship to his subject matter differs appreciably in degree, if not in kind, from the natural scientist's. These propositions are hardly novel. Herbert Spencer advanced some of them in his *The Study of Sociology* when he wrote:

> Here, then, is a difficulty to which no other science presents anything analogous. To cut himself off in thought from all his relationships of race, and country, and citizenship—to get rid of all those interests, prejudices, likings, superstitions, generated in him by the life of his own society and his own time—to look on all the changes societies have undergone and are undergoing, with reference to nationality, or creed, or personal welfare; is what the average man cannot do at all, and what the exceptional man can do very imperfectly.[13]

What is unique about our formulation is the effort to detail the manifold implications of these issues for social research and, moreover, to accomplish this within an explicitly sociology of knowledge orientation. In addition, we utilize this analysis as a means for suggesting improvements in various research procedures.

The positivists tend to assume, as do some neo-idealists as well, that simply stating that a scientist *qua* scientist must be objective is sufficient to attain this goal. Thus Lundberg, Schrag, and Larsen argue:

> It is not the business of the sociologist, in his work of arriving at scientific laws of group behavior, to permit himself to be influenced by

[13] Herbert Spencer, *The Study of Sociology* (New York: Appleton-Century-Crofts, 1877), 74.

considerations of how his conclusions will coincide with existing notions or what will be the effect of his findings on the social order. However, the sociologist can exert his influence *as a citizen* to insure that scientific findings will be used only for the benefit of the community.[14]

But they do not effectively demonstrate how this objectivity (specifically the separation between the scientist role and the citizen role) can be achieved.[15] True, the positivists may utilize the experimental method (including measuring instruments) as a means for overcoming some of the scientist's biases. At the same time, such an orientation presupposes that the scientist is fully acquainted with his own and the society's impact upon the experimental design. Moreover, there are circumstances where even experimental designs are insufficient to overcome the biases that stem from the position of the scientist as a "variable" in social research.

Although extensive documentation regarding the scientist's impact upon the research design will be provided in succeeding chapters, we should take note here of Bramson's *The Political Context of Sociology*.[16] This study makes it clear that the changing value system in American society has been associated with shifts in the sociologist's research orientation. More narrowly, Krupp in his *Pattern in Organization Analysis*[17] documents the effect of unstated social premises, or ideological commitments, upon the study of large-scale organizations in the United States. In turn, Hirsch has shown that in totalitarian systems social scientists are more vulnerable to power considerations than are physical scientists (though the latter are far from immune to manipulation).[18]

We contend that the positivists must become more, rather than less, empirical if they are to attain the ideal of objectivity that they (and we) hold in such high esteem. Moreover, we believe that social scientists should be able to check upon one another's results. But to achieve this, scientists often must do more than simply set forth their formal research design and their hypotheses. They must also detail their assumptions about man and society and the resultant pathways they have chosen in constructing their design. Their doing so will

[14] George A. Lundberg *et al., Sociology,* rev. ed. (New York: Harper & Row, 1958), 17.

[15] William R. Catton, Jr., *From Animistic to Naturalistic Sociology* (New York: McGraw-Hill, 1966). Catton, a contemporary exponent of the heritage of positivism, also fails in this text, except in passing (342–343), to examine the issue of how objectivity can be attained in the social sciences.

[16] Leon Bramson, *The Political Context of Sociology* (Princeton, N.J.: Princeton, 1961).

[17] Sherman Krupp, *Pattern in Organization Analysis* (Philadelphia: Chilton, 1961).

[18] Walter Hirsch, "The Autonomy of Science in Totalitarian Societies," *Social Forces,* 40 (October, 1961), 15–22.

enable other scientists to determine more adequately whether the means a particular scientist has selected is congruent with his end (that is, his findings). Currently scientists are called upon to accept all too many aspects of the research process simply on faith.[19]

Faced with the overwhelming evidence that the mere desire to be objective does not ensure objectivity, we purposively seek to formulate a methodology that will make possible greater objectivity in social research. In other words, some method must be developed for controlling the biases mentioned by Spencer, among others. It is to attain this objective that we turn to the sociology of knowledge orientation. A critical examination of the impact of the researcher upon the research design is the first step toward objectivity. After all, rational thought, critical inquiry, and objectivity are all intimately related. To achieve greater objectivity we must draw upon aspects of the nonpositivist tradition— upon the works of Dilthey, Weber, and Mannheim, who assumed that fundamental differences exist between the natural and the social sciences.

The Sociology of Knowledge Orientation

Inasmuch as we rely so heavily upon this particular theory, some explication of our use of it seems in order. Although this viewpoint was in greater or lesser degree expressed in the writings of Spencer, Durkheim, and Marx, among other early social scientists, we shall, for purposes of our own analysis, rely upon the works of Mannheim, who generally is credited with the first full-scale exposition of the sociology of knowledge perspective.[20]

Mannheim's work on the nature of knowledge has been a source of pride and consternation to social theorists, for his theory both resolves problems and creates others of its own. Mannheim, although influenced considerably by Marx, also drew upon the *Geistswissenschaften* school of Dilthey and others, particularly in his methodology and his development of the notion that knowledge is a product of one's social and cultural setting. More specifically, for Mannheim knowledge is a product of one's social position, especially one's social class, within a society.

[19] Cf. J. W. N. Watkins, "Confession Is Good for Ideas," *The Listener*, 69 (Apr. 18, 1963), 667–668.

[20] Karl Mannheim, *Ideology and Utopia*, trans. by Louis Wirth and Edward A. Shils (New York: Harcourt, Brace & World, 1949). For an analysis of various schools of thought within the sociology of knowledge tradition, see Merton, *op. cit.*, chaps. 12 and 13, and Kurt H. Wolff, "The Sociology of Knowledge and Sociological Theory," in Llewellyn Gross (ed.), *Symposium on Sociological Theory* (New York: Harper & Row, 1959), chap. 18. See also the much neglected work by Stanley Taylor, *Conceptions of Institutions and the Theory of Knowledge* (New York: Bookman, 1956).

A major failing of the sociology of knowledge perspective is its tendency to lapse into a kind of historicism.[21] For if the social scientist's knowledge is simply a product of his own role in the sociocultural setting, how are "universal" generalizations to be achieved? Indeed, uncritical acceptance of the sociology of knowledge theory leads one to deny "rationality" altogether, to assume that men are not the creators of ideas or masters of their fate but are simply mirrors of social forces and traditions over which they can wield no control.

Mannheim, to his credit, recognized the dilemma inherent within his theory. He sought to resolve it by arguing that "unattached intellectuals" can and do arise and that they are capable of creating a science of politics.[22] In his view, the free-floating intellectual achieves this status by virtue of his detachment from any particular social class, for Mannheim, like Marx, viewed class as the crucial determinant of any intellectual's theoretical system.

But Mannheim's solution can be faulted on several counts. One of the major deficiencies of his argument stems from his failure to examine the scholar-scientist's relationships to social systems on a crossnational or crosscultural basis.

Our solution to the difficulties posed by the sociology of knowledge perspective differs from Mannheim's. We shall utilize this orientation not as an end in itself but rather as a methodological device. Our main hypothesis is that with this tool the scientist can move beyond his own system to a degree, provided he employs the sociology of knowledge as a mirror in which to examine himself in crosscultural perspective. If the researcher compares his own actions with those of scientists in other sociocultural settings or in an earlier era within his own society, he can attain an understanding of the universal problems that face anyone who seeks to analyze human action.

By examining the social forces that impinge upon the social researcher, we can at the very least objectify them and thus bring them to the level of consciousness. This objectification of the social pressures upon the scientist is a necessary, if not a sufficient, condition for achieving some measure of control over them. Sheer knowledge of the hidden biases makes it possible to bypass them or eliminate them completely from the research design. This procedure is in one sense analogous to the eidetic method of the phenomenologists whereby one peels away the many layers of bias in the search for objective knowledge.

That knowledge is to be preferred to ignorance is an underlying postulate of this study. If this assumption is accepted, the sociology of knowledge perspective can be employed as a tool to further rationality as opposed to irrationality. Viewed as a methodological tool, the sociology of knowledge perspective not only prevents any lapse into an antiscientific, historicist position but permits one

---

[21] Cf. Helmut R. Wagner, "Mannheim's Historicism," *Social Research, 19* (September, 1952), 300–321.

[22] Mannheim, *op. cit.,* 136–158.

to avoid, at least to a degree, becoming a captive of one's own time and place.

Although this approach will not resolve all the dilemmas inherent in the sociology of social research orientation, it will lay bare neglected issues and take certain steps toward the solution of problems that have too long been shunted aside.

A Forward Look

The main themes of this study will be developed as follows. In some chapters we shall focus on the theoretical and logical bases of social inquiry, in others, on the sociology of social research perspective. The perspectives as developed in these chapters are used in our interpretation and evaluation of the procedures involved in (1) the collection, (2) the analysis, and (3) the diffusion of social data.

Specifically, Chapters 2 and 3 deal with certain broad issues relating to the theoretical and logical bases of inquiry. In one of these chapters we consider the historical basis of science: the assumptions underlying the scientific method, and the nature of theory and of data. In the other we focus upon the logic of inquiry—deduction, induction, and discovery—as well as upon the major assumptions (the logico-theoretical constructs) that scientists make about their own methods, the nature of man, and the nature of reality and which provide the framework within which substantive generalizations regarding social life are developed.

The next major section begins with Chapter 4, "The Researcher and the Social System." Here we elaborate upon the sociology of knowledge, or sociology of social research, perspective in light of the preceding discussion of the logic of inquiry and the ensuing chapters on data collection and analysis.

Chapters 5 through 8 form more or less a single unit, dealing as they do with the isues of project formulation and data collection. Herein we consider the matter of why sociologists select certain projects and not others, the problems involved in sampling, and the specific kinds of data collection that we term direct observation and indirect observation. Although we theorize concerning these procedures, we take cognizance of what social researchers actually do, not just what they say they should do.

The matter of data collection having been discussed, we proceed to the problems of data analysis. Chapter 9 considers the use of cases and numbers, whereas Chapters 10 and 11 deal with conceptual analysis in social research, including the matter of explanation and prediction. In all three of these chapters, we are forced to retrace some of the steps in the preceding sections as we seek to keep foremost the fact that the various phases of social research are interwoven in complex ways.

The final chapter is addressed to the problem of the diffusion of research findings. One point stands out: the dissemination of one's results to other researchers is a responsibility of the scientist: without this science cannot advance.

CHAPTER 2

Basic Orientations Toward the Scientific Method

A brief sketch of the history of the scientific enterprise provides us with a perspective on modern science and at the same time serves as a backdrop against which we can review the basic postulates underlying the scientific method as well as the conceptions of theory and data among sociologists.

Science Has a History[1]

If science today embodies an approach to knowledge that is far more disciplined and calculated than the ordinary inclinations of humans, it has become so only after a slow passage through many painful stages of development. The earliest step, taken in some remote prehistoric age, was the discernment of predictable patterns in the natural environment. Even this bit of knowledge proved useful to man in his efforts to push outward the very narrow confines nature imposed upon his activity. Earliest man, like his modern descendants, functioned with a mixture of idealism and realism.

Preliterate man's advances, over several millennia, occurred mainly in two spheres: technology (which includes not only material objects such as tools but also the objective knowledge of how to use them) and social organization. The

---

[1] Our discussion in this section is based on the multivolume work of Charles Singer *et al.* (eds.), *History of Technology* (Fair Lawn, N.J.: Oxford, 1954–1958); A. C. Crombie (ed.), *Scientific Change* (New York: Basic Books, 1963); Gideon Sjoberg, *The Pre-industrial City* (New York: Free Press, 1960); and others.

roster of technological inventions is long: These range from the primeval use of fire to the extraction and working of metals and the development of techniques in animal husbandry and agriculture. These technological innovations both depended upon and led to the creation of complex social organizations. For example, large-scale irrigation systems seem to have required the coordinated activity of hundreds of persons operating under an effective leadership. In turn, the economic surplus made possible by such irrigation systems permitted the development of specialists who could direct activities in the technological sphere.

Out of some of those human settlements with a more complex social organization cities ultimately emerged. Concomitantly, the expanding body of knowledge now demanded, and made possible, a small literate group with sufficient leisure time to sustain and add to the society's accumulated body of learning. It is with the rise of cities and the formation of a literate urban elite that civilization, as we know it, evolved.

The invention of writing, among other factors, accelerated greatly the tempo of social and technological change. The impetus given to human knowledge and intellectual activity by the ability to maintain records cannot be overestimated.[2] The written word not only enabled man to build more readily upon his achievements, but it also facilitated greatly the diffusion of learning across regions and across cultures.

From the time of the emergence of the earliest cities about 5500 years ago up to the scientific and industrial revolution in Europe a few centuries ago, advances occurred on many fronts. As we review the course of man's creativity since the dawn of recorded history, we are impressed by his inventions in the realm of abstract thought. The development of the concept of zero and of such logical systems as that of Aristotle laid the groundwork for the modern scientific revolution. Nor should we minimize the contributions of speculative philosophy. Although many theories closed men's eyes to new ideas and knowledge, speculative thought, on the whole, extended man's range of curiosity, to the profit of later generations seeking to break through the stubborn crust of ignorance.

Alongside these more abstract contributions to human thought, which arose primarily out of society's intellectual or learned class, were the more practical technological contributions of the artisans and merchants. Particularly within the urban environment, the commingling of men of diverse perspectives sparked the formation of new ideas and techniques. Arising out of these preindustrial

---

[2] Although preliterate man's thought system has been a complex one, it is obvious that it is literate (especially literate-industrial) man who evaluates the preliterate's world view in terms of some broad perspective. The reverse is simply not possible. For literate man possesses the advantage of written records. These provide him with a scope and a vision that can never be attained merely through reliance upon the spoken word. Nor could mathematics or logic ever have reached their current heights without the use of writing, a medium by which one is able to recall (and recheck) complex thought processes.

cities, too, were certain major feats of engineering, such as the aqueducts and roads of the Roman Empire.[3] And not to be overlooked were the improvements in weaponry, which made possible the expansion and destruction of empires. In turn, of course, these technological achievements rested upon advances in man's organizational skills and knowledge.

Although a considerable accretion of knowledge occurred before the dawn of the "modern era," preindustrial civilized societies, those in China, India, the Middle East, and even in Europe, were fundamentally distinct in form, if not in content, from the social orders that took shape in Western Europe after the sixteenth century with the beginning of the scientific and industrial revolution.

In the preindustrial civilized order the nature of thought and action was intimately linked with the society's social structure, notably the power structure, and overall value orientation. Thus, the literati, the small learned group who made up an important segment of the privileged elite, were little interested in applying their ideas to problems on the practical and mundane level. Typically, these persons were either part of or strongly influenced by the religious structure, one that was committed to perpetuating the traditional, sacred body of learning, not to the formulation of new ideas or critical evaluation of the learned heritage.

Just what was the traditional system of knowledge? Primarily it reflected a particular orientation to the social and physical environment. Generally, these latter were assumed to be fixed and immutable, beyond man's immediate control. Indeed, the natural order was viewed as sacrosanct: One could seek to manipulate it only with dire consequences. The educated man, therefore, typically did not experiment either with nature or with society. Instead, he sought to adapt himself to forces whose workings were beyond his immediate comprehension.

Quite in harmony with this conceptualization of reality are magical practices, utilized in varying degrees by all ranks of the preindustrial civilized order. We must recognize that there is a fundamental distinction between magic and science. Magical practices are predicated upon the assumption that man cannot intervene directly in the functioning of the natural order; rather he seeks to adjust to the natural order and, with the aid of supernatural forces, to maintain the "balance" in nature or restore this balance when "evil" forces have acted to upset it.

The history of medicine, for example, exemplifies the general failure of the literati to seek to manipulate nature directly. In China, India, and traditional Europe complicated medical theories were developed to explain the functioning of the human body. But rarely were these theories tested against reality. Not only did learned men assume that they could not change the sacred and/or natural order directly, but they had a disdain for physical labor, for such was considered the proper activity of the lower classes and outcaste groups. Conse-

---

[3] See, e.g., James Kip Finch, *The Story of Engineering* (Garden City, N.Y.: Doubleday, Anchor Books, 1960).

quently, the early physicians and scholars in the field of "physiology" and medicine rarely resorted to dissecting human or animal cadavers in order to acquire new knowledge or verify existing theories. Hippocrates, although he treated biological factors in naturalistic terms by removing them from the realm of the sacred, nevertheless shied away from the dirty business of dissection. Even Galen, the Roman physician whose writings on anatomy remained the final authority on the subject for thirteen centuries, used only animals to check his theories about the functioning of the human body. When finally his ideas were tested in the sixteenth century by Andreas Vesalius, the first scholar to systematically dissect and study the human cadaver, they did not stand up. The struggles of Vesalius with his empiricist views against the traditions of the ages (for example, to obtain cadavers he often had to resort to theft) have recently been detailed in a compelling manner by O'Malley, a medical historian whose work sheds much light on the evolution of modern science.[4]

But the field of medicine is only one among many that have undergone marked revision since the preindustrial civilized period. Although the Greeks made progress in other realms of natural science, it was typically in areas such as astronomy or botany where considerable description could be accomplished with little need to experiment. To be sure, some historians of science, such as De Solla Price,[5] see certain Greeks as manipulating the natural order to a degree; however, we side with Gillispie, who, among other scholars, stresses the fundamental novelty of the modern scientific revolution:

> Greek science was subjective, rational, and purely intellectual. It started inside the mind whence concepts like purpose, soul, life, and organism were projected outward to explain phenomena in the familiar terms of self-knowledge. . . . Greek science scarcely knew experiment and never thought to move beyond curiosity to power. Modern science, on the other hand, is impersonal and objective. . . . Modern science has not abandoned rationality, but it is first of all metrical and experimental. Related to this is its association with technology as a continuation of that generalized thrust toward mastery of the world which began in the West with the Renaissance.[6]

And bear in mind that the intellectual activity of classical Greece was far advanced over the efforts of earlier preindustrial societies which erected large-scale barriers against any independent probing of the sacred or natural order. If the progress of the Greeks has seemed impressive it is because their activities so

---

[4] C. D. O'Malley, *Andreas Vesalius of Brussels, 1514–1564* (Berkeley: University of California Press, 1964).

[5] Derek J. de Solla Price, *Science Since Babylon* (New Haven: Yale, 1961).

[6] Charles C. Gillispie, *The Edge of Objectivity* (Princeton, N.J., Princeton, 1960), 10.

markedly contrasted with what had transpired before as well as with what was accomplished during many centuries afterward. Their attainments in the field of "science," however, are all too readily exaggerated.

But what about the nature of social science in preindustrial civilized orders? Here some of the same patterns obtained as in natural science. The philosophical skills of various intellectuals—their contributions in the moral, theological, and philosophical realms—rank in the forefront of man's most constructive endeavors. The great religions of the modern world all have been associated with major intellectual achievements of one sort or another. At the same time, the heavy commitment of the intellectual elite in the preindustrial order to the sacred learning tended to vitiate the evolution of any social science—of any "objective" and "value-free" enterprise geared to accumulating knowledge and discovering principles grounded in empirical reality, by which man could manipulate his social environment and thus command a higher degree of control over his own destiny. Instead, the intellectuals, dominated usually by the priestly group, were intent upon upholding traditional values. And given the nature of the social order to which they belonged, one that resisted rapid social change, the intellectuals were able to isolate themselves from conflicting cultural values and, therefore, many of the issues that trouble modern thinkers.

Here again we can cite deviations from the general pattern, notably in classical Greece. The works of certain Greek theorists suggested important leads for later social scientists. The Arabs, too, had their social philosopher, Ibn Khaldun, who wrote such discerning commentaries on the social order of his time that some scholars believe that he, as much as anyone, is entitled to be called the "founder of sociology."[7] Still, in all the varied writings that have come out of preindustrial civilized societies one searches in vain for certain of the crucial tenets that form the basis of modern social science.[8]

Twentieth-century social science and the fledgling endeavors of the preindustrial era differ fundamentally in the kinds of data employed. In most preindustrial urban societies the literati compiled histories, but these were primarily genealogies or records of the leading families and the royal court. Governments amassed certain kinds of data on the operation of the system, materials which are of some sociological value today. And of course there were accounts of military and other events of significance for the society.[9]

[7] Pitirim A. Sorokin, Carle C. Zimmerman, and Charles J. Galpin (eds.), *A Systematic Source Book in Rural Sociology*, vol. 1 (Minneapolis: University of Minnesota Press, 1930), 54.

[8] Of course, modern social science did not develop in a vacuum. Thus John Howland Rowe, "The Renaissance Foundations of Anthropology," *American Anthropologist, 67* (February, 1965), 1–20, believes that Renaissance writers were instrumental in creating a "perspective distance" by which antiquity or more recent cultures could be understood.

[9] See e.g., D. G. E. Hall (ed.), *Historians of South East Asia* (London: Oxford,

But there was a remarkable lack of interest in the society's lower class and outcaste groups. The few records that exist are apt to be the observations of foreign visitors. For the most part, the educated groups rarely interested themselves in the commoners, some of whom were so far below the elite that they hardly held the status of human beings.

Indeed, few scholars wrote about the social order at all, excepting again certain major military, political, and social events. Their all-consuming interests, as we intimated earlier, lay in philosophical and theological issues. Of course, the fields of theology, philosophy, and logic all border on what we consider to be social science, but major efforts at objectively describing or analyzing a society's social structure are rare indeed. Furthermore, the theoretical treatises were often cast in highly stylized and abstruse language. The intellectuals were writing only for themselves and for God—not for the common man, who, in any case, was unable to read or write.

So much for the upper class and its orientation toward social and natural phenomena. The numerically dominant section of society was made up of the lower class and certain outcaste groups, who carried out the menial and defiling tasks and made possible the leisure enjoyed by the literate, privileged elite. In addition, various practical pursuits, including the work of artisans and merchants, were essential if the social system was to be sustained. What is significant is that these practical tasks often involved some manipulation of the natural order. Thus, for example, it fell to members of the lower class, such as barbers, to engage in bloodletting and other crude forms of surgery. The tools that have come down to us from the preindustrial past are mute testimony to the creativity that existed in the practical, workaday world—creativity that had little or no grounding in theory—as the ordinary man attempted, through trial and error, to construct and perfect devices to help him in his battle against nature. Again let us stress that this practical knowledge on the part of the common man was seldom, if ever, conjoined with the theoretical insights of the intellectuals.

Yet the centuries did witness a considerable accumulation of both theory and practical knowledge within the context of preindustrial civilized societies.[10] It was this knowledge that finally laid the basis for the scientific revolution

---

1961). Cf. C. H. Philips (ed.), *Historians of India, Pakistan and Ceylon* (London: Oxford, 1961); and W. G. Beasley and E. G. Pulleybank (eds.), *Historians of China and Japan* (London: Oxford, 1961). There are of course differences among traditional civilized societies, but the patterns enumerated above generally hold.

[10] The manner in which knowledge has been accumulated and sustained is itself worthy of study. Knowledge has followed the spread of empires. Thus, after the "fall" of Greece and Rome, many of the ideas and tools that were employed therein were not only preserved but elaborated upon by peoples in the Eastern Roman Empire and the various empires that arose in the Arab world. A number of these ideas and inventions were reintroduced into Europe especially after the tenth century, there to form the basis of the scientific and industrial revolution that followed some centuries later.

which began to take shape in the fourteenth and fifteenth centuries in Western Europe and culminated in what is termed the industrial revolution.[11] The striking advances that led to the formation of modern science resulted from a merging of theory, or abstract conceptualization (earlier the exclusive province of scholars), with more practical pursuits (the domain of artisans and members of certain service groups). The process, however, was a slow and painful one. Students of the history of engineering argue that even in seventeenth-century Europe most engineering activities were still being carried out largely on an "inductive," hit-or-miss, trial-and-error basis, with little theoretical foundation.[12]

It is significant that the crucial interplay between the theoretical and practical traditions took place at the time of the breakup of the medieval world. As men shed much of their belief in absolutes, they became more willing to attempt to manipulate and control the physical and the social orders for their own ends. In turn, experimentation with the "natural order" led to the introduction of new and heretical ideas. But the traditional social structure did not take kindly to this undermining of the established system of knowledge, with its particular world view. The Catholic Church, for example, often reacted strongly against these new developments—note the severe pressures exerted on Galileo Galilei.[13] Various forms of social control, some subtle and others not so subtle, ranging from censorship and ostracism to capital punishment itself, were employed to stem the flow of ideas that were eroding the fundamental premises of the medieval world.

The crumbling of the old order was fostered and intensified by the heightened contacts with diverse cultures that characterized the golden age of exploration. Europe after the fourteenth century became a receptacle for new ideas that were carried back by travelers from strange and distant lands. Inevitably this growing awareness of the existence of diverse customs hastened the secularization process. In time, scholars such as Vico and Montesquieu began to

---

[11] A number of historians distinguish between the scientific and the industrial revolutions. See J. Bronowski and Bruce Mazlish, The Western Intellectual Tradition (New York: Harper & Row, Harper Torchbooks, 1962), chap. 7. Scholars assign different dates to the origins of the scientific revolution. Some date it as early as the fourteenth century and some as late as the sixteenth. Herbert Butterfield, The Origins of Modern Science, rev. ed. (New York: Collier, 1962), places its beginnings at about 1300. Almost all writers view the industrial revolution as having begun in eighteenth-century England. Although the distinction between the scientific and the industrial revolutions is analytically useful for some purposes, we view the two as part of one process, with the industrial revolution an extension of the scientific one.

[12] See, e.g., A. Rupert Hall, "Engineering and the Scientific Revolution," Technology and Culture, 2 (Fall, 1961), 333–341.

[13] See, e.g., Ludovico Geymonat, Galileo Galilei, trans. by Stillman Drake (New York: McGraw-Hill, 1965); and Giorgio de Santillana, The Crime of Galileo (Chicago: University of Chicago Press, 1955).

reflect upon the reasons for the differing customs and beliefs in other parts of the world. This process led intellectuals to see their own society in different perspective. The foundation for a science of society, as we know it, was being laid.

Although scholars from almost all parts of Europe contributed to the intellectual renaissance, it was in England and northwestern Europe that the scientific and industrial revolution finally came into its own. In England the conditions were even more propitious than on the Continent. The British value system, including that of the Puritans, may, as Merton suggests, have provided a fertile seed-bed for the growth of science.[14] But more significantly, the hiatus between the social classes and the intellectual's separation from the world of practical affairs were not so marked in England as in the more tradition-bound countries on the Continent. And England's contacts with the outside world, reinforced by her growing dependence upon trade, did much to further this atmosphere of change.

The scientific-industrial revolution was destined to affect the entire world. It brought about drastic changes in the European social structure and set the stage for a permanent, ongoing revolution. Indeed, science can be viewed as a social movement in its own right. Scientific activity has for some centuries been supported by a loose, though effective, social organization, and its supporters have had an ideology of their own, tinged with a utopian dream of a more perfect society. If we accept Feuer's somewhat controversial thesis, the supporters of the scientific revolution, as it faltered and was revived in different times and places, had a strong commitment to a "hedonist-libertarian" ethic. Feuer, moreover, contends that only when scientists became firmly committed to such a value system did science really begin to prosper.[15]

The scientific-industrial revolution made social science possible, but the emergence of a true science of society was perhaps more directly abetted by what can be viewed as a by-product of this scientific-technological change: namely, the French Revolution. Without doubt, much of European sociology in the 1800s was a reaction to the upheaval that followed from the destruction of traditional authority and power structures.[16]

---

[14] Robert K. Merton, *Social Theory and Social Structure*, rev. ed. (New York: Free Press, 1957), chap. 18. The reasons for (or preconditions of) the scientific-industrial revolution have been a matter for wide debate. Merton's thesis has been subject to extended discussion. For a relatively recent bibliographical guide to the controversy, see Joseph Ben-David, "The Scientific Role: The Conditions of Its Establishment in Europe," *Minerva, 4* (Autumn, 1965), 54.

[15] Lewis Feuer, *The Scientific Intellectual* (New York: Basic Books, 1963).

[16] See, e.g., Robert A. Nisbet, *The Sociological Tradition* (New York: Basic Books, 1966), chap. 2; and Bruce Brown, "The French Revolution and the Rise of Social Theory," *Science and Society, 30* (Fall, 1966), 385–432.

Such a context makes it easier to understand why the social movement that carried forward the scientific-industrial revolution engendered countermovements of its own. Some of these appeared in the early stages of modern scientific development, during the Renaissance; others came to the fore during the French Revolution; still others were reflected in the negative reaction to Darwinism during the nineteenth century.[17]

Although significant pockets of resistance to the application of the scientific method persist,[18] particularly with respect to social data, the goals and ideals of science have become legitimized in the industrial-urban orders of the West. The physical sciences have achieved startling results, and significant advances are apparent in social research as well.[19]

But at the very time that science has emerged victorious, serious questions are being raised about its proper place in society. Whereas in the nineteenth century a significant number of intellectuals looked to science for a utopian solution to human ills, there are fewer today who would argue that salvation will come solely through the advancement of the scientific method.

World War II, and the events surrounding it, did much to erode the utopian elements in scientific thinking. It became clear that empirically verified knowledge about the social and physical orders could assist various types of nations in attaining their particular goals—be they Nazi Germany's destruction of the European Jews or America's use of nuclear weapons in defeating Japan.

The Nazis employed the advances of natural science, as well as some of the principles we associate with scientific management, to engineer one of the greatest feats of mass destruction in human history: the systematic elimination of five to six million Jews, plus several million Poles, Russians, and other non-Aryans. Hilberg, perhaps more than any other scholar, has documented the Nazis' use of scientific knowledge as a means for achieving "the final solution to the Jewish problem."[20] So too, the development of nuclear weapons has posed a

---

[17] See, e.g., Charles C. Gillispie, "Science in the French Revolution," in Bernard Barber and Walter Hirsch (eds.), *The Sociology of Science* (New York: Free Press, 1962), chap. 5; and John C. Greene, *Darwin and the Modern World View* (New York: New American Library, Mentor Books, 1963).

[18] See, e.g., Giorgio de Santillana, "Galileo and J. Robert Oppenheimer, Jr.," *The Reporter, 17* (Dec. 26, 1957), 10–18.

[19] The development of systematic social research, which sets off the twentieth from the nineteenth and earlier centuries, is beginning to be documented. See, e.g., A. Oberschall, *Empirical Social Research in Germany, 1848–1914* (New York: Basic Books, 1965); and Paul F. Lazarsfeld, "Notes on the History of Quantification in Sociology—Trends, Sources and Problems," *Isis, 52* (June, 1961), 277–333. See other articles in this issue of *Isis* for the history of quantification in psychology and economics.

[20] Raul Hilberg, *The Destruction of the European Jews* (Chicago: Quadrangle Books, 1961). Hilberg describes in great detail how the Nazis relied upon the advances in natural science and upon rational bureaucracy (with its stress upon efficiency) in their killing center operations (esp. chap. 9).

dilemma unique in the history of science. Ironically, scientists are now able to destroy the very social structure that has made the advancement of science possible.

The Basic Postulates of Science

An understanding of the history of science is essential for any analysis of the fundamental premises of the scientific method. For the premises (or postulates) of the method one employs are in part a product of one's image of the evolution of the scientific enterprise.

Actually, there are efforts afoot to reevaluate the premises of science and the scientist's relationship to the products of his method. As some scholars have come to recognize, the invention of nuclear devices capable of destroying the scientific community itself immediately outdated traditional formulations.

In light of the evidence, it would be a mistake to confuse scientifically based knowledge with wisdom, as did some of the utopian thinkers of the nineteenth century. Wisdom involves sound ethical direction, the exercise of good taste, and distinguishing the worthwhile from the not so worthwhile. The scientific method (in the narrow sense) does not tell us how to use empirically verified knowledge other than to further the ends of science; however, by utilizing more of the empirically validated knowledge and less of the unverified and often fiat knowledge of other epistemologies the cause of humanity may be advanced.

It is by detailing the premises of the scientific method, as we shall now attempt to do, that we can gain a more adequate understanding of this method and its place in modern society.

Like the logical positivists, we believe in the unity of science; but our formulation differs considerably from theirs. The logical empiricists have conceived of this unity in terms of a common method; the natural and social sciences are seen as similar because they employ similar procedures in their research.[21] Our belief in the unity of science, however, is derived from assumptions on a higher level of abstraction (or generality).

A minimum set of assumptions (often left unstated) which underlie the application of the scientific method are (1) that there exists a definite order of recurrence of events, (2) that knowledge is superior to ignorance, (3) that a communication tie, based upon sense impressions, exists between the scientist and "external reality" (the so-called "empirical assumption"), and (4) that

---

[21] This view finds expression in the writings of many philosophers of science. See, e.g., Carl G. Hempel, *Aspects of Scientific Explanation* (New York: Free Press, 1965); and the writings of such sociologists as George A. Lundberg, *Foundations of Sociology* (New York: Macmillan, 1939), and William R. Catton, Jr., *From Animistic to Naturalistic Sociology* (New York: McGraw-Hill, 1966).

there are cause-and-effect relationships within the physical and the social orders. Moreover, (5) there are certain "observer" assumptions: (a) that the observer is driven to attain knowledge by his desire to ameliorate human conditions, (b) that the observer has the capacity to conceptually relate observations and impute meanings to events, and (c) that society will sustain the observer in his pursuit of knowledge. These assumptions, which the scientist more or less takes for granted, are in the last analysis largely understandable as "functional fictions." Their usefulness in the acquisition of knowledge is the primary raison d'être.

THE ASSUMPTION OF ORDER IN THE "NATURAL" WORLD

Science, in so far as it seeks to generalize and predict, depends upon the existence of some degree of order in the physical or social world under study. That which it cannot describe as a manifestation of regularity it must define as some describable departure from regularity. Such reasoning assumes that events are ordered along certain dimensions. To be sure, all systems of knowledge rest upon the assumption of order in the universe, but this may be of greater significance for science than for other systems of knowledge. After all, scientists spend most of their time differentiating among classes of relative uniformity and relating these one to another. Even within a rapidly changing, revolutionary system there is a degree of order. And change itself displays patterns that can be described and analyzed.

The assumption of order leads the social scientist, if he is to remain a scientist, to eschew historicism. Those who advocate the historicist position in its extreme form assume that every cultural system must be studied as a separate entity and that, moreover, no regularities obtain across cultures. Of course, even the historicist admits there is a uniformity of sorts, for he recognizes that each system has its own laws of development.

The notion of order is closely related to the concept of a "natural universe." In our sketch of the history of science, we observed that a major breakthrough occurred when scholars were able to conceive of the physical and social environments in naturalistic terms, that is, as functioning independently of factors in the spiritual realm. This was an essential step in modern man's development of the means to manipulate and positively control aspects of the social and physical spheres.

In contrast, when one assumes the presence of "supernatural forces," one opens up the possibility of capricious change that cannot be studied via scientific procedures—let alone controlled to any degree. In the days when men, including scholars, perceived of their environment as laden with spirits, friendly or hostile, any direct manipulation of these (as opposed to magical practices, which usually attempt to correct the imbalances in nature through indirect means) was assumed to have grave consequences for all concerned. Today scientists believe that they can manipulate and control the natural and social worlds.[22] Concern with nonnatural forces becomes the province of other epistemologies—theology and philosophy.

KNOWLEDGE AS SUPERIOR TO IGNORANCE

This assumption underscores the fact that the chief goal of science is the search for knowledge. It is perhaps the key premise underlying all scientific activity.

The contention that knowledge is eminently preferable to ignorance does not imply that all the mysteries of the universe can or ever will be resolved; rather the scientist assumes that his knowledge of the social and physical worlds can be continually enlarged, at times by accretion, at other times via more revolutionary thrusts.

Of necessity the pursuit of knowledge rests upon the somewhat arbitrary assumption that knowledge is to be desired even where the short-range consequences of new ideas or data are emotional or social trauma for individuals or for the broader society. A corollary of this assumption is that the alternative to knowledge—ignorance—is undesirable and even detrimental to man's well-being. From this it follows that man could overcome the threat of nuclear war, not by lapsing back into ignorance but by acquiring more adequate knowledge.

The assumption that knowledge is superior to ignorance frequently places those who support the scientific method at odds with the proponents of those epistemologies who define knowledge according to their own particular criteria. Certainly the ideal that human dignity is enhanced when man is restless, inquiring, and "soul-searching" conflicts with a variety of belief systems that would strive toward a closed system, one based on absolute truth. The history of modern science and its clash with absolute systems bears testimony to this proposition.[23]

The concept of the happy, ignorant, implicitly trusting individual doing what arbitrarily assumed authority tells him to do is challenged by the central notion of the scientific method—that knowledge is superior to ignorance. This is the main reason why persons who already "know" and feel no need for further inquiry are threatened by the ongoing scientific revolution. It is also the reason why persons disposed to political authoritarianism must argue that science, al-

---

[22] Most social scientists—positivists and nonpositivists alike—seem to agree that some manipulation or control of the social order is possible. But the positivists or naturalists also are committed to a deterministic conception of the social world. Man simply responds to the course of events. We believe that one consequence of man's ability to use scientific knowledge to control his sociocultural milieu is that he can at times transcend what appear to be deterministic situations.

[23] Cf. R. E. Gibson, "Our Heritage from Galileo Galilei," *Science, 145* (Sept. 18, 1964), 1271–1276.

ready too strong to dispose of, should at least be kept on a leash, so that if "wrong" knowledge develops, it can be outlawed or suppressed, or at least condemned as heresy.

The assumption that knowledge is clearly preferable to ignorance ranges scientists against those groups that glorify "closed systems"—those that encourage bookburning, censoring, and antiintellectualism in general. And science, to survive, must deplore any censoring even of persons who speak out against science in the name of other epistemologies. It follows from this position that science gives man more credit for the ability to judge matters for himself and arrive at decisions based upon his own interpretation of the evidence than is normally granted by the adherents of other epistemologies. For science is fundamentally optimistic about human capacities. It is no mere happenstance that modern science and mass democracy are intimately associated. Democracy, in theory, calls for an open society, with an emphasis upon human dignity. This reinforces some of the assumptions that underlie the scientific method. In turn, the scientific method with its negation of absolutes lends support to democracy.

That the scientific method is also processual and dynamic leads it to clash with many traditional epistemologies. Science must always assume that its findings are tentative, that new evidence may change or even reverse existing theoretical formulations. An important corollary to this is that science cannot harbor fanaticism, that scientists must sustain a highly rational orientation toward their subjects of study and toward any new evidence that is brought to light. Only thereby can science sustain the ideal of knowledge as paramount.

With respect to the preservation of the scientific method, the skeptical outlook toward absolute truth is both a strength and a weakness. It is a strength in the sense that presumably rational man will in the long run act to correct his own errors. It is a weakness in that scientists, not being so confident of the validity of their own assertions as is the general public, may, in those frequent periods when social crises threaten public security, be overrun by absolutists. Science is often temporarily helpless when its bastions are stormed by overzealous proponents of absolute systems of belief.

THE EMPIRICAL ASSUMPTION

Science assumes that a communication tie between man and the external universe is maintained through his own sense impressions. Knowledge is held to be a product of one's experiences, as facets of the physical, biological, and social world play upon the senses. Negatively stated, this premise denies that knowledge about the world is instinctive or inborn, that knowledge necessarily precedes experience. Such an assumption is not unassailable, for it depends upon one's definition of "knowledge." Still, from a historical perspective, the notion that knowledge is based upon some form of empirical test was a reaction against the belief that knowledge, particularly moral understanding, has been innate in human beings. Today almost all learning theory is based upon the "empirical" assumption.

CAUSE-AND-EFFECT RELATIONSHIPS

Although the concept of "cause and effect" has been the target of considerable criticism since Hume first argued that no one can observe "causation," although a number of scientists have chosen not to write in cause-and-effect terms, and although numerous thorny issues have been involved in the use of this concept even among those scholars who concede its existence, it is still difficult, and often well-nigh impossible, to avoid the assumption that some kind of cause-and-effect relationship does exist. Implicit in the application of the scientific method is the notion that some events occur prior to or concurrently with others and that the former have an impact upon the latter, thereby generating, or causing, specific reactions.

OBSERVER ASSUMPTIONS

Much less emphasized, but equally essential to the success of the scientific method, are certain assumptions about the scientist himself—what we call "observer assumptions."

We have already mentioned that one of the premises underlying science is the superiority of knowledge over ignorance. Closely related to this premise is the notion that scientific activities in the long run benefit the scientist-observer and his social order. Although conceivably a scientific method that is not dedicated to humanistic goals might develop, the fact remains that science is man's own creation and he is therefore likely to apply the scientific method in terms of his own interests, or, more accurately, in terms of what he perceives to be his own interests. Man, therefore, seems motivated to acquire scientifically based knowledge by the desire to ameliorate his own social condition. Much historical evidence can be adduced in support of the proposition that numerous scientists have been motivated by the belief that science would eventuate in some kind of utopia. Although the specific content of this utopian dream varies considerably, almost always the ideal condition is one that emphasizes freedom, the dignity of man, and the like. Implicit here is the notion that science is not a dehumanizing activity but on the contrary permits man to fulfill some measure of his nobler capacities.

A second observer assumption is that man is or can be made a proper instrument for performing the ratiocinations involved in the application of the scientific method. It is assumed that he can observe, relate, and impute meanings to events—that he can remember, compute, imagine, compare, differentiate, integrate, and thereby place events in their proper perspective.

If man is incapable of performing these tasks, then the requirements of the scientific method are unrealistic and he might as well resign himself to more suitable epistemological undertakings. However, even where man's innate capacities are limited, he may still possess the wherewithal to create instruments that extend his capabilities or in other ways reduce the restrictions placed upon the exercise of his talents. Indeed man has, by recognizing his own weaknesses and then seeking to circumvent them, greatly advanced the cause of science.

A third observer assumption is that the social conditions essential for the application of the scientific method can be sustained. These include not only tolerance of free inquiry but such positive conditions as provision of the machinery and other facilities to meet the needs of scientific endeavor and the presence of a climate of opinion that permits the scientist to function without undue strictures or political pressures. Scientists, like the clergy, may be toughened by persecution, but they hardly flower under it. The necessary conditions for science do not, however, include passivity in the sociopolitical realm, for scientists may have to assume an active role in developing and maintaining the social circumstances conducive to the scientific enterprise.

IMPLICATIONS

We have attempted to isolate those premises underlying the scientific method that are *common* to both the natural and the social sciences. The common assumptions should be kept in mind as we build up to our main thesis: namely, that major differences exist between the natural and the social sciences *in the application* of the scientific method.

Also, looking back upon the premises underlying the scientific method, we must emphasize the limitations these impose upon the activities of scientists. Science does not and cannot reach beyond its own assumptions. It is therefore inadequate for dealing with ultimate causes and other problems so dear to human beings. As with all fields of knowledge, an understanding of the premises permits one to comprehend both the weaknesses and the strengths of the scientific method.

The Nature of Theory and Data

Our sketch of the development of modern science emphasized that its emergence can be traced to that point in time and space when speculative thought and theorizing became systematically linked with empirical data on the technological level, in the practical, workaday world. Theory, as a system of concepts or ideas, is of course not unique to science but is basic to all systems of philosophy and religious thought.

An essential difference, perhaps the only one, between theories in science and in other belief systems lies in the method of validation employed. Scientific theories are necessarily subject to validation through empirical observation, not by fiat or on the basis of tradition.

Although scientists would agree that theory and data are essential features of the scientific method, they disagree, as have philosophers since the days of Hume and Kant, over the relative weight to be assigned to each and over the relationships between the two. Herein we are concerned with the nature of theory and of data in modern sociology and in social science more generally.

THE NATURE OF SCIENTIFIC THEORY

Today most social scientists speak glowingly of the utility of theory. Yet, when we seek an answer to the question, "What is meant by theory in social science?" we encounter definitions that are contradictory or, at best, ambiguous. Moreover, such terms as "theory," "theoretical orientation," "theoretical frame of reference," "theoretical sketch," or "model" are on occasion employed synonymously, at other times with only fine shades of difference.

One group of social scientists would identify, at least implicitly, any kind of conceptualization with theory. Such concepts as "status," "role," "culture," or "public opinion," when defined and utilized in the interpretation of research materials, are equated with social theory. In this sense, theory comes to be defined as almost any thought process as opposed to the observation of facts per se. Although all theory involves conceptualization, and although concepts are the building blocks for theory, to equate conceptualization in general, or isolated concepts in particular, with scientific theory seems inutile.

Another group of social scientists tends to identify theory with the writings of classical scholars such as Marx, Weber, Durkheim, Pareto, and Spencer.[24] Granted that modern sociologists frequently overlook some of the advances made by earlier scholars, equating the "history of ideas" with social theory can serve little purpose.

Still other social scientists attempt to define or identify theory in more rigorous terms. To them the term "theory" is applicable only to a "formal" or "logico-deductive" system, one that involves a set of postulates from which testable hypotheses (or propositions) can be derived. In this category belong sociologists such as Zetterberg, Homans, and Schrag,[25] who reason, in lesser or greater degrees, along the lines of such philosophers of science as Popper and

[24] See, e.g., Margaret Wilson Vine, *An Introduction to Sociological Theory* (New York: Longmans, 1959). The work of Andrew Hacker, *Political Theory* (New York: Macmillan, 1961), also seems to belong to this tradition.

[25] Hans L. Zetterberg, *On Theory and Verification in Sociology,* 3rd ed. (Totowa, N.J.: Bedminster, 1965); George C. Homans, "Contemporary Theory in Sociology," in Robert E. L. Faris (ed.), *Handbook of Modern Sociology* (Chicago: Rand McNally, 1964), chap. 25; Clarence Schrag, "Elements of Theoretical Analysis in Sociology," in Llewellyn Gross (ed.), *Sociological Theory: Inquiries and Paradigms* (New York: Harper & Row, 1967), 220–253.

Merton, *op. cit.*, 96 ff., has on occasion identified theory with the logico-deductive system. However, as we shall observe in Chapter 9, this reasoning is by no means similar to the logic of the structural-functional orientation which Merton has so ardently championed.

Hempel;[26] the latter in turn have taken modern physics as the "model" to emulate (see Chapter 3). Writers who equate theory with a logico-deductive system often refer to other conceptual systems as "theoretical orientations," "frames of reference," or "theoretical sketches."

This narrow definition of theory, though it has some appeal, raises difficulties of its own. By relegating to the class of "nontheory" all conceptualizations other than the logico-deductive sort, sociologists may inhibit rather than advance the cause of science. Such thinking would lead us to reject certain kinds of logical systems—notably the logic of the dialectic—as inappropriate to social investigation and would blind us to certain types of conceptualizations that have proved useful for coping with specific problem areas. Most significant of all, the narrow definition of theory advocated by Zetterberg,[27] among others, ignores the assumptions scientists make about their method and their data, assumptions that do much to structure the total research process and the interpretation of one's results. These assumptions are elaborated upon in Chapter 3.

In a broad sense, a scientific theory serves to link apparently discrete observations. More specifically, it refers to a set of logically interrelated "propositions" or "statements" that are "empirically meaningful," as well as to the assumptions the researcher makes about his method and his data. Thus, there are three dimensions to theory in science: (1) the broad logical structure, or the form; (2) the generalizations or propositions concerning the patterning of the empirical world (the specific content); and (3) the assumptions regarding the scientific method and the nature of the data.

We equate theory neither with isolated concepts nor with logico-deductive systems. Rather, our definition is broad enough to encompass such classificatory schemes as those of Parsons (his pattern-variable or system-problem formulations)[28] as well as the more rigorous logico-deductive schemes. Obviously, theories may take different forms: They may be rigorous or loose, general or specific, and so on.

Moreover, our definition of theory includes an aspect of theory building which, as suggested above, has been slighted by methodologists and philosophers of science: the assumptions that scientists make concerning their methods and their data.[29] These assumptions cannot be relegated to the sphere of "meta-

[26] Karl R. Popper, *The Logic of Scientific Discovery* (New York: Wiley, Science Editions, 1961); Hempel, *op. cit.* Also, R. B. Braithwaite, *Scientific Explanation* (New York: Cambridge, 1953).

[27] Zetterberg, *op. cit.*

[28] Talcott Parsons, *The Social System* (New York: Free Press, 1951), and his "General Theory in Sociology," in Robert K. Merton *et al.* (eds.), *Sociology Today* (New York: Basic Books, 1959), chap. 1.

[29] Our usage of the term "assumption" differs from that of Schrag, *op. cit.*, 221 ff. Schrag distinguishes between two kinds of generalizations or propositions: (1) descriptions of previous observations and (2) "lawlike assumptions" about events not yet observed

theory," or theorizing about theory, since they affect the nature of one's propositions and, more specifically, the very selection of the problem and collection and analysis of the data. For example, sociologists who conceive of social reality as fluid and constantly evolving are committed to a set of research procedures that tend to be rejected by those who see social relationships as fundamentally stable and fixed. The general disregard of this dimension of theory building, a point upon which we elaborate in succeeding chapters, has done much to hinder the advance of methodology in sociology.

To reduce the terminological confusion in this area, we should also comment briefly upon concepts such as "model" and "explanation." Some writers use these as synonyms for theory. Yet the term "model," for instance, has acquired a number of rather different meanings.[30]

Sociologists often speak of a "model" in common-sense terms: as something to be emulated. Thus, Communist China has become a model of economic development for certain recently emergent nations. But a model may also refer to a miniature physical representation of reality, as in chemistry. Or the sociologist's sociogram serves as a physical representation or model for a small group.

A number of writers conceive of this representation in conceptual rather than physical terms. It is in this sense that a model is frequently equated with a logico-deductive system.[31] But even within this framework finer distinctions can be made. For instance, the economist Papandreou distinguishes between a model and a theory. For him a theory is a logico-deductive system that can be falsified, whereas a model is a conceptual system that cannot be falsified but is capable only of empirical confirmation.[32]

The notion of "explanation," which we analyze at some length in a later

---

or examined. He uses the term "assumption" specifically in this context. Our usage is more theoretical and on occasion more "philosophical" in nature.

[30] For a discussion of the use of the concept, "model," see May Brodbeck, "Models, Meaning, and Theories," in Llewellyn Gross (ed.), *Symposium on Sociological Theory* (New York: Harper & Row, 1959), chap. 12. Cf. Merle B. Turner, *Philosophy and the Science of Behavior* (New York: Appleton-Century-Crofts, 1967), chap. 9; E. A. Gellner, "Model (Theoretical Model)," in Julius Gould and William L. Kolb (eds.), *A Dictionary of the Social Sciences* (New York: Free Press, 1964), 435; and Michael Banton (ed.), *The Relevance of Models for Social Anthropology*, A.S.A. Monographs 1 (London: Tavistock, 1965).

[31] Not all social scientists equate the notion of conceptual model with the logico-deductive formulation. Some seem to identify "model" with one's assumptions about data and method, as, e.g., M. Brewster Smith, "Anthropology and Psychology," in John Gillin (ed.), *For a Science of Social Man* (New York: Macmillan, 1954), 64–66. And Karl W. Deutsch, "On Communication Models in the Social Sciences," *Public Opinion Quarterly*, 16 (Fall, 1952), 356, sees models as structures of symbols and operating rules which are supposed to match certain relevant points in an existing structure or process.

[32] Andreas G. Papandreou, "Explanation and Prediction in Economics," *Science, 129* (Apr. 24, 1959), 1096–1100. He writes: "Economists construct models, not theories. Their models may be confirmed by reference to empirical data, but they cannot be refuted. Therefore, they are strictly explanatory in character" (1099).

chapter, is frequently used as a synonym for theory: often, theory = logico-deductive system = explanation.[33] Although theories have explanatory power, the notion of theory, as we have defined it, encompasses more than explanation: It includes in addition the underlying premises.

THE NATURE OF DATA

From the time of Durkheim and his concern with "social facts" up to the present day, a long-standing controversy has been brewing over just what is the proper field of study for the sociologist. Most would agree that the sociologist does not study biological or physical phenomena but concentrates upon social or cultural data. But what are social or cultural data? What is a social or cultural fact?

The concept "fact" is not easy to define. The field of philosophy contains a considerable body of literature on the subject, and a controversial one at that. Moreover, what is a fact for a particular social scientist is a product of his own theoretical assumptions. Durkheim's well-known dictum, "Consider social facts as things,"[34] is a case in point. In this utterance Durkheim was reacting to the subjectivist orientation of the utilitarians of his time, and he was intent upon placing sociology on a scientific footing. Although scholars quarrel over the precise meaning of Durkheim's maxim, it seems clear that for Durkheim social facts were external to the observer and the actor alike, and they were capable of being observed in a highly objective manner.

More narrowly, Brodbeck defines a fact as follows: "A 'fact' is a particular thing, characteristic, event, or kind of event, like Johnny's I.Q. or the proportion of home owners, or the size of the Republican vote. To state a fact, then, is to state that a concept has an instance or a number of instances."[35] Implicit in Brodbeck's definition is the notion that a fact is conceptually defined or ordered. More broadly, these sense impressions can be transformed via concepts into statements or propositions (for example, "There are over 180 million people in the United States") which then are viewed as facts.

Yet problems remain. There are, after all, different kinds of facts: those that are general and those that are specific, those that are positive and those that are negative. Kenneth Burke, among others, has stressed the role of the negative in human symbol systems.[36] The idea of "nothingness" seems to be central to much of social experience. Social scientists cannot ignore the existence

---

[33] See, e.g., Hempel, *op. cit.*

[34] Emile Durkheim, *The Rules of Sociological Method,* trans. by Sarah A. Solovay and John H. Mueller, 8th ed. (New York: Free Press Paperback, 1964), 14.

[35] Brodbeck, *op. cit.,* 377.

[36] Kenneth Burke, "Definition of Man," *Hudson Review,* 16 (Winter, 1963–1964), 498–503 and his *Grammar of Motives* (Englewood Cliffs, N.J.: Prentice Hall, 1945), 294–297.

of negative facts. Nonaction is a negative fact (or nonevent) that may have considerable relevance for social inquiry. The failure of a citizen to vote or of the groom to kiss the bride are illustrative of such negative facts in American society.

But to get at the facts, just what do social scientists observe? They observe physical behavior, such as walking, waving of the arms, facial expressions, and patterned sounds, and the results of physical behavior, such as writing or tools. Yet these physical movements (or the products thereof) are meaningful to the observer only in terms of his own conceptualization and acquired knowledge of the actor's interpretation of them. Scientists thus observe in terms of some conceptual system—some set of common understandings—which orders or connects disparate physical movements, movements which are taken as indicators of underlying patterns.[37]

Some radical empiricists (including the materialists among them) would remove the subjective element, or meaning, entirely from sociological investigation.[38] Although in so doing they are perpetuating a theoretical perspective that reaches back over several centuries of social thought, the evidence, as we argue in succeeding chapters, is ranged against the validity of such a viewpoint. To deny the legitimacy of the subjective as an area of scientific investigation is to downgrade the role of conceptualization and ultimately of the scientific method itself.

RELATIONSHIPS BETWEEN THEORY AND DATA

It is difficult, if not impossible, to discuss in any meaningful way the role and nature of theory without giving some consideration to the role and nature of data, and vice versa. But which has priority in the research process: theory or data? Undoubtedly the social scientist's particular theoretical assumptions mold the formulation of his problem and even structure the findings. The phenomenologist and the extreme empiricist will inevitably arrive at different conclusions. More generally, those scientists who work within the Kantian tradition give priority to concepts and theory, whereas those who are committed to the views of Locke and Hume and their contemporary expositors stress observation and data rather than theory. In practice, most researchers tend to be either neo-Kantians or neo-Humeans.

---

[37] See, e.g., Karl Mannheim, *Essays on the Sociology of Knowledge,* trans. and ed. by Paul Kecskemeti (New York: Oxford, 1952), 53–63; and Harold Garfinkel, "Common-Sense Knowledge of Social Structures: The Documentary Method of Interpretation," in Jordan M. Scher (ed.), *Theories of the Mind* (New York: Free Press, 1962), 689–712.

[38] One current effort to eliminate the subjective element in scientific inquiry is that of Otis Dudley Duncan and Leo F. Schnore, "Cultural, Behavioral, and Ecological Perspectives in the Study of Social Organization," *American Journal of Sociology,* 65 (September, 1959), 132–146. The authors point to the ecological approach as nonsubjective, while admitting that the subjective enters into, say, the behavioral orientation.

A comparison of the writings of Lazarsfeld and Parsons sheds light on one dimension of the theory-data controversy within sociology. Parsons, a champion of the relative priority of theory, has been responsible for sensitizing several generations of sociologists to the crucial role of theory in social research.[39] Examining the functions of theory, he recognizes it as a beacon researchers employ when charting a course through the murky depths of social systems. One must know what to study and what not to study. Theory, moreover, becomes essential when we seek to interpret our observations. And it is theory that illuminates the gaps in our observations of the social world.

The function of theory in structuring the researcher's observations is readily grasped when we compare the divergent approaches of different scientists toward a particular complex of social activities[40]—for instance, the fishing patterns of a tribe of South American Indians. A medical doctor might examine the effect of the tribe's fishing habits upon the people's diet, whereas a geographer could study the fishing patterns from the perspective of the group's adaptation to the physical environment. Or one ethnologist might consider their activities from the viewpoint of the society's economic system, while another might examine their interrelationships with, say, religious ritual and beliefs.

Although sociologists such as Lazarsfeld do not question the significance of theory, their emphasis is upon the role of data in the scientific process. Consequently, Lazarsfeld tends to utilize "natural classes" in his research.[41] He would, when carrying out a public opinion study, for example, employ a classification scheme that reflects the natural breaking points within his data. Parsons, on the other hand, in examining the same materials, would tend to impose his own classificatory system upon them. Of course, Lazarsfeld's so-called natural classes are partly a product of his theoretical commitment, for he would not utilize or perhaps even recognize those classes that fall outside his own conceptual or theoretical framework.

[39] Charles Ackerman and Talcott Parsons, "The Concept of 'Social System' as a Theoretical Device," in Gordon J. DiRenzo (ed.), *Concepts, Theory, and Explanation in the Behavioral Sciences* (New York: Random House, 1966), chap. 2. In this essay co-authored with Ackerman, Parsons contends that "We select, we ascribe importance; and both our selection and our ascription of importance are in a sense unnatural since the array of reality itself does not supply the criteria for the selection or the ascription" (26), a perspective that diverges considerably from that enunciated by Lazarsfeld.

[40] Cf. Ely Devons and Max Gluckman, "Conclusion: Modes and Consequences of Limiting a Field of Study," in Max Gluckman (ed.), *Closed Systems and Open Minds* (Edinburgh: Oliver & Boyd, 1964), 158 ff. "The different social and behavioural sciences are in the main distinguished not by the events they study but by the kinds of relations between events which they seek to establish" (160).

[41] See, e.g., Paul F. Lazarsfeld and Allen H. Barton, "Some General Principles of Questionnaire Classification," in Paul F. Lazarsfeld and Morris Rosenberg (ed.), *The Language of Social Research* (New York: Free Press, 1955), esp. 91–93.

The split between those scientists who stress theory over those who empha-size observation (or data) reflects to some degree the cleavage between scholars who are committed to a logico-deductive approach in science and those who are oriented toward discovery (an issue we consider in the next chapter). More generally, Merton,[42] among others, has, in an effort to build a bridge between the theoreticians and the empiricists, argued at some length that theory and data are in constant interaction. Such a position is widely acclaimed today. But the idea of such interaction has become almost a cliché in some circles. We can readily concur that it is inherent within the scientific method, but in reality we know little about the specific content or form of this interplay between theory and data.

An understanding of the relationship of theory and data rests in large part upon a firm grasp of the nature of perception. For it is perception that con-nects the data with one's conceptual knowledge of the latter. Perception media are the senses by which human beings see, hear, touch, smell, and taste. There are at least three aspects to this process: (1) the quality of man's perception media, (2) the impact of conceptualization upon perception, and (3) the nature of the data being studied.

A major deterrent to scientific inquiry lies in the selective quality of the senses. Roughly speaking, the senses pick up some sound waves, light waves, odors, and so on, emanating from or reflected by physical objects, but fail to pick up others. We must either remain oblivious to the latter or infer their pres-ence via instruments or, in some instances, deduce their existence from other observable phenomena. Some of the limitations upon human observation have been examined by psychologists. Although methodologists have given little at-tention to the latter's findings, the experiments of psychologists have certainly elucidated some of the barriers to human perception. One of them is the "Three Men" test, whereby the placement of three individuals with respect to certain geometrical configurations leaves the observer with the impression that they are of different sizes, even though "in reality" all three are the same.[43] We also have experiments in which lines of the same length appear to observers to be of differing lengths, simply because of the manner in which the lines are portrayed.

A second and more insidious kind of influence upon perception stems from one's own conceptual system. Clearly, we perceive objects or behavior largely in terms of prior conceptualizations or categories. This proposition has been docu-mented by crosscultural research.[44] A number of studies have supported the idea that persons in different cultures may perceive the color spectrum, geometric

1457984

[42] Merton, *op. cit.,* chap. 3.

[43] See, e.g., M. L. Johnson Abercrombie, *The Anatomy of Judgment* (New York: Basic Books, 1960), 30–31.

[44] See the review of the literature, as well as the original research that was conducted, by Marshall H. Segall *et al., The Influence of Culture on Visual Perception* (Indianapolis: Bobbs-Merrill, 1966). This is a truly valuable work.

forms, etc. somewhat differently. So, too, they may classify and impute meaning to particular human behavior in rather different ways. Yet if persons from divergent cultures perceived in radically divergent ways one could not distinguish between total failure of communication and total difference in perception. It is because we perceive and respond essentially alike that we can take note of the differences that result.[45]

The impact of conceptualization upon perception *within* broad cultural systems has also been documented through various experiments. For instance, several groups of observers are told different stories about a given picture before they are shown the object. As we might expect, the different groups perceive the picture in terms of patterns that reflect the themes they have been told the picture portrays. This line of reasoning also suggests the crucial influence of the "social situation" upon perception. That an individual's perceptions of objects or of the behavior of other persons is structured by his "expectations" of others has been a conclusion of a number of social psychologists.[46]

Actually, there appear to be various levels of "consciousness" with respect to one's conceptual categories. Some phenomenologists seem rightly to distinguish between those situations wherein a person can conceptualize his observations and disseminate them to others and those wherein a person is "intuitively aware" of objects or reactions but is unable to conceptualize, order, and communicate what he "observes." One may, for example, walk into a room after, say, a year's absence and be aware that changes have occurred in the arrangement of the furniture, and even communicate this awareness to others, but be unable to specify the particular rearrangement that has occurred. Field workers, thus, may be aware of patterns long before they are able to specify or order their observations into well-defined categories.

These fine distinctions aside, it is the overall impact of one's conceptual system upon perception that makes a sociology of knowledge orientation so essential to the methodology of social research. We have already suggested that a significant part of the scientist's overall environment is made up of the concepts held by other persons in his sociocultural milieu. These concepts have an empirical existence of their own in the sense that they are discoverable and can be communicated. It is the scientist's total conceptual environment, not just the concepts he acquires during his scientific training, that structures his observations. For us, the sociology of knowledge perspective is a methodological device that

[45] Fred L. Strodtbeck, "Considerations of Meta-Method in Cross-Cultural Studies," *American Anthropologist, 66,* part 2 (June, 1964), 225. This issue of the *American Anthropologist* is a special publication, "Transcultural Studies in Cognition," ed. by A. Kimball Romney and Roy Goodwin D'Andrade.

[46] See, e.g., A. Paul Hare (ed.), *Handbook of Small Group Research* (New York: Free Press, 1962), 26 ff.; Renato Tagiuri and Luigi Petrullo (eds.), *Person Perception and Interpersonal Behavior* (Stanford, Cal.: Stanford, 1958).

serves to objectify this broader conceptual system so that we may properly gauge its impact upon the scientific observer.

A third element of the perception process is "what is observed." The research of social psychologists lends support to the proposition that, where one's "reality" being observed is relatively fixed or stable, the influence of other persons' conceptual orientations upon one's own observations will be less than where this reality lacks any well-defined reference points and is highly amorphous.[47] We would therefore expect the degree of consensus among scientists to vary with the amount of stability and permanence in the social order they are studying.

But the relationships of conceptualization to perception and to the social environment itself are more complex than we have indicated. There is another element that enters into the picture: language (the nature of which has also been the subject of considerable debate). Following Saussure,[48] we define "language" as a system of signs that link concepts to specific sounds or sequences of sounds. One can hear or utter given sounds, yet fail to attach any specific concepts, or meaning, to these, if he lacks knowledge of the language, or system of signs.

Language, as a system of linguistic signs that serves to convey meaning among speakers, has a structure of its own. This structure, which includes phonemic, morphemic, and syntactic patterns, seems to influence the perception process and conceptualization itself. The perception of certain aspects of social reality may be more readily achieved through some kinds of structural systems than through others. And although, as we observe in the following chapter, it is easy to exaggerate the impact of different language structures upon conceptualization, that they may differentially shape thought patterns in some areas is a proposition that cannot be ignored.

In the end, the broader theoretical system, the specific concepts contained therein, and the language which conveys these concepts all interact in complex ways. Refinement of isolated concepts can lead to improvements in the overall theoretical system, and in turn improvements in the latter may help to refine certain concepts, and, in the process, one's perception of particular phenomena. Moreover, refinement in the system of linguistic signs can lead to advances both in the concepts and in the broader theory, as occurred, for example, in Europe with the adoption of the Hindu-Arabic decimal system in place of the unwieldy Roman numerals. This change did much to facilitate the breakthroughs in mathematics that came in the succeeding centuries. Of course, these achievements in mathematics itself were made possible only by the much earlier reduction of spoken language to written form. And without the invention of writing, science as we know it could never have developed. For writing enabled man to greatly

[47] See, e.g., Muzafer Sherif and Carolyn W. Sherif, *An Outline of Social Psychology,* rev. ed. (New York: Harper & Row, 1956), 81 ff., 103 ff., *passim.*

[48] Ferdinand de Saussure, *Course in General Linguistics,* trans. by Wade Baskin (New York: Philosophical Library, 1959).

transcend the very narrow limits of his own memory span and to build upon the accumulated knowledge over the millennia.

Ultimately, if we are to understand more fully the relationships between theory and data, we must have a better grasp of the conceptualization process. With a sounder knowledge of conceptualization, we could effect many improvements in the scientific method. The ongoing research in psychology may help scientists widen their grasp of this knotty problem. Certainly, the studies in concept formation by Piaget, Bruner, and so on have blazed a trail through this area that methodologists should not ignore.[49]

So too, the efforts that have been made to apply our knowledge of computers—by drawing an analogy between these and the human brain—to the study of thought and the thinking process will in due time also expand our knowledge of conception (as well as perception). As Goldstine observes:

> Many workers in the field are at present trying to explore what is called artificial or machine reasoning or intelligence. In effect they are trying to see how far a computer can go in doing tasks which we normally class as human ones. . . . It is characteristic of all these efforts, though, that so far the investigators have been unable to deduce any general principles from their results.[50]

Yet eventually this work will likely extend our understanding of the rudiments of conceptualization and in turn of the scientific method itself.

[49] For a brief survey of some of this literature, see Roger Brown, *Social Psychology* (New York: Free Press, 1965), chap. 7.

[50] Herman H. Goldstine, "Computers and Perception," *Proceedings of the American Philosophical Society, 108* (August, 1964), 290.

CHAPTER 3 ⎯⎯⎯⎯⎯⎯⎯⎯⎯⎯⎯⎯⎯⎯⎯⎯⎯⎯

The Logic of Inquiry
and the Nature
of Theoretical Systems

In the preceding chapter we outlined the three elements of social theory: the logical form, the substantive generalizations, and the theoretical assumptions. We shall now elaborate upon the first and last of these. If sociologists are to advance substantive theories and to effectively design research projects, whether in ecology, social psychology, social organization, and so on, they must be cognizant of the logic of theory building and hypothesis testing. They must also be aware of the logical-theoretical constructs (the sets of assumptions that researchers make about their methods and their data) within which generalizations about substantive empirical matters are made. This chapter provides the basis for much of the succeeding discussion, particularly the section on theoretical analysis.

The Nature of Logical Systems

Scientific inquiry involves one or more logical systems which define the research situation by setting artificial boundaries upon the processes of observation and analysis. The scientist, by objectifying the logical system he employs, can maximize its usefulness as well as recognize the limitations it places upon his own investigations.

Actually, the term "logic" is a troublesome one. Philosophers have been of many minds concerning what it should or should not encompass. So writes Bocheński:

For apart from "philosophy" there is perhaps no name of a branch of knowledge that has been given so many meanings as "logic." Sometimes the whole of philosophy, and even knowledge in general, has been thus named, from metaphysics on the one hand, cf. Hegel, to aesthetics ("logic of beauty") on the other, with psychology, epistemology, mathematics etc. in between.[1]

We shall use the term "logic" rather broadly to refer to any *system of rules* for organizing thought and expression. But we also recognize that logical systems, ranging as they do from relatively loose and semiformalized systems to highly formalized ones, display different degrees of "power" and rigor.

We begin our discussion of logical systems by considering natural languages; after that we treat artificial languages of the deductive sort. This should set the stage for the ensuing section on the problem of inference.

NATURAL LANGUAGES AND LOGICAL SYSTEMS

Given our definition of logic, it is possible (even necessary) to view natural, or ordinary, languages as logical systems. Such languages, after all, posseess their own rules for organizing thought and expression. Through various sets of phonemic, morphological, syntactical and semantic rules, users of these systems are enabled to understand one another.

Natural languages as logical systems, as means of ordering knowledge about man and society, should not be lightly dismissed. Their very lack of rigor often permits scientists to perceive interrelationships among variables that might go unnoticed in rigorously formalized logical systems, which tend to guide observations and analysis along too narrow a pathway. Indeed, the vagueness of natural languages may at times prove invaluable. Here, Quine's remarks are pertinent:

> Vagueness is an aid in coping with the linearity of discourse. An expositor finds that an understanding of some matter A is necessary preparation for an understanding of B, and yet that A cannot itself be expounded in correct detail without, conversely, noting certain exceptions and distinctions which require prior understanding of B. Vagueness, then, to the rescue. The expositor states A vaguely, proceeds to B, and afterwards touches up A, without ever having to call upon his reader to learn and unlearn any outright falsehood in the preliminary statement of A.[2]

---

[1] I. M. Bocheński, *A History of Formal Logic,* trans. and ed. by Ivo Thomas (Notre Dame, Ind.: University of Notre Dame Press, 1961), 2.

[2] Willard V. Quine, *Word and Object* (Cambridge, Mass.: M.I.T. Paperback, 1964), 127. Also, George C. Christie, following Quine's leads, argues for the importance of

Furthermore, natural languages convey shades of emotion and thereby communicate data about human action that cannot be captured via highly formalized logical systems. In striving to understand or describe the cultural values of a society other than his own, the scientist may find it mandatory to rely upon a natural language rather than some highly stylized medium; we suspect that natural languages are indispensable in these circumstances.[3] Even the logical empiricists who advocate the use of artificial languages in scientific discourse must for many purposes rely upon natural languages. Sociologists, for instance, have not yet devised any formal means of effectively communicating to researchers the techniques to be used in interviewing. Such education must be carried out largely through the medium of ordinary language. We would not term this process as "nonlogical."

Some sociologists would contend that we are irrevocably committed to the use of natural languages. The proponents of this view include a number of symbolic interactionists such as Blumer who have championed the use of "sensitizing concepts."[4] For them, sensitizing concepts are empirically realistic, for they reflect the actor's usage. Even where scientists can define concepts more rigorously than do laymen, they must often convey meaning through terms that are defined by their context and at best are lacking in rigor.

Still, natural languages, as such, have decided limitations. Out of the search for increased rigor in the sciences, for methods of coping with the numerous ambiguities presented by natural languages, several schools of thought have emerged. One has taken ordinary language and has sought through analysis of language structure and content to reduce the ambiguities inherent in daily discourse and thus achieve greater precision in the use of words. This school of thought includes many of the present-day semanticists as well as the linguistic philosophers who have held forth in England (and to an extent in the United States) during the past several decades.[5] Their contribution lies mainly in having called to the attention of social scientists the looseness and lack of precision of many terms they employ.

The linguistic philosophers have done much to clarify the general confusion

---

vagueness in legal language. See his "Vagueness and Legal Language," *Minnesota Law Review,* 48 (April, 1964), 885–911. "Vagueness is sometimes an indispensable tool for the achievement of accuracy and precision in language, particularly in legal language" (911).

[3] The works of Oscar Lewis on the "culture of poverty" are a case in point. See his *The Children of Sánchez* (New York: Random House, 1961) and his *La Vida* (New York: Random House, 1966).

[4] Herbert Blumer, "What Is Wrong with Social Theory?" *American Sociological Review,* 19 (February, 1954), 3–10.

[5] For a brief discussion of the possible relationships between language analysis and social theory, see Whitaker T. Deininger, *Problems in Social and Political Thought* (New York: Macmillan, 1965), chap. 15.

that has reigned in the area of ordinary language. Yet they display a fundamental weakness, as commented upon in Gellner's critical work.[6] In their preoccupation with the Oxford dictionary, with the meaning of words, they have lost sight of the fundamental problems of philosophy and social theory. Their focus upon English, and the consequent failure to generalize about (or to) other languages, has meant an unusually heavy stress upon particulars as against universals.

ARTIFICIAL LANGUAGES AND LOGICAL SYSTEMS

Another school of thought would, at least in its extreme form, reject the use of natural language in science. Its main goal is to create artificial languages that are free of the inadequacies of ordinary discourse. Those who advocate the use of artificial languages look to symbolic logic or mathematics as the means for building more effective theories in science.

To understand this group we must pause for a moment to consider the evolution of logical (or mathematical) languages over time. Long before the birth of the scientific revolution, learned men in such divergent civilizations as the Greek and the Indian sought to overcome the ambiguities of natural languages by formalizing the reasoning process, by insisting upon clearly defined terms and well-stated premises, and by objectifying the steps in formal reasoning from one set of premises to another—rules by which valid inferences can be drawn.

Although the traditions of logic and mathematics have tended to merge in recent decades, they were rather separate during their early development. Thus, few formal intellectual ties existed between Aristotelian logic and Euclidian geometry. Yet both traditions emphasized deductive reasoning and the establishment of "absolute truth," the primary goal of scholars until a mere few centuries ago.

Although a number of advances in logic were achieved after the time of Aristotle, including the development of the "logic of propositions," it was only during and after the Renaissance in Europe that logic and mathematics both underwent a revolutionary change that was associated with (and laid the basis for) the scientific revolution.[7] With the work of Leibnitz, and especially after 1800, a marked shift occurred in Western man's orientation toward mathematics and formal logic. The resultant intellectual breakthroughs have left their mark upon the physical sciences and bid fair to remake the theoretical structure of many fields in social science as well.

Within the tradition of mathematics an upheaval occurred with the for-

---

[6] Ernest Gellner, *Words and Things* (London: Gollancz, 1959).

[7] For histories on the development of formal logic, see, e.g., Bocheński, *op. cit.;* and William Kneale and Martha Kneale, *The Development of Logic* (Fair Lawn, N.J.: Oxford, 1962). Also, the brief review by P. H. Nidditch, *The Development of Mathematical Logic* (New York: Free Press, 1962).

malization of non-Euclidean geometries. The work of Gauss, Lobachevski, and Riemann demonstrated that viable deductive systems could be established upon other axioms than those tied to the concept of physical space. Euclid's lines that remained "parallel unto infinity" were not the self-evident truth that earlier scholars had assumed. The early nineteenth-century mathematicians' attack upon Euclidean geometry undermined the absoluteness that earlier scholars had associated with mathematics. It also opened up new vistas for the mathematician. It freed him from his former dependence upon some "empirical referent," since prior to the nineteenth century mathematicians had been primarily committed to "describing" aspects of the empirical world. Now mathematics could be viewed as an intellectual exercise, a challenge to men's minds, and mathematicians were free to formulate all manner of deductive schemes, so long as these were consistent within themselves. Then too, the emergence of new geometries (along with the advances in symbolic logic, noted below) in the latter part of the nineteenth century stimulated increased interest in the limitations of Euclid's formulations. Mathematicians set about to explicate the hidden assumptions in this system, to make explicit the undemonstrated propositions and undefined terms that older scholars had taken for granted. This movement culminated in the emergence of what is frequently called "axiomatics."[8]

In a somewhat different intellectual tradition, one that connects with the formal logic of Aristotle, are the steps toward a new logic in the mid-nineteenth century. One especially important advance was made by Boole, who, by treating logical problems algebraically, opened up the field of symbolic logic for investigation. Supplementing Boole's logic of classes was De Morgan and Pierce's logic of relations. And the contribution of Frege, among others, was an essential stepping stone to Whitehead and Russell's *Principia Mathematica*. The latter, a landmark in modern thought, sought to demonstrate that it was possible to reduce mathematics to logic. Thus, at the very time that new mathematical and logical systems were flowering, the intellectual traditions associated with mathematics and logic were merging. Nevertheless, the question of the specific relationships between mathematics and logic still evokes controversy.

> If logic is understood clearly to contain the theory of sets (and this seems to be a fair account of what Russell had in mind), then most mathematicians would accept without question the thesis that the basic concepts of all mathematics can be expressed in terms of logic. . . . But perhaps of greater significance is the consensus of mathematicians that there is much more to their field than is indicated by such a reduction of mathematics to logic and set theory.[9]

[8] Robert Blanché, *Axiomatics* (New York: Free Press, 1962).

[9] Leon Henkin, "Are Logic and Mathematics Identical?" *Science, 138* (Nov. 16, 1962), 793.

In any event, the outpouring of new logical systems has resulted in some major intellectual discoveries the implications of which for social research still await exploration. One such development was Gödel's theorem, wherein he demonstrated that there are systems for which closure is logically impossible.[10] This discovery relativized logic still further and ended, at least for the present, the search for absolutes via deductive systems.

Finally, when discussing the varieties of logical systems, we cannot ignore one that typically stands outside the tradition of formal logic and mathematics— the Hegelian dialectic with its stress upon thesis, antithesis, and synthesis. Although of little or no importance in the natural sciences, it has been the basis of some of the most significant theory building in social science, including the works of the materialist Marx and the neo-idealist Sorokin.[11] Traditional Marxists have, in fact, vigorously objected to the formalism associated with symbolic logic. One reason dialectical thinking has been disjunct from formal logic (although a few philosophers have attempted to merge the two traditions) is that the notion of "implication," so vital to formal logic, cannot effectively be applied to dialectic thought.[12]

THE PRESENT STATUS OF LOGICAL RELATIVISM

The flowering of a variety of logical systems during the past century and a half has led a number of scholars to champion the cause of logical relativism. With the breakdown of traditional sociocultural patterns and the overthrow of a belief in absolutes, which was fundamental in classical logic, many scholars have rejected the notion of a constant among logical systems. For example,

[10] Ernest Nagel and James R. Newman, "Gödel's Proof," in James R. Newman (ed.), *The World of Mathematics,* vol. 3 (New York: Simon and Schuster, 1956), 1668–1695.

[11] For a discussion of the logic of the dialectic and its relevancy for social inquiry, see, e.g., Georges Gurvitch, *Dialectique et sociologie* (Paris: Flammarion, 1962); Louis Schneider, "Toward Assessment of Sorokin's View of Change," in George K. Zollschan and Walter Hirsch (eds.), *Explorations of Social Change* (Boston: Houghton Mifflin, 1964), chap. 15; Pitirim A. Sorokin, "Comments on Schneider's Observations and Criticism," in Zollschan and Hirsch, *op. cit.,* chap. 16; Herbert Marcuse, *Reason and Revolution,* 2nd ed. (Boston: Beacon Press Paperback, 1960), esp. the preface, "A Note on Dialectic"; and Nicholas Georgescu-Roegen, *Analytical Economics* (Cambridge, Mass.: Harvard, 1966), 27–29.

[12] In general, those who subscribe to the logic of the dialectic question Aristotle's law of noncontradiction—the statement that a phenomenon may not have an attribute and its opposite at the same time. Indeed, the supporters of the logic of the dialectic and of formal logic tend to go their separate ways. But we would adhere to the position set forth by Claude Lévi-Strauss, *The Savage Mind* (Chicago: University of Chicago Press, 1966). He writes: "I do not regard dialectical reason as *something other than* analytical reason . . . but as *something additional in* analytical reason." (246).

Spengler in *The Decline of the West*[13]—a dour, pessimistic, and highly controversial study—attempted to demonstrate that in one major discipline after another (mathematics, architecture, music, and so on) the logical system that had been developed in ancient Greece, was restricted in both time and space. (Here we use the term "logic" in a very broad sense.) By implication, Aristotelian logic was suited to the classical tradition, but it proved inadequate for modern Western civilization with its different perspective and aspirations.

According to Spengler, "number worlds," or systems of logic, are essentially "products" of the cultures that generate them and thus differ according to time and place; they are committed to, and reinforce, a particular view of reality or *Weltanschauung*. Accordingly, as cultures undergo fundamental change so also do their systems of logic. Little wonder that Spengler made himself unpopular with scholars who clung to a belief in absolutes. At the same time, Spengler found himself arguing for logical relativism as a universal principle, for he contended that his logic was universal. And his extreme historicist view is out of step with a science of society, which must assume that aspects of logical systems remain constant across cultures and that some procedures have universal applicability.

Whorf[14] was another ardent supporter of logical relativism, but his approach to the problem diverged from that of Spengler. Spengler viewed logic as a product of the broader cultural order, as changing with modifications in the culture. Whorf argued that it is language, the linguistic structure of Chinese, Navajo, Nahuatl, or whatever, that determines the logical or cultural categories and not the reverse. Thus, the linguistic categories, a language's morphology, syntax, and vocabulary, Whorf theorized, shape the categories of thought and the logical structure of reality to the point that speakers of radically different languages who are confronted by "similar" social and physical phenomena tend to perceive and interpret these in markedly different ways.

Although the Whorfian hypothesis has attracted considerable attention from social scientists, Whorf's fellow linguists are among his severest critics. Some use the argument that it is possible to translate all cognitive experience and classifications from one language to another without any real loss of content.[15] Admittedly, considerable circumlocution may at times be required, for languages express specific concepts and ideas with different degrees of complexity and

---

[13] Oswald Spengler, *The Decline of the West: 1. Form and Actuality,* trans. by Charles F. Atkinson (New York: Knopf, 1926), chap. 2.

[14] Benjamin L. Whorf, *Language, Thought, and Reality* (Cambridge, Mass.: Technology Press, and New York: Wiley, 1956).

[15] See, e.g., Harry Hoijer (ed.), *Language in Culture,* American Anthropological Association Memoir No. 79 (Menasha, Wis.: American Anthropological Association, 1954). Also see the informative essay by J. W. Swanson, "Linguistic Relativity and Translation," *Philosophy and Phenomenological Research,* 22 (December, 1961), 185–192.

effectiveness. Yet this is far from saying that particular problems can be dealt with only by particular languages.

Spengler and Whorf not only underscored the loss of faith in logical absolutes; they also dramatized the opposing viewpoint of logical relativism, one manifestation of the theory of cultural relativism. Their writings also point to the serious impasse that faces logical relativism. For ultimately the supporters of this view challenge the validity of any science of society. But if this approach to knowledge were carried to its logical conclusion, we would find ourselves with Japanese, Russian, Chinese, Hindu, and Turkish sociologies, and with no bridge to link these different heritages. Full acceptance of logical relativism denies the premises of the unity of mankind and any kind of crosscultural universals.

Recent research in anthropology suggests that there is a unity to human cultures that transcends the obvious diversity. It seems advisable, therefore, to speak, as does Bocheński, of "varieties"[16] of logical systems rather than of different kinds of logical systems. Certainly some patterns, or rules, seem to be common to all. Unless this is accepted as a working assumption, scientists committed to divergent logical systems (natural or artificial) could never communicate with one another.

The Relevance of Varieties of Logical Systems for Social Research

Congruent with this concept of unity in diversity is the position that various logical and theoretical systems (for example, Boolean algebra, graph theory, and calculus) all have a place in social research. Each may prove useful for solving specific kinds of sociological problems. This pragmatic view of logic, held by Dewey,[17] among others, remains a useful perspective.

More broadly, we would not reject either natural or artificial languages. Nor would we deny the utility of the Hegelian dialectic as a logical system for analyzing or explaining certain aspects of the social order. The logic of the dialectic, in fact, may be an essential tool for interpreting many kinds of social processes.

The new logics do not, of course, lead us to discard the older forms— Aristotelian logic, for example. The latter is still much in evidence. Rather than being an all-embracing system, however, classical formal logic has come to occupy a niche in the larger universe of logics. Certainly, in the empirical sciences the canons of classical logic must be heeded where they are pertinent for establishing the intermediate fabric of meaning, as when one reasons from premises to conclusions. Such rules as the law of contradictions, which state that a condition and its denial cannot be held simultaneously, and the law of the excluded

[16] Bocheński, *op. cit.*

[17] John Dewey, *Logic: The Theory of Inquiry* (New York: Holt, Rinehart and Winston, 1938).

middle are still with us. Without them the instruments for establishing proofs would be inadequate. There is in fact little in classical logic, other than a belief in this logic as the road to absolute truth, that does not form part of the newer logical systems.

The newer systems, however, do not duplicate the outlook of the classical logics but rather respond to the conceptual needs of the modern scientific world. Therefore, little effort is currently expended in establishing logics as the base from which to draw all rational conclusions or to set up some all-encompassing system of absolutes.

The newer logical systems do resolve issues and further the development of empirically based knowledge in a manner superior to that of the classical formulations. Different logical systems may be equally "true" (that is, self-consistent), but they are not necessarily of equal value in empirical investigations. Scientists are in fact continually searching for more useful or more powerful ones. Often scientists may conceive of an empirical area of application and attempt to construct a logical system to resolve the particular problems involved, or they may draw upon existing logical systems that have been developed without reference to any specific empirical application. In either case, we should recall that logical systems are in themselves formal and general; they are, consequently, never the exclusive property of researchers in any one empirical realm. Rather they may be applied in many different contexts. The theoretical requirement these systems share is that each must be internally self-consistent; the practical requirement is that they must facilitate conceptualizalion in ways that enable theory to increase our empirically based knowledge.

Zeno's paradoxes were unsolvable via traditional logic but became solvable with the introduction of newer logical forms. Scholars of antiquity, seriously or half-seriously, formulated problems but found the avenues to their solution too alien to bear credence. Zeno, among others, saw change as a unidimensional variable and never adequately grasped a condition that is now considered obvious, that of a rate of change in which converging time increments can be compared. The logical systems of the Greeks could not cope with the concepts of continua, infinitesimals, irrationals, or any part of present-day mathematics that deals with the dynamics of change.

Another difference between the newer and the older logics arises from the fact that sybolic logic is able to cope with relational statements in addition to statements in predicate form: It can handle statements that involve notions of "more than" or "less than." Such a logical system is proving to be particularly useful in the analysis of many facets of sociocultural data.

More generally, the newer logic has led to an emphasis upon the axiomatic method in social research. Such an approach has been diffusing rapidly within sociology and psychology, and this trend is likely to become more pronounced in the years ahead.

The elements of the axiomatic method include (1) a system of postulates or axioms, based upon previous research or studied guesses, that enter logical systems as "hypotheses"; (2) the definition of key terms in the axioms or postulates as well as a statement of undefined terms; and (3) the theorems (or hypotheses or propositions) that are logically derived from the axioms or postulates and which are subject to "test" through empirical observation.

The nonstandardized terminology of the so-called axiomatic method is troublesome. Some writers distinguish between axioms and postulates, employing the former to refer to self-evident truths; however, many others use these terms synonymously.[18] At times, axioms and postulates are equated with hypotheses, but most frequently hypotheses are equated with theorems or propositions. A proposition or hypothesis, as we employ it herein, refers to a statement (particularly one concerning the relations among variables) that can be empirically demonstrated to be true or false; it is therefore to be distinguished from a tautology, a statement that is true by virtue of the rules of language alone.

Several gains accrue from use of the axiomatic method. One is greater parsimony and economy. But more than this, the method has proven especially useful in exposing defects in one's reasoning process and in forcing the researcher to explicate his assumptions so that they can readily be checked by other scholars. More broadly, commitment to the axiomatic method leads researchers to integrate otherwise segmented observations into a coherent whole.

Although a number of sociologists are employing the axiomatic method in a verbal manner, others are proceeding a step further, translating natural languages into symbolic form. Symbolic logic, because of the slimness of the notations, permits us to cope with a more complex set of postulates, and consequently the deductive inferences that are drawn (the theorems, propositions, or hypotheses) are likely to possess a much higher degree of psychological novelty than would otherwise be the case. It is this psychological novelty that fulfills one of the major functions of the deduction process, for through deduction those assumptions that are implied in the postulates are made explicit in the theorems.

This reasoning suggests one limitation of the axiomatic method. Deduction per se yields no information that does not appear in the original postulates from which the theorems or propositions are drawn. It is this fact that has led scientists to analyze the process of induction or inference.

The Problem of Inference

The subject of logic or logical systems in science sooner or later leads us to consider the actual steps in scientific inquiry. Isn't there, we would like to know, a distinguishing set of steps, a structured logical prescription, which

[18] See, e.g., Blanché, *op. cit.,* 9 ff.

produces new and valid empirically based knowledge?

For a long time the proper response to this question was to argue that science is inductive, that it extracts out of nature an order to produce "truth," whereas other modes of analysis impose certain characteristics upon nature and are therefore subjective. This outlook harks back to the initial formulations of the scientific method. Some of the earliest statements regarding the inductive method, such as that by Hume, were attacks upon classical rationalism (although Aristotle implicitly provided much of the justification for the new objectivity). Commitment to some of the early formulations of the scientific method, such as Bacon's *Novum Organum,* long obscured the fact that induction could never be made to suffice for anything like a complete method. More recent thoughts on the nature of induction have reshaped the earlier conceptions almost beyond recognition. Still, philosophers of science and methodologists in sociology and related disciplines argue endlessly about the nature of induction and inference. And the controversy shows no signs of abating.

Although we cannot hope to resolve the problems relating to the logical basis of inference, it is possible to isolate those issues about which all researchers should be aware. We adopt a pragmatic approach, much as we did with deduction, for we believe that several conceptualizations regarding inference contribute to the explication of the research process in sociology. More significant still, the commitment of the researcher to a particular view regarding induction or inference shapes the formulation of his problem and influences the kinds of hypotheses he employs, the type of research procedures he favors, and the mode of analysis he undertakes.

DEDUCTION AND THEORY TESTING

Induction, as traditionally conceived, was the procedure of reasoning from "facts" to theories or, more technically, from singular statements to universal ones. Karl Popper has perhaps been the most ardent critic of this formulation.[19] Not that Popper is opposed to using empirical data. Quite the contrary.

Popper sets out to resolve the controversies between the empiricists, such as Hume and Locke (who stressed observations apart from concepts), and the rationalists, such as Descartes (who emphasized theory and ideas but gave minimum weight to empirical evidence). Moreover, Popper links his methodology to a particular political ideology: pragmatic democratic liberalism.[20] Popper, as much as or perhaps more than any other methodologist, has attempted to establish a causal connection between his logical system and his own political orientation. Certainly, the idea that a given logical system is inter-

[19] Karl R. Popper, *The Logic of Scientific Discovery* (New York: Wiley, Science Editions, 1961).

[20] Karl R. Popper, *Conjectures and Refutations* (New York: Basic Books, 1962), 5 ff. and 34–37.

related with a particular kind of political system deserves far more attention than it has received or than we can devote to it herein.

Our concern at this point is with the more formal aspect of Popper's theory. Popper sharply scores those scientists who think along traditional lines regarding induction.

> According to the view that will be put forward here, the method of critically testing theories, and selecting them according to the results of tests, always proceeds on the following lines. From a new idea, put up tentatively, and not yet justified in any way—an anticipation, a hypothesis, a theoretical system, or what you will—conclusions are drawn by means of logical deduction. These conclusions are then compared with one another and with other relevant statements, so as to find what logical relations (such as equivalence, derivability, compatibility, or incompatibility) exist between them.
>
> We may if we like distinguish four different lines along which the testing of a theory could be carried out. First there is the logical comparison of the conclusions among themselves, by which the internal consistency of the system is tested. Secondly, there is the investigation of the logical form of the theory, with the object of determining whether it has the character of an empirical or scientific theory, or whether it is, for example, tautological. Thirdly, there is the comparison with other theories, chiefly with the aim of determining whether the theory would constitute a scientific advance should it survive our various tests. And finally, there is the testing of the theory by way of empirical applications of the conclusions which can be derived from it.[21]

Popper in fact contends that a logical procedure for induction as such is nonexistent. He does *not,* however, deny the existence of an empirical science. What Popper is arguing is that scientists proceed along lines of the logico-deductive method. Popper's logico-deductive system, however, is of a particular sort.

Specifically, Popper avers: "To give a *causal explanation* of an event means to deduce a statement which describes it, using as premises of the deduction one or more *universal laws,* together with certain singular statements, the *initial conditions."*[22] This has also, until recently, been the position advanced by Hempel.[23]

[21] Popper, *The Logic of Scientific Discovery, op. cit.,* 32–33.

[22] *Ibid.,* 59.

[23] Carl G. Hempel, *Aspects of Scientific Explanation* (New York: Free Press, 1965).

In more technical terms, there are two parts to this kind of formulation: the *explanadum,* or description of the phenomenon to be explained, and the *explanans,* or statements accounting for the phenomenon. The *explanadum* is deduced from the *explanans.* The latter is composed of two parts: (1) the statement of the antecedent conditions that give rise to the event to be explained and (2) one or more universal laws. The premises that Popper terms universal laws must be statements that are true irrespective of time and place as well as empirically falsifiable.[24]

To clarify Popper's orientation, permit us to construct a highly adumbrated and crude model:

Law: Rapid industrialization always leads to rising expectations.
Law: Political revolutions always develop in societies that experience rising expectations.
Condition 1: Nigeria is experiencing rapid industrialization.
Conclusion or theorem: Nigeria will experience a political revolution.

Assuming we could define the various terms to everyone's satisfaction, we could disprove this logico-deductive system (or theory) if Nigeria does not experience a political revolution. One negative case is sufficient to disprove this deductive system because of the presence of the covering laws.

The notion of falsifiability is central to Popper's argument.[25] No theory, according to Popper, can ever be proven "true" with finality, but it can be proven "false" with finality. Popper thus equates the scientific method with negation of a particular type of logico-deductive system and its reconstitution in light of negative evidence or else the recourse to some entirely new theory. Essentially, Popper argues that the accretion of new knowledge occurs through modification and revision (in greater or lesser degree) of earlier explanatory systems in light of new empirical data.

Where the scientist is unable to uncover negative evidence, he must proceed *as if* the theory were true. The notion of "as if" arises because of the ever-present possibility of discovering a negative case.

Popper's concern with the principle of falsifiability is part of his reaction to the theories of Marx and Freud, among others.[26] To Popper, the proponents of these theories were always able to find some confirmatory data to support their vague, essentially loose formulations. Only by restating these theories

---

[24] Dray has employed the apt phrase "covering law theory" for this kind of orientation. William Dray, "The Historical Explanation of Actions Reconsidered," in Sidney Hook (ed.), *Philosophy and History* (New York: New York University Press, 1963), chap. 7.

[25] Popper, *The Logic of Scientific Discovery, op. cit., passim.*

[26] Popper, *Conjectures and Refutations. op. cit.,* chap. 1.

in such a manner that they can be falsified is it possible to demonstrate their inherent weaknesses.

But what about the situation that involves probability? Here Popper contends that probability as such does not attach to hypotheses but rather to reality and that what is required in this situation is a methodological rule decreeing that only reasonably represented elements are permissible.[27] Therefore, even within the context of probability statements Popper continues his search for universal laws, for his rule forbids any predictable and reproducible occurrence of systematic deviations.

It must be borne in mind that Popper has taken physics, rather than sociology, as the basis for his analysis. In the physical world, atoms, for example, though they "behave" randomly, nonetheless function consistently within certain ascertainable limits: they have consistently reproducible results. In time, a theory of this sort may be developed to account for social events, but it does not exist at present.

Although Popper's analysis (of which only the bare skeleton has been presented here) has served to objectify the logical steps in the scientific method, it still leaves us with many vexing problems. For instance, if we view Popper's formulation as an *ideal,* there are still many deviations from this logical structure on both the theoretical and the practical levels (see Chapter 9). Moreover, Popper dismisses as impossible of solution problems such as, "What transpires between the time a hypothesis is overthrown and the time a new explanatory system is constituted?" In Popper's view this question is not subject to logical analysis. Moreover, Popper devotes little attention to the "weight of evidence" issue, one of long-standing interest to sociologists.

THE NATURE OF DISCOVERY

To fill in gaps in Popper's reasoning, and particularly to understand the procedures social researchers employ under certain conditions, we turn to Hanson's *Patterns of Discovery.*[28] Hanson takes issue with some of Popper's views, notably the view which denies the logic of discovery. True, as Michael Polanyi argues,[29] there are acts of personal judgment in scientific discovery that cannot be replaced by any "operation of explicit reasoning." Nevertheless, Popper's belief that one cannot prescribe a logic of inquiry must be challenged. One can explicate the discovery process in at least a broad sense. If nothing else, discovery favors the well-prepared mind.

Hanson, in his argumentation, follows in the footsteps of the renowned

[27] Popper, *The Logic of Scientific Discovery, op. cit., passim.*
[28] Norwood R. Hanson, *Patterns of Discovery* (London: Cambridge, 1958).
[29] Michael Polanyi, *Personal Knowledge* (Chicago: University of Chicago Press, 1958).

American logician Peirce, whose concept of "abduction" or "retroduction" refers to the observation of "facts" and the construction of a theory to explain these facts.[30] Here one is faced with a set of data that cannot be adequately accounted for; one therefore reasons back from the observations in order to construct a theory that will account for them. Hanson devotes considerable space to detailing the process by which Kepler determined the true orbit of Mars, which Peirce describes as "the greatest piece of retroductive reasoning ever performed." This search for an explanatory link between what appeared to be discrete facts did in fact go on over a period of many years.

Hanson succinctly describes this retroductive process:

> A theory is not pieced together from observed phenomena; it is rather what makes it possible to observe phenomena as being of a certain sort, and as related to other phenomena. Theories put phenomena into systems. They are built up "in reverse"—retroductively. A theory is a cluster of conclusions in search of a premiss. From the observed properties of phenomena the physicist reasons his way towards a keystone idea from which the properties are explicable as a matter of course. The physicist seeks not a set of possible objects, but a set of possible explanations.[31]

In the Peirce-Hanson terms, we are herein attempting to "retroduce" the nature of scientific discovery itself, for while discovery occurs untold times, we understand only in a very approximate way the logic behind it. Our focus upon the sociocultural factors in research may assist us in this respect, if in no other way than that we may be able to hold these factors constant and thereby achieve a clearer understanding of the logical process of discovery.

But let us probe further into the matter of retroduction. Peirce viewed "induction," in contrast to retroduction, as the test or verification of a theory, as when an inductive inference results in the confirmation of a prediction. Induction, in Peirce's view, occurs only after the theory is fully developed; it does little to influence the theory. Of course, Peirce makes it clear in his treatment of retroduction that induction adds something substantive to the scientific process, that it is more than just the simple test of a developed theory. Nevertheless, Peirce dismisses it a little too hastily, for induction, or some similar process by another name, usually refers to a series of corroborative observations that despite their neutral appearance do inject something into the theory. It seems to us that retroduction would be free of induction if, and only if, persons like Kepler

[30] Hanson, *op. cit.* We rely primarily upon Hanson's interpretation of Peirce.
[31] *Ibid.*, 90.

didn't keep returning to their data. Here is a feedback situation, which implies influence in two directions: The theory compels us to continue looking, and the data force us to modify the theory.

Although Peirce perhaps overdraws this distinction between induction and retroduction, he was essentially correct in divorcing retroduction from the problem of "the weight of evidence" or "the adequacy of evidence"; that is, from the question, "What kind of evidence, and how much, is required to reject or confirm a theory?"

INDUCTION AND ADEQUACY OF EVIDENCE

Although both Popper and Hanson approach the problem from divergent perspectives, they are fundamentally interested in the logical structure of theory building, in developing a set of logically interrelated statements concerning the nature or patterning of events. But there is another facet to the logic of inquiry: the adequacy of the evidence. Methodologists in social science who concern themselves with induction frequently focus upon this particular issue.

When analyzing the adequacy-of-evidence question, we must first of all differentiate among types of propositions or hypotheses: statements than can be demonstrated to be true or false empirically. These stand in contrast to tautologies, which are true by reason of the rules of language alone.

To differentiate among hypotheses, we must distinguish between "eliminative" and "enumerative" induction, a terminology that goes back to Bacon and continues to find adherents among modern logicians such as Von Wright.[32] This distinction has been carried over into the social sciences by Znaniecki, who speaks of enumerative induction in contrast to "analytic induction," the latter being another way of saying eliminative induction.[33]

In eliminative induction, hypotheses are stated as "universal generalizations," so that ideally they can be falsified by a single negative case. Thus, contrast the simple hypothesis, "All adult males in North Borneo are over $4\frac{1}{2}$ feet tall," with that stated in enumerative terms, "Over 50 percent of the adult males in North Borneo are over 5 feet tall." To test the latter hypothesis, one would have to employ enumeration.

Znaniecki, as well as earlier logicians, seem to have equated enumerative induction with what we now term "descriptive" statistics.[34] They did not consider the principle underlying modern inductive statistics: probability sampling. (Popper, because of his stress upon universal generalizations, has attempted to fit probability statistics into the eliminative inductive framework; this approach

[32] Georg Henrik von Wright, *A Treatise on Induction and Probability* (London: Routledge, 1951), chap. 4.

[33] Florian Znaniecki, *The Method of Sociology* (New York: Farrar & Rinehart, 1934).

[34] *Ibid.*

is not that employed by most social researchers who utilize inductive statistics.)

In practice, it is perhaps unwise to draw too sharp a distinction between eliminative and enumerative induction. For example, take the hypothesis, "*All* large-scale organizations in industrial urban societies contain more men than women." In order to disprove the hypothesis, we would have to count noses in various organizations, in the process employing enumerative induction.

Yet it is also clear that researchers need to distinguish among different kinds of hypotheses. In later chapters we observe that scientists often employ different research designs when they seek to reject or falsify an hypothesis in contrast to situations where they seek to provide confirmatory data in support of a particular proposition or hypothesis.

In addition to distinguishing between hypotheses one seeks to reject in contrast to those one seeks to confirm, we can separate hypotheses relating to "form" from those relating to "content." Compare, for instance, the proposition, "A middle class is found in all industrial societies," with "In all industrial societies, the majority of the people belong to the middle class." Upon reflection it will become apparent that most universal, crosscultural generalizations deal with form rather than content. The greater the specificity demanded, the more difficult it becomes to formulate testable and valid universal hypotheses. Thus, we can more readily hypothesize that all societies have a family system than that certain types of relationships among husband and wife and children hold for all social orders.

Within the context of hypothesis formation and the adequacy of evidence, topics we have been discussing here, we ultimately encounter the problem of experimental inquiry and John Stuart Mill's methods of inductive inference.[35] Mill, in an effort to refine the logical structure of eliminative and enumerative induction, elaborated a set of rules of proof which he believed formed the basis of discovery.

Mill differentiated among the method of agreement, the method of difference, the method of residues, and the method of concomitant variations. The first two, the method of agreement and the method of difference, have become the basis for modern experimental designs, with emphasis upon comparison of control and experimental groups. The method of concomitant variation finds contemporary expression in the correlation techniques of statistics.

Although Mill claimed too much for his rules as procedures for discovery, these methods have become the basis for standardizing the nature and kind of evidence scientists accept in the testing of hypotheses. Certainly, Mill's argument brought to the fore the importance of experimental controls.

[35] John Stuart Mill, *Philosophy of Scientific Method* (New York: Hafner, 1950), 211–233.

INFERENCE—A REASSESSMENT[36]

We are now in a position to evaluate our discussion and to refine some of our arguments. Whether or not sociologists continue to find the idea of "induction" useful, they must recognize that numerous ambiguities and controversies surround employing the idea. Recent discussions have, at the very least, made it impossible to accept the traditional notion that knowledge can be generated by some elementary operational process or that scientists reason inductively or (in any such simple fashion) from singular statements to universal ones. Relying primarily upon research in the natural sciences, philosophers of science, such as Popper, Peirce, Hanson, and Von Wright have sought to abstract the *ideal* structure of scientific research. Their formulations provide social scientists with the basis for a clearer understanding of the logic of scientific inquiry, including the various deviations from the ideal structure.

Popper's emphasis upon the logico-deductive method has much to commend it. It lends emphasis to the priority of a logical and/or theoretical framework in scientific research. Social researchers who claim to proceed inductively often fail to discern the many universal generalizations from which they actually deduce their specific hypotheses. They work within an implicit theoretical framework, one which, if explicated, would become more useful to them.

Nevertheless, Popper's analysis has several limitations. Although we would agree with the priority he places upon theory, his framework is too narrow. For one thing, he fails to objectify the manner in which logico-theoretical constructs—the set of assumptions scientists make about the nature of man, of reality, and so on—influence the application of the logico-deductive method. The logical-theoretical constructs (discussed in detail below) are on a different level of abstraction than the postulates regarding substantive matters.

Popper may neglect these broader assumptions because he is committed to a particular view of man and of reality, one he associates with his logico-deductive approach. But social scientists employing divergent logical-theoretical constructs utilize the logico-deductive method, and this results in divergent interpretations of their empirical findings (see Chapter 9).

Rigid adherence to Popper's formulation would also force us to reject the logic of the dialectic, so significant in sociology as a mode of analysis. Moreover, as suggested above, Popper's particular logico-deductive system is an ideal which cannot be adhered to in practice. More specifically, an overcommitment to

---

[36] Various aspects of the nature of induction have not been considered herein. Many of the ongoing arguments among philosophers have implications for social research, but these lie outside the purview of our analyses. See, e.g., Henry E. Kyburg, Jr., and Ernest Nagel (eds.), *Induction: Some Current Issues* (Middletown, Conn.: Wesleyan University Press, 1963).

Popper's orientation makes it difficult, if not impossible, to distinguish between those researchers who begin with a logico-deductive system and falsifiable hypotheses and those who proceed with only vaguely defined problems or broad questions to guide them. Polanyi's analysis seems to call for such a distinction.[37] And we would agree with this reasoning. Otherwise, much exploratory research, guided by vague questions and hunches, may come to be regarded as improper or nonscientific. Such an approach would stifle, rather than encourage, certain significant social research.

Popper has, in fact, retreated from the strong stand he assumed in *The Logic of Scientific Discovery*. He now admits that "we may sometimes, for example in archaeology, advance through a chance observation"[38]—through an observation apart from any well-defined theory. Surely, here, as in the case where theories are falsified, retroduction of some kind of theory becomes vital. And we return to our position that the arguments of Hanson and Peirce and Von Wright are necessary supplements to the Popper view.

Of course, there are aspects of the logic of inference that still await objectification. Koestler in *The Sleepwalkers*[39] argued that some of the major scientific discoveries of the past arose from the unconscious reconstruction of theories after observation had occurred, somewhat in line with the retroduction of theories but with emphasis upon the unconscious. So too, Poincaré contended that the unconscious mind collates and sorts random possibilities among pertinent variables at a rate that defies the much too slow efforts on the conscious level.[40] Poincaré's suggestion seems inspiring in view of the recent knowledge that pulse electronics can actually move information at approximately the speed of light, as in the high-speed automatic computer. Perhaps the human psyche does, in a more or less random way, trace out consequences by systematically correlating through a wide range of possible logical combinations a number of variables that observing scientists consider to be pertinent—"gating,"[41] for example, the relatively few noncontradictory or logically acceptable relationships to a level available to the conscious mind, where they can emerge as "seemingly likely hypotheses" worthy of testing. This or some similar principle, if found to be true, would take the metaphysics out of intuition and aid in the formulation of a more rigorous logic of retroduction. Logicians of science might

[37] Michael Polanyi, "The Unaccountable Element in Science," *Philosophy*, 37 (January 1962), 1–14.

[38] Popper, *Conjectures and Refutations, op. cit.*, 28.

[39] Arthur Koestler, *The Sleepwalkers* (New York: Macmillan, 1959).

[40] H. Poincaré, *The Foundations of Science*, trans. by George B. Halsted (New York: The Science Press, 1913), 387–394.

[41] Roger Nett and Stanley A. Hetzler, *An Introduction to Electronic Data Processing* (New York: Free Press, 1959), 128.

begin to study cybernetics as a basis for a clearer explication of the logic of science.

Theoretical Assumptions and Logical-Theoretical Constructs

With the discussion of the broad logical form of theory building in hand, we can now turn to the assumptions or premises that researchers make concerning their method and the nature of the reality they study.

Ordinarily the scientist's assumptions combine to form some kind of logical system, or what we would term "a set of logical-theoretical constructs." In sociology, structural-functionalism, symbolic interactionism, and positivism all involve, for example, certain assumptions about reality, the nature of man, and the scientist's relationship to his empirical data—assumptions that are usually linked together logically to some extent. These sets of assumptions serve as paradigms (to appropriate Kuhn's terminology)[42] or frameworks within which the sociologist proceeds to formulate or test his substantive generalizations. The assumptions not only influence the scientist's choice of research methods but affect his interpretations of the data as well.[43]

Here we are not attempting to analyze, as did Merton, the interaction between theory and data.[44] Actually, when Merton discussed "serendipity," he was concerned, in somewhat the Hanson-Peirce tradition, with the logical structure of research. We are intent upon examining a quite different problem; namely, those theoretical assumptions that are not necessarily associated with any substantive research area.

These assumptions, although generally more abstract than generalizations regarding substantive matters, can be also ordered into different levels of abstraction. Some of the premises, such as those regarding the particular relationship of the scientist to his data of observation, seem amenable to empirical test. Certainly some are potentially more subject to empirical scrutiny than are others; for example, the ultimate nature of social reality seems subject only to indirect empirical verification or to logical analysis.

What is significant for our purposes is that these theoretical assumptions guide the researcher both in his choice of topics of study and in his research pro-

---

[42] Thomas S. Kuhn, *The Structure of Scientific Revolutions* (Chicago: University of Chicago Press, 1962).

[43] Actually, one's assumptions about the nature of social reality may influence the manner in which particular concepts are defined and employed. This emerges from the analysis by Peter Nettl, "The Concept of System in Political Science," *Political Studies,* 14 (October, 1966), 305–388.

[44] Robert K. Merton, *Social Theory and Social Structure,* rev. ed. (New York: Free Press, 1957), chap. 3.

cedures, including on occasion even the specific techniques, such as the type of interviewing, employed. At the very least, specific research methods or techniques are more compatible with some logical-theoretical constructs than with others. So it is with the procedures used in analyzing and in interpreting data.

The following categories, though not exhaustive, include those that continually recur and which strongly influence the specific course of the research enterprise.

ASSUMPTIONS ABOUT SOCIAL REALITY. These rank among the most significant of the premises in social research. Analysis of this category, however, is complicated by the presence within it of several subdimensions: (1) fluidity or stability, (2) integration or conflict, (3) materialism or idealism, and (4) the individual or the group as the basic unit of observation and analysis.

1. The assumption of fluidity or of stability in the social order. The choice here is a matter of long-standing debate among sociologists. There are some sociologists, like Blumer,[45] who, while conceding that there is a degree of order in the social world, stress the ever-changing nature of social reality and see the social order as in a state of becoming. In firm opposition to this stance are those scholars who believe that social reality is basically fixed and stable.[46] This last-mentioned orientation is perhaps the dominant one in contemporary sociology. Those who adhere to it answer the question, "How can social systems be orderly and patterned when scientists have formulated so few well-defined laws?" by contending that sociology is a young science, that sociologists have yet to formulate the methodology and the theory that are essential if we are to grasp the order that lies hidden below the surface. These sociologists grant that social systems appear to be in disarray. But they argue that sociologists will in time be able to uncover the fixed order that actually exists.

Associated with the premise of fluidity or of rigidity are the conflicting assumptions concerning the extent of man's control over his environment. Those sociologists who posit a stable order generally assume that man simply responds to such an order. Others, such as Mead and Blumer, object to this reasoning; instead their emphasis has been upon fluidity and the actor's ability to reshape his environment. That Blumer objects to operational definitions of concepts and advocates the use of "sensitizing concepts" is consistent with his image of social reality.[47]

2. The assumption of integration or of conflict. For the integrationists, represented by Parsons in many of his writings, man strives toward harmony and

---

[45] Blumer, *op. cit.*

[46] Such a writer as William R. Catton, Jr., *From Animistic to Naturalistic Sociology* (New York: McGraw-Hill, 1966), seems to fall into this category. Most social scientists stand somewhere between Catton and Blumer, (*op. cit*).

[47] Blumer, *op. cit.*

cooperation and shuns tension and conflict.[48] This viewpoint stands in sharp contrast to the perspective of such conflict theorists as Marx and Simmel, who generally assumed that human beings or social systems are continually at odds with one another. Surely this latter viewpoint leads one to analyze the social order in terms quite different from those of sociologists who stress integration and cooperation. Not only are the conflict theorists much more likely to utilize dialectical logic, but many disavow the notion of equilibrium, unlike most integrationists, who tend to adhere to this notion. Even when the conflict theorists posit the presence of an equilibrium, they conceptualize it somewhat differently than do the integrationists.[49]

To be sure, theorizing at times may become rather complex. We have only to examine the theorists within the Marxian tradition. While Marx seems to have rejected the notion of equilibrium, such writers as Bukharin, though committed to materialism and a conflict view of reality, nonetheless assumed the existence of an "unstable equilibrium" within society.[50]

3. The assumption of materialism or of idealism. A third premise that pervades social science literature separates the materialists from the idealists or neo-idealists. Although most physical scientists work comfortably with the assumption of materialism,[51] social scientists typically have found it difficult to accept the notion that the material world is the ultimate reality.

The Marxists have been the leading exponents of a materialist interpretation of reality. Even so, there is considerable disagreement over just what they mean by materialism and what are the implications of this position for the study of social life.[52]

[48] Although some of Parsons' supporters, such as Robin Williams, have defended him against the charge of ignoring strains, even they acknowledge his preoccupation with order, stability, and equilibrium. Robin M. Williams, Jr., "The Sociological Theory of Talcott Parsons," in Max Black (ed.), *The Social Theories of Talcott Parsons* (Englewood Cliffs, N.J.: Prentice-Hall, 1961), 71. It is significant that Williams uses terms such as "strains" and "inconsistencies" but not "conflict." Yet it is conflict that Parsons shies away from analyzing. One reason is that Parsons ignores the notions of "negative" and "counter-system."

[49] For an informative review of five different usages of "equilibrium" within social science, see Pitirim A. Sorokin, *Social and Cultural Dynamics,* vol. 4 (New York: American Book, 1941), 677–693. Each of these usages seems to be associated with different assumptions about the nature of man and social reality.

[50] Nikolai Bukharin, *Historical Materialism* (New York: International Publishers, 1925), 74–77.

[51] Cf. John G. Kemeny, *A Philosopher Looks at Science* (Princeton, N.J.: Van Nostrand, 1959), 219.

[52] See, e.g., A. K. Saran, "The Marxian Theory of Social Change," *Inquiry, 1* (Spring, 1963), 70–127; A. Zvorikine, "Technology and the Laws of its Development," *Technology and Culture, 3* (Fall, 1962), 443–458; Alfred G. Meyer, *Marxism* (Ann Arbor, Mich.: University of Michigan Press, Ann Arbor Paperbacks, 1963); Paul Tillich, "Marx's View

Today within sociology the chief battle ground for the materialist-nonmaterialist controversy has been the field of human ecology. At one pole stand those writers who insist we cannot analyze spatial activities or structures without recourse to the actor's interpretation thereof.[53] They regard the conceptual world as the ultimate reality. But a number of ecologists have assumed a counterposition. Duncan and Schnore, for instance, posit the main variables of technology, environment, demography, and social organization, and even the last named must be studied without recourse to values or beliefs.[54] They conceive of impersonal forces that lie beyond the interpretation and understanding of the actors as the major determinant of, say, man's orientation to space. Although these sociologists share one key premise—materialism—with the Marxists, they do not assume, as the latter do, that the social order is in a state of conflict.

There are of course other variants of this materialist-nonmaterialist debate. Many sociologists, for instance, work within the framework of dualism. And there are phenomenologists who regard the fundamental reality as not the material world or one's system of concepts but instead the relationships (or link) between the two.[55]

4. The assumption of the basic unit of study as the individual or the group. Although some sociologists would dismiss this argument as lacking in significance, the issue refuses to subside. The recent exchanges between Homans and Parsons point to the persistence of this particular debate.[56] Homans, as well as a number of philosophers of science, rejects the idea of a group or social system as the basic unit of analysis. Many of these writers believe that the whole (or the group) is merely the sum of its parts. Certainly, this premise will structure both one's collection and one's analysis of data.

---

of History," in Stanley Diamond (ed.), *Culture in History* (New York: Columbia, 1960), 631–641; Erich Fromm, *Marx's Concept of Man,* with a translation of Marx's *Economic and Philosophical Manuscripts* by T. B. Bottomore (New York: Ungar, 1961); and Raymond Aron, *Main Currents in Sociological Thought,* trans. by Richard Howard and Helen Weaver (New York: Basic Books, 1965), esp. 153–155.

[53] Walter Firey, *Land Use in Central Boston* (Cambridge, Mass.: Harvard, 1957); and Sidney M. Willhelm, *Urban Zoning and Land-Use Theory* (New York: Free Press, 1962).

[54] Otis Dudley Duncan and Leo F. Schnore, "Cultural, Behavioral, and Ecological Perspectives in the Study of Social Organization," *American Journal of Sociology,* 65 (September, 1959), 132–146. Cf. Jack P. Gibbs and Walter T. Martin, "Toward a Theoretical System of Human Ecology," *Pacific Sociological Review,* 2 (Spring, 1959), 29–36.

[55] See, e.g., Alfred Schutz, *Collected Papers. 1. The Problem of Social Reality* (The Hague: Martinus Nijhoff, 1962).

[56] Talcott Parsons, "Levels of Organization and the Mediation of Social Interaction," *Sociological Inquiry,* 34 (Spring, 1964), 207–220; and George Homans, "Commentary," *op. cit.,* 221–231.

ASSUMPTIONS ABOUT THE NATURE OF MAN AND HIS POTENTIALITIES. This major assumption[57] overlaps with, but is also somewhat distinct from, the assumption about social reality.

One group of social scientists have stressed the irrational dimension of man's nature and his actions. Those in the Freudian tradition, for instance, believe that man has created a society which represses his biological urges to his own detriment. For Freud, man was propelled by hidden motives and drives that we can understand only by examining the unconscious. Thus, Freud's method of interviewing (see Chapter 8) was founded upon the assumption that man is fundamentally irrational. On the other hand, Freud the scientist attempted to impose a rational order upon man's irrational actions.

Although the attention given to irrationality in modern social psychology looms large, numerous social scientists, including many economists and some political scientists and sociologists, have regarded man as a rational being. Parsons in his *The Structure of Social Action* belongs in this category.[58] That the influence of Freud and the concern with the irrational became more pronounced in some of Parsons' later writings is indicative of the long-standing struggle by scholars to explain these rather divergent aspects of man.

Another division among social scientists regarding the nature of man pits the followers of Hobbes, who conceived of man as "treacherous" and at all times pursuing his interest at the expense of others,[59] against those scholars who, like Sorokin, have regarded man as willing to sacrifice his own ends and to contribute to some larger good.[60]

Finally, some sociologists are "pessimistic," others are "optimistic," regarding man's ability to improve himself or his environment.[61] In large part the perspective of these social researchers is associated with their assumptions regarding the nature of reality. For example, it is easier for sociologists within

[57] Schools of psychology have arisen around differing conceptions of man, and these in turn are related to somewhat different views of reality. See, e.g., T. W. Wann (ed.), *Behaviorism and Phenomenology* (Chicago: University of Chicago Press, 1964), and the multivolume work edited by Sigmund Koch, *Psychology: A Study of a Science* (New York: McGraw-Hill, 1959–1963), for a modern expression of some long-standing controversies.

[58] Talcott Parsons, *The Structure of Social Action,* 2nd ed. (New York: Free Press, 1949). Also, William H. Riker, *The Theory of Political Coalitions* (New Haven: Yale, 1962) for a somewhat different perspective on rationality.

[59] Gerhard Lenski, *Power and Privilege* (New York: McGraw-Hill, 1966), builds his theory of stratification on the assumption that men act in terms of "self-interest."

[60] Pitirim A. Sorokin, *Altruistic Love* (Boston: Beacon Press, 1950).

[61] From one perspective the positivists or naturalists who take a deterministic view of social reality are pessimistic in that they do not believe that man can control his own destiny. Yet most of these scholars seem to concede that in the long run the application of the scientific method will lead to a better existence.

the Mead-Blumer tradition to think of man as capable of self-improvement than for sociologists who are committed to a conception of a fixed set of relations in the social order to do so. The former conceive of man as re-creating or remaking his environment during the course of action; man is not merely a billiard ball who responds to external social forces. The Marxian materialists, for instance, face a dilemma as they strive to reconcile their materialistic (or external) determinism of human action with the notion that man can restructure his environment through revolutionary efforts or indeed that Marxian ideas play a positive role in human affairs.

ASSUMPTIONS CONCERNING THE OBSERVER'S RELATIONSHIPS TO OBSERVED SOCIAL PHENOMENA. Every social researcher makes some assumption, often only implicitly, concerning the scientific observer vis-à-vis social reality. In the first chapter we took cognizance of the marked divergence between the logical empiricists and the adherents of the *verstehen* approach. The former typically assume that the observer is able to remove himself from what he observes, that he can and does function independently of the reality he studies. The *verstehen* group, on the other hand, contend that the observer influences, and is in turn influenced by, the social world he observes. We have, it will be recalled, attempted to construct a position midway between these two views. We believe that the observer influences and is influenced by the social order he studies, but that he can, by objectifying this interrelationship, eventually exert some degree of control over it and thus attain in relatively high degree the objectivity that the logical empiricist takes for granted but actually rarely achieves.

Some adherents to positivist thought press their argument further by contending that it is possible to study social action without regard to "meaning" or "mentalist" considerations. This position continues to be criticized by numerous social scientists, many of whom point to the fact that material objects and formal social relations vary considerably according to the meaning the actor imputes to them—according to the actor's cultural values and beliefs and his definition of the situation.

Then there are those sociologists who tend to impose "scientific categories" upon their data, under the assumption that the categories exist prior to the observations. In extreme form, this viewpoint has few champions. However, sociologists such as Parsons approach this position in their writings.[62] In opposition to these are sociologists such as Znaniecki who assume that the social order exists apart from the scientist and that he discovers this order via observa-

[62] Talcott Parsons, *The Social System* (New York: Free Press, 1951); and Charles Ackerman and Talcott Parsons, "The Concept of 'Social System' as a Theoretical Device," in Gordon J. DiRenzo, *Concepts, Theory, and Explanation in the Behavioral Sciences* (New York: Random House, 1966), chap. 2.

tion, that the categories inhere in the data.[63]

ASSUMPTIONS CONCERNING THE LEVEL OF THEORY.   Whether one should work with simple isolated hypotheses, utilize abstract or grand theoretical systems, or employ "middle-range" theories continues to elicit controversy in sociology, psychology, and anthropology. One's choice in this matter structures the whole research process.

The scientist's level of theory is intimately linked with his image about the growth of knowledge. A number of researchers in the narrow empiricist tradition have conceived of knowledge as accumulating piece by piece, with many of the elements eventually falling into place.[64] This reasoning is somewhat at odds with the logico-deductive orientation championed by Popper and outlined above. In Popper's view the scientist must take a more active role in ordering scientific knowledge.[65] Actually, it is possible to conceive of the scientist's utilizing the isolated hypotheses as the building blocks for a more elegant deductive edifice.

Still another view could be imputed to writers such as Sorokin who seem to believe that it is only through grand theoretical schemes that the various discrete bits and pieces of knowledge are merged into some integrated or meaningful whole.[66]

Another variant of the sociologist's image about the growth of knowledge is held by some *verstehen* sociologists. Implicit in their conception of social science is the idea that relatively little *accumulation* of knowledge as such occurs. Although we continually extend the range and amount of information about societies and cultures, we do not, as do the natural scientists, typically use smaller hypotheses or theories to build more all-encompassing explanatory schemes.

The different conceptions regarding the level of theory are frequently associated with different orientations toward the validity of social data. Some logical positivists, for instance, argue that only when data have been quantified can these be accepted as reliable and valid evidence in testing scientific hypotheses; measurement becomes a necessary and sufficient condition for a science of society. At the opposite extreme stand those sociologists who argue that it is impossible to quantify effectively social experience; yet, we must keep in mind that they still fancy themselves empiricists. Between these two poles are ranged a

---

[63] Znaniecki, *op. cit.* Cf. Paul F. Lazarsfeld and Allen H. Barton, "Some General Principles of Questionnaire Classification," in Paul F. Lazarsfeld and Morris Rosenberg (eds.), *The Language of Social Research* (New York: Free Press, 1955), 83–93. Lazarsfeld apparently stands closer to Znaniecki and many symbolic interactionists than he does to Parsons.

[64] Cf. Marvin Bressler, "Some Selected Aspects of American Sociology, September 1959 to December 1960," *The Annals, 337* (September, 1961), 154–156.

[65] Popper, *Conjectures and Refutations, op. cit.,* chap. 1, or his *The Logic of Scientific Discovery, op. cit.*

[66] Sorokin, *Social and Cultural Dynamics,* 4 vols., *op. cit.*

variety of social scientists. Our own position is that quantified data serve as one kind of evidence among many.

ASSUMPTIONS ABOUT CAUSAL OR EXPLANATORY VARIABLES.   The kind and nature of the variables that the researcher employs reflect, among other things, his assumptions about the nature of reality and the proper level of theorizing.

The researcher's formulation of his explanatory variable (or variables) certainly depends upon his substantive area of investigation—whether it be personality systems, social systems, or cultural systems—and the assumed relationships among the types of social phenomena. But the substantive area of study is in large measure a reflection of the scientist's conception of what is the basic nature of social reality. Materialists would explain social change in terms of variables such as Marx's "means of production," whereas the neo-idealists would stress such variables as values or ideas.

Sociologists are likely to employ one or more of the following as their key independent (or explanatory) variables:[67]

1. *The historical variable.*   A number of social scientists, particularly some anthropologists, continue to assume that each culture has its own laws and, therefore, that we can understand the patterning of a cultural system only if we conceive of it as a relatively self-contained entity persisting over time. This assumption, stressing as it does the dependence of the present upon the past, commits the scholar to historical research and to some evolutionary framework as a means for understanding the present or "predicting" the future.

2. *The economic and/or technological variable.*   Many social scientists have taken the industrial revolution as the primary varable for explaining the changing structure of societies. Some writers believe that the economic variable is analytically distinct from the technological, and they tend to emphasize one or the other. Marx and his followers, on the other hand, have spoken of the "means of production," incorporating within this notion both technological and economic factors, with apparent stress upon the latter.

But matters actually can become complicated. Whereas Marx treated both the technological and economic variables as materialistic, other scholars in the neo-idealistic tradition view the technological variable in a very different manner. For it is possible to examine technology in terms of the system of ideas and knowledge by which the material objects are manipulated.

3. *Cultural values.*   This is perhaps the most widely agreed-upon variable for explaining differences among societies. Max Weber relied upon the value and

---

[67] For a discussion of some of the variables mentioned herein in terms of a specific substantive field of sociology, see Gideon Sjoberg, "Theory and Research in Urban Sociology," in Philip M. Hauser and Leo F. Schnore (eds.), *The Study of Urbanization* (New York: Wiley, 1965), chap. 5.

belief system in his analysis of the relationships between religion and the economic system in various societies around the world. Parsons and his students have followed in a similar tradition and thus stand in rather sharp opposition to scholars who give priority to materialistic factors.

4. *Social power.* Many political scientists and sociologists, particularly those influenced by Pareto, Mosca, and Michels, believe that social power can be employed to account for the principal structural arrangements within and among systems. Power, as an explanatory variable, was used by Marx to supplement his emphasis upon the means of production and by Weber to supplement his emphasis upon cultural values.

5. *Other variables.* We could elaborate upon a host of variables—population size, the city, age and sex structures, the family, the suburbs, bureaucracy—that some sociologists have relied upon to explain a particular set of social phenomena. Indeed, the wide range of variables employed becomes a source of considerable confusion when we seek to classify types of social research. For one thing, many of the variables are not upon the same level of abstraction. Some are more concrete, or specific, than others, inasmuch as some sociologists prefer to work within low-level theoretical frameworks.

IMPLICATIONS OF THE THEORETICAL ASSUMPTIONS

The aforementioned premises (as well as others that have not been mentioned) enter into such logical-theoretical constructs as structural functionalism, symbolic interactionism, and dialectic materialism. Even the "social problems" construct harbors a number of hidden assumptions. Although this scheme is of limited analytical power and is loosely formulated, it is one of the widely used logical-theoretical constructs in modern sociology. Inherent within it are such assumptions as (1) man can control his own destiny if he can understand his problems, (2) problems in the system under study are defined by actors in that system, and (3) modern industrial systems would be "the best of all possible worlds" if only their limitations were corrected.

This line of reasoning suggests another proposition implicit in the foregoing discussion: that many theoretical assumptions are associated with the scientist's broader ideological orientation and with his social position within the society. It is often difficult to separate the theoretical assumptions a person makes in his role as a scientist from the ideological assumptions he makes in his role as a member of the broader society that supports the scientific enterprise. This confusion is especially transparent with respect to the premises regarding the nature of man. Here a sociology of knowledge orientation becomes essential in order to expose the unstated assumptions.

But more significant at this point is the proposition that the advocates of the logico-deductive method cannot avoid making theoretical assumptions that, unlike the postulates or axioms which involve statements about certain empirical regularities, are not subject to empirical test. The failure of philosophers of science to examine these theoretical premises stems from the following facts: (1) that they are (as in the case of Popper) advocating certain assumptions of their own,[68] (2) that most of them are logico-empiricists and thus consider many of the assumptions as metaphysical, or (3) that in the natural sciences these theoretical premises often may be conveniently ignored. It is quite clear that the theoretical assumptions cannot be ignored in the formulation and testing of logico-deductive schemes in the social sciences.

In human ecology, for example, the neo-idealists, committed as they are to studying the actor's definition of time and space, must elicit via questionnaires or other interviewing procedures the actor's definition or interpretation of the spatial and temporal order. The materialists dismiss subjective factors as irrelevant and rely instead upon population composition, technology, and other variables, which they contend can be analyzed independently of the values and beliefs of the actors in the system.

In addition to the impact of theoretical assumptions upon the development of axiomatic theories, we must recognize that there is an association between the scientist's theoretical assumptions and the logical structure the scientist employs. And deductive systems are not the only logical systems used by social scientists. Sociologists may also apply the logic of the dialectic, and those who do are committed to a conception of reality wherein the social order is evolving or in a constant state of flux rather than consisting of a fixed set of relationships.

Yet, the relationship between some logical systems or systems of inference may be very complex. Znaniecki in *The Method of Sociology* sought to link the method of analytic induction (or eliminative induction) with a particular concept of social reality, one which was relatively independent of the observer's conceptual system.[69] The researcher discovers these patterns through the negative case approach. Although this argument is informative, the negative case method is not necessarily associated with the view of reality as espoused by Znaniecki. Popper, it will be recalled, employed the negative case approach when calling for falsifiable hypotheses;[70] but Popper's assumptions as well as his logic of theory building differ considerably from those of Znaniecki.

Obviously, methodologists face major difficulties in analyzing the relationships of theoretical assumptions to logical systems, substantive generalizations, and specific research procedures. One reason is that the assumptions can be combined in a variety of ways. Even trained sociologists find themselves entangled in a web of confusion when they attempt to classify the logical-theoretical constructs that make up contemporary social theory. But there are compelling reasons

[68] Popper, *Conjectures and Refutations, op. cit.*

[69] Znaniecki, *op. cit.*

[70] Popper, *The Logic of Scientific Discovery, op. cit.*

for the dearth of agreed-upon classificatory schemes.

Illustrative of this confusion are the positions taken by sociologists who classify themselves (or are classified by others) as positivists. Aside from the old-line Comteans, who are no longer represented on the contemporary scene, there are sociologists who would insist that description of social patterns is sufficient and that ultimately the empirical findings will fall into some meaningful whole. In addition, the sociologists who follow in the footsteps of Bridgman and Lundberg have as their primary objective the testing of hypotheses operationally; and the contemporary logical empiricists, such as Schrag and Zetterberg, emphasize the significance of the axiomatic method in social research, although they retain an emphasis upon operationalism when testing their propositions.[71]

Still other subgroupings within positivism could be delineated. There are, for instance, those positivists who can be classed as materialists. And within this group some stress discovery, while others employ the logico-deductive approach.[72] At the same time, both are concerned with "aggregates," or "collectivities." Granted that they study aggregates as if they were "individuals" (being unconcerned with relating parts to wholes); these scholars nevertheless differ from positivists in the field of social psychology who take the individual as the ultimate unit of analysis.

At this point the question arises: Is there in all this confusion any semblance of order? Yes, and for this reason: If a sociologist makes certain assumptions about social reality, for example, he sets limits upon the other kinds of assumptions he can make. Thus we can discern in *ideal-type* terms certain major schools of thought with respect to the logical-theoretical constructs that are employed. We have already delineated two of these major groupings in our introduction when we contrasted the *verstehen* school with the positivists.[73] The former conceive of social reality as fluid and emerging, with no sharp division between the scientist and the data of observation. They utilize the actor's frame of reference in collecting and analyzing their data. Ultimately they utilize understanding in testing the validity of their theory. The positivists, on the other hand, tend to view reality in mechanistic terms and assume the existence of a sharp dividing

---

[71] Clarence Schrag, "Elements of Theoretical Analysis in Sociology," in Llewellyn Gross (ed.), *Sociological Theory: Inquiries and Paradigms* (New York: Harper & Row, 1967), 220–253; and Hans Zetterberg, *On Theory and Verification in Sociology,* 3rd ed. (Totowa, N.J.: Bedminster, 1965).

[72] Cf. Otis Dudley Duncan *et al., Metropolis and Region* (Baltimore: Johns Hopkins, 1960), and Jack P. Gibbs and Walter Martin, "Urbanization, Technology, and the Division of Labor: International Patterns," *American Sociological Review, 27* (October, 1962), 667–677.

[73] Although there are variations in the way these basic schools of thought are treated, and in the way individual scholars are classified, there is good reason why this division should be a basic organizing principle for many works in theory. See, e.g., Don Martindale, *The Nature and Types of Sociological Theory* (Boston: Houghton Mifflin, 1960).

line between the scientists and the data of observation. They tend to ignore the actor's perspective. In the end, the positivists would judge a theory's validity in terms of its predictability.

Although we recognize the presence of many complications in classifying theories according to their major assumptions, we believe that the distinction between the *verstehen* sociologists and the positivists is a convenient tool for developing the arguments in the succeeding chapters. As mentioned earlier, we attempt to draw upon both viewpoints in formulating a methodology for social research.

CHAPTER 4

The Researcher
and the Social System

To comprehend the manifold dilemmas confronting the social scientist as he collects and processes his research materials, we must do more than merely examine the history, assumptions, and abstract rules of scientific inquiry. We must determine how the rules are actually applied by their perpetuators: the scientists themselves. In so doing, we consider not only the professed ideals of science—those stating what scientists *ought to do*—but also what scientists *do*.

We begin with the postulate that scientists act in accordance with certain norms. In turn, to understand these norms we must examine not only the "associations" through which scientists sustain the normative order but the effect of scientists' roles and statuses upon their adherence to (or deviation from) the norms. Our analysis forms the basis for the treatment in later chapters of the impact of social forces on project selection, on data collection, and on the analysis and publication of research findings.

Science as a System of Norms

The rules, procedures, and methods of science are norms—analogous to the norms in religious, governmental, and other institutions. From the perspective of the means-end schema, some of these norms function as conditions ruling out certain actions as nonpermissible; others serve as means for achieving ends.[1] Some norms are highly "abstract"; others are relatively "concrete." The latter

[1] Sidney M. Willhelm, *Urban Zoning and Land-Use Theory* (New York: Free Press, 1962), 34–40. Willhelm has reconceptualized Talcott Parsons' theory of action as stated in *The Structure of Social Action*, 2nd ed. (New York: Free Press, 1949), 44 ff., in a useful manner by arguing that means are norms.

include the means, or specific methods, the scientist employs in his collection and analysis of data. For example, the social scientist may select from among available norms (or sets of norms) such procedures of unit selection as random sampling or the case study approach—whatever he believes will enhance the search for "truth" or empirically grounded knowledge. In positively valuing certain methods and negating others, he is influenced not only by his theoretical commitment but by his role and status in the society. To treat the scientist as a non-person is to ignore social reality.

Although scientist and layman alike act in accordance with social norms, the two differ in some fundamental respects. Ideally the former far more than the latter strives to understand the assumptions underlying his own actions so as to explicate and objectify, and, wherever possible, to formalize, the rules and procedures that govern his actions. The layman, on the other hand, tends to disregard these or take them as given.

From this perspective, sound methodology in social science is perforce sound sociology as well. Unlike some sociologists, we believe it is impossible to draw a fruitful analytical distinction between the sociology of science and the methodology of social research.[2] For as long as researchers are human beings engaged in the study of their fellow men, they must examine their own values and their roles, both in science and in the society at large. In the language of social research, the scientist is a significant variable in his own investigations.

After all, the norms of science are human constructs; even logical systems, absolute within themselves, are up to a point relative to time, place, and purpose. Granted that scientific procedures are much more highly formalized and explicit than are the rules that govern one's nonscientific activities, an element of arbitrariness still attaches to most of the techniques of science. The recourse to fixed levels (say, the 1 percent and 5 percent level) as a basis for rejecting or accepting a statistical hypothesis is a case in point.

It is mainly through the conventionalization of research procedures that scientists are able to achieve consensus, a point the operationalists rightly stress. Moreover, standardization of norms in science eases the diffusion of research methods and findings across divergent cultural boundaries. When we speak of science as ideally a crosscultural enterprise, we mean that the norms of science can be readily understood and applied by persons in a variety of cultural settings.

[2] Roy G. Francis, *The Rhetoric of Science* (Minneapolis: University of Minnesota Press, 1961), 8. Some philosophers of science have also attempted to draw a distinction between the sociology of science and methodology. See, e.g., Herbert Feigl, "Philosophy of Science," in Roderick M. Chisholm *et al., Philosophy* (Englewood Cliffs, N.J.: Prentice-Hall, 1964), 472–473. More generally, what is "scientific" cannot be set apart from what is "social"—yet such a distinction has been advanced by, for example, Robert K. Merton in his "Social Conflict over Styles of Sociological Work," *Transactions of the Fourth World Congress of Sociology, 1959,* vol. 3 (Louvain, Belgium: International Sociological Association, 1961), 34.

Inasmuch as the methods in social science are less conventionalized than those in the natural sciences, the diffusion of the sociologist's research procedures and findings has fallen far short of the intended goal.

The matter of conventionalization forces us to confront a dilemma within the scientific method itself: the presence of contradictory requirements, the struggle between order and creativity. Although the development of science depends upon creativity, one form of which is discovery, scientists can "create" consensus by employing measures that will ensure conformity. And without some conformity in scientists' actions, there could be no commonly agreed upon body of knowledge.

A source of considerable difficulty stems from the temptation to view the norms that constitute the scientific method as possessing some sort of ontological status. The neophyte, as he becomes socialized into the scientific system, often comes to accept, albeit unconsciously, many of the norms (both the means and conditions) as "absolute," or "sacred." Consequently, some scientists become prototypes of organization men, strongly committed to the status quo and viewing as a threat persons who, in the search for truth, reject the prevailing normative order or segments thereof. In the end we must be cognizant of both the gains and the losses that accrue from rigid adherence to, and deviation from, what is at any given moment accepted practice.

IDEAL VERSUS ACTUAL NORMS

Within science, as within other social systems, we can distinguish analytically among various kinds of norms. There are, for instance, the "ideal norms," the collective expectations of how people *ought to act,* and the "actual norms," the collective expectations of how people *will act.*[3] (The term "actual norm" is not fully satisfactory, but neither are such possible synonyms as "informal," "*sub rosa,*" or "compromise norm.")

Both ideal and actual norms should be distinguished from behavior. Social scientists observe behavior or products of behavior, but they study norms.[4] Norms involve some conceptualization of what should or will be. There are, after all, many kinds of behavior that sociologists never think of analyzing. For example, of the wide variety of physical movements on the part of the individual, only those that are socially or culturally relevant, those that are normatively oriented, are, or can be, studied.

The ideal norms are those that methodologists are prone to enunciate and

[3] These definitions are based, with certain modifications, upon Jack P. Gibbs, "Norms: The Problem of Definition and Clarification," *American Journal of Sociology,* 70 (March, 1965), 586–594.

[4] Our orientation is in line with Weber's definition of social action. Max Weber, *The Theory of Social and Economic Organization,* trans. by A. H. Henderson and Talcott Parsons (New York: Free Press Paperback, 1964).

that researchers are enjoined to follow, whereas the actual norms are those which researchers adhere to in carrying out their daily chores.[5] Though the two may correspond, they frequently do not. We would stress that much of the behavior we observe deviating from the ideal expectations is far from formless. If it were, sociologists could not study it. Therefore, we employ the concept of norm when talking about social action that does not fit the ideal expectations, to emphasize that this reflects a certain standard of conduct that has come to be regularized and accepted as legitimate. Both the functions of and interrelationships between the ideal and the actual have many unnoticed implications for methodology.

Certainly science cannot prosper without standards or norms. Yet, scientists may be at odds among themselves over what the ideals are or should be. Moreover, in many situations the norms are not objectified or are at best in a muzzy state. If we are to understand the character of the ideal norms and how and why they are compromised, the normative order must be raised to the level of "conscious reflection."

With respect to the sources of ideal norms, some of the most abstract ones stem from the general unity of science itself. More narrowly, the social sciences have looked to the natural sciences for the proper interpretation of what the normative order should be—in fact, for specific research methods (or norms). Early sociologists looked largely to classificatory biology, but as physics has achieved such great success in unfolding the secrets of nature, this has become the primary model for many sociologists (and other social scientists as well). In recent years, philosophers of science have been the main interpreters of natural science methods for social scientists. Of course, the methods of the more successful social science investigators also serve as the models for their colleagues.

The actual norms in scientific research also have several origins. First, in the absence of any ideal norms, actual norms arise more or less informally to guide the researcher in his data collection and analysis. Some of these patterns have arisen in the sampling of working, or specific, universes (see Chapter 6). Second, actual norms may arise from inconsistencies within the scientific enterprise; for example, they emerge as compromises among incompatible ideal norms. One instance of incompatibility is that between the ideal of systematized knowledge—the formalized research procedures—and the ideal of creativity. To achieve the latter, it is often necessary to violate certain ideal research procedures. Researchers do in fact consistently experiment with means for circumventing the limits that ideal norms impose. Frequently these deviations become formalized and routinized, and in time they may replace the older ideals.

Third, other actual or compromise norms, particularly those that stand in contrast to ideal ones, may owe their existence to scientists' adherence to the

---

[5] Kaplan recognizes some aspects of the overall problem with which we are grappling when he distinguishes between "reconstructed logic" and "logic-in-use." Abraham Kaplan, *The Conduct of Inquiry* (San Francisco: Chandler, 1964), 6–11.

ideals of various nonscientific reference groups. Even when the scientist utilizes the norms of science, he functions within an intricate web of social relationships. And a scientist's commitment to norms stemming from power and ethical considerations within the broader society may induce him to seek a compromise between these and the ideal research procedures. Social scientists are particularly vulnerable in this respect. Not that natural scientists are immune; we need only recall how Lysenko's commitment to Marxian ideology and the Communist power structure led to actions other than the ideal in genetics.[6] Still, the social scientist, because of the nature of his subject matter, is undeniably subject to greater pressures in both democratic and totalitarian social orders.

These actual norms, consisting partly of sound knowledge and partly of lore, must usually be sought outside the pages of published works on research methods. Yet these norms are implicit in the oft-repeated maxim of professors to their students: "One learns research by doing, by getting one's hands dirty, not by sitting in the classroom or reading books."

Often these actual or compromise norms are difficult to formalize and elevate to the plane of reflective consciousness. One learns them or, perhaps more accurately, gains sensitivity to them only through repeated exposure.

Some of the most significant compromise norms pertain to highly delicate aspects of social action. The touchy matters relating to out-of-bounds research projects[7] or to intellectual dishonesty seldom receive a formal airing in the literature. Most discussion of these topics is confined to personal conversations or to the gossip that goes the rounds.

A few scholars object to public discussion of the informal norms. They view these as improper subject matter for the uninitiated, or the public at large, who cannot be expected to appreciate the social pressures that give rise to these norms. Thus, if the layman is aware of the *sub rosa* norms, he is likely to misinterpret the actions of scientists, and, if he is influential, he may even cause withdrawal of support from scientific research—or so the argument runs.

Other scientists object to exposure of the actual norms as a means of protecting their own ego and security. This motive may be one reason for the overreaction on the part of some sociologists to the blunt criticisms of writers such as Mills.[8]

---

[6] For a discussion of one aspect of this case, see David Joravsky, "The Lysenko Affair," *Scientific American, 207* (November, 1962), 41–49.

[7] Some attention has been given to highly sensitive research areas; e.g., Norman L. Farberow (ed.), *Taboo Topics* (New York: Atherton, 1963). Of course, what is out of bounds in research varies over time within a sociocultural system and across systems.

[8] Although Mills himself did not shrink from harsh criticism of persons with whom he disagreed, one cannot but be struck by the highly personal tone of, for instance, Edward Shils, "The Great Obsession," *The Spectator, 211* (July 5, 1963), 20–21. Shils writes of Mills' "fictitious 'heroism,'" and he refers to Mills as a "demagogic simplifier."

Anyone who examines the divergencies between the ideal and the actual typically invites criticism. A common technique for rationalizing the hiatuses between what ought to be and what is is negation of persons who discuss them. Nonetheless, science claims as one of its ideals the encouragement, rather than the discouragement, of self-criticism. Science ultimately depends for its advancement upon objectification of the values and norms that guide it.

In practice, ideal and actual or compromise norms perform distinctive functions. Without ideal norms the scientific method could not progress and the system would soon lose its vitality. For sooner or later all scientific endeavor is judged according to the ideal, or more enduring, standards. The latter are the chief guideposts for the scientist, setting the limits, or conditions, within which he should act as well as providing the means for achieving the goals of truth and knowledge. We need to know much more about those situations wherein it is possible for scientists to adhere to the ideal norms.

But knowledge of compromise or actual norms also is essential. Indicative of this is the maxim: "The purist cannot effectively carry out research." The wise researcher knows that he cannot always adhere to the ideal research design if he is to show tangible results for his efforts. Insufficiency of resources, pressures from the broader society, and the like force him to choose the "least of the evils."

By bringing actual norms onto the level of reflective consciousness, we can formalize those patterns that have proved useful or use these as the basis for the creation of ideal norms. Many of the gains in research methodology are due to just such procedures. One of our primary goals in the chapters on sampling, direct and indirect observation, and numerical and conceptual analysis is clarification of the nature of the actual norms in the research process. In other instances we shall see that both actual and ideal norms are vague, and at present the most that can be accomplished is to clarify the problems involved.

Explicit recognition of the actual in contradistinction to the ideal also clarifies the functional limits of the ideal norms in social research. For instance, ideal research procedures that seem workable on paper may prove quite otherwise within the kiln of bitter experience. Rather than cling stubbornly to these ideal methods we should reshape them to fit reality. Or, if the divergency between the ideal and the real continues to widen, the scientist may be well advised to concede that there are drawbacks to certain methods and to search for others that will prove more useful.

Then too, attention to the actual norms enables us to examine the interaction between the ideal and the real, and how they complement each other. A degree of tension between scientists who uphold the ideals and those who act in terms of the informal or compromise norms is perhaps inevitable. Researchers, to procure results, to cope with various idiosyncratic factors in the fieldwork situation, will continue to make concessions to expediency. Yet, in so doing, they invite criticism from those who defend the ideals. Typically, the latter look for discrepancies between the actual and the ideal and, if they find none, they attempt to establish more stringent procedures. Many a scathing book review has, wittingly or no, implemented the ideal norms by attacking the researcher's efforts, by demanding conformance to standards of perfection.[9] If the ideal norms are to be meaningful, they must somehow be reinforced, and such is achieved primarily through negation of research activities that contravene the ideals. Durkheim long ago recognized the need for negation against violators of the norms if the latter are to be sustained.[10] Without some kind of sanctions, extreme relativism in science, and consequent willingness to accept all research as of equal worth, is a clear and present danger.

But it must be emphasized that the upholders of the ideal norms and the infringers of these both, in their own way, contribute to scientific knowledge. We would not wish to rid science of this neverending dialectic.

Scientists and Their Associations

In order to sustain and to enforce the normative structure of science, scientists must cooperate with one another. Such a process spurs the development of organizations of various kinds. Some of these are highly informal, whereas others—departments, universities, or scientific associations like the American Sociological Association, the American Anthropological Association, and the American Psychological Association—tend to become highly structured. In turn, these formal associations are intermeshed with the broader societal structures, particularly the governmental system, and these social links exert subtle influences upon the actions of scientists.

We would do well to realize that not all scientists belong to a university department or scientific association. The common practice today of equating members of the American Sociological Association or members of sociology departments with the actual practitioners of the "science of sociology" is misguided. Members of other disciplines may be pursuing scientific studies of a sociological nature. In other societies particularly, sociological research as Americans know it may be carried out by persons who classify themselves as anthropologists, geographers, and so on.

[9] See, e.g., Alexander W. Astin, "Review of Torsten Husén (ed.), *International Study of Achievement in Mathematics,* 2 vols. (Stockholm: Almqvist & Wiksell, and New York: John Wiley, 1967)," *Science, 156* (June 30, 1967), 1721–1722. Also, the various review symposia in the *American Sociological Review,* 1966 and 1967—especially the one on Marion J. Levy, Jr., *Modernization and the Structure of Societies,* 2 vols. (Princeton, N.J.: Princeton, 1966), in the December, 1966 issue, 857–861.

[10] Emile Durkheim, *The Rules of Sociological Method,* trans. by Sarah A. Solovay and John H. Mueller, 8th ed. (New York: Free Press Paperback, 1964).

Science in the ideal does not admit of formal educational or organizational bars. The only qualifications it demands of its practitioners is that they understand its norms and commit themselves to the pursuit of empirically grounded knowledge. Today more and more scientists are acquiring the formal trappings of scientific status, notably the Ph.D., and are functioning within formalized bureaucratic structures. But this was not always so. Many of the early social scientists, for example, carried out their activities more or less as an avocation. Nor did they prepare for this work by fulfilling specific course requirements that confer on one the title of sociologist, anthropologist, or whatever. Still, even today some persons who are contributing to social science lack the formal educational prerequisites and work quite independently of any bureaucratic setting. Morgenthau has argued that the most creative political theorists are those functioning outside the halls of academia.[11] And then there is Eric Hoffer, author of *The True Believer*.[12] Although his celebrated work is not a scientific treatise in the narrow sense, numerous social scientists who possess the formal trappings of scientific status have relied upon it for inspiration in the areas of mass movements and collective behavior. It is significant that Hoffer lacks a college education and has for many years been a longshoreman on San Francisco's waterfront.[13]

Today of course most scientists work through formal associations. In America the university structure is the setting for much scientific activity. It is academia that indoctrinates the young scholar into the norms of science. Professors, acting as both judge and jury, can make or break the budding scientist. And they do much to instil in students certain theoretical constructs and assumptions and to shape their orientation toward research methods. Some of the controls professors exert are informal and subtle in nature; others are highly formalized. But the result is the same: Limits on thought and on action are established, and deviation from these is not only discouraged but punished to some degree. Moreover, a host of pressures within the department and on the broader university scene affect the conceptual and methodological orientation of the neophyte social scientist. After he receives his degrees, he may continue within the university context, or, as social scientists are increasingly doing, he may find employment in some governmental, business, or other bureaucratic organization.

Most scientists also affiliate themselves with scientific associations of a national or regional sort. A particularly vital function of the scientific association is sponsorship of publications through which scientists' research findings are diffused to others within the fraternity. The regular conventions of these associa-

---

[11] Hans Morgenthau, "Review of Louis Halle, *Men and Nations* (Princeton: Princeton University Press, 1962)," *New York Times Book Review*, May 6, 1962, 3.

[12] Eric Hoffer, *The True Believer* (New York: Harper & Row, 1951).

[13] Calvin Tomkins, "Profiles: The Creative Situation," *New Yorker*, 42 (Jan. 7, 1967), 34–77.

tions, moreover, tend to reinforce and revitalize the collective representations of the membership.

The functions of scientific associations have, however, been the object of extended debate.[14] On the one hand these societies are committed to the maintenance of scientific endeavor per se, on the other to more narrow, "guild" concerns. Signs of the struggle have erupted within several of the social sciences in the United States, particularly within psychology and sociology, and are bound to affect the nature and future course of social research.[15] As researchers seek to apply scientific principles within the broader society, they must formalize their relationships with the bureaucracies that utilize their services. And the federal government, for instance, because it finds it difficult to deal with individual scientists, often looks to the scientific associations to provide qualified spokesmen for the discipline as a whole.[16] Conversely, if scientists are to have their say in the political realm they must engage in lobbying activities. In these situations the scientists' formal organizations play a strategic role.

Scientific associations attempt to cope with these practical problems in various ways. Some of the issues involve questions of how much conformity and deviation should be permitted the member scientists, both within the association

[14] Everett C. Hughes, among others, has argued that the American Sociological Association should remain a scientific discipline, whereas Talcott Parsons and others have argued for the professionalization of sociology. For general discussions of the professional versus the scientific orientation of social science organizations, see William J. Goode, "Encroachment, Charlatanism, and the Emerging Profession: Psychology, Sociology, and Medicine," *American Sociological Review,* 25 (December, 1960), 902–914; and Irving Louis Horowitz, "Mainliners and Marginals: The Human Shape of Sociological Theory," in Llewellyn Gross (ed.), *Sociological Theory: Inquiries and Paradigms* (New York: Harper & Row, 1967), 358–383. Goode and Horowitz refer to much of the relevant literature.

In addition to the scientific versus professional dilemma, another issue has emerged within some scientific associations in recent years. Some groups have urged that the associations take stands on major social issues which concern the broader society (for instance, the American involvement in the Vietnam war). Both the American Sociological Association and the American Anthropological Association have openly struggled with this problem. See, e.g., "Correspondence," *Fellow Newsletter,* American Anthropological Association, 8 (February, 1967), 7–8, as well as letters in subsequent issues. If we look at this debate in the most general sense, the fundamental question is, "What steps, if any, should a scientific association take to ensure a proper social climate or structure which will facilitate scientific investigation?"

[15] Severe strains and tensions, resulting from a marriage of strictly scientific concerns with more narrow, guild considerations, have come to the fore in the American Psychological Association. See the comments by various psychologists in "The Scientific and Professional Aims of Psychology," *American Psychologist,* 22 (January, 1967), 49–76.

[16] Cf. Wallace S. Sayre, "Scientists and American Science Policy," in Bernard Barber and Walter Hirsch (eds.), *The Sociology of Science* (New York: Free Press, 1962), chap. 36.

and in the broader social order. We have already suggested that what is "good" methodology (at any given time) is a matter of social consensus. One could say that Lazarsfeld and Stouffer have been viewed as "good" methodologists because the procedures they invented and employed have been admired and emulated by many other sociologists. At the same time, a few social scientists want to "impose" consensus through organizational controls. They believe that if scientific associations achieve consensus and thus reduce their internal bickering and strife, the prestige and status of a particular discipline, or of social science in general, will be enhanced in the public eye. Internal disputes, these scientists argue, lead outsiders to question the adequacy of the procedures and the conclusions of social science.

A number of social science associations have in recent years sought to extend their controls into the broader society by insisting that they should determine, through official certification, or licensing, just who can call himself a sociologist, psychologist, or whatever. Psychologists and sociologists in particular have been concerned with "imposters" who claim to *apply* the theory and methods of social science. More generally, these associations have moved or are now moving toward restraining certain unethical practices among their members—a practice which has a subtle impact upon the research process.[17]

Some facets of the conformity-deviation dilemma in scientific associations bear directly upon the methodology of social research. In this context we should like to review the debate that took place at the organizational meeting of the methodology section of the American Sociological Association in Chicago, 1959. We shall not identify the participants and shall concede the possibility of errors in our observations and interpretations.

At this organizational meeting the question was raised as to who should be eligible for membership in the methodology section and what services this section should perform. The discussants were primarily sociologists who, through their writings and research, consider themselves to be methodologists and generally are viewed as such by their colleagues.

The discussants were rather evenly divided between those who argued for tight restrictions on the membership and those who sought to sustain a broader membership base. The former contended that a high degree of restrictiveness would enhance the prestige of the section. What is significant is that some of these sociologists felt that the methodology section should in time come to judge what is good and bad in research. One member of the restrictionist bloc

---

[17] The problems facing scientific associations as they develop codes of ethics are manifold. See, e.g., Ralph L. Beals *et al.,* "Background Information on Problems of Anthropological Research and Ethics," *Fellow Newsletter,* American Anthropological Association, 8 (January, 1967), 2–13. Also Talcott Parsons, "The Editor's Column," *American Sociologist, 2* (August, 1967), 138–140, as well as communications to the editor by E. H. Volkart and Edgar A. Schuler in the same issue (162–163).

specifically advocated that the methodology group take upon itself the task of determining for the entire field of sociology just what is good (and bad) research. By implication, this function could be carried out effectively by members of the methodology section only if sociologists saw this group as comprising exclusively the "elite" methodologists. Other, somewhat more generous, members of the restrictionist camp suggested that the section might function in an advisory capacity to help sociology refine its methodological and field research tools.

As we interpret these remarks, a few sociologists saw themselves as censors for the entire field, as sole judges of the methods to be employed and the actions to be enjoined. But this perspective violates the principle that science and its methods must be open to examination by all interested parties. More to the point, what are good and bad research procedures cannot be legislated by a select body of scientists. Ultimately such a decision must stem from reason and empirical test.

Scientific associations, if they are to advance the cause of science, must remain loosely organized, heterogenous bodies. Although scientific knowledge is never the product of a single individual but is achievable only by scientists functioning as a group, dissent and negation are essential ingredients of the scientific method. Remember, much of yesterday's "knowledge" is the substance of today's "myths" and "superstitions." The history of science, and its incessant reevaluation of men and ideas, should endow us all with humility when passing judgment on the validity of new hypotheses or speculative theories.

Of course, it is not just the scientific method that tends to keep scientific associations fluid. Contradictory pressures emanating from the pluralistic society in which modern science is embedded help to sustain a diversity of opinions among scientific practitioners. Specifically, the diffusion of social power in the broader society appears to be one necessary condition for maintaining heterogeneity within the scientific association, for such diffusion leads to a commitment by sociologists and others to divergent political and economic ideologies.

The Scientist's Role and Functions

Scientists, we have argued, strive toward certain goals by adhering to given norms, whether ideal or actual, and by interacting, formally or informally, with other scientists. By so doing, they give rise to associations which are in turn embedded within a broader societal context.

But a schism occurs within science between those scientists who are committed first and foremost to the scientific method and its ideals and those who identify mainly with scientific associations or with other sectors of the broader society. It is our thesis that the role orientation of the researcher affects the selection of his theoretical assumptions and the application of his research methods and does much to structure his analysis and the manner in which he writes up his findings.

COMMITMENT TO SCIENCE

Earlier we reasoned that science has as one of its assumptions that knowledge is preferable to ignorance and that, by implication, knowledge should be disseminated. So far so good. But deeper probing suggests that the goal of the "pure" scientist is knowledge for its own sake. This is not meant to imply that he opposes the application of scientific findings, but for him this is secondary to the desire to know. And this goal is associated with certain positively valued ideal norms such as impartiality and universalism in the evaluation and dissemination of scientific data.

Persons for whom knowledge for its own sake is paramount tend to slight the role of the practitioner or applied scientist. Typically they urge others to avoid entanglement in immediate day-by-day concerns and to devote themselves to the quest for new knowledge.

Unquestionably, imbuement with the ideals of science strongly orients one to the future, to generations yet unborn who will be both the judges and the beneficiaries of one's efforts. More than others, researchers with this focus recognize that their findings are highly tentative and, moreover, that new ideas, even scientific truths, may at first fail to win acceptance. It was Max Planck who observed that even in the physical sciences one never converts one's opponents; the opposition simply dies off.[18] Conversely, new ideas may spring up and achieve popularity for a time, only to fade within a few decades. This is a recurrent pattern in the social sciences.

Not a few social scientists, at least in the United States, take a dim view of the notion of writing for posterity. Such a goal is out of keeping with the current preoccupation with pragmatism and the general societal emphasis upon immediate gratification as opposed to the striving for highly deferred goals. Small wonder, then, that recent research suggests that many sociologists find it difficult to sustain their productivity for any length of time; most of their work is accomplished in the years immediately following receipt of the Ph.D., and it declines thereafter.[19] Numerous social scientists apparently have as their prime goal the furthering, via publication, of their own security and status within a bureaucracy—be this a university or some governmental agency. This goal achieved, they derive little satisfaction from working for longer range, ill-defined ends. Certainly the notion of the search for truth (even empirically defined

[18] Max Planck, *Scientific Autobiography and Other Papers,* trans. by Frank Gaynor (New York: Philosophical Library, 1949), 33–34.

[19] Leland J. Axelson, "Differences in Productivity of Doctorates in Sociology," *Journal of Educational Sociology,* 33 (October, 1959), 49–55.

truth) as a goal is a diffuse one. For the dedicated scientist there is little assurance of eventual reward. Even the highly creative person may achieve little acclaim during his lifetime. Given these facts, we can more readily comprehend why the purist looks askance at the applied scientist.

Commitment to the purist role also inspires a dedication to creativity. Merton has detailed the reasons why science is dependent upon the ingenious and the creative rather than upon the replicators and synthesizers.[20] Yet the creative person is likely to deviate and to challenge currently accepted theory and methodology. By definition creativity involves rejection of the status quo.[21] That the original thinker may find support from other scientists difficult to muster should occasion no surprise.

Pursuant to the matter of science's emphasis upon creativity, Merton has argued that one index of fame in science is the attachment of one's name to some notable law or discovery.[22] Thus we speak of Einstein's theory of relativity, Darwin's theory of evolution, and Mendel's law of genetics. This pattern is less developed in the social sciences, in part because new discoveries in this area are more difficult to define. Still, we have the Thurstone scale and the Guttman scale. More typical of the social sciences is the identification of a person's name with some concept he has developed—for example, Merton and serendipity, Sumner and folkways and mores, and Redfield and the folk society.

The link between creativity and a futuristic orientation should be apparent. The very association of a scientist with a particular theory dedicates him to posterity, making him part of the scientific heritage of coming generations. So too, creativity finds its fulfillment not in the immediate present but in futurity. In light of these patterns, we can better understand the bitterness of the arguments in science over the priority in inventions: He who achieves recognition for a given discovery first will be the one to be acclaimed by generations to come.

More generally, the purist attempts to assist humanity in the broad rather than the narrow sense and may be concerned less with promoting his own image for posterity than with combatting the pessimism of those who in the name of expediency sell humanity short. The purist's quarrel with the practitioner is not over practice per se but over short-range versus long-range goals.

The purist's chosen path is not an easy one to tread. If he pursues problems that seem significant to him but diverge from current modes of thinking within the discipline and the broader society, he must often forego immediate rewards and can entertain few hopes for long-range recognition. It is not just his prestige

20 Robert K. Merton, "Priorities in Scientific Discovery," *American Sociological Review* 22 (December, 1957), 635–659.

21 Cf. André Bennett, "Science: The Antithesis of Creativity," paper presented at the annual meeting of the American Sociological Association, Miami, Fla., August, 1966.

22 Merton, *Priorities in Scientific Discovery, op. cit.*, 642 ff.

that is at stake. Financial support for research that deviates from the tried and true may be at times difficult to secure.

The pure scientist who elects to search for knowledge for its own sake—paying little heed to, and frequently coming into conflict with, his departmental colleagues, administrators, and politicians—must assume a kind of elitist stance, for he reasons that in some areas at least, he and he alone is qualified to judge whether a given project is worthy of investigation or the methods appropriate to the undertaking.

The scholar who identifies with the scientific community per se also comes to support certain ethical values or ideals. Some of these are quite revolutionary. For the purist justifies his research and writing not in terms of the concerns of his own society but in terms of the long-run ideal of the search for knowledge and truth that will serve mankind as a whole. In this respect, the pure scientist resembles on occasion a member of a religious sect who feels impelled to spread his doctrines regardless of the firmness of the society's opposition.

Although the pure scientist is committed to the search for empirical truth even in the face of countervailing political pressures, and although certain ethical norms inhere in this commitment to truth, we should also recognize that the scientific method can not empirically determine the ends or goals, or "what ought to be" in human experience.

Yet, the notion that a pure scientist cannot empirically determine the "ought to be" does not, as we have already suggested, mean that he is without social and moral commitments. For example, his role orientation is such that he has an obligation and a duty to associate with other scientists, irrespective of their particular religious and political identifications or class positions. The scientific associations he cultivates, in so far as they support the ideals of science, hurdle various religious, ethnic, and political barriers.[23] Science itself can never be viewed as the product of a single culture or political unit. Yet, because of this, the researcher often experiences conflicts between his commitment to the scientific community and his commitment to the broader society of which he is a part. Clearly the transnational orientation of the pure scientist reduces the efficacy of the society's efforts to control him. So the consequences of the actions of the purist, who adheres to the norm of scientific neutrality in his research, are frequently far from ethically neutral from the perspective of the broader society.

That contradictions inhere in the purist's role should be apparent. His elitist position tends to seal him off from the very social order he seeks to study and explain and also from the very persons on whose support he ultimately depends. Much has been written about the need for a scientific and intellectual

[23] The struggle to harness modern scientists to the nation-state system, to assert the priority of the national political structure over the scientific community, appears in many forms. For one example, see Don K. Price, *The Scientific Estate* (Cambridge, Mass.: Harvard, 1965).

elite in modern society. But the existence of such an elite would not necessarily be conducive to scientific research. Especially is this true for social scientists. The very conflicts and struggles they experience in society provide them with insights into the workings of the system. The balance point, of course, is difficult to determine. On the one hand, scientists require a certain degree of immunity from societal pressures if they are to pursue certain types of research; yet on the other, they must maintain a keen awareness of the workaday world if they are to comprehend its actual operation.

The pure scientist also encounters the problem of legitimizing his role to his university or research organization, to his community, and to the society. In some respects the early social scientists had an easier task than their modern counterparts. In the early stages of sociology the notion prevailed (at least in Europe) that the educated man occupied a privileged position and thus did not have to constantly justify his existence to the mass populace. But today, with the extension of industrial urbanization and democracy, the common man has achieved a degree of power and authority undreamed of in the feudal past. And the pure scientist must garner some support from the man in the street if he is to function effectively.

To achieve such legitimization is perhaps more difficult for social scientists than for natural scientists. Unlike the latter, with their electronic devices, nuclear weapons, and so forth, the former have few tangible products to show for their efforts and with which to impress the public. They do have such spectaculars as public opinion polls, but the slightest failure of these may appear as a debacle. Social scientists, then, must continually justify their activities to the society at large. Therefore in most societies, particularly in industrial-urban democracies, the purist depends upon his practically oriented colleagues to legitimize his scientific activity.

COMMITMENT TO THE BROADER SOCIETY

Applied social scientists are ordinarily more willing than the purists to make concessions to the ideal norms in science on behalf of the associational structure and the broader society that underwrites scientific activity. And they are likely to be closely attuned to the shifting social and cultural changes that influence the course of their research.

Not unexpectedly, we find significant differences among sociocultural systems in the kinds of roles applied social scientists carry out. Three types, however, seem universal: These are the roles of *moralizer, mediator,* and *technician.*[24]

24 For another formulation of role types, see William H. Form, "On the Sociology of Social Research," *Rassegna Italiana di Sociologia* (September, 1963), 463–481. Other discussions of, and materials on, the various roles of sociologists can be found in Arthur B. Shostak (ed.), *Sociology in Action* (Homewood, Ill.: Dorsey, 1966); and Alvin W. Gouldner and S. M. Miller (eds.), *Applied Sociology* (New York: Free Press, 1965).

THE RESEARCHER AS MORALIZER. As indicated above, most methodologists reason that the scientific method cannot be employed to determine empirically what is right and what is wrong, particularly with respect to ultimate values and goals. The scientific method, however, can aid one in making rational selections from alternative means (once an end is given), and it can open up alternative values and ends for consideration.

In recent decades a few philosophers have challenged the traditional conception of the scientific method, which has been dominant since Kant's time.[25] Also, the Marxists, perhaps the most avid critics of the Kantian view, contend that the scientific process cannot be severed from moral judgments in the social world. The Marxist position is of more than passing interest, for it has been highly influential among social scientists in numerous societies, particularly developing ones.

Even where sociologists champion the ideal of scientific neutrality, deviation from this norm is marked. We should remember that the discipline arose, as the writings of Comte, Durkheim, Weber, and Marx witness, as one means of grappling with the societal dilemmas that have resulted from the changeover from a preindustrial to an industrial base. Actually, Comte conceived of sociology as a "secular religion" that could resolve the problems of the new order, one that in Comte's day was struggling not only with the beginnings of industrialization but with the ideological impact of the French Revolution. Indeed, many of the most influential sociologists have been those who, like Marx, based their social analysis upon a definite ideological stand.

Social scientists today moralize primarily within a reformist tradition;[26] however, some writers, particularly in developing nations, who have been influenced by Marxian thought or by pressing problems of their own, adopt a more antisystem framework. In the United States, perhaps the most ardent spokesman for moralization (in the reformist as well as revolutionary tradition) in recent decades has been C. Wright Mills.[27] In his view, empirical data should be employed for specific moral ends: primarily for constructing a better world, the nature of which is to be defined by sociologists like himself. In his *The Sociological Imagination* Mills attacked not only the purists but also the brokers and the technicians; only the moralizing scientist who grapples with the crucial issues

---

[25] See, e.g., F. S. C. Northrop, *The Logic of the Sciences and the Humanities* (New York: Macmillan, 1948); and C. West Churchman, *Theory of Experimental Inference* (New York: Macmillan, 1948).

[26] Thus Ralph H. Turner, in his *The Social Context of Ambition* (San Francisco: Chandler, 1964), states, "Liberal democratic values have inspired a major portion of sociological research and have already been affected by its conclusions" (xiii).

[27] Mills is in the tradition of such sociologists as Robert S. Lynd, *Knowledge for What?* (Princeton, N.J.: Princeton, 1939).

of the day emerged unscathed.[28] Mills attempted to practice what he preached: see his *Listen, Yankee*.[29]

But Mills has by no means been alone in this venture, no matter what methods texts may aver. Though prone to exaggeration and careless exposition, his writings were more open and frank than those of many social scientists. Moral judgments fairly leap from the pages of journals like *Human Organization*. And a number of these authors are concerned with broader values and ends.

Sociologists in such fields as political sociology, race relations, and mental health have advanced their share of moral judgments. Those concerned with race relations have on more than one occasion reflected the "liberal orientation" of mid-twentieth century American society as they have analyzed Negro-white relationships.[30] A number of social scientists writing on mental illness have taken value judgmental stands on the nature of normality or have advocated policies that they believed would aid in resolving mental health problems.

Although much moralization in both European and American sociology has been within the reformist tradition, a number of sociologists have moralized in favor of the *status quo* and, particularly, against revolutionary change.[31] Most early American sociologists were reformers, in that they wanted to modify laissez-faire capitalism.[32] Yet this also meant that they were among the early supporters of what was to become corporate capitalism. And it appears that many social scientists (including sociologists) have, in recent decades, become increasingly identified with, and integrated into, the resultant structure, particularly the large-scale bureaucratic apparatus of American society. One of the most unusual efforts to moralize in favor of modern American society is that of Nathan Glazer. He admits that he can envisage no alternatives to the solution of current "social problems" other than simply extending present-day bureaucratic tendencies, and he looks forward to the day when social scientists will function as "philosopher kings."

[28] C. Wright Mills, *The Sociological Imagination* (New York: Grove, Evergreen Books, 1961).

[29] C. Wright Mills, *Listen, Yankee* (New York: Ballantine, 1960).

[30] See the exchange between Horton, who questions the existing orientation, and Williams, who tends to defend it. John Horton, "Order and Conflict Theories of Social Problems as Competing Ideologies," *American Journal of Sociology*, 71 (May, 1966), 701–713; and Robin M. Williams, Jr., "Some Further Comments on Chronic Controversies," *op. cit.*, 717–721.

[31] One of the most interesting expressions of this position is the statement of W. I. Thomas issued upon his dismissal from the University of Chicago. *Chicago Examiner*, April 22, 1918, 1, 10. He did "not believe in social reform by the way of revolution," and he did "not believe in the reduction of the members of society to one class, but in a hierarchization of social classes based on efficiency" (10).

[32] Dusky Lee Smith, "Sociology and the Rise of Corporate Capitalism," *Science and Society*, 29 (Fall, 1965), 401–418.

This is the vision. At the top there will be the analysts and researchers and programmers and computers and the huge machines into which many kinds of data now guarded in the files of separate organizations will constantly be fed and out of which will flow guides and aids to action.[33]

But the question here is, Why this high degree of moralization in social science? A number of social factors are responsible for this situation. In the most extreme instances (in societies beset with revolutionary change), the political climate makes it impossible for a social scientist to sustain the search for objective truth. Here the conflicting parties will not concede that neutral, objective observers exist—so intense are the feelings. It is hardly surprising that certain social scientists in revolutionary orders come to take firm stands against the old order and in favor of the present regime.

Yet social scientists, even in nonrevolutionary societies, must constantly advance value judgments. Earlier we observed that researchers must justify and legitimize their actions to the general public. But these persons find it difficult to comprehend the meaning of the scientific method and the ideal of seeking objective truth. In order to rationalize their role, they often speak in terms of what is good and bad for the social order. This the layman can understand.

American social scientists have also justified certain research on the grounds that ultimately the data will aid in improving the lot of the common man. We might at this point draw an analogy from the efforts of contemporary Russian social scientists to justify their empirical research on ethnic minorities in the Soviet Union. They argue that the resultant knowledge will speed replacement of the traditional norms by Communist ones and, by inference, contribute to the welfare of these minorities.

This argument was revealed in a conference of Soviet social scientists wherein more intensive study of the Muslim urban populations of Central Asia was urged—because the Soviet regime had failed to make satisfactory progress in obliterating the traditional (feudal) beliefs and practices.[34] For it is increasingly apparent that the older economic, familial, and religious patterns have not faded away as rapidly as the governmental leadership had assumed they would. Here, then, is a situation where social researchers justify their actions by arguing that, by collecting more adequate data, they can assist in demolishing the older forms and thus bring minority peoples more completely in line with the broader Soviet system.

Although the content of social science in the United States and in the

[33] Nathan Glazer, "The Good Society," *Commentary, 36* (September, 1963), 231.

[34] See, e.g., A. Bennigsen, "Traditional Islam in the Customs of the Turkic Peoples of Central Asia," *Middle East Journal, 12* (Spring, 1958), 227–233.

Soviet Union diverges, the underlying form is not too different. After all, the more data we have on lower-class and ethnic-minority life styles in the United States, the more easily we can reshape these populations into the middle-class mold, making them, so some scientists assume, a healthier and happier lot. Rationalizations of this sort are understandable, but let not the researcher with this orientation assume that his position is "value free."

Often the scientist also moralizes because of his role as a citizen. Some sociologists, to be sure, assume that one can readily doff one hat and don another.[35] But in practice this is far from easy. For the scientist seems to function most effectively as citizen-moralizer when he is enfolded in the cloak of scientific enterprise and its concomitant prestige and status. When the scientist speaks as an expert, the layman listens. What is more, power and authority tend to accrue to the scientist who moralizes, who seeks to shape men's actions (the ultimate goal of moralization). Under these circumstances, it more or less follows that scientists, as rational citizens, should select the most effective means at their disposal for maximizing the impact of their message.

Conversely, the layman faced with a grave moral issue or crisis finds it incomprehensible that the experts, men of superior training in a given field, should hesitate to take a stand on what they believe to be right or wrong. All the more disconcerting is the position of the scientist whose own actions may in some way be responsible for a particular crisis, for example, the physicists who unleashed the forces of nuclear activity upon the world. Here scientists are indeed in a quandary—one to which we return in later chapters. Does the attempt to maintain "ethical neutrality" justify disinterest in the consequences of one's actions? The scientist who answers this affirmatively could not be supported by any moral order.

In the end, the fundamental dilemma facing the scientist is the need to moralize in order to sustain and to legitimize the scientific method and its use in the search for objective truth. This role orientation is perhaps more trying for the social than for the natural scientist. Certainly social scientists must strive to create (and sustain) a climate of intellectual freedom, one with a minimum of political controls and censorship, if they hope to carry out scientific research. Yet they must also rationalize their research to the very groups they propose to study. In turn the public's image of them as moralizers or as objective scientists

---

[35] If we can judge by the manner in which he signs his name to articles, Coser has been engaged in a rather unique attempt at role differentiation. His articles in the *American Sociological Review* and the *American Journal of Sociology* have been signed Lewis A. Coser, whereas those in the journal of socialist opinion, *Dissent* (he is on its editorial board), have carried the name Lewis Coser. Recently, however, he included one of his articles originally published in *Dissent*, "Prospects for the New Nations," 10 (Winter, 1963), 43–58, in a book, *Political Sociology* (New York: Harper & Row, Harper Torchbooks, 1966), which he edited under the name of Lewis A. Coser.

is likely to influence informants' responses and even scientists' opportunities for field research. So the very process of self-justification can structure one's scientific findings. Similarly, the researcher wishing to give a good account of himself may limit his studies to those that conform to, or at least do not clash with, the moral stance of the group or society he is researching. But this, too, may detract from the validity of his findings.

That, contrary to the ideal norms enunciated by many social scientists, some must moralize if others are to sustain their scientific neutrality and objectivity is a compromise norm that often goes unrecognized.[36] Clearly we should avoid succumbing to the belief that all the actions of sociologists are neutral in character.

THE RESEARCHER AS MEDIATOR.   The mediator, or broker, is another kind of researcher-scientist whose commitment is to the broader society, or, if he functions on the international scene, to various societies. The mediator formally espouses a neutral, objective position relative to divergent interest groups. His task is to provide the public or decision makers with the data upon which to base their judgments and formulate policy. The broker's ultimate purpose is to assist in alleviating the conflicts and strains that inhere in the relations among groups, particularly in pluralistic, industrial orders. As such the researcher-broker has much in common with many newsmen who see themselves as supplying the citizenry with the facts they must have for democracy to function effectively.

A pluralistic industrial order apparently requires some persons who strive to achieve scientific neutrality, who eschew rigid ideological commitments. Implicitly the mediator assumes that although people may disagree over the application of knowledge they can reach some sort of compromise on the nature of the evidence itself. In practice the empirical validity of this assumption is not readily demonstrable. Yet, unless the members of divergent interest groups of a society are willing to entertain the possibility of objective observation—even as a social fiction—democracy, at least as we know it, could not function. Only by assuming that some persons, such as broker-researchers, are neutral and can provide objective data is it possible to build a bridge of understanding that will permit otherwise antagonistic groups to work with one another.

Modern industrial societies have experienced a vast proliferation of mediator roles. Thus, in the United States a number of skilled functionaries—variously termed arbitrators, mediators, fact-finding board members—attempt to bring together competing groups such as labor and management. Social researchers frequently work hand in glove with these neutral players. So too, researchers are more and more being called upon by politicians to provide data on which various competing factions can agree.

---

[36] Lundberg and those who have followed in his footsteps have not dealt with the issue we have posed. George A. Lundberg, *Social Research,* 2nd ed. (New York: Longmans, 1942), 53–54.

But tensions inhere in the mediator role. As a specialist, the social scientist may wield considerable power and authority, but in the negotiation process the combatants often try to co-opt him, each side seeking through a variety of means, overt and covert, to gain his support. Or, as a neutral player he may become the focus of hostility on the part of one or both factions. During periods of stress the antagonists may provide false information and suppress certain facts. The mediator, with his objective reporting and analysis of events, thus poses a distinct threat from the point of view of the combatants.

The problems that have confronted social scientists in South Africa are instructive. There have been those who have aligned themselves with the Afrikaners, and others who have taken their stand with the opposition. There also seem to have been some who have sought through objective research to provide a basis for reducing the conflicts that pervade the South African racial situation. However, as the power structure has become increasingly rigid, the mediator role has become exceedingly difficult, if not impossible, for scholars to sustain. For objective reporting threatens this kind of system.

Indeed, the social scientist as mediator is dependent upon a democratic order. He in turn supports it and does much to justify the essentiality of social research in this kind of society. The mediator role is a convenient link between pure and applied science, for the pure scientist can assume the mantle of the broker, or mediator, more readily than he can that of any other kind of applied functionary.

The pure scientist can, in theory at least, pursue the question of truth without attaching himself ideologically to any vested interest group and can nourish the hope of amassing in the process a fund of relatively objective data. The moralizer, on the other hand, finds it most difficult to play the role of broker because his position of nonneutrality is apparent.

THE RESEARCHER AS TECHNICIAN.   Another type of applied scientist is the technician who, though he makes a moral commitment to a "nonscientific" organization by accepting employment in it, seeks in the course of his research to discover through objective study the best means for achieving a given end.

Whereas the pure scientist, and to some extent the broker, does not formally align himself with a specific bureaucracy, and the moralizer either may or may not, the technician most often does so. Not infrequently the technician commits himself to an organization without really questioning its goals.[37] This is more and more becoming the norm for social scientists who function as experts in

[37] This role commitment in the field of industrial sociology has engendered more than its share of controversy. See, e.g., Clark Kerr and Lloyd H. Fisher, "Plant Sociology: The Elite and the Aborigines," in Mirra Komarovsky (ed.), *Common Frontiers of the Social Sciences* (New York: Free Press, 1957), 281–309. Also, Conrad M. Arensberg and Geoffrey Tootell, "Plant Sociology: Real Discoveries and New Problems," in *Ibid.*, 310–337.

modern, large-scale bureaucratic structures, be these governmental, business, or educational. In these situations, the norms of the organization often define for the researcher what kinds of data are required, permitting him little or no control over the choice of problems.

Although many social scientists fancy themselves pure scientists, in reality they often structure their research, select their topics, design their research projects, and write their reports in terms of the demands of the organizational apparatus rather than those of the scientific community. What gains pure science derives from the efforts of the technician frequently are mainly by-products of the ongoing research initiated by various bureaucracies for their own special and immediate goals.

Nonetheless, the technician, like the broker, does contribute to scientific knowledge. In addition to rationalizing scientific activity to the public by demonstrating that it can indeed implement specific organizational goals, the technician focuses attention upon certain issues that the pure scientist, withdrawn into his ivory tower, would overlook or disregard. Thus in the field of industrial sociology, knowledge of certain topics—for example, the social sanctions imposed by workmen upon one another—has been advanced through the researcher's concern with the practical problems of management.

One of the salient requirements of the technician is that he be highly skilled in the techniques of research; he must know how to draw samples, code materials, punch cards, sort materials, and so on. His role commitment is such as to minimize interest in abstract theorizing.

The industrial-urban society presents an enormous range of problems the proper study of which demands a large body of technically skilled researchers. Thus, modern democracy, necessarily concerned with public opinion, has given rise to a wide gamut of public opinion pollsters.[38] Certainly, American politicians depend upon pollsters and their findings as they seek to formulate issues, campaign for elections, and so on. And we see polling becoming part of the political scene in England, although the patterns there differ to some extent from those in American society.[39] Even the Soviet system is slowly but surely beginning to feel the pulse of its citizenry, for the latter's views cannot be disregarded in the decision-making process.

But industrial-urban society's need for data far exceeds what the pollsters can provide. As we sought to explain earlier, science in the modern sense arose through efforts to control and manipulate the natural and social worlds. Although attempts to reshape the social order have lagged behind those geared to

[38] See, e.g., Louis Harris, "Polls and Politics in the United States," *Public Opinion Quarterly,* 27 (Spring, 1963), 3–8; George Gallup, "Polls and the Political Process—Past, Present, and Future," *Public Opinion Quarterly,* 29 (Winter, 1965–1966), 544–549.

[39] Mark Abrams, "Public Opinion Polls and Political Parties," *Public Opinion Quarterly,* 27 (Spring, 1963), 9–18. Abrams analyzes the uses of polls in Britain.

revising elements of the physical world, results of the former have slowly but surely materialized. Consider the economic system in the Western world. The laissez-faire economists assumed that the economic order had its own inherent laws that functioned independently of man's efforts at control. But with the eventual demise of this belief (in part as a result of great depressions), a vast expansion has occurred in purposive social action designed to bring the economic order more into line with man's needs and desires. The whole field of social planning, whether in the economic sphere or in some related area, has had revolutionary effects upon social science. For today it is assumed that adequate data are essential if planning is to proceed in a rational manner. Social planning, therefore, demands countless technicians who can provide this information. This relationship between planning and social research has also become quite apparent in the Soviet Union. More and more bureaucratic leaders believe that they cannot act without detailed statistics on the economy and other facets of the social structure.

To be sure, the technician role has its own built-in tensions as the technician-researcher strives to maintain his scientific integrity in the face of the incessant political demands of the organization.

Status of the Scientist

Not only does the scientist's role serve to guide his research, but his status, or social position, markedly affects the manner in which he carries out the obligations of a particular role, be he engaged in pure or in applied research.

Within American society the status of the sociological researcher, particularly his position in the power structure, has undergone considerable change during the past few decades. In part this has resulted from the heightened incorporation of social scientists, primarily as technicians, into modern bureaucratic structures. The implications of this trend for scientific research are many, not the least of which is a perceptible shift in the relationships between investigators who function as teams and those who are "lone wolves."

A backward glance over the history of sociology in the United States reveals that within the space of only a few decades the direction of this discipline has changed dramatically. Many of the early American sociologists were not well integrated, nor did they identify, explicitly or otherwise, with the then existing power structure. They were seeking to revise the older order in keeping with the changing nature of capitalism and the emergence of an industrial-urban way of life. So too, many European social scientists tended to align themselves with movements seeking to revise the feudal order, thereby advocating a new utopia based on industrialization and urbanization.

These early social scientists for the most part were individual entrepreneurs.

Although the pre-World War I period witnessed a few major group research efforts like those of the Booths in England, large-scale projects are a relatively recent phenomenon.

The transition within American sociology is informative in this regard. Even during the 1920s, during the heyday of the Chicago School, most research was conducted by individuals; thus "participant observation" became a significant research tool. The trend toward large-scale group research was accentuated during the Great Depression of the 1930s, and it was more or less institutionalized during World War II.[40] Sociologists such as Samuel Stouffer were instrumental in selling sociology to the federal government, especially to the military. Such a study as *The American Soldier* was not only a landmark in social research but a turning point in the way in which research was to be conducted. For after World War II, more and more large-scale research came to be supported by the federal government (as well as other governmental units). Also, big business has come to accept sociology as a legitimate enterprise.

This general movement of sociologists into and upward within the business and governmental sectors has coincided with the bureaucratization of universities and the emergence of large research institutes. More and more research is being carried out within these bureaucratic systems, systems which, significantly, have complex ties with other formal organizations in the society.

Sociologists not only have become an essential part of the research apparatus in American society, but their voices are being heard as never before. Although persons formally designated as sociologists have not attained the pinnacle of influence held by certain economists (for example, those holding formal positions in the President's Council of Economic Advisers), the former have ascended the power scale considerably during the past half-century, especially in the post-World War II era. Sociologists are now being consulted by leading decision makers in the society.

Moreover, sociologists (and sociology) have become the topics for discussion in such magazines as the *New Yorker* and *Time*. Sociological findings and ideas are thus being diffused to an ever wider audience.

The upward mobility of sociologists that has brought them closer to Comte's vision of them as the ruling element in society is not, however, without significant liabilities. For one thing, sociologists continue to be the target of severe

---

[40] Alpert has traced the U.S. federal government's recognition and acceptance of social science research. Harry Alpert, "The Government's Growing Recognition of Social Science," in Donald M. Valdes and Dwight G. Dean (eds.), *Sociology in Use* (New York: Macmillan, 1965), 477–487. For a discussion of some of the early struggles to institutionalize social science (especially sociological research) as an activity of the federal government, see Richard S. Kirkendall, *Social Scientists and Farm Politics in the Age of Roosevelt* (Columbia, Mo.: University of Missouri Press, 1966). This work includes some valuable data on the rise and decline of the Bureau of Agricultural Economics.

criticism. Indeed, we can expect a degree of "anticlericalism" to emerge as they attempt to impose their own views concerning the management of modern societies.

New schisms in sociology have followed upon the shift in status. Accompanying the alignment of more researchers with large-scale bureaucracies, and the growth of large-scale research efforts, has been a decline in the independent researcher's role. In the process a rift has appeared between the independent researchers and those who pursue their activities as members of teams. Yet both the independent and the group researcher are essential to the furtherance of scientific knowledge. Obviously, some types of research, including large-scale social surveys, cannot be conducted by "loners." At the same time, as we indicate in succeeding chapters, large-scale organizations have given rise to dilemmas which are political and ethical and unquestionably methodological in character. Thus the researcher who goes it alone still has an essential role to play. Theory is still largely an individual effort, and the individualist is the most effective critic of the research process (as well as of the broader society).

It is quite apparent that the shifting status of social researchers (and here we are primarily concerned with sociologists) has resulted in changes in the way they select and conceptualize their research problems. Unlike their forebears, sociologists have during the past several decades been intent upon contrasting actual patterns with ideal ones, the latter usually remaining unquestioned. While some changes in orientation may be taking place, researchers in general do not compare the past with the present; they are not concerned with change over time. Sociologists, in so far as they moralize (implicitly or explicitly), deplore deviations from the ideal and shy away from any critical evaluations of the ideals themselves.

Sociologists, as a result of their shift in status, are able to study power groups in the United States to a greater extent than ever before. Military leaders, big businessmen, legislators, doctors, and lawyers have become accessible to sociological researchers as the latter have become part of the mainstream of modern society. This situation, though it has certain advantages, is nonetheless likely to make it difficult for sociologists to sustain their objectivity when studying the poor within their own society, and particularly when analyzing the problems of people in developing nations. The interests of such nations may well run counter to the interests of the organizational apparatus upon which modern sociologists depend so heavily for their prestige and support.

At this point we must draw another distinction—that between scientists and administrators. Many administrators call themselves scientists, but the scientific and the administrative roles are analytically, and often empirically, distinct. Scientists are committed to the search for empirically based truth, administrators to the development and maintenance of systems. Although the technician-researcher typically accepts the administrative structure as a given, the commitment of other types of scientists runs counter to the goal of "system maintenance" that administrators typically hold so dear. If we are to understand the application of the scientific method in modern society we must recognize the built-in tensions between the pure scientist, in particular, and the administrator (whether of a nation or of a research institute). On the other hand, scientists and administrators depend upon each other in modern society. What emerges is a kind of love-hate relationship.[41]

[41] The scientist's role is in this respect analogous to that of a newsman. Cf. Bernard C. Cohen, *The Press and Foreign Policy* (Princeton, N.J.: Princeton, 1963).

CHAPTER 5

Selection and Preliminary Formulation of a Research Project

Methodologists, when they treat the matter of project selection, do little more than reiterate, or take as a given, the ideal norm which states that the scientist exercises free choice in his selection of topics for research but is obligated to choose those that are potentially the most significant for scientific knowledge. However, scientists do not enjoy absolute freedom to study what they will. Social scientists, in particular, are affected by a variety of cultural and social strictures, particularly those of an ethical nature.

A serious bar to understanding the methods by which research projects are formulated has been the reluctance of many practitioners themselves to reveal the nature of the activity in its early stages—the various meanderings of thought and action that precede the actual shaping and execution of the research design. But we are beginning to acquire some detailed information on the natural history of project selection and formulation.[1] This chapter attempts to stimulate further investigation by delineating some of the major issues involved.

[1] See, e.g., Phillip E. Hammond (ed.), *Sociologists at Work* (New York: Basic Books, 1964); Arthur J. Vidich *et al.* (eds.), *Reflections on Community Studies* (New York: Wiley, 1964); and Stewart R. Perry, *The Human Nature of Science* (New York: Free Press, 1966).

Critical Factors in the Formulation of Research Projects

THE ROLE OF CHANCE

With the accumulation of further, detailed data on the matter of project selection, we may discover that certain patterns that we now attribute to chance do in fact stem from definite social factors. Nevertheless, it is unlikely that chance (or accident) will ever be completely ruled out as a variable in the choice of research projects.

Chance has been a factor in determining the course of many significant studies. Whyte, in his oft-quoted *Street Corner Society*, details some of the fortuitous events that led him to "stumble upon" his gang in an Italian slum district of Boston.[2] Likewise C. K. Yang and his students literally "fell into" their research on a Communist village in the Canton region of China, an area where, prior to the Communist conquest, they had planned to carry out field work of a sort.[3] No one could have fully anticipated the subsequent chain of events. Professor Yang did not plan the resultant "social experiment," nor did he say to himself: "I will go to X village, for in the year 194– the Communists, like the Mongol hordes before them, will sweep over China, and I must be on hand to record the momentous changes that will ensue." He could hardly have foreseen that the new rulers would permit him to remain in the village long enough to provide the scientific world with a permanent record of the dramatic transformation this community underwent as it exchanged its traditional ways of life for Communist ones; nor, finally, could he have predicted that he would find the opportunity to escape and subsequently publish his findings in the outside world.

Instances of projects arising from chance factors are recorded now and again in the natural sciences.[4] For example, the Newtonian theory concerning the nature of the color spectrum has within the past decade been challenged by a chemist who, while concerned with more mundane matters, happened to juxtapose certain filters in his projectors and discovered that the resulting color combinations were not those that existing theories about the color spectrum would lead one to expect. The researcher's first reaction was to discount his findings as an optical illusion. But he was sufficiently disturbed to ask other

[2] William Foote Whyte, *Street Corner Society*, 2nd ed. (Chicago: University of Chicago Press, 1955), appendix.

[3] C. K. Yang, *A Chinese Village in Early Communist Transition* (Cambridge, Mass.: Technology Press, 1959).

[4] Bernard Barber and Renée C. Fox, "The Case of the Floppy-Eared Rabbits: An Instance of Serendipity Gained and Serendipity Lost," *American Journal of Sociology*, 64 (September, 1958), 128–136.

persons what they saw when these filters were juxtaposed, and they confirmed the original observations.[5]

Chance factors also go back into the lives of individuals. The scientist's training and conceptual orientation, as well as the society's receptivity to new findings, all play a role in the creative process. Probably neither Whyte nor Yang would have written or published their particular kinds of studies had they not been trained in social science. With respect to the findings that overturned the prevailing theories on the color spectrum, it is an arresting fact that industrial technicians had, some decades earlier, made these discoveries and utilized them in movie-making, and some had even discussed them in the popular literature. But, lacking knowledge of theory in physics, they did not recognize the manifold implications of their findings. Nor did the published findings of the technicians, so far as we know, come to the attention of the scientists.

THE DEVELOPMENT AND PERSISTENCE
OF PARTICULAR THEORETICAL ORIENTATIONS

The scientist, like other persons, is the product of an extended socialization process involving his family, childhood peer groups, social class, community ties, and so on. That these factors in one way or another mold his research interests is presumed by most sociologists.

Merton has outlined the existence of national styles in sociology, a pattern that is well documented within the literature.[6] Furthermore, within nations, differential association patterns affect the sociologist's research orientation. Mills, for instance, observed a rather well-defined relationship between the social backgrounds of a selected group of sociologists and their orientation toward the study of social problems.[7] These particular scholars reflected the values of the small towns and rural areas in which they had grown up.

More specifically, graduate departments in American universities appear to be the prime mechanism for molding the thoughtways of the would-be scientist.

---

[5] For a popular account of this discovery, see Francis Bello, "An Astonishing New Theory of Color," *Fortune*, 59 (May, 1959), 144–147 f.

[6] See, e.g., Robert K. Merton, "Social Conflict over Styles of Sociological Work," *Transactions of the Fourth World Congress of Sociology, 1959*, vol. 3 (Louvain, Belgium: International Sociological Association, 1961), as well as vol. 1 of this Congress. Numerous essays dealing with sociology in specific nations lend empirical support to Merton's general proposition. See, e.g., Richard A. Peterson, "Sociology and Society: The Case of South Africa," *Sociological Inquiry*, 36 (Winter, 1966), 31–38; George Fischer, *Science and Politics: The New Sociology in the Soviet Union* (Ithaca, N.Y.: Cornell University, Center for International Studies, 1964); and Howard Becker and Alvin Boskoff (eds.), *Modern Sociological Theory in Continuity and Change* (New York: Holt, Rinehart and Winston, 1957), part 5.

[7] C. Wright Mills, "The Professional Ideology of Social Pathologists," *American Journal of Sociology*, 49 (September, 1943), 165–180.

Through course work, examinations, and other rites of passage the student is introduced to particular constructs and research procedures. Not infrequently, graduate departments also orient the student to the specific role he will fill after his period of apprenticeship.

University departments that socialize budding scientists into the scientific method also display a subculture that reflects the way of life of a particular discipline, be it sociology, anthropology, or whatever.[8] Thus graduate students in sociology departments are introduced to the greats of yesteryear: Durkheim, Weber, Simmel, Sumner, and others. In time the student becomes indoctrinated into the salient theories of this field regarding suicide, the nature of rational bureaucracy, interaction in small groups, and other subjects frequently debated in books and journals. For these are the topics that the sociological fraternity today defines as relevant, a viewpoint that is reinforced and shaped by the concerns of the broader industrial-urban order.

Outside the hard core of this intellectual heritage lie, in Sorokin's terminology, the fads, fashions, and foibles.[9] We need to recognize the validity of his argument: that within sociology, for example, marked shifts in research interests occur over time. These changes result from progress in scientific investigation itself, from status rivalries within the associational structure that supports the scientific enterprise, and from sociocultural innovations within the broader society.

University departments, as socializing agencies, blend the new fads into the older intellectual heritage of the discipline in distinctive ways. Each department tends to champion or represent one or at most a few schools of thought. That is, in their teaching and research, departments tend to regard particular logical-theoretical constructs and research methods as superior to others and encourage their students to do likewise. As a result, graduate students in logical-positivistic halls of learning come to stress the efficacy of method over theory and to select their research problems accordingly; those in other departments may proceed quite differently, holding the problem to be studied as relatively more important than either theory or method.

Departments can become so stereotyped that young sociologists may be known as Chicago men, Columbia men, Harvard men, and so on. Although in practice most such departments are staffed by professors of diverse hues, a stereotype emerges because of the tendency for one or a few dominant personali-

---

[8] The nature of styles within disciplines in American society can be inferred from essays such as that by Dennison Nash, "The Ethnologist as Stranger: An Essay in the Sociology of Knowledge," *Southwestern Journal of Anthropology, 19* (Summer, 1963), 149–167; and John Walton, "Discipline, Method, and Community Power: A Note on the Sociology of Knowledge," *American Sociological Review, 31* (October, 1966), 684–689.

[9] Pitirim A. Sorokin, *Fads and Foibles in Modern Sociology and Related Sciences* (Chicago: Regnery, 1956).

ties to leave their stamp upon students. Thus at Harvard we find Parsons, and at Columbia Merton and Lazarsfeld, and so on. This means that not only do graduates emerge with a given point of view but incoming students at times enroll in departments whose orientation they anticipate.

Consequently, not only after graduation but also during the training period students tend to pursue projects that in one way or another reflect the interests of their professors. Students may at times be told outright that the department expects them to pursue certain types of studies; those who are unwilling to do so are encouraged to enter other departments or fields.

Many advanced students become quite conscious of their selection of professors under whom to work. Within the limits permitted by the system, the student gravitates toward certain faculty members and may even avoid others. Implicitly, if not explicitly, he asks himself before aligning with a particular professor (or professors) questions such as the following: (1) Will this professor provide me with employment while I am in graduate school? Even for the dedicated graduate student, Sumner's initial observation in his *Folkways,* "the first task of life is to live," remains paramount.[10] (2) Is the professor part of the power group in the department? Here the student's concern relates to whether the attitude of other members of the department toward the sponsoring professor will help or hinder the student in having his efforts accepted by the department. (3) How respected is the professor nationally? The answer to this question tells the student much about the professor's ability to sponsor him in his immediate post-Ph.D. career, specifically to help him secure a first-rate position. At this point, such a variable as age comes into play, for students may shy away from older men who they think will not be around to assist them in the early years of their career. (4) How difficult to please, and how fair, is the professor? This question has several dimensions, but lack of prejudice in grading and the use of "reasonable" standards rank foremost. (5) What is the professor's primary field of interest and competency?

A number of graduate students appear to develop particular fields of interest and acquire knowledge of given theoretical constructs and research procedures without being exposed to the range of possible alternatives. Or their theoretical orientations may be shaped by social factors that bear only indirectly upon what might be considered theoretically significant research from the standpoint of either science or society.

Ideally students are rewarded for independent thought, but in practice they are often expected to conform to general and sometimes to specific orientations.[11]

---

[10] William Graham Sumner, *Folkways* (Boston: Ginn, 1940), 2.

[11] For a highly critical review of the conformist orientation in American graduate schools, see Theodore Solotaroff, "The Graduate Student: A Profile," *Commentary, 32* (December, 1961), 482–490. Materials by sociologists on the socialization process in graduate schools are slowly becoming available. See, e.g., Charles R. Wright, "Changes

They may find "survival value" in developing fields of interest that are not their own but which emanate from others in the bureaucracy. To be sure, enterprising students may spawn their own ideas and research designs, all the more when a professor encourages such even though his own views may be challenged. Still, even the more independent student is unlikely to act until he has carefully reconnoitered the prejudices of the professors concerned—and wisely so. Students do (and at times must) probe the "enemy lines" with all the perspicacity of well-trained soldiers looking for hidden mine fields or snipers. Even where professors champion the ideal of freedom of inquiry, pressures from, say, other departmental members tend to reduce the actual degree of freedom the student enjoys. For example, a professor may attack a colleague by sniping at the latter's graduate students.

The norms of the discipline or even of the broader society also impinge upon professors and thus serve to structure the student's choice of research topics. One rather general norm in present-day sociology, already crystallized in some university departments, calls for graduate students to write empirical rather than strictly theoretical dissertations. This practice reflects in part the discipline's struggle for status as a science. Furthermore, theoretical dissertations are apt to be controversial and thus more difficult to move through the departmental structure. We have heard more than one professor remark: "Write an empirical dissertation, for even if the other members of the committee disagree with your interpretation, they cannot challenge your data."

At the same time, the departments themselves (through which the norms of the discipline and the broader society tend to be filtered down to the student) are changing, mostly in the direction of greater complexity.[12] Large-scale research projects have become major adjuncts of many sociology departments.[13] As a result, more and more professors expect (some in fact insist) that students select their thesis and dissertation topics—in effect, shape their research interests and methods—to fit the demands of the department's bureaucratic apparatus. A few students even feel constrained to list the directing professor as coauthor in later publications they may develop from the data.

Students working under the aegis of these departmental bureaucracies bear witness to the priority of group research projects over individual creativity.

---

in the Occupational Commitment of Graduate Sociology Students: A Research Note," *Sociological Inquiry*, 37 (Winter, 1967), 55–62; and the papers by John Pease and Bernard Rosen and Alan P. Bates in the same issue.

[12] For a survey of graduate education in American sociology, see Elbridge Sibley, *The Education of Sociologists in the United States* (New York: Russell Sage, 1963).

[13] See, e.g., Paul Lazarsfeld (in collaboration with Sidney S. Spivack), "Observations on Organized Social Research in the United States," A Report to the International Social Science Council, August, 1961 (mimeo.).

Thus, within the graduate school setting, the neophyte soon becomes socialized into the norms of the technician's role. The pattern has become so widespread that Weaver, a graduate school dean, after conducting a survey of graduate schools in the United States, was moved to remark that one function of post-doctoral programs is to provide a broader education for students who spent their Ph.D. candidacy functioning as technicians.[14]

The ultimate effect of a student's graduate training is that so frequently it largely shapes his postdoctoral research orientations. This is most apparent in the scientist's basic theoretical and methodological orientations. Therefore we find considerable continuity in the specific fields of interests of sociologists, in addition to a high degree of consistency over time in their theoretical orientation. In practice, many graduates accomplish little more than spinning out some of the loose strands of their dissertation, or they may devote themselves to testing the theories of other scholars, often their own mentors. Such of course are worthy endeavors as long as they result in the refinement of particular methodological and theoretical perspectives.

Actually, there is a definite continuity in outlook even among the major figures in sociology. It is unusual to find a marked shift in a person's basic theoretical assumptions in the course of his career.[15] But there are some striking exceptions. Sorokin wrote as a Pavlovian behaviorist in his *Sociology of Revolution* (1925) and as a neo-idealist in his *The Ways and Power of Love* (1954).[16] In 1939 Bierstedt was an ardent advocate of the natural science approach to sociology in his "The Means-End Schema in Sociological Theory," but by 1960 he had reversed his position in "Sociology as Humane Learning."[17]

But why the strong tendency toward continuity in theoretical outlook? Some persons simply lack the ability to create new perspectives. Others adhere

[14] John C. Weaver, "Some Dilemmas in Graduate Education," A Report to the Carnegie Corporation of New York on a Travelling Fellowship, 1957–1958, n.d.

Indeed, the generalization might be hazarded that the present rapid growth of the postdoctoral fellowship idea is, at least in part, a direct result of many of our Ph.D.s having been trained in too-large groups, in overextended graduate departments, and under "team research" circumstances. Having failed properly to achieve the purposes of a doctor's degree in gaining the understanding and maturity to undertake independent research, they are compelled to return to an academic setting to learn what they should have learned before their degree was granted (57–58).

[15] Even Philip Selznick, while disavowing somewhat his early anarchist leanings, nevertheless recognizes his intellectual continuity with this past. See his introductory note to his essay "Revolution: Sacred and Profane," in Irving Louis Horowitz (ed.), *The Anarchists* (New York: Dell, 1964), 563.

[16] Cf. Pitirim A. Sorokin, *Sociology of Revolution* (Philadelphia: Lippincott, 1925), with his *The Ways and Power of Love* (Boston: Beacon Press, 1954).

[17] Cf. Robert Bierstedt, "The Means-End Schema in Sociological Theory," *American Sociological Review*, 3 (October, 1938), 665–671, and his "Sociology as Humane Learning," *American Sociological Review*, 25 (February, 1960), 3–9.

to the theories and methods acquired in graduate school for purely social considerations. It is noteworthy that the continuity between graduate school and the scientific career is reinforced by the scientist's own colleagues. At conventions, for instance, the young scientist is frequently asked: "Where did you get your degree and under whom did you work?" If he is a product of a well-known department and studied under an illustrious professor, his theoretical constructs and research interests are more or less taken for granted—all of which reinforces the scientist's self-image. Furthermore, young scientists are often recruited on the basis of the fields of specialization of the professors with whom they worked most closely. Or a person may be hired because he represents a particular school of thought. And as departments become increasingly specialized and bureaucratized,[18] their members are more likely to look askance at anyone who works in a field other than what is viewed as his specialty.

Another factor perpetuating a scientist's use of logical-theoretical constructs through time is the traditional student-teacher bond. Although in industrial societies strong personal ties are by no means as binding as their counterparts in the preindustrial civilized order, where ideally the student is devoted to his guru for life, certain bonds persist. It is somehow improper even in the United States for a student to criticize the work of his professor (or professors) strongly in print. However, the humble attitude of the former student vis-à-vis his former mentors is dropped, and the student is even expected to "cut the cord" to a degree. As a result the professor-student tie is more in the nature of an unspoken mutual assistance pact. The student is particularly dependent upon his academic sponsor during the initial period of his professional career.[19] Under these circumstances, it may be, as one sociologist expressed it to us personally, "intellectual suicide" for one to break with the school of thought that nurtured him. Conversely, the professor has a stake in the placement and future success of his "products."

Then too, the scientist's adherence to certain theoretical constructs and a given methodological orientation stems from the ties the emergent scientist maintains with his fellow students from graduate school days.[20] These sociointellectual bonds can be politically useful in helping him climb within the associational structure that supports scientific activity.

We have in a sense come full circle. Within the associations that support

[18] For a discussion of the bureaucratization of higher education in general, see Herbert Stroup, *Bureaucracy in Higher Education* (New York: Free Press, 1966).

[19] See Theodore Caplow and Reece J. McGee, *The Academic Marketplace* (New York: Basic Books, 1958).

[20] The sociometric relationships of symbolic interactionists have been traced by Larry Reynolds and Ted R. Vaughan, "The Sociology of Symbolic Interactionism," unpublished manuscript. From their data one can surmise the existence of certain links between graduate student education and commitment to a particular theoretical orientation.

scientific activity the student tends to identify with his former professor (or professors), as well as with his classmates—all of which aligns him with a given school of thought. In turn, the more status the scientist achieves within the associational structure as a result of these links with a particular school of thought, the firmer his commitment to continuing research along particular lines, the ideals of science to the contrary. Although there are countervailing tendencies in science and the broader society, the scientist does have a vested interest in defending and propounding a given point of view.

Additional, more elusive factors may explain the continuity of theoretical perspectives in social science. In sociology, for instance, the longer one thinks and acts in terms of a specific set of logical-theoretical constructs, the more difficult it may be to shake off tradition and devise a new orientation. This in part may result from the sociologist's use of his theoretical constructs to interpret his everyday existence; to the extent this occurs, any revision of these constructs involves a change in his day-by-day actions. Moreover, the vagueness of social data and the general inability of sociologists to devise research designs that will ensure a firm testing (especially in the sense of falsification) of hypotheses derived from the theories of Parsons, Marx, Freud, and so on, makes it easier for social than for natural scientists to think and act in accord with their traditional formulations.[21] These theories, when they can not be disproved, continue to have a degree of plausibility.

THE SEARCH FOR NEW IDEAS OR HYPOTHESES

Despite the "cake of custom," the scientific method is essentially dynamic. Numerous forces are at work effecting changes in the scientist's selection and formulation of his project or, on occasion, his theoretical constructs. Some of these pressures for change inhere within science; others emanate from the associational structure supporting science, including the broader society.

With respect to the scientific method, the ideal of creativity runs counter to tradition. Indeed, an essential aspect of the scientific method is the negation process, one involving continual reevaluation of existing hypotheses or traditional research procedures and, where these are found wanting, replacement of them with "better" ones. The pure scientist strives to achieve this goal even in the face of firm resistance to change.

In addition, the purists in particular constantly seek to deal with the contradictions and conflicts among various theoretical orientations in science. Efforts are made either to resolve these differences through development of a higher order of theory or to explain why they must prevail.

---

[21] Hyman has observed that "whether we are discussing social psychology or sociology, the influence on research of *systematic* theory, whether unified into one general theory or fragmented into several less inclusive and partial systems, seems to have been small." Herbert H. Hyman, "Reflections on the Relation between Theory and Research," *Centennial Review,* 7 (Fall, 1963), 436.

That the search for consistency, along with the continuing availability of new empirical data, has led to revisions in theory is aptly demonstrated in the history of structural-functional analysis. Merton, especially, has explicated some of its underlying assumptions and has sought to bridge some of the differences among such writers as Parsons, Malinowski, and Radcliffe-Brown.[22] In the process, he has sought to make the theory more useful for interpreting empirical data. It is more difficult to cite a theory that has been refuted outright. However, drawing upon the instinct school of McDougall, we find that advances in social theory and research have led to the virtual demise of this perspective. Although this school may be experiencing a regeneration (at least as reflected in popular literature), the crude biological assumptions of McDougall's formulation are unlikely to enlist long-standing support in sociology.

Or consider research procedures. Sociologists today are far wiser in the area of field research methods than were their predecessors in the Chicago School of the 1920s. There have been major innovations in the study of the community, particularly in the use of more rigorous sampling procedures.

The changes resulting from the application of the scientific method are intensified by social patterns within the associational structure that supports science. One widespread phenomenon is "status seeking" on the part of scientists. Thus, a sociologist who has developed a new idea or new perspective and seeks to prove to the world that he has scored a major theoretical breakthrough attempts to enlist support not only from his students but from his peers as well. If he is able to use a prestigious university as his platform, he is more assured of success than if he speaks as a member of a lesser-light organization.

For example, W. Lloyd Warner during the 1940s led a "movement" promoting the notion that the social class system in industrial-urban America was becoming more rigid. This campaign, based at Harvard and later at the University of Chicago, brought with it widespread publicity.[23] However, in time other scholars came to belabor the views of Warner and his associates. As a result of these vigorous criticisms as well as his own research, Warner modified his conception of the American social class system.[24] Yet the extremist nature of the movement in its early stages helped to put across an important idea.

New ideas are also generated by the argumentation between scientists aligned with the formal associational structure that supports science, and intellectuals of the free-floating variety. The latter have often been highly critical of formalized social research and of persons who are enamored of the technical apparatus of science. And while some social scientists have reacted strongly to

---

[22] Robert K. Merton, *Social Theory and Structure,* rev. ed. (New York: Free Press, 1957), chap. 1.

[23] See, e.g., Milton M. Gordon's chapter "The Warner School," in his *Social Class in American Sociology* (Durham, N.C.: Duke, 1958), chap. 4.

[24] W. Lloyd Warner and James C. Abegglen, *Big Business Leaders in America* (New York: Harper & Row, 1955), chap. 11.

this criticism, they have nevertheless drawn upon the unattached scholar's ideas. That those who are formally labeled sociologists rely upon outsiders for creative inspiration in a number of areas is not sufficiently acknowledged. For instance, significant theories regarding the impact of automation upon society have been formulated by scholars who stand apart from the formal sociological tradition in American society.[25]

Morgenthau, a political scientist, perhaps as clearly as anyone has pinpointed the role of the nonprofessional in generating new ideas:

> It is significant that the few creative efforts to understand the contemporary political world have in the main not been made by the academic professionals, but either by theologians, such as Reinhold Niebuhr, or by outsiders, such as Hannah Arendt, Bertrand de Jouvenel and Walter Lippmann. Unencumbered by the weight of academic traditions and unrestrained by the shackles of professional conformism, they have been able to view the contemporary political world in the light of the heritage of our civilization.[26]

Implied in the foregoing is the impact of the broader sociocultural system upon social scientists. Although rapid changes in the broader society, notably social crises, may cause some social scientists to become more conservative in their choice of projects and content to struggle with petty problems, these forces can have the opposite effect upon others. In the main the kinds of modifications that ensue depend upon the scientist's role and status (and upon his ethical orientation, discussed below). But in general the scientist's substantive research interests are more subject to change than are his theoretical and methodological premises.

Changes in the broader social order on occasion result in research areas disappearing before the scientist's very eyes. Many anthropologists who have taken as their focus the American Indian and his assimilation into the broader society are slowly but surely being forced to cast about for new research problems. Some have fastened onto the study of large-scale social orders such as American society. This shift has led them to revise aspects of their theory and methods, for some of the procedures of anthropologists for the analysis of small communities (for example, direct observation) have proved inapplicable to the study of large-scale social systems.

[25] See, e.g., Ad Hoc Committee on the Triple Revolution, "The Triple Revolution," in Wilbert E. Moore and Robert M. Cook (eds.), *Readings on Social Change* (Englewood Cliffs, N.J.: Prentice-Hall, 1967), 141–151. Although Everett C. Hughes was a member of this committee (which published its statement in 1964), most of the participants were so-called nonprofessionals.

[26] Hans J. Morgenthau, "Review of Louis J. Halle, *Men and Nations* (Princeton, N.J.: Princeton University Press, 1962)," *New York Times Book Review*, May 6, 1962, 3.

Societal changes may also reorient the scientist in his choice or interpretation of explanatory variables. Until recently sociologists stressed the factory system as the primary dimension of industrialization. Today, however, many are coming to recognize that the scientific method (or science more generally) is the key ingredient of industrialization. This reconceptualization has resulted from changes in the very fabric of modern society, including the rise of automation, the enormous expansion of the white-collar group, the proliferation of scientists and technicians, and the relative decline of the old-line factory system.

More narrowly, many social scientists are crisis-oriented. Wars or depressions affect not only the researcher who identifies with the broader society but the purist as well. What scientists take as their "independent" or "dependent" variables is frequently a product of social crises.

Illustrative of the effect of crises on social research are the shifts in orientation among social scientists in the United States during the period 1930–1960. The Great Depression of the 1930s was taken, time and again, as a key independent variable by scientists seeking to examine its impact upon familial, religious, governmental, economic, and other structures. But with the advent of World War II the situation changed dramatically: Now war became the crucial variable. More recently the Cold War, though to a somewhat lesser degree, has left its impact upon the social scientist's choice and formulation of research projects.

A link between social crises and social research has been forged by the organizational revolution and by social scientists' growing identity with non-academic bureaucracies in modern society and the research operations of these, in part because many such organizations have made funds available to social researchers.[27] During any great crisis, research funds tend to flow to scholars who are willing to investigate the pressing problems of the moment (problems that are defined to a degree by the organizations themselves).

This overall trend serves to generate a body of social scientists who skip from topic to topic as money for these becomes available.[28] Certainly the process has been heightened by the increased support the federal government has given to research.[29] Again, funds appear to go primarily to those researchers who are

[27] The growth of such organizations as the Rand Corporation in America is one expression of this trend. See Bruce L. R. Smith, *The Rand Corporation* (Cambridge, Mass: Harvard, 1966).

[28] Cf. Peter H. Rossi, "Researchers, Scholars and Policy Makers: The Politics of Large Scale Research," *Daedalus, 93* (Fall, 1964), 1142–1161. Also the comments by James A. Davis, "Great Books and Small Groups: An Informal History of a National Survey, "in Hammond, *op. cit.,* 212–215.

[29] For the emergent role of the federal government in social research, see the special issue "The Federal Government in Behavioral Science," *American Behavioral Scientist, 7* (May, 1964). Also, A Staff Study for the Research and Technical Programs Subcommittee of the Committee on Government Operations, *The Use of Social Research in Federal*

willing to investigate topics that result in the accumulation of a body of knowledge that can be employed by administrators to resolve problems of immediate interest to them. This trend suggests that we must look closely at the procedures by which the ongoing social order supports social scientists and how they influence, even shape, the destiny of social research.

Research Grants, Bureaucracies, and Project Formulation

We have already indicated that in industrialized societies, social research, as a source of data upon which rational decisions can be based, is today not only desirable and essential but also economically feasible—far more so than in centuries past.

That research grants influence the course of social science is apparent enough. One of the most obvious effects is the realization, through large-scale subvention, of research involving the collection of data from large numbers of persons within or across nation-state systems. Such projects of national and international scope were impossible in the era of the small research grant—for example, during the Chicago School era of the 1920s.[30]

The expansion of large-scale research has been associated with the rise of complex bureaucracies—not only grant-giving agencies but also research institutes. The latter, which Lazarsfeld regards as one of the chief innovations furthering social research in recent decades, have emerged either as appendages of the departmental structures of universities or as more or less independent agencies.[31] Many departments have in recent years sought to sustain these research organizations as one means of supporting their gradaute programs, thus providing employment for students as well as enabling professors to engage in specialized types of research. These tendencies have been exaggerated by the demands of the broader university, which depends upon these grants for its success and economic well-being. Consequently, we have witnessed the rise of research administrators whose prime function is neither teaching nor research but rather administration.

Although complex, large-scale organizations, along with considerable financial support, are prerequisites to realizing certain kinds of research, the resultant

---

Domestic Programs, 4 parts (Washington, D.C.: GPO, 1967), provides data on many of the complexities of the relationship of social scientists to the federal government. This is a highly useful compilation.

[30] See Ernest W. Burgess and Donald J. Bogue, "Research in Urban Society: A Long View," in Ernest W. Burgess and Donald J. Bogue (eds.), *Contributions to Urban Sociology* (Chicago: University of Chicago Press, 1964), 5–7.

[31] Paul F. Lazarsfeld, "The Sociology of Empirical Social Research," *American Sociological Review,* 27 (December, 1962), 757–767.

bureaucracy does not always articulate well with the ideal norms of science.[32] Administrators of research grants find themselves committed not only to carrying out scientific research but also to sustaining their own bureaucracy. Thus, situations emerge wherein administrators seek grants not to investigate a particular theory or some significant societal issue but rather to acquire funds in order to "keep the team together." For some continuity is essential if bureaucratic efficiency is to be sustained. So when the administrator discovers that funds are available for such and such a project, he is tempted to tailor his research to fit the requirements of the donor agency. Similarly, agencies may approach a research administrator with a request that he pursue certain types of projects— projects that may contribute little to basic knowledge but which the agency wants carried out as a means of resolving its own administrative problems. Wishing to encourage the donor's interest in supporting research projects, the research administrator may find himself justifying the project as worthwhile.

These patterns have given rise to persons whom De Takats, a medical doctor, labels "grant eaters."[33] Using the field of medicine as an illustration, he has drawn a Parkinsonian caricature of this kind of researcher. Like all caricatures, this one is an exaggeration; nevertheless, De Takats points up the prominence of persons whose prime goal is obtaining and spending money. Indeed, we have heard numerous discussions at sociological conventions concerning how much money such and such a research project involves. Here the attainment of a scientifically valid body of knowledge may be subordinated to the striving for other gains.

To determine the impact of grants upon social research, we must also examine some of the actual norms governing the grant-bestowing process.[34] For although the supporting agencies are influenced by shifting sociocultural patterns in the broader society, they do acquire an identity of their own, and the rules they apply in the grant-giving process uniquely affect the course of research.

One clue for determining which scientists are most apt to receive grants can be found in the adage: "Success breeds success." Once a scientist receives a grant and publishes his findings, and assuming that these are reasonably satisfactory, he is slated for further assistance. A related factor is the prestige of the

---

[32] This conclusion can definitely be drawn from Jane Cassels Record, "The Research Institute and the Pressure Group," in Gideon Sjoberg (ed.), *Ethics, Politics, and Social Research* (Cambridge, Mass.: Schenkman, 1967), chap. 2.

[33] Geza de Takats, "Parkinson's Law in Medicine," *New England Journal of Medicine,* 262 (Jan. 21, 1960), 126–128.

[34] There are all too few studies in this problem area. Clues to the grant-bestowing process can be found in such sources as Ernest M. Allen, "Why Are Research Grant Applications Disapproved?" *Science, 132* (Nov. 25, 1960), 1532–1534; and Richard Colvard, "Foundations and Professions: The Organizational Defense of Autonomy," *Administrative Science Quarterly, 6* (September, 1961), 167–184.

grant seeker. If he does not enjoy sufficiently high prestige, he tends to enlist the assistance of those who do. From one perspective this is rational action, in that one should grant funds to persons who, as far as is known, can make the most effective use of them.

This policy of course tends toward closure. It is to be expected that scientists who are consulted as to the disposition of research funds will direct them toward persons whom they know rather than to persons of unknown quality. And it is "natural" that one will judge his own friends to be competent—few could describe them otherwise. At the same time, cleavages within the scientific community have worked toward greater openness, and the federal government, for example, has become concerned with distributing grants somewhat more equitably (at least by states).

Then there is the matter of the grantee's familiarity with the bureaucratic structure. Grant-dispensing agencies are apt to view certain formats for research proposals as definitely superior to others, and applicants who are familiar with the rules and with the preferences of the fund dispensers, or who have acquaintances who can inform them about these norms, are the most likely to satisfy the requirements of these agencies or otherwise create a favorable impression. Moreover, government bureaus and certain private foundations, in particular, are constantly shifting their emphasis in grant-giving programs, making knowledge of the most recent policy crucial for attracting funds.

In addition to such special knowledge, the aspirant's associational affiliation may be a critical variable in the procurement of funds. A scientist who claims as his home base a high-status university holds distinct advantages over one from a less prestigious institution. Not only does one's associational affiliation reinforce (or detract from) one's personal prestige, but it is frequently assumed (and with considerable justification) that high-status universities have more of the basic resources and facilities for conducting research than do less prominent centers of learning.

Another variable affecting the procurement of grants is the nature of the project and its design. Here foundations do differ among themselves. Some grant-dispensing agencies carefully circumscribe their activities, supporting only narrowly specified kinds of projects, whereas others cover a much wider range. Yet some general patterns seem to emerge: (1) Projects with a practical (or policy) orientation more readily gain support than those that are essentially theoretical; (2) research projects utilizing natural science procedures, rather than the more traditional humanistic ones, are usually given priority; and (3) group efforts tend to be favored over individual ones.

The practical orientation of much grant-giving—especially on the part of governmental and business organizations—reflects a concern with resolving "visible" problems. Many administrators are not interested in abstract principles but rather in solutions to specific difficulties they encounter. Also, in a democratically oriented society, where both private foundations and governmental agencies must take account of the pulse beat of the voting public and the voices of the politicians, it is easier to justify allocating funds for research whose immediate gains in terms of societal "progress" are apparent than for studies whose results may not be forthcoming for generations, if at all.[35]

A second factor entering into grant-giving is the general preference in our technologically oriented society for projects in the natural science tradition, as opposed to those in the humanistic realm. The National Science Foundation, especially in its formative years, dispensed funds primarily to social scientists whose methods most closely approximated those of the natural scientists.[36] Thus, studies stressing the use of statistics, along with experimental or quasi-experimental designs, have been heavily favored over other approaches in social research. Here the method, far more than the problem, is given priority.

One consequence of this stress on method is the favoring of certain theoretical constructs in social science over others. Hence the very course of the scientific method is affected by the policies of the grant givers. We might even argue that the humanistic tradition within social science has declined in recent years in part because its practitioners have failed to secure adequate financial support. Specifically, the symbolic interactionists, whose founders include Mead and Cooley, appear to have lost ground because their field of study is relatively unamenable to experimentation and/or statistical analysis.[37]

A corollary of this emphasis upon method is the complaint of some grant seekers that they are called upon to detail their method and research design at the outset, leaving little room for later interaction between theory and data, or indeed for discovery itself. Supportive agencies in a sense expect solutions to research problems before the investigation has even begun. Such a policy does much to reduce the risk of failure. However, as one natural scientist, commenting upon the criteria for acceptance and rejection of projects submitted to the National Institutes of Mental Health, has observed, many of the eminent scientists of yesteryear could not (for methodological and other reasons) gain support today for projects that in the past yielded highly significant scientific discoveries.[38]

[35] *National Science Foundation, Fifth Annual Report, Fiscal Year 1955* (Washington, D.C.: GPO, 1955), 60. One of the four criteria the foundation used for establishing a program of support of the social sciences was the "national interest"; namely, that projects should be directly related to the responsibilities of the federal government with respect to national welfare and national defense.

[36] *Ibid.,* 60–61.

[37] There have, of course, been sociologists like Manford H. Kuhn who have reformulated symbolic interactionism to bring it more in line with logical empiricist reasoning. See the special issue of the *Sociological Quarterly, 5* (Winter, 1964).

[38] Johan Bjorksten, "Letter to the Editor: Criteria for Research Grants," *Science, 133* (Apr. 7, 1961), 1040.

As indicated above, some fund-dispensing agencies favor group projects over those carried out by individuals. Partly this trend is a product of the organizational revolution in modern society—the assumption that groups can resolve problems more readily than can lone individuals. Partly this trend is a matter of economy. One large grant is less costly to administer than several small ones. Then too, there is less risk involved in giving money to organizations rather than individuals. A large-scale organization will persist even if some personnel abandon the project. Of course, as we have already noted, certain kinds of large-scale projects seem to require large-scale bureaucratic operations for their very execution.

In practice this tendency toward bureaucratization of research reinforces the need to delineate the research design in advance of data collection and analysis. In some instances the grant-dispensing agency's demands for periodic reports commit the researcher to designs that have not been fully tested in the field. For once the project is under way, administrative considerations make it difficult to revise the research design. Permitting new ideas and issues to filter up and down the bureaucratic hierarchy and incorporating these new notions into the research design may not be feasible—not because the researcher is unreceptive to new ideas but rather because the routinization of bureaucratic activity would be seriously impaired. The demands of bureaucracies on occasion override the demands for scientific creativity and even objectivity.[39]

With respect to the aforementioned criteria, certain countervailing trends can be observed. Some programs have been initiated to provide small grants for exploratory projects, and efforts are under way to provide more funds for the humanities. Also, universities and foundations have sought to sustain individual research activity in the face of bureaucratization by setting up research professorships. Nevertheless, the patterns we have delineated seem to dominate in the grant-giving and grant-receiving process.

Cultural and Social Strictures on Social Research

Some of the restrictions upon the research process have already been outlined. For example, the scientist can never completely shed his own conceptual apparatus. He observes phenomena in terms of some set of concepts which delimit and define what he observes. Other strictures, including the existing state of

[39] Herbert Hyman in his *Survey Design and Analysis* (New York: Free Press, 1955) has argued: "It is an interesting feature of research organization that the very conditions of work, the occurrence of interaction whether the individual wills it or not, *insures* that the scholar becomes aware of his bias" (34). The difficulty with this argument is that Hyman fails to recognize that bureaucracy is governed by the principle of dominance, with the result that the occupants of lowly positions in the hierarchy will be reluctant to state their views openly to persons who wield power and authority.

knowledge, inhere within science itself. After all, many kinds of studies require the prior accumulation of much basic data as well as the development of certain kinds of research techniques. For example, the urban ecological studies of Shevky and Bell[40] presuppose the existence of census data on cities, the ordering of this information into special areal units, and knowledge of certain measurement procedures.

More subtle, but no less real, restrictions on research reside in the nature of social reality. It is difficult to analyze social data with the precision physical data afford: The former are simply not as ordered as the latter. Here, however, we are concerned with the strictures upon the scientist's freedom of choice in research that stem from cultural values and from social structure and social power.

CULTURAL VALUES

Some social scientists assume that only totalitarian political systems impose restrictions on social research. However, all societies, and their subsystems as well, set various kinds of limits on research. This is true even in democratically oriented industrial social orders, where social research has achieved its greatest advances.

It must be recalled that no social system is completely secular. Every society comes to regard some areas as too sensitive or sacred to be investigated. Although in a totalitarian system the realm of the sacred is broader and more clearly defined than it is in the more democratic order, social scientists nonetheless encounter obstacles in the latter as well. We shall focus upon the ways in which cultural values narrow the scope of social research, especially in democratic orders.

Central to the sociology of knowledge orientation is the issue: How can a scientist remove himself from his own milieu and achieve a degree of objectivity? Mannheim hypothesized that only the unattached intellectual, one lacking any firm anchorage in the class structure, could attain this goal.[41] But Mannheim's formulation is too narrow; for example, he devoted almost no attention to the crosscultural aspect of this problem. For every social scientist experiences grave difficulties when he seeks to move beyond the premises of the social system—especially the nation-state system within which he functions.

Consider a striking illustration: In 1962, some 17 years after World War II, Laqueur was able to write:

> In the Soviet Union not a single book dealing with the nazi regime, the party, its leaders, the SS, the Gestapo, the concentration

---

[40] Eshref Shevky and Wendell Bell, *Social Area Analysis* (Stanford, Cal.: Stanford, 1955).

[41] Karl Mannheim, *Ideology and Utopia,* trans. by Louis Wirth and Edward A. Shils (New York: Harcourt, Brace & World, 1949).

camps, has been published—strictly speaking there is not even a history of Germany covering that period (apart from lecture courses).[42]

This neglect by Russian scholars may have been due to the fact that the Communists have had no acceptable explanation for the rise of fascism.[43] From the viewpoint of Marxist theory, fascism should never have arisen in a nation with a large industrial proletariat. Hence, faced with a problem that lies outside the set of categories or premises of the societal dogma, Soviet scholars remain silent.

Nor are American social scientists immune to the influence of values associated with nationalism. Thus some prominent social scientists comparing the United States and the Soviet Union have in effect taken the position that the United States would *not* violate its own democratic ideals when dealing with foreign powers.

The difficulty of escaping from the premises even of subsystems within a society has been raised by the economist Boulding in his review of a book by two former members of the Rand Corporation.[44] He argues that the authors took for granted the main premise of this corporation—that national defense constitutes a feasible social system—in initiating their study of the economics of national defense. What is needed, Boulding argues, is a similar study by researchers who are members of a corporation committed to building a world free of armies and threats of war.

After all, social scientists acquire not merely a set of logical-theoretical constructs peculiar to their own discipline but also a whole range of premises (often unstated or unarticulated) that stem from the broader sociocultural order or from particular organizations within which scientists carry out their research. In this manner the researcher's immediate social setting circumscribes the application of his theoretical constructs.

The efforts to protect salient values or ideals within the society foster another set of restrictions upon research. Even those persons who support the ideal of democracy may (because of other ideals) strive to inhibit some kinds of social research. For research often exposes discrepancies and contradictions in

[42] Walter Laqueur, "Russia and Germany," *Survey*, no. 44–45 (October, 1962), 9.

[43] That changes have been occurring in the Soviet Union (especially since the Stalin era) is suggested by the work of Anatoly Kuznetzov, *Babi Yar: A Documentary Novel*, trans. by Jacob Guralsky (New York: Dial Press, 1967). Cf. Anatoly Kuznetzov, "The Memories," *New York Times Book Review*, Apr. 9, 1967, 4–5 f.

[44] K. E. Boulding, "Review of Charles J. Hitch and Roland McKean, *The Economics of Defense in the Nuclear Age* (Cambridge: Harvard University Press, 1960)," *Bulletin of the Atomic Scientists, 17* (March, 1961), 115–116. Cf. Jerome Laulicht and Norman Z. Alcock, "The Support of Peace Research," *Conflict Resolution, 10* (June, 1966), 198–208.

the value system, which may lead some persons to question the society's basic orientation.

For example, the ideal of classlessness became a goal in the 1950s toward which everyone in India was expected to strive. Laws were passed ruling out the more "obnoxious" features of the caste system. In part as a result of this policy, questions regarding caste affiliation were omitted from the 1951 census, a practice that was continued in the 1961 census—this despite objections from some Indian social scientists who believe such information is essential for understanding present-day Indian society.[45] Yet the presentation of detailed information about caste in a census would have lent more or less official sanction to exposing the limited impact of the present laws.

In the United States, threats to "sacred values" have also led to strictures upon social research. The negative response to the jury study in Wichita, Kansas, conducted by persons affiliated with the University of Chicago Law School is a case in point. This group, intent upon examining the decision-making process of juries in a federal courtroom, had received permission to observe the workings of the jury without the jurors' knowledge. The permission was hedged about by precautionary rules designed to protect all parties involved. Nevertheless, the procedure contravened the value of privacy (discussed below) and also exposed to public scrutiny a basic assumption of the democratic heritage as it has been elaborated in England and the United States, that one's peers can rationally evaluate one's actions and arrive at a just decision regarding one's guilt or innocence. In effect, the jury study sought to lay bare a structure that the society has viewed as indispensable, even sacred. Though the empirical data collected apparently supported the assumption of rationality on the part of the jurors, the findings were considered by many as threatening to undermine the traditional jury system. The entire research operation was investigated by the United States Congress, which subsequently passed legislation that made these kinds of studies illegal.[46] The threat to fundamental values led to a reassertion of the police power of the state.[47]

A further restriction can be traced to inherent contradictions in the value system that supports research. Democratic values have greatly encouraged social

---

[45] See, e.g., N. R. Sheth, "The Census and Social Reality," *Economic Weekly, 11* (March 21, 1959), 417–418.

[46] For a detailed analysis of this case, see Ted R. Vaughan, "Governmental Intervention in Social Research: Political and Ethical Dimensions in the Wichita Jury Recordings," in Sjoberg, *op. cit.,* chap. 3.

[47] Other instances have arisen where the U.S. Congress has acted to make certain kinds of research "off-limits." As a result of the furor surrounding Paul Kecskemeti's *Strategic Surrender* (Stanford, Cal.: Stanford, 1958), a bill was adopted "forbidding the use of public moneys for any study dealing with a U.S. surrender under any circumstances" (Smith, *op. cit.,* 96).

research; yet these same values often impose strictures upon the activities they encourage. Democracy, at least as it has been interpreted in the West, has proclaimed freedom as one of its central values. Used to justify the scientist's activities, the concept of freedom also provides persons or systems with a rationale for objecting to certain kinds of research. Freedom serves as a basis for the individual's claim to (1) the right to a degree of privacy, (2) the right to avoid being "manipulated," and (3) the right to oppose others, including social scientists.

The average citizen's claim to privacy is, at least in American society, one of the main reasons given by interviewees for declining to answer questions on family life, sex habits, religious beliefs, and so on. The field worker is told: "That's a private matter." Of interest, in light of this claim to privacy, have been the actions of a number of sociologists who were intent upon having the United States Census Bureau include a question on religious affiliation in the 1960 census. It is noteworthy how infrequently sociologists recognized that this kind of question might impinge upon the rights of some citizens. In the end, certain religious groups did voice objection to any question on religion, contending that this would violate fundamental principles of the American Creed, and the census was taken without it.

What is considered a private matter, of course, varies not only among cultures but over time.[48] Today Americans apparently are quite willing to discuss facets of their actions that were taboo subjects a mere few decades ago. The trend is most apparent in the realm of sex mores. Shrouded in relative secrecy at the beginning of this century, the sex behavior of Americans has now become a "best-seller" in the publishing and entertainment fields. The revolution has been so marked that by the late 1950s Freedman and his associates could carry out a study on birth control and family planning with apparently little objection from informants that their privacy was being violated. The percentage of respondents in this survey compared very favorably with that in national studies.[49]

On the other hand, the demand for privacy has perhaps intensified in other areas. During the McCarthy era of the 1950s, many Americans (including college professors) became wary of discussing their political views in public, whereas 10 to 15 years earlier these same problems had engendered the liveliest of debates. Of more general significance is the growing concern among members of many professions in industrial-urban societies with the problem of privacy,

[48] The whole issue of privacy and social research has come to the fore in recent years. See, e.g., *Special Inquiry on Invasion of Privacy,* Hearings Before a Subcommittee of the Committee on Government Operations, House of Representatives, June 2, 3, 4, 7, 23 and September 23, 1965 (Washington, D.C.: GPO, 1966). Also the special issue on "Privacy," *Law and Contemporary Problems,* 31 (Spring, 1966).

[49] Ronald Freedman *et al., Family Planning, Sterility, and Population Growth* (New York: McGraw-Hill, 1959), 14.

in, say, doctor-patient or lawyer-client relationships. To the extent that privacy in these relationships is respected, social research is inhibited.

The notion of freedom is also used to justify one's antipathy to manipulation. Democracies, in the ideal, decry manipulation of the individual. But experimentation, the basis of modern science, involves manipulation. Such a conflict of interests creates numerous difficulties.[50] One such stems from the "exploitation" of subjects (at times without the consent of the latter) in prisons, mental hospitals, and schools. In universities particularly, behavioral scientists have a ready-made set of subjects—students—and the temptation is strong to use them for research in ways that might not be possible among other elements of the population.

Another value that limits the range of social research, one that is closely linked to the value of personal freedom, is that whereby democracy in the ideal encourages, even protects, those who voice objection to ongoing action within the society, including that by social scientists. Without such institutionalized opposition, democracy, as the Western world knows it, would not exist. As a result, the hostility of some social scientists, particularly those in academic circles, to criticism from politicians or the general public can hardly be defended. Although social scientists must continually assert their freedom to investigate elements of the social order, they must concede to others the right to question or oppose their actions. To assume that the scientist's work is immune to examination by the broader society is to adopt an elitist stance that contravenes the values that support social research.

Social scientists, to the extent that they accept the premises of a democratic order, must concede that elected officials have the right (and duty) to challenge and question scientific activities, just as social scientists in turn have the right to study politicians (among other groups) in the society. To adhere to this view is not to condone an inquisition but simply to clarify the scientist's relationship to the broader society. He has no special claim to exemption from criticism. In turn the vulnerability of social scientists to criticism leads us back to the point made in a previous chapter: Social scientists, to justify their existence and to avoid undue criticism from the public that supports them, are compelled to engage in moralization.

SOCIAL STRUCTURE AND SOCIAL POWER

Cultural values, significant though they may be, effectively inhibit research only when they articulate with the structural arrangement through which social

---

[50] See, e.g., Executive Office of the President, Office of Science and Technology, *Privacy and Behavioral Research* (Washington, D.C.: GPO, 1967); Herbert C. Kelman, "Human Use of Human Subjects: The Problem of Deception in Social Psychological Experiments," *Psychological Bulletin*, 67 (1967), 1–11; and J. Kenneth Benson and James Otis Smith, "The Harvard Drug Controversy: A Case Study of Subject Manipulation and Social Structure," in Sjoberg, *op. cit.*, chap. 5.

power is wielded. Such a condition is most dramatically displayed in totalitarian societies: for example, Communist China. The Communist regime, once it had usurped societal power, demanded unswerving loyalty from the intellectuals. Those social scientists who wanted to continue carrying out research capitulated to these demands. The career of Fei, the leading anthropologist in pre-Communist China, is enlightening here. During the early period of Communist rule, Fei apparently became an ardent supporter of the regime. However, during the "Hundred Flowers Movement," he accepted Mao's call for critical analysis. Subsequently, when the regime dropped the iron curtain of thought control, Fei, along with others, was repudiated and allowed to continue his intellectual endeavors only after public confession of his "crime."[51]

But totalitarian states, industrial or preindustrial, are not alone in restricting or channeling the course of social research. Social power within a democratic society such as the United States and its subsystems also may have telling effects upon science, though to a much lesser degree than in nondemocratic orders.

The use of national power was very much in evidence during the McCarthy era in the United States, particularly in the Congressional investigation of Owen Lattimore, a social scientist specializing in Asian studies who was charged with aiding and abetting the Communist cause.[52] This inquiry set social scientists against other social scientists, and undoubtedly these hearings made some scholars more cautious in their choice of problems.

More generally, as we suggested earlier, the demands of various social organizations—be they nations or universities—may only partially articulate with the demands of pure science. What is essential from an administrative viewpoint may not be functional to the advancement of the scientific enterprise. Thus, the strictures upon travel to various countries imposed by the State Department in line with its foreign policy surely have limited social inquiry into certain highly sensitive subjects.

But even the power structure of modern universities may limit research activities. Departmental power systems may be such that some members effectively discourage others from engaging in research which may impinge upon their special domains. And the concerns of the overall university bureaucracy loom large.[53] In some instances, universities have applied informal censorship

[51] Elise Hawtin, "The 'Hundred Flowers Movement' and the Role of the Intellectual in China. Fei Hsiao-t'ung: A Case History," *Papers on China,* vol. 12 (Cambridge, Mass.: Center for East Asian Studies, Harvard University, 1958), 147–198.

[52] *State Department Employee Loyalty,* Hearings Before a Subcommittee of the Committee on Foreign Relations, United States Senate, 2 parts (Washington, D.C.: GPO, 1950).

[53] The view that deviation and conflict are detrimental to a university bureaucracy has been voiced by Logan Wilson, "The Inhabitants of Academe; Some Aspects of a University as a Social Organization," *Graduate Journal,* 4 (Fall, 1961), 429–430. Wilson does not seem to recognize that truly creative thought is by nature deviant and disruptive.

of social science research.[54] Yet, more subtle and pervasive controls stem from the fact that most social scientists are reluctant to embarrass administrators by engaging in research that might antagonize the general public or the alumni who provide the system with the funds it requires. In some respects, an implicit contractual obligation arises between the scientist and the public that supports him—thereby limiting the scientist's freedom to carry out research.

Most bureaucratic structures object to being studied in depth—except perhaps when the diffusion of results can be carefully controlled—because social research tends to expose their practices to outsiders, including competitors and opponents. Obvious strictures are thus placed on the intelligence activities of even democratic nations. And whenever there are competitive relations among business organizations, between government and business, and so on, the accepted practice calls for controls upon the information to be released to outsiders.[55] Inasmuch as formal organizations are reluctant to expose their operations to public scrutiny for fear that politicians will object to or misinterpret various practices and consequently withdraw their support, social scientists tend to study relatively weak organizations. When they do study the very powerful ones, they usually skirt the sensitive issues. Thus, most studies of major bureaucracies in the United States have been of the middle-level management and not of the elite decision makers. Also relevant is the difficulty in gaining access to the power elements, unless one relies upon marginal informants.[56]

The public exposure function of social research may lead otherwise friendly groups to oppose the scientist's activities. One of the authors had occasion to discuss with a leading official of a Negro organization problems attendant upon the study of race relations in Southern communities. This official indicated that he had sought to keep sociologists out of a particular strife-torn city, not because he opposed sociological research, but because such a study at that time could have upset the delicate negotiations being carried on between the opposing factions.

Actually, there is considerable disagreement among sociologists as to their freedom to carry out research. Some believe that they enjoy considerable latitude; others feel quite bound by numerous social constraints. Much of this disagreement hinges upon varying definitions of "freedom." Those who believe that

---

[54] Record, *op. cit.*, points to some of the strictures operating within research institutes. Also see Henry Anderson, *A Harvest of Loneliness* (Berkeley, Cal., Citizens for Farm Labor, 1964), 1–12. Although it is very difficult to judge the validity of Anderson's charges, these kinds of materials need to be collected and evaluated.

[55] For a discussion of the impact of the confidentiality factor on data relating to Canadian manufacturing, see James M. Gilmour, "The Joint Anarchy of 'Confidentiality' and Definitional Change," *Canadian Geographer, 10* (1966), 40–48.

[56] For a discussion of the procedures that were used to bypass the power structure, procedures which in themselves raise ethical issues, see Melville Dalton, "Preconceptions and Methods in *Men Who Manage,*" in Hammond, *op. cit.*, chap. 3.

they are free to study what they so choose, implicitly or explicitly accept the idea that man is most free when the norms are clearly defined and adhered to. These sociologists accept and adhere to the norms of the university administration and the broader community that define what is legitimate and open to formal investigation.

There is, however, another definition of freedom, one wherein the actors consider the range of *theoretically* possible alternatives. According to this criterion (which we consider to be more meaningful from the standpoint of the scientific method), scholars are by no means as free as they may often assume. In fact, the first-mentioned definition of freedom, if pushed to the extreme, would mean that a scientist in a totalitarian state is freer than one in a democratic order.

Rarely can structural and power factors be sidestepped completely.[57] American social scientists have, as a result of their own increased identification with the "establishment," managed to circumvent some of the barriers to research emanating from the power structure. Inasmuch as the researchers today are thought to be less likely than those in the past to disturb the status quo, the power groups are more willing to accept them and their social investigations.

The Ethics of Project Selection

To just what extent the researcher should accept the society's normative constraints is a delicate ethical question for which there seems to be no satisfactory answer. Although the scientific method is incapable of empirically determining what "ought to be," we must constantly be aware that it has a built-in ethic and that scientific activity has moral consequences. Social scientists, whether

---

[57] Certain strictures upon data collection come to be supported by the legal system of a nation. Certainly limits are imposed upon reporting of many forms of deviant behavior in the United States. Here the comments of the journalist Thompson concerning drug use among youth are worthy of note:

A journalist dealing with heads is caught in a strange dilemma. The only way to write honestly about the scene is to be part of it . . . . Yet to write from experience is an admission of felonious guilt; it is also a potential betrayal of people whose only "crime" is the smoking of a weed that grows wild all over the world but the possession of which, in California, carries a minimum sentence of two years in prison for a second offense and a minimum of five years for a third. . . . it is not very likely that the frank, documented truth about the psychedelic underworld, for good or ill, will be illuminated at any time soon in the public prints (124).

Hunter S. Thompson, "The 'Hashbury' Is the Capital of the Hippies," *New York Times Magazine*, May 14, 1967, 29 f. Cf. Richard A. Brymer and Buford Farris, "Ethical and Political Dilemmas in the Investigation of Deviance: A Study of Juvenile Delinquency," in Sjoberg, *op. cit.*, 311–313.

they admit it or not, continually make decisions of an ethical character. The very precepts "scientific neutrality" and "objectivity" involve certain moral commitments. Frequently, so-called objective research results in exposure of norms and values, with adverse consequences for some persons or groups.

Ethical decisions confront the scientist at every stage of the research project. Here we focus upon those that clamor for attention in the initial stages of project selection and formulation. Every researcher faces, if only implicitly or by default, the question: What are the possible impacts upon science, upon the group being studied, and upon the broader society of my data collection, analysis, and subsequent publication? In answering this question, the scientist must often cope with the rather fuzzy, on occasion conflicting, ethical norms current among scientists, among the subjects studied, and within the broader society.

Another reason for the ambiguity in the researcher's ethical values arises from his shifting status in American society (a trend mentioned earlier). Historically, sociologists, for example, have tended to align themselves with the social reformist tradition (though not with radicalism). Although articulate conservatives have always prevailed, most major sociologists of the past have sought to justify their studies on the grounds that they were attempting to build a better, even utopian, tomorrow. The accumulated body of research has been viewed as a means by which the evils of the emergent industrial order (and of capitalism) could be eliminated.

But the mature industrial-urban system that earlier social scientists envisaged is now upon us. Many social scientists today, at least in the United States, find themselves living in a society where they are more and more becoming part of the power structure. This transition has spelled discomfiture for many sociologists, for some of the earlier bases for rationalizing project selection can no longer be adduced.

To restate the argument: A dilemma every researcher must resolve at one time or another in his choice of a project is whether to select those that are "safe" or one that may lead to exposure of, say, discrepancies between the ideal and the real or in some other manner threaten the very apparatus being studied.

But we have already implied that from one perspective, examination of the divergencies between the real and the ideal implies acceptance of the basic tenets of the system and thus involves relatively conservative types of research. Many American social scientists have in one sense come to "the end of ideology." Yet they have adopted an ideology, still largely unarticulated, that calls for adherence to the system. Consequently, American social scientists are likely to find themselves more and more at odds with the revolutionary orientation, particularly in the underdeveloped world, wherein certain social scientists become a major vehicle for change, even of outright destruction of the traditional social order.

Although the overall ethical orientation of social scientists in the West has generally shifted in emphasis, we cannot overlook the continuing disagreements among them concerning the ethical standards in the discipline. For purposes of analysis, we shall speak of "conservative" in contrast to "liberal" scientists. In terms of their role and status, most purists (in the ideal) would tend to assume a liberal stance, along with the moralizer who negates the traditional, or existing, structures. Conversely, some *moralizers,* most *mediators,* and most *technicians* (at least to the extent that they adhere to the ideals of their role) tend to espouse a conservative cause in that they seek order rather than change for the social system *within* which they live and work.

These orientations influence the selection of projects. The conservative position, essentially a cautious one, decries any upsetting of the moral order by scientists who have no constructive and acceptable substitute to offer. More central still to the conservative's argument is the belief that the scientific enterprise must be protected from any bitter controversy. The conservative emphasizes the associational apparatus (the universities, the scholarly organizations, even the broader society) that supports and sustains the scientific method. These scholars would contend that without a viable supportive structure science cannot survive and prosper. Thus its practitioners should eschew any social research that might weaken these associational underpinnings. Technicians and the more bureaucratically oriented scientists are prone to think this way, for they are particularly dependent upon the supportive structure.

Researchers who uphold the liberal ethic, either as purists or as reformers vis-à-vis the existing order, hold that scientists must strive to carry out research even in the face of formidable opposition. Defenders of this orientation turn to history for documentation of their case. Clearly, many major advances in both the natural and the social sciences would never have been achieved if some men had not been willing to flout, or at least question, the existing social arrangements.

Although the ideal of the purist, with its emphasis upon knowledge as preferable to ignorance, serves to challenge the status quo, it is significant that some sociologists, notably the positivists, may avoid sensitive or controversial topics because of their commitments to certain research procedures. The positivists argue fervently for rigor and a highly predictive social science. But some of the most controversial topics, including many facets of social power, are frequently the most difficult to research via the rigorous procedures the logical empiricist commends. Of course, this is not always the case, and there are some notable exceptions to the pattern.[58]

Both the more conservative and the more liberal social scientists encounter

[58] See, e.g., Samuel A. Stouffer, *Communism, Conformity, and Civil Liberties* (New York: Doubleday, 1955).

serious ethical dilemmas. Because the more conservative social scientist seeks to avoid controversy, and because social research by its very nature involves a degree of exposure, and therefore controversy, the conservative's actions may contravene some of the ideals of science, particularly that calling for freedom of inquiry. Moreover, the mere acceptance of the broader society's definition of what is right may lead one to support and advance policies that are fundamentally at odds with "man's welfare." Thus, many German scientists, who passively accepted the goals and norms of Nazism, were instrumental in aiding and abetting, through their work, the destruction of millions of Jews.

On the other hand, the more liberally inclined may find themselves challenging through their research and analysis their own associational structure— the very system that underwrites and supports the scientific method. The liberal scientist may unwittingly collect data that could be used to question or challenge the democratic political system, some form of which is essential for sustaining social research.

The scientist will find no ready solution to these dilemmas. But at the very least he should be cognizant of the implications of his unstated ethical assumptions. These should be made explicit, for they provide other scholars, or even the public at large, with a sounder basis for evaluating the methods, as well as the results, of social research. Our own position is that although both the conservative and the liberal scientists have telling points to make, the latter group has the more persuasive argument: namely, that knowledge is preferable to ignorance. In so far as the scientist adheres to this ideal—without which science would lose its very raison d'être—he must gravitate toward the liberal rather than the conservative pole.

At the same time, we must recognize the presence of serious contradictions. For instance, the scientist who carries the liberal position to the extreme will find himself in the position of championing the thesis that the ends justify the means. Some compromise on the part of the liberals seems essential if the associational structure that supports science is to be sustained. Even the scientist who values freedom will experience grave difficulties in justifying the destruction of the associational apparatus that enables him to engage in the search for truth. Moreover, the atmosphere of freedom to conduct research also makes it possible for potential subjects to oppose being studied; the freedom to do research in a sense also restricts that research. It is unlikely that scientists can fully overcome these contradictions, but they can reduce the impact of the latter.

Up to now we have examined ethical issues as these relate to the scientist and the social system that sustains him. Of a more concrete nature are those problems that stem from the interpersonal relationships of scientists with one another.

One of the most sensitive topics revolves about the question: Who is to be given credit for a given research effort? With the popularity of large-scale research projects involving dozens of persons, this has become an increasingly pressing issue. Once again internal contradictions within science come into play, not to mention the perennial schism between the purists and certain applied scientists.

Science ideally calls for widespread dissemination of knowledge. But it also seeks to give due recognition to the inventor or discoverer of new knowledge. In a sense science is the history of great men and their discoveries.

The concern with priority occasionally leads to charges (whether legitimate or not need not concern us here) that scientist X stole such and such an idea from scientist Y. Some of the charges and countercharges concerning such pilfering of ideas and data reach into the top echelons of American social science: Witness, for example, Sorokin's intimation that Parsons had used his ideas in the book, *The Social System*, without giving proper credit.[59]

However, it is often difficult to decide just who has prior claim to a particular idea. Within university departments conversations on scholarly matters take place among scientists and their students to the extent that in the course of time it may be impossible to determine how much of one's thinking is original with himself. Even where professors in a department have little formal contact with one another, there are seminars and informal sessions where students become vehicles for the diffusion of ideas to other students and professors. Compounding the problem is the current *Zeitgeist*, including the set of ideas afoot in the discipline or in the broader society. That several scientists may make the same discovery at approximately the same moment in history should occasion no surprise.

A particular source of controversy concerns the professor-student or supervisor-assistant relationship. Professors can, and occasionally do, utilize their political power in the associational structure supporting science to exploit students' ideas (and time) without proper credit or reimbursement. The greatly expanded bureaucratization of social research has accentuated this trend. Students are hired to work on a specific project, and because they receive financial remuneration for their services, the project director may assume that their assistance and intellectual contributions require little or no formal acknowledgment.

This practice has long been not only condoned but encouraged in the federal government, where a bureau head may claim full credit for the original research of his underlings. The latter may not only collect and analyze the data but they may even write the final report on which the director lists himself as sole author.

---

[59] Pitirim A. Sorokin, *Sociological Theories of Today* (New York: Harper & Row, 1966). Sorokin was more explicit about his feelings in an earlier mimeographed version that he distributed.

L'AFFAIRE VIDICH

This case, which became a *cause célèbre,* highlights the liberal-conservative clash in social science as well as the difficulties of determining who should receive credit for a particular research effort. It was first broached in an unsigned editorial (presumably by William Foote Whyte) in *Human Organization,* published at Cornell University.[60] The editorial engendered counterattacks from the chief antagonist, Vidich, as well as comments by others.

According to the original editorial,

> Vidich spent two and a half years living in "Springdale" as field director of a Cornell project. . . . As a result . . . Vidich published several articles, but the official report in book form regarding the project did not materialize during his tenure at Cornell and is only getting into print at this writing. Some time after he left Cornell, Vidich began work on a book of his own, in collaboration with Joseph Bensman, who had had no previous association with the project.
>
> The Vidich manuscript gave rise to considerable controversy between the author and the Springdale project director. . . . The points of controversy were essentially these:
>
> 1. Should individuals be identified in the book?
> 2. If individuals were identified, what—if anything—should be done to avoid damage to them?
> 3. Did Vidich have a right to use—or should he be allowed to use —project data which he did not gather himself? Who "owns" project data?
>
> . . . . While all of the Vidich characters are given fictitious names, they can easily be identified within Springdale. . . .
>
> In addition to his objections regarding the anonymity pledge, Bronfenbrenner claimed that certain individuals were described in ways which could be damaging to them. . . .
>
> Bronfenbrenner took the position that Vidich had no right to— and should not be allowed to—use project data beyond that which he personally had gathered. When Vidich wrote that, while he did not agree with Bronfenbrenner's reasoning, "Wherever possible I will delete the material you consider objectionable," Bronfenbrenner responded by writing that, in this case, he would not object to having other project data used in this book. However, a comparison of the book with Bronfenbrenner's written objections indicates that, in most cases, changes were not made.[61]

---

[60] "Editorial: Freedom and Responsibility in Research: The 'Springdale Case,' " *Human Organization,* 17 (Summer, 1958), 1–2.

[61] *Ibid.*

Vidich and Bensman replied to these charges on two rather distinct levels. They observed that Vidich, in addition to his duties as project director, "was allowed to do field work on his own initiative, using informal methods of research not subject to the formal mechanism of data collection."[62] In the course of the field work, Vidich and Bensman discussed various aspects of the research, and out of these conversations emerged a number of problems worthy of further exploration. Later they completed in draft form an analysis of the community's class structure and a monograph-length report on the political structure. "The project expressed no particular interest in these writings, or in the ideas which they represented, because they did not fall within the scope of its research design and theoretical focus.[63] They continued working on this material after Vidich left the project, and only after a time did the thought of publishing a book emerge.

Vidich and Bensman announced to the project staff their intention of writing such a book:

> There were no objections to this enterprise, and it was not only understood, but also specified, that all work was to be forwarded in manuscript form, as it was completed, to the project, which of course we did.
>
> About a year and a half later, only after we had presented a manuscript, complete except for a few chapters, were any objections made. A project policy was then formulated: . . .
>
> Previously, the project had let us use selected project data which did not fall within the purview of the project's central focus. When the project's permission to use their data was revoked, we went through the manuscript before typing a final draft and cut substantial portions of their data which we had used for illustrative purposes. . . . We felt we were successful in these excisions in almost all cases, but we know that there are six quotations on pages 125, 151, 157, 161–163, 173–174, 182–186, and the two census-like tables on pages 17 and 18, which technically were the property of the project. If there is any feeling that we have not given due credit for the use of this data, we wish to do so now.[64]

So much for one aspect of their argument. But other matters are methodologically more significant. Vidich and Bensman state in their defense that

---

[62] Arthur Vidich and Joseph Bensman, " 'Freedom and Responsibility in Research': Comments," *Human Organization,* 17 (Winter, 1958–1959), 3.

[63] *Ibid.*

[64] *Ibid.,* 3–4.

One of the principal ideas of our book is that the public atmosphere of an organization or a community tends to be optimistic, positive, and geared to the public relations image of the community or the organization. The public mentality veils the dynamics and functional determinants of the group being studied. Any attempt in social analysis at presenting other than public relations rends the veil and must necessarily cause resentment. Moreover, any organization tends to represent a balance of divergent interests held in some kind of equilibrium by the power status of the parties involved. A simple description of these factors, no matter how stated, will offend some of the groups in question.

The only way to avoid such problems is not to deal with articulate groups who will publicly resist the attention which research gives to them, or to deal with the problems in such a way that they are inoffensive. Research of this type becomes banal, irrespective of its technical and methodological virtuosity.[65]

Furthermore,

If social science is to have some kind of independent problems and identity and, if a disinterested effort is to be made to solve these problems, a certain number of social scientists, presumably residing at universities, must be willing to resist the claims for planned, popular, practical research.[66]

Other social scientists contributed to the debate[67] Bronfenbrenner, for instance, contends that Vidich was shown copies of a code of professional ethics which had been developed for the project (later published in the *American Psychologist,* 1952), and that he should therefore have conducted himself differently.[68] This line of reasoning at first glance appears impressive, but more careful scrutiny reveals that Bronfenbrenner does not indicate just what if any agreement was reached on these principles, which, as stated, are subject to differing interpretations by men of good will.

We have elaborated upon this case at some length and would encourage the interested reader to consult the writings in *Human Organization.* The case,

[65] *Ibid.,* 4.

[66] *Ibid.,* 5.

[67] See, e.g., the comments by Robert Risley, Raymond E. Ries, and Howard S. Becker, *Human Organization, op. cit.,* 5–7.

[68] Urie Bronfenbrenner, " 'Freedom and Responsibility in Research': Comments," *Human Organization, 18* (Summer, 1959), 49–50. Cf. Arthur J. Vidich, " 'Freedom and Responsibility in Research': A Rejoinder," *Human Organization, 19* (Spring, 1960), 3–4.

as we mentioned, serves to magnify the conservative-liberal dilemma in the researcher's choice of subjects for study. It also demonstrates that ethical considerations must be faced squarely during the *earliest stages* of the research design: Otherwise dissension and disagreement will result. Clearly, neither Vidich nor Bronfenbrenner was explicit concerning the initial agreements. One wonders whether Vidich's arguments are not rationalizations after the fact, and also why Bronfenbrenner and his coworkers seem to have revised the rules concerning the use of project data after the field research was in full bloom. One also entertains second thoughts about the personality conflicts involved and wonders whether Bronfenbrenner did not react to Vidich's work in part because this was the first major publication to result from the project.

Several conclusions emerge from this case study. Problems arise from the absence of an agreed-upon set of ethical norms that serve to guide scientists in drafting their research designs, and it is unlikely that full agreement can ever be established. At the same time, the scientist's ethical commitments are an essential ingredient of the research design and, as such, cannot be ignored.

CHAPTER 6

Selection of Units
and Sources of Data

During the past half-century, social scientists have made striking advances in formalizing the procedures for selecting their "universes" and the units within these. Nevertheless, many facets of the selection process require clarification. Such clarification can be achieved by recognizing the impact upon the selection of universes and units therein of the scientist's theoretical assumptions and his conception of the scientific method. Much can also be gained by objectifying the role of ideal and informal norms in the selection procedures.

Most lay observers fail to appreciate many of the technical procedures involved in sampling, for some of these depart markedly from common-sense thinking. Perhaps the greatest difficulty the scientist experiences in effectively utilizing the material collected by lay observers results from the failure of the latter to specify just how informants are chosen. For the more clearly the researcher envisions his universe and the more carefully he selects its component parts, the more likely is his research to be successful and the more readily can others verify his findings. To be sure, the researcher may choose his universe prior to formulating his specific research design. Thus an anthropologist whose curiosity centers on a little-known preliterate group can hardly formalize the procedure for sampling informants until he has arrived on the scene. All the same, some prior plan of action, however tentative, is necessary.

The Special Versus the General Universe

Before selecting the social units from or about which data are to be collected, the researcher should have a clear conception of the ultimate range of his generalizations. He must decide which groups (or kinds of groups) of structures or events are to be the bases of his generalizations. We must remember that the scientist rarely studies groups per se. Although sociologists speak of studying, for instance, the family or a community, in practice few, excluding perhaps a few phenomenologists, search for the "essence" of group life. Primarily they are concerned with various outward manifestations of group activities. It follows that, to select social units rationally, one must make explicit which manifestation of a group or system one proposes to treat. Certain facets of group life may be more homogeneous and stable through time than others, and this fact influences the selection of units.

An essential step in conceptual clarification of the selection procedure is distinguishing between the special, or working, universe and the general one. The *special* (or *working*) *universe* is that specific, concrete system (or subsystem) from which one selects his units of study, notably his respondents. Statisticians refer to such a system as a *universe* or *population,* and usually they are content to work within its narrow boundaries. On the other hand, any theoretically oriented social scientist envisions still another kind of universe. If he studies a particular group or social system, he entertains the notion that his findings will, in part at least, hold for other groups or systems—not just in the United States but in other parts of the world as well. For his ultimate goal is establishing generalizations that extend beyond any time-bound social setting. We therefore define the *general universe* as that abstract universe to which the scientist assumes, however tentatively, that his findings will apply.[1] Put another way, every sample is a subsample of a broader type—mankind being, for purposes of generalization, the ultimate category.

The distinction between these two universe types holds in all fields of social science. Let us assume that the researcher defines his special universe as a particular community, nation, bureaucracy, or whatever, and carefully draws his respondents from this universe according to certain formal prescriptions (to be discussed below). Once he has chosen his sample, he can relate it to his special universe through well-known statistical techniques. However, in most cases he or others will proceed to generalize his findings to other communities or nations, as the case may be. Thus Warner's studies of Yankee City and Jonesville and those by the Lynds on Middletown[2] have for some decades served as the basis for considerable social science generalization, particularly by textbook

---

[1] Margaret J. Hagood and Daniel O. Price, in their *Statistics for Sociologists,* rev. ed. (New York: Holt, Rinehart and Winston, 1952), 193–195, 287–294, 419–423, are among the few methodologists who have considered the problem of the general universe. However, their analysis—constructed around the notion of the "hypothetical universe"— differs from our own.

[2] W. Lloyd Warner and Paul S. Lunt, *The Social Life of a Modern Community* (New Haven: Yale, 1941); W. Lloyd Warner *et al., Democracy in Jonesville* (New York: Harper & Row, 1949); and Robert S. Lynd and Helen M. Lynd, *Middletown* (New York: Harcourt, Brace & World, 1929), and their *Middletown in Transition* (New York: Harcourt, Brace & World, 1937).

writers, not only about other American communities but about American society as a whole.[3] Nor is this practice limited to the community field. Selznick's *TVA and the Grass Roots* and Gouldner's *Patterns of Industrial Bureaucracy*[4] have spawned numerous generalizations by researchers concerning large-scale social organizations or bureaucratic structures in the United States. Social scientists have treated the original working universes of the authors *as if* they were more general ones—at least they have done so until contradictory data have come to light. But if they did not do this, social science would be narrowly restricted to particulars, to a crude form of nominalism.

But when the researcher draws his sample from a total society, do not the general and specific universes coincide? No, usually they do not. For although the scientist may be concerned only with generalizing about the United States, for example, he usually is not content to generalize about the social order only for the specific time when the sample was drawn. That is, although social scientists may interview a set of persons on a particular day of a given month and year, they do assume some consistency over time: They consider their findings to be valid for a somewhat greater time span. Thus the study by North and Hatt served as a basis for generalizations about American occupational prestige, years after the original national sample was drawn.[5] In the process, sociologists have constructed, often without recognizing the logical leap, a quite different kind of universe: a general one. The working universe becomes a case study within a broader context.

A sample drawn from American society at a given point in time may be related to a general universe of still another kind: a crosscultural one. Here one nation serves as the basis for generalizations about other nations or kinds of societies, even about mankind. Not infrequently, sociologists take the United States as their case study when constructing a typology of industrial-urban society.

To place our argument in sharper focus, we quote from the work of Goldsen, Rosenberg, Williams, and Suchman—methodologists all—who distinguish between their special and their general universes as follows:

---

[3] Some writers, like Warner, carried this position to an extreme. He and his associates argued that "To study Jonesville is to study America" in *Democracy in Jonesville, op. cit.,* xv.

[4] Philip Selznick, *TVA and the Grass Roots* (Berkeley: University of California Press, 1949); and Alvin W. Gouldner, *Patterns of Industrial Bureaucracy* (New York: Free Press, 1954).

[5] Cecil C. North and Paul K. Hatt, "Jobs and Occupations: A Popular Evaluation," in Logan Wilson and William L. Kolb, *Sociological Analysis* (New York: Harcourt, Brace & World, 1949), 464–474. This work has been brought up to date by Robert W. Hodge, Paul M. Siegel, and Peter H. Rossi, "Occupational Prestige in the United States: 1925–1963," in Reinhard Bendix and Seymour M. Lipset (eds.), *Class, Status, and Power,* 2nd ed. (New York: Free Press, 1966), 322–334.

We have often referred in this book to "the college campuses." At this point it is time to remind ourselves of the disclaimer appearing in the introduction: the campuses we studied are not representative of American colleges and universities. Interpreted, however, in the light of sociological principles of how societies function, develop, and change, the findings of this research nevertheless illuminate trends that are dominant in American society as a whole.[6]

Observe that although the authors admittedly did not select their campuses in a manner that would ensure "representativeness," they nonetheless assume that their data and analysis shed light not just on all college campuses but on American society at large—rather an ambitious theoretical jump. Much of the validity of their argument, of course, hinges on the meaning of "illuminate," a concept subject to various interpretations. Yet the authors seem to assume that their study "explains" certain social processes or relationships that transcend their particular working universe. Although this position is subject to challenge, Goldsen *et al.* have formally stated a premise that most writers implicitly adopt —namely, that the generalizations they draw from their data are applicable beyond their special, or working, universe—despite the fact that this universe cannot be demonstrated to be typical, random, or representative in any rigorous sense.

Several factors account for the readiness of researchers to make this facile leap from the special to the general universe. One is that scientists implicitly or explicitly assume a fundamental invariance in the social relationships, or social phenomena, under study. That is, they assume a degree of stability through space and time in the processes being investigated. Not that they would go so far as to state, or even imply, that the particular quantitative patterns they uncover in their special universes hold for the general ones as well. But they proceed *as if* they believe that similar patterns, if not specific content, obtain in both.[7]

Our argument suggests that if social scientists could deal with homogeneous social systems, or if they could isolate certain invariant relationships, they would be able to disregard the issue of randomness or representativeness.

The research procedures in some of the natural sciences are pertinent to our reasoning here. Significantly, some natural scientists seem to make little use of

[6] Rose K. Goldsen *et al., What College Students Think* (Princeton, N.J.: Van Nostrand, 1960), 196.

[7] See, e.g., Richard T. Morris, *The Two-Way Mirror* (Minneapolis: University of Minnesota Press, 1960); and Seymour M. Lipset and Reinhard Bendix, *Social Mobility in Industrial Society* (Berkeley, Cal.: University of California Press, 1959), esp. pt. 2. Note the caveats and the manner in which Lipset and Bendix generalize beyond the findings of their Oakland study.

random sampling. When conducting experiments with water, for example, the chemist assumes that, given similar conditions, water molecules the world over will respond similarly. Inasmuch as he can to a large extent control the variables, he can ensure such similar conditions. The chemist is not obliged to test samples of water from Lake Baikal, Lake Tahoe, or the Red Sea when generalizing about the behavior of water molecules. Nor does he when placing litmus paper in an acid solution worry about whether the paper and the solution are each representative of their respective universes, for he is studying certain invariant phenomena.

Our discussion has brought to center stage a theoretical proposition of major import to every methodologist: that is, a functional relationship exists between one's conceptual analysis and one's selection of social units. The more social scientists conceptually isolate invariant relationships, the less they need concern themselves with the interrelationships between special and general universes and the position of social units (particularly respondents) vis-à-vis the special universe.

However, intensive comparative research by anthropologists, among others, has demonstrated the rather wide diversity of human activity historically and temporally across cultures. Given this situation, it behooves us to examine the typicality and representativeness of any working universe we employ. This applies also to research within a sociocultural system, for here too we may study social action that evinces considerable variation: for instance, the opinions of the citizenry relative to politics or education. At the same time, the limits upon this variation makes social science feasible.

Defining the Special Universe

On the whole, social scientists find it more difficult to define, and rationalize the selection of, the working universe than to define the units therein. The barriers in the realm of social organization are especially imposing. As the social scientist, seeking to encompass other sociocultural systems within his working universe, vaults the boundaries of his own culture, the route to success becomes still more precipitous.

But even with respect to a single society, the researcher may encounter serious difficulties in defining and selecting the working universe. First, his particular theoretical and methodological commitment will intervene: The kind of working universe achieved will reflect his own theoretical assumptions. Second, the stability of the reality being studied is a decisive factor. It is easier to define a special universe in a social order with highly institutionalized or highly standardized patterns of social activity than in a society characterized by vague and highly complex social arrangements.

A few empirical illustrations should clarify our discussion. One concerns the manner in which scientists engaged in the study of social power define the universe of key decision makers, or leaders, in the United States on either the community or the national level. We could, as did Stouffer, assume that the key decision makers are those who occupy high positions in the community; thus the mayor and other city officials would be included in our sample.[8] But data from various community studies indicate that informal king makers at times wield greater power and influence than do persons occupying the formal seats of authority. Floyd Hunter, attempting to cope with this informal power structure when isolating his universe of key leaders, utilized another kind of selection procedure. He acquired four lists of names (of civic, governmental, business, and status leaders) from relevant organizations and selected informants. Then fourteen judges were used to select the top leaders in each of the lists.[9] However, Hunter's use of this procedure has been challenged by various writers;[10] for one thing, some of Hunter's leaders may have enjoyed more prestige than influence in the decision-making process. Of course, if no discrepancy between the formal and informal power structures existed, difficulties such as this would not arise.

Other striking dilemmas assail those who seek to define working universes for other groups in American society. For instance, who are the intellectuals in America today? Within social science literature and in popular writings we find a considerable range of definitions, each including, or excluding, different persons or roles.[11] Some writers define the intellectual operationally; thus, an intellectual is one who claims to be an intellectual or who is considered such by others. Yet, for certain purposes this may prove quite unsatisfactory. Some so-called intellectuals may disclaim any allegiance with other so-called intellectuals. On the other hand, if all persons in a system, intellectuals and nonintellectuals alike, could agree upon the meaning of the term, these difficulties would largely evanesce and the delineation of the universe would accordingly be simplified.

In the realm of crosscultural research the difficulties of delineating one's

[8] Samuel A. Stouffer, *Communism, Conformity, and Civil Liberties* (New York: Wiley, Science Editions, 1966), 17, 244–249.

[9] Floyd Hunter, *Community Power Structure* (Chapel Hill: University of North Carolina Press, 1953), esp. 268–269.

[10] See, e.g., Nelson W. Polsby, *Political Power and Political Theory* (New Haven: Yale, 1963).

[11] For illustrations of different usages of the term "intellectual," see George B. de Huszar (ed.), *The Intellectuals* (New York: Free Press, 1960), especially the articles by Joseph A. Schumpeter, Raymond Aron, Russell Kirk, and John Lukacs. Also Lewis A. Coser, *Men of Ideas* (New York: Free Press, 1965); Seymour M. Lipset, *Political Man* (Garden City, N.Y.: Doubleday Anchor Books, 1963); and Eric Hoffer, *The Ordeal of Change* (New York: Harper & Row, 1963).

working universe loom especially large.[12] Murdock and his associates have engaged in what is perhaps the most ambitious effort to study societies crossculturally,[13] and their research highlights some of the compromises that are mandatory if research is to be accomplished. Their working universe includes societies on which substantial data are available. When data on a social order do not exist, the order simply has to be omitted from the working universe.

Murdock and others who have developed the Human Relations Area Files have experienced additional difficulties in defining (and selecting) their special universe. At times it is not easy to determine whether particular social systems are independent units or whether they should be treated as one. Then too, complex preindustrial societies pose problems that cannot be effectively resolved. Some writers still do not recognize that villages are not representative of the *dominant* values and structures of the broader social order. The urban centers are the fulcrum of preindustrial civilized (as well as industrial) systems. More generally, communities in these societies, be they rural or urban in character, are part systems and therefore are not comparable to preliterate systems, which tend toward political and economic closure.

For some purposes, as in the study of informal group relationships, the peasant village and the more self-sufficient folk order may be viewed as similar, but for other purposes this is decidedly a less-than-satisfactory arrangement. It may in fact be more logical, when seeking an understanding of, say, economic organization, to contrast the Trobriand Islanders with a modern nation or even with such a broad category as Western civilized society.

Nor does the problem of crosscultural comparison revolve solely about what constitutes a society. Every substantive problem of sociological import presents some kind of conceptual difficulty. A crosscultural survey of the family, for example, requires a definition of this phenomenon that is sufficiently all-encompassing to cope with all the cultural variations, yet specific enough to make empirical research practicable. And just what is a family has been the subject of considerable disputation by anthropologists and sociologists.[14]

Even when we narrow our perspective to industrial-urban societies, we encounter considerable variation on the empirical plane. If, for instance, we are intent upon delineating a working universe of unemployed persons in the European and American industrial systems, we immediately must decide what is the meaning of the term "unemployed." Yet various nations define the con-

[12] Cf. Robert M. Marsh, *Comparative Sociology* (New York: Harcourt, Brace & World, 1967), esp. chap. 9.

[13] Frank W. Moore (ed.), *Readings in Cross-Cultural Methodology* (New Haven: HRAF Press, 1961).

[14] Morris Zelditch, Jr., "Cross-Cultural Analyses of Family Structure," in Harold T. Christensen (ed.), *Handbook of Marriage and the Family* (Chicago: Rand McNally, 1964), chap. 12, esp. 465–467.

cept in somewhat differing fashions for the purpose of census taking.

Still, although the investigator often cannot adhere to rigorous definitions, he can with ingenuity reduce the number of possible discrepancies. He can arrive at definitions that represent fairly adequate first-approximations that are well in advance of common-sense formulations. Kingsley Davis and his co-workers, for example, have sought to compare cities in a wide range of societies. By avoiding the category of "urban" (for the definition of "urban" in the censuses of different nations varies widely), and by analyzing instead "metropolitan areas," defined as having 100,000 or more inhabitants plus other rather well-defined characteristics, these researchers were able to achieve some standardization for purposes of crosscultural comparison.[15] Although such broad categories may not lend themselves to certain kinds of analysis, and although Davis and his associates made strategic compromises in utilizing data on cities in some societies, this kind of orientation is essential if crosscultural research is to be carried out.[16]

Selecting a Special Universe

Methodologists have made few if any systematic efforts to cope with the problem of selecting the working universe. On this level the ideal norms are largely nonexistent, or muzzy at best. Here, then, is an instance where objectification of the actual norms of scientists is a prerequisite to delineating more abstract, ideal procedures. For analytical purposes we separate the more theoretical and logical considerations in the selection of a working, or special, universe from the more pragmatic considerations.

LOGICAL OR THEORETICAL BASES
FOR SELECTING A SPECIAL UNIVERSE

A perusal of research reports that consider the selection of a special universe points up a variety of operating factors, both logical and theoretical. In the main we can say that the researcher's original theoretical commitment, as well as his research design, determines the selection of his universe. Scientists committed to discovery are likely to approach the selection process quite differently than those seeking to test existing hypotheses or theories either by searching for confirmatory evidence or by attempting to disprove them. At times, of course, the various criteria are used in conjunction with one another. However, it is significant that we speak of "random sampling" not with respect to the selection of a special universe but with reference to the selection of the units within it.

---

[15] International Urban Research, *The World's Metropolitan Areas* (Berkeley, Cal.: University of California Press, 1959) 25, *passim*.

[16] See *Ibid.*, 31 f., for a discussion of some of the compromises that were made.

The following are the common logical or theoretical reasons social scientists employ in selecting a working universe.

As a basis of discovery.   One compelling reason for selecting a particular universe is the hope of uncovering new factual data or the germ of a new theory. Here the researcher may enter the field with various alternative hypotheses, even hunches, none of them clearly formulated, but with the expectation that new ideas may emerge from this effort at discovery.

Anthropologists may be interested, for instance, in detecting survivals of earlier cultures in a society such as Mexico. They are led, then, to select some out-of-the-way community as their working universe, for such a subsystem is most likely to be a reservoir of ancient traits. But the researcher may have no well-defined hypotheses to test and only the vaguest of hunches concerning what he will uncover.

In recent years some anthropologists have reasoned that rather than study a variety of communities, the social scientist should concentrate upon a single community, even to the extent of encouraging others to continue in this setting for decades.[17] The assumption here seems to be that knowledge of a detailed sort, amassed over a long period of time, will provide us with new and different insights into and perspectives on social and cultural change.

The testing of hypotheses or theories.   Several rather distinct approaches fall under this rubric.

1. To illustrate or confirm a theory.   Whereas some researchers are seekers, others are believers convinced that a particular social pattern or process holds for a given societal type. The latter may resolutely set out to demonstrate the validity of a given hypothesis. While scientists can never "prove" a hypothesis conclusively, they frequently proceed to demonstrate the validity of a given hypothesis or theory by seeking confirmatory data.

Warner and Lunt, commenting on the methodology used in the selection of Yankee City as a working universe, remark: *We sought above all a well-integrated community,* where the various parts of the society were functioning with comparative ease. We did not want a city where the ordinary daily relations of the inhabitants were in confusion or in conflict [Italics added].[18] Although Warner details other criteria that he and his colleagues employed in the selection process, the chief criterion was the community's high degree of integration. It is hardly surprising, therefore, that Warner found this community, admittedly a well-integrated one, to have a well-defined class system.

What is of even greater moment, Warner, and many other social scientists who have relied upon the findings in Yankee City, have generalized freely from

[17] See, e.g., Evon Z. Vogt, "On the Concept of Structure and Process in Cultural Anthropology," *American Anthropologist,* 62 (February, 1960), 29.

[18] Warner and Lunt, *op. cit.,* 38.

this community to numerous facets of the total American society, particularly to the American class structure. In so doing they have in the main ignored the primary criterion used in the original selection of the working universe. It is certainly doubtful that American cities have been well integrated. In order to generalize about the broader society, Yankee City should have been a typical rather than a deviant community.

2. *To disprove a hypothesis or theory.*   In light of the importance of the negative orientation underlying the scientific method, it is rather surprising that relatively few researchers explicitly seek a working universe with the intention of disproving a particular hypothesis. However, some anthropologists have used this approach as a basis for challenging various crosscultural generalizations. Although Leach is somewhat vague in his exposition, his choice of a Ceylonese community of Pul Eliya as the focus of his study seems to have been influenced by a search for negative evidence.[19] He was looking for a small community which lacks a unilineal descent system, for he apparently believed that certain theories of Radcliffe-Brown and Fortes regarding social structure relied too heavily upon data from perliterate societies having such unilineal descent groups.

One reason that Lipset and his associates selected the particular union they studied was that it provided the basis for challenging Michels' hypothesis regarding "the iron law of oligarchy."[20] Other researchers have used the negation criterion at least indirectly. Even Warner in his aforementioned study of Yankee City appears to have sought to disprove the prevailing idea that America lacked a class structure.[21] His selection of an integrated community becomes much more meaningful from this perspective.

3. *To retest existing hypotheses or theories.*   Some researchers are primarily intent upon checking the validity of earlier findings or interpretations. Some of these cases fall under the heading of seeking confirmatory data, others under the heading of seeking data that will disprove existing propositions. We distinguish this category from the other two, for in this situation researchers stress the need for replicative research, especially the restudy of the working universes of others.

Lewis' study of Tepoztlán, a small town in Mexico, was in large part an effort to determine the validity of Redfield's earlier findings.[22] And as is well

---

[19] E. R. Leach, *Pul Eliya: A Village in Ceylon* (London: Cambridge, 1961), esp. chaps. 1 and 8.

[20] Seymour M. Lipset, "The Biography of a Research Project: *Union Democracy*," in Phillip E. Hammond (ed.), *Sociologists at Work* (New York: Basic Books, 1964), chap. 4. It is also true that Lipset's father was a lifelong member of that union.

[21] Warner and Lunt, *op. cit.*

[22] Oscar Lewis, *Life in a Mexican Village: Tepoztlán Restudied* (Urbana, Ill.: University of Illinois Press, 1951). There have been other restudies of communities. See, e.g., Art Gallaher, Jr., *Plainville Fifteen Years Later* (New York: Columbia, 1961).

known, Lewis' findings led him to challenge many of Redfield's interpretations, including the latter's folk-urban continuum.

But the notion of replication brings to the fore some strategic theoretical issues that are easily overlooked. For is a given working universe really the same after a period of time has elapsed? The answer seems to be yes and no. Some elements of the past do survive, but others are lost and replaced by new forms. At the very least, some people die and others are born.

Inasmuch as no system's structure is perfectly static, the community itself is never the same from one point in time to the next. It therefore behooves the researcher to critically examine his theoretical categories, to ask himself whether or not the sector of the social order which he is supposedly restudying has in fact remained unchanged.

Even if we grant these and other strictures upon replication, studies of this type, which commit the researcher to selecting his special universe in terms of previous efforts, do much to advance the cause of social science. Replication not only serves as a check upon extant findings or hypotheses but serves indirectly to expose the biases stemming from each researcher's cultural background and personality structure.

THE SEARCH FOR TYPICALITY. In this situation the researcher is concerned with avoiding a deviant or aberrant working universe. Instead he is concerned with discovering, via the typical working universe, certain common patterns about a general universe or with supporting hypotheses regarding these patterns.

One of the prerequisites for choosing a working universe which is typical of a general one is extensive knowledge about the latter.

We could cite a number of instances wherein a working universe was selected on the basis of typicality. Dore, for instance, when he took a particular neighborhood in Tokyo as his special universe, sought to demonstrate through the use of "external" evidence involving "a few easily quantified characteristics" that his neighborhood possessed a set of traits typical of the city of Tokyo and in some respects of Japan as a whole.[23]

Katz and Lazarsfeld, more than many researchers, have taken considerable pains to explain just how they came to study Decatur, Illinois, the setting for their publication, *Personal Influence*.[24] "The problem then is to select the most 'typical' town (or the few most typical towns) from cities in the Middle West with a population of around 60,000."[25] They chose this figure for financial

---

[23] R. P. Dore, *City Life in Japan* (Berkeley, Cal.: University of California Press, 1958), 4, chap. 2.

[24] Elihu Katz and Paul F. Lazarsfeld, *Personal Influence* (New York: Free Press, 1955).

[25] *Ibid.*, 335.

reasons: Their budget did not permit study of a larger community. But why a city in the Midwest? The authors' reasoning was that this region, more than any other, has tended to be representative of the United States, because, in their words, it is "least characterized by sectional pecularities."[26]

Applying the following criteria (as well as two additional ones) to this broad sociogeographic sphere, they settled upon Decatur as the community to investigate.

1. We first listed all the cities in seven Middle Western states (Ohio, Michigan, Indiana, Illinois, Wisconsin, Iowa, Kansas) with a population from 50,000–80,000. . . .

2. From this group we eliminated all the suburban or near-suburban towns, i.e., all those dominated by a large city.

3. We were then left with eighteen cities, which constituted the group for final study. From each of them, we collected data on some thirty-six social indices selected because of their relevance to the problem under study. The broad clusters of social characteristics included in the analysis . . . are . . . COMPOSITION OF THE POPULATION . . . ECONOMIC STATUS . . . COMMERCIAL STRUCTURE . . . COMMUNICATIONS BEHAVIOR . . . GENERAL QUALITY (MISCELLANEOUS).

4. For each of these indices an average was computed for the eighteen towns as a group. This average for each index was then taken as 100 and the ranking of each of the eighteen cities was computed on this basis. . . .

5. Averages were then figured for each *cluster* of characteristics in order to gauge the representativeness of the towns in each broad group of social indices. . . .

6. Finally, a grand average of all the indices was computed on the basis of the averages for the different clusters of characteristics.[27]

Application of these and other criteria yielded several communities. Then, in the final selection, the authors resorted to a negative approach. On the basis of certain negative considerations they eliminated the most unsatisfactory "units," for no one city was perfect in every respect. Thus was Decatur selected.

This study points up the difficulties of determining what is a typical working universe; it indicates the painstaking effort required to select a special universe when representativeness or typicality is a primary concern; and it dramatizes the need for extensive data concerning the broader general universe.

Moreover, if we view the Decatur study as providing sociologists primarily

26 *Ibid.*
27 *Ibid.*

with theoretical propositions regarding mass communication in an industrial-urban society (the "two stage" pattern of information diffusion), then Decatur becomes a case study not merely within the United States but also within the general universe of industrial-urban societies. From this perspective, the effort of Katz and Lazarsfeld to isolate a community that was typical of America loses much of its significance.

USE OF AN EXPERIMENTAL DESIGN.[28]   The scientist's commitment to the use of an experimental design—whether of a natural or an artificial (that is, laboratory) sort—will affect his choice of a special universe. Consider for a moment the natural experiment. While ideal natural experiments are rare, some useful approximations are possible. Thus, when the Harvard group of social scientists selected as a site for their investigations the Rimrock area of New Mexico (a relatively homogeneous physical setting in which peoples representing five different cultures had been subject to the same historical process), they evidently sought to hold the physical environment and certain historical factors constant as they examined the impact of the value systems of the Navahos, Zunis, Spanish-Americans, Texan and Oklahoman homesteaders, and Mormons upon the actions of their respective members and upon the natural environment.[29] Here the choice of specific communities (that is, the special universe) to be studied was governed by the need for a situation wherein certain factors were constant while others varied.

SOCIAL FACTORS AFFECTING
THE SELECTION OF A SPECIAL UNIVERSE

These factors, though having theoretical overtones, seem rather distinct from the more formal theoretical and logical ones. Yet, the following pragmatic variables, stemming largely from the fact that the scientist functions within the context of a broader social order, are at times of paramount consideration (or so it would seem from an examination of certain research reports).

AVAILABILITY OF DATA.   For one group of sociologists, apparently a growing element, the sheer existence of a substantial body of data on a subject may be the overriding factor in the choice of a particular working universe. This is frequently true in comparative, or crosscultural, research. We all know that numerous countries have recently undertaken censuses and that many employ researchers for extensive polling operations. However, the data obtained are

---

[28] For a useful discussion of experimental designs in social research, see Donald T. Campbell and Julian C. Stanley, "Experimental and Quasi-Experimental Designs for Research on Teaching," in N. L. Gage (ed.), *Handbook of Research on Teaching* (Chicago: Rand McNally, 1963), chap. 5.

[29] Evon Z. Vogt and Ethel M. Albert (eds.), *People of Rimrock: A Study of Values in Five Cultures* (Cambridge, Mass.: Harvard, 1966), 1–2.

not only uneven in quality but relate to quite divergent kinds of problems. In some societies, certain issues may be examined in great detail; in others, they may be completely ignored. Therefore if one is interested in, for example, the movement of people into and out of the central city on a given day, the availability of data may force one to select some particular working universe, even though for theoretical reasons one may have preferred to make a different choice. The principle is equally applicable to the selection of a special universe within a society. Kephart, in his studies of divorce, used data on Philadelphia, not just because of convenience but because in Philadelphia, where city and county are coterminous, various agencies had collected specific kinds of data that enabled Kephart to test certain hypotheses regarding the relationships between occupational level and frequency of marital disruption.[30]

Then too, researchers may select a working universe because it has been previously studied by other scientists. Here the rationale does not rest upon replication of the previous study but upon foreknowledge that certain background data are available and that certain data can be uncovered through field work. Cohn's choice of a village in India as his working universe in large part stemmed from the fact that this community had previously been carefully researched by other anthropologists.[31]

RESOURCES.   Certainly, if a sociologist hopes to actualize his research plans, he must pay special heed to his resources—time, money, and manpower. That monetary considerations strongly influence one's choice of a working universe is generally taken for granted by methodologists. Even those scientists who seem to command vast resources work within rather narrow limits. In fact, from their perspective, these strictures can be as stifling as those affecting researchers with much lower aspiration levels.

CONVENIENCE.   This variable, closely related to that of resources, enters into most research proposals. Indeed this criterion often determines not only the special universe but the topic of study itself. No matter how theoretically oriented the researcher, this is one very practical consideration he cannot ignore.

The Studies of Detroit that have emanated from the social science departments at the University of Michigan illustrate this generalization. It is hardly surprising that Detroit—and not Chicago, New York, Tokyo, London, or Delhi —was selected by Michigan-based social scientists as a laboratory for urban studies. Although some of the studies on Detroit have opened up new vistas for

---

30 William M. Kephart, "Occupational Level and Marital Disruption," *American Sociological Review,* 20 (August, 1955), 456–465. For a discussion of the methodological issues, see William M. Kephart and Thomas P. Monahan, "Desertion and Divorce in Philadelphia," *American Sociological Review,* 17 (December, 1952), 719–727.

31 Bernard Cohn, *The Camars of Senapur: A Study of the Changing Status of a Depressed Caste* (Ann Arbor, Mich.: University Microfilms, 1954).

investigation, certain of the results have been questioned by researchers who use national polling data.[32]

That a working universe selected primarily for reasons of convenience can, unless the researcher takes proper precautions, lead to some unwarranted generalizations is more clearly documented by the early sociological studies of Chicago. Although we would not wish to depreciate these pioneering ventures, it is also clear, notably in the work of the ecologists, that some writers made too little effort to relate their findings to the data that were available (in America and elsewhere). Had they done so, they might have been more cautious in their theorizing. As it was, only after the passage of several decades, and with a growing body of research on American cities and on those in other societies, did American sociologists seriously seek to reevaluate some of the Chicago findings and the conclusions drawn therefrom by Burgess, Park, Wirth, *et al.*[33] Even today, a surprising number of their propositions, though discredited by recent research, persist in general introductory texts.[34]

CONCERN WITH PRACTICAL ENDS. Social scientists, notably those who identify more with the broader society than with the scientific community per se, often have their special universe selected for them by nonscientists. That is, their very reference group tends to define their working universe. On this basis we might predict with some certainty that a social scientist employed by General Motors will study problems relating to this corporation and will focus most of his research directly upon it as a working universe. So too, scientists who receive grants for research with the proviso that their findings should benefit a particular group are limited in the kind of working universes they can investigate.

CHANCE, OR FORTUITOUS FACTORS. Though exceedingly difficult to treat, the factor of chance cannot be ignored. West, in his *Plainville, U.S.A.,* describes how the community he studied was one that he "stumbled across" while traveling in search of an appropriate setting.[35] He happened upon Plainville because his automobile had broken down in the vicinity and he had to stay a couple of days for repairs. Although West relied upon other criteria in making his choice, it was literally an accident that led him to focus upon this particular community.

Fortuitous factors influence the choice of a working universe in still other ways. In recent years a number of sociologists have investigated the impact of

---

[32] Gerhard Lenski, *The Religious Factor,* rev. ed. (Garden City, N.Y.: Doubleday, Anchor Books, 1963); and Norval D. Glenn and Ruth Hyland, "Religious Preference and Worldly Success: Some Evidence from National Surveys," *American Sociological Review,* 32 (February, 1967), 73–85.

[33] See, e.g., Robert E. Park *et al., The City* (Chicago: University of Chicago Press, 1925).

[34] See, e.g., Everett K. Wilson, *Sociology* (Homewood, Ill.: Dorsey, 1966), 281–295.

[35] James West, *Plainville, U.S.A.* (New York: Columbia, 1945), vii–viii.

natural disasters upon communities or subsystems thereof. The researcher cannot choose his community beforehand: The tornado, hurricane, flood, or whatever, selects the working universe for him.

FURTHER REFLECTIONS

We have not exhausted the list of pragmatic, or social, variables that enter into the selection of a special universe. The power structure within the broader society and the ethical commitment of the scientist are other factors that must be evaluated when choosing a universe for study. Nevertheless, our argument seems clear: Extrascientific norms play a major role in the selection of a special universe, and these tend to bend or distort the theoretical or logical rules, those that might be viewed as "ideal." Although there is little hope for eliminating some of these social factors, the researcher should, when evaluating his findings, objectify the role these variables play and thus achieve some measure of control over them.

Selection of Units Within a Special Universe

When selecting units within the special or working universe, we must distinguish between the case and the statistical approach. This permits us to indicate how the research design, notably the kinds of hypotheses that are formulated, influences the way a sample is drawn. At the same time, we continue to emphasize the impact of the scientist's theoretical assumptions and the social setting upon the method of sampling.

CASE SELECTION

When sociologists speak of the case study method—as it was popularized by the early studies of the Chicago School of Sociology during the 1920s and as it has been carried out by various social scientists until the present day—they generally refer to the selection of cases *within* a working universe. Above we discussed the selection of a working universe and observed how this special universe generally becomes a case study within a more general universe. Many of the principles enumerated for the selection of the special universe hold for the selection of cases within this universe. Thus cases are selected with an eye to discovery, or to the testing of hypotheses, either to provide confirmatory data or to reject the hypothesis in question.

Implicit in our previous discussion was a typology of cases: the *typical,* the *deviant,* and the *extreme* types. Knowledge of these types is required if we are adequately to select cases within any given universe.

The notion of typicality can be equated with the idea of what is representative. Actually, in a social order, normal and deviant cases are always defined in terms of one another, but what is normal and deviant in one context is not always so construed in another. If we study deviant cases with respect to personality, we can speak of psychotics as deviants. But if we consider only psychotic personalities, we can speak of normal psychotics.

In the aforementioned situations the typical and deviant cases are discussed in terms of some underlying continuum or statistical distribution. But we can think of deviant cases without reference to a statistical distribution. We do so in various all-or-none generalizations. In the hypothesis "All societies have incest taboos," there is implicit the idea of a normal state of affairs, but not normal in the sense of typical or representative for there is no implied statistical distribution. It is in these situations that one deviant case serves to overthrow hypotheses. Indeed, some anthropologists and sociologists have spent time searching for cases of societies where no incest taboos exist.[36]

The extreme cases can be distinguished from both the normal and the deviant types. In the extreme case, certain variables are "eliminated" or "controlled." Consequently this type of case is the social scientist's substitute for the natural scientist's experimental design. Under extreme conditions it is possible to observe social patterns or processes that are otherwise obscured.

The Nazi concentration camps were an extreme case with respect to man's manipulation of his fellow man. And it was Frankl's own concentration camp experience that led him to reject many features of Freudian theory and to build a therapy geared to the role of meaning and purpose in human action.[37]

In Chapter 10 we shall attempt not only to relate these various types of cases to the logic of theory building but also to demonstrate that certain kinds of theoretical perspectives (for example, structural functionalism) are more congruent with the case study method than are others.

SAMPLING

For all the advantages of the case method, it poses special problems for the researcher. For example, in many areas it is unfeasible to formulate universal propositions (even for a single complex society), for these become so abstract as to have little empirical relevance. Then too, the representativeness of one's units looms exceedingly large when complex societies constitute one's working universe. Even relatively small working universes may become unmanageable without a refined set of rules for ensuring a representative selection of respondents or other data sources.

It would be impossible for Gallup or Roper to achieve a complete enumeration of persons in the United States each time they sought to study the opinions

[36] See, e.g., Russell Middleton, "Brother-Sister and Father-Daughter Marriage in Ancient Egypt," *American Sociological Review, 27* (October, 1962), 603–611.

[37] Victor E. Frankl, *Man's Search for Meaning* (Boston: Beacon Press, 1963).

of the citizenry. Financial considerations alone force even the most affluent of pollsters to limit their sample size.[38] Any increase in sample size beyond, for example, 4000–5000 leads to only small increases in the reliability of the results for the working universe as a whole, although the reliability of the analysis of various subgroups might be enhanced considerably by a larger sample.

Yet, as indicated earlier, the unmanageability of populations is merely one variable fostering the use of sampling. The heterogeneity and fluidity of modern social systems make it imperative that representativeness be sought wherever possible. If all carpenters thought and acted in a similar manner and if all sociologists were alike, a single case would suffice for generalization about each of these occupational groups. It is the complexity and disarray in social systems that generate problems for the researcher. Interestingly, the democratic industrial-urban order, encouraging as it does the flowering of social research, also abets pluralism, heterogeneity, and fluidity. Such complexity makes representative sampling a must for social scientists but simultaneously erects barriers to the realization of this goal.

If one were to draw a sample for unwed mothers, he would face this paradox. Because of the societal complexity, we must be concerned with representativeness. Until recently it was widely assumed that unwed mothers usually came from the disadvantaged sector of society or psychologically disturbed backgrounds. But Vincent, employing a different sampling design than his predecessors, selected his unwed mothers from doctors' files and was able to question seriously these long-held hypotheses regarding the characteristics of unwed mothers.[39] Yet, Vincent's sample is, as he acknowledges, not a representative one. Given the fact that American society permits many unwed mothers to cover up their condition through a variety of means, the difficulties of drawing a representative sample of unwed mothers are almost incalculable.

In addition to complexity, still other factors lead researchers to engage in sampling. One, frequently overlooked, relates to the social organization of the research team itself. The report of the procedures of the first census in the Sudan states:

> Such intractable problems as the scarcity of suitable enumerator and supervisors, the shortage of transport, the difficulties of enumerating

[38] For example, in the *Gallup Political Index,* Report No. 14, July, 1966, it is noted that Gallup's national survey results are based on interviews with a minimum of 150 adults. The variation in size of national surveys has been considerable, but those with an *I* of over 5000 are uncommon. See "Listings of American Surveys: The Roper Publ. Opinion Research Center," Williamstown, Mass., Williams College, n.d. (mimeo.), which contains a listing of the *N*s used in various polls through the early 1960s.

[39] Clark E. Vincent, "The Unwed Mother and Sampling Bias," *American Sociologic. Review, 19* (October, 1954), 562–567.

nomads and people living in widely scattered tukls (as they do in the south)—all these, and many other, problems were overcome by the use of sampling methods. In addition, sampling methods made possible a much closer supervision of the work of enumerators and supervisors.[40]

Although this report *overstates* the case (sampling did not by any means overcome the difficulties of enumerating nomads, for instance), it nevertheless seems clear that greater reliability and validity can be achieved through dependence upon a few highly trained persons than upon a large group of untrained interviewers and analysts—a consideration of special moment in many modernizing countries that lack a pool of trained researchers.

Probability Sampling

It is through probability sampling that scientists attempt to achieve representativeness. That is, they look for a set of cases that reflect the complexities of the particular working universe they are investigating. We will consider briefly some of the more commonly employed sampling procedures: simple random sampling (the classic form of probability sampling), systematic sampling, stratified sampling, and area sampling. We will then be in a position to examine some of the barriers to probability sampling and, most important of all, to indicate means of bypassing some of these.

SIMPLE RANDOM SAMPLING

The notion of probability is fundamental to random sampling. In simple random sampling, units—be these individuals, families, or communities—must be drawn from the working universe in such a manner that each unit (and combination of units) has an equal chance of being selected. Significantly, this procedure assumes that the units themselves are equal.

It is perhaps of more than passing interest that this notion of equality of units articulates with certain premises underlying democratic industrial orders. Here, theoretically at least, "every man is entitled to his opinion" and "every man's vote is of equal weight." This pattern explains in part the popularity of random sampling. But it also suggests certain difficulties. All men's opinions do not carry equal weight in a democracy, especially in predicting decisions by governmental leaders.

The premise of equality of units presents a difficulty of another sort, for instance, in crosscultural research. Here such units as "community" or "family" are difficult to standardize.

[40] Roushdi A. Henin, *First Population Census of Sudan, 1955/56, Methods Report,* vol. 1 (Khartoum, Sudan: Department of Statistics, 1960), 8.

As to the specific means of ensuring a random sample: If the working universe is relatively small, and if we possess detailed knowledge of it, we can number each unit and then resort to one of several tables of random numbers. This method is the most effective one a social scientist can employ to approximate the ideal of a random sample.

Experience has, of course, demonstrated the unreliability of some traditional, popular means of selecting random samples. One that has been partially discredited consists of placing numbered slips of paper in a goldfish bowl, mixing them up, and then having a neutral party pick out the slips. It has been demonstrated empirically that this technique has built-in biases: It is apparently very difficult to mix the slips in a random manner.

In the end, whatever procedure the researcher utilizes in drawing a random sample, two facts remain uppermost: (1) A simple random sample cannot be attained without adherence to strict rules or norms. (2) The more information one has about the working universe the more likely it is that the ideal of a random sample will be attained.

SYSTEMATIC SAMPLING

The paucity of data on the working universe, the complexity of the latter, and/or limited finances may force the researcher to rely upon procedures other than the above. Systematic sampling, which consists of taking every *k*th sampling unit (houses on blocks, cards in files, and so on) after a random start, is, given the structure of modern bureaucratic society, a widely used selection procedure. But some writers doubt whether this procedure should be classed as probability sampling; systematic sampling is, therefore, occasionally referred to as "pseudo-random" selection. At the same time, Kish writes:

> If the population units were thoroughly shuffled or mixed before they were ordered on the list, the systematic sample would be equivalent to a simple random sample. Though short of this ideal, in some populations the overwhelming proportion of the variance of survey variables is irregular and haphazard, and the result of a systematic sample can be accepted for practical purposes as a good approximation for random choice.[41]

STRATIFIED SAMPLING

An inherent limitation of simple random sampling is the researcher's inability at times to introduce sufficient controls to ensure representativeness. When, for example, we select units from a complex, heterogeneous universe, certain subgroups in our universe, perhaps strategic ones, may be excluded from

[41] Leslie Kish, *Survey Sampling* (New York: Wiley, 1965), 118.

the sample simply as a result of chance factors. Thus, if we are studying a community with a variety of ethnic groups, we must make certain that each appears in sufficient numbers to make our analysis meaningful.

Stratification of the working universe is one means of ensuring the representation of specified subgroups within the overall sample. We can, for instance, divide our universe into various subcategories (ethnic, economic, or whatever) and then draw random samples from each subclass. As a result, a predetermined number of persons within each subclass will be included in the total sample, the number being proportionate to the size of the group vis-à-vis the working universe or according to some other proration. But here again, if the researcher is to achieve a valid stratified sample, he must have at his command information adequate to delineate the various strata from which he draws his random samples.

AREA SAMPLING

Another form of probability sampling, of more recent vintage, is that based on areas. Here, rather than selecting units with specified social attributes such as ethnic or occupational, one draws a sample from a set of social areas. As illustrative of this procedure we quote from one of the studies of Detroit carried out by the University of Michigan:

> The sampling design for Detroit consisted of multi-stage probability sampling. (1) A random sample of census tracts was drawn from the entire metropolitan area of Detroit and its densely populated suburbs. (2) A random sample of five or six city blocks was drawn from each tract. (3) Within each block, a random start was made and every *nth* dwelling unit selected for interviewing. Each household in the community had one chance in 900 of being selected.[42]

With this kind of sampling design, the researcher can instruct the interviewer to select a specific person in house X of block Y of census tract Z, permitting the interviewer no freedom in the choice of interviewees.

However, implicit in this procedure, though frequently unexplicated, is the premise that a definite relationship obtains between a given set of social characteristics and their spatial patterning. Materials from the field of human ecology indicate that this premise is often open to question on empirical grounds. For example, urban census tracts, commonly employed as areal units by researchers in the United States, are often quite heterogeneous in their social composition. At the same time, researchers may have the data necessary for drawing an area sample but lack the kinds of information essential for stratifying the sample by social groupings.

[42] Robert O. Blood, Jr., and Ronald M. Wolfe, *Husbands and Wives* (New York: Free Press, 1960), 269.

SIZE OF SAMPLE

When the researcher sets out to draw a random, stratified, or area sample, one of the first questions he must answer is, "How large should the sample be?" For this there is no neat formula. As Stephan and McCarthy observe: "It all depends."[43] It depends upon one's finances, one's problem, the categories to be employed in the analysis, the nature of the working universe (whether it is homogeneous or heterogeneous), and the ultimate purpose for which the data have been amassed (whether for theoretical or for practical ends).

If, for example, the researcher intends to analyze his data according to numerous subcategories, a larger sample is required than if the categories are relatively few in number.

Another critical facet of sample size is the amount of error variance the researcher is willing to tolerate. There is, however, a law of diminishing returns relative to the spread in the distribution of estimates; this spread is expressed as the square root of the reciprocal of the sample size. A 20 percent increase in size produces only a 10 percent reduction in this spread in the distribution of estimates.[44] Obviously, the goals of the research are critical for the final decision concerning sample size. If numerous subgroups are to be analyzed, a much larger sample is required. Also, if a sample is to be used by managers of business or governmental agencies, the sample size may have to be increased—not for any inherent scientific reason, but because these decision makers find they cannot use a small sample (relative to the size of the working universe) to rationalize their actions to their constituency. The latter may be unwilling to accept the principles of scientific sampling.

Our discussion suggests another issue confronting the scientist: the controversy over the merits of large versus small samples. Those researchers who utilize the latter (say, those of 100 units or even of 30 units or less) tend to assume that a small sample permits the exercise of more stringent controls over the collection and analysis of data than does the large one.[45] But the proponents of large samples, who also advocate precision, question the validity of small samples in many areas of contemporary social research. The heterogeneity and looseness of many social systems make it difficult to achieve representativeness through the use of small samples. For many kinds of sociological problems, nonprobability samples which have built-in controls to ensure selection of a diversity of persons (or other units) in a working universe may provide us with more information than carefully drawn probability samples from a limited universe.

---

[43] Frederick F. Stephan and Philip J. McCarthy, *Sampling Opinions* (New York: Wiley, Science Editions, 1963), 103.

[44] *Ibid.,* 104.

[45] Robert F. Winch, *Mate-Selection: A Study of Complementary Needs* (New York: Harper & Row, 1958), 106.

SAMPLING AND EXPERIMENTATION

If sociologists could experiment freely with their subjects or with social systems in general, they could dispense with probability sampling, for ultimately probability sampling serves to control, or to hold constant, certain variables. However, in a democratic order, ethical and political considerations inhibit the use of experimentation. Indeed, it would require experimentation on, say, the order of the Nazi concentration camps to hold certain sociocultural factors constant. There is the underlying premise, among a number of social psychologists, for example, that experimentation makes it possible to examine the "universal aspects" of the human personality. But many of the findings based on experiments employing small groups in the United States will be called into serious question once subjects are selected from diverse cultural backgrounds.[46]

This is not to say that limited types of experimentation will not prove useful. Moreover, researchers can resort to matching certain variables (at times termed "covariables") so that any differences which appear can be ascribed with reasonable confidence to the effects of the factor under investigation. One could match an experimental group of parolees, for example, with a control group on the basis of such covariables as age, education, type of crime, and so forth, covariables whose significance is suggested by prior research. However, the limitations of the matching procedure are quite apparent. The greater the number of covariables utilized in matching units in the experimental and control groups, the more difficult it becomes to find units with the desired traits. Then too, given the present state of knowledge, we cannot be confident that we have matched the units according to the relevant covariables.

Deviations from the Ideal in Probability Sampling

Deviations from the ideal norms abound in probability sampling, and, what is significant, these are more or less accepted practice in sociology, psychology, and political science. Some of the most widely acclaimed studies in recent years have only approximated a probability sampling design. Among these are Stouffer's *Communism, Conformity, and Civil Liberties* (where community leaders were not selected in terms of a probability sample)[47] and Lazarsfeld and Thielens' *The Academic Mind*.[48] Moreover, we find numerous sociologists apply-

---

[46] Much more interest is being displayed today by social psychologists in cross-cultural research, to judge by a cursory examination of the relevant journals.

[47] Stouffer, *op. cit.*

[48] Paul F. Lazarsfeld and Wagner Thielens, Jr., *The Academic Mind* (New York: Free Press, 1958). While the authors contend that "Probability procedures were used throughout" (371), they also state:

Once the schools were drawn in the home office they were assigned to the interviewing agency which had the best supervisor in the vicinity. If colleges were located more than

ing the techniques of inductive statistics—which assume probability sampling—when in fact the sampling design involves only a crude form of randomization.[49]

These distortions, however, have become institutionalized, accepted as legitimate by many social scientists, for both theoretical and practical considerations. In exploratory research, where the investigator is intent upon formulating tenable hypotheses rather than formally testing them, or where he is searching for new ideas, a probability sampling design may not be in order. Here concentration upon deviant, or nonrepresentative, cases may be far more rewarding than the analysis of representative cases.

If the investigator's goal is to discover the extremes of human action with respect to a given norm, probability sampling is usually not a desideratum. For extreme cases may not be included in a random sample. And, as we will enlarge upon when we discuss "Sampling and the Study of Social Norms," certain types of social inquiry are most effectively advanced when the researcher relies upon strategic informants who would not be located through any random sampling procedure.

Also, if the researcher intends to establish universal propositions, random sampling is not applicable at all. In this instance, both the nature of the hypothesis and the logical structure of inquiry determine the scientist's sampling procedure.

In addition to the aforementioned theoretical reasons, a range of social factors restrict or inhibit the use of random sampling. These include disarray within, or lack of data on, the special universe; the researcher's own lack of resources; and the value system and power structure of both the society within which the researcher functions and the special universe he is studying.

One critical assumption implicit in probability sampling is that the working universe displays some kind of internal order. Certain kinds of disorder, particularly where combined with restricted financial and human resources, may make probability sampling unfeasible.

Two illustrations should clarify our argument. It is common practice for researchers studying industrial-urban centers to select every *n*th house when drawing a systematic sample. But even this kind of unit selection (which has been referred to as a "pseudosample") could not be duplicated in the cities of

---

eighty miles from either a Roper or N.O.R.C. interviewing station, and if more accessible but closely comparable schools in a stratum existed, substitutions were made. Approximately 15 per cent of the schools in the final sample were chosen in this manner (372).

Other major deviations from their probability sampling design, with reference to the colleges, could be noted (372–373).

[49] Cf. Leslie Kish, "Confidence Intervals for Clustered Samples," *American Sociological Review*, 22 (April, 1957), 165. An instructive case of ideal versus actual practice can be found in Hodge, Siegel, and Rossi, *op. cit.* In discussing their sample of 651 cases, the

many underdeveloped nations, where houses are scattered about willy-nilly, with a chaotic numbering system or none at all.[50] Unless one first plotted and numbered all the houses within the city, field workers often would find it impossible to locate house X in area Y. Another example concerns the study of collective behavior. How does one draw a random sample of persons in an acting mob? The confusion and disorder would obviate any such attempt. This may explain why few formalized statistical studies have been accomplished in the field of collective behavior. Thus, to state the case in more theoretical terms, probability sampling presupposes a certain kind of social order.[51]

Then too, the sheer paucity of data on the special universe may make it impossible to draw an adequate probability sample. We have already mentioned the crosscultural research undertaken by the Human Relations Area Files. Once societies of the past were defined as part of the special universe, even an approximate random sample became unattainable. For on numerous social orders adequate data are nonexistent.[52] Even in less extreme instances, the paucity of data on one's working universe is a formidable barrier. The Useems, in their study of foreign-educated Indians in Bombay State, encountered just such a problem in the selection of their subjects. "We were faced with the fact that no one knows with any certainty the number and distribution of the foreign-educated in Bombay State."[53] Or consider the case of Thorndike and Hagen.[54]

---

write: "Even the sample was selected according to the outmoded quota sampling methods employed in 1947." Then, in a footnote on the same page, they state: "Justification for our claim that 651 cases suffice to give a reliable intertemporal comparison can be derived from an examination of sampling error estimates based on the assumption of a random sample" (323).

[50] In a number of countries the enumeration of houses becomes a prerequisite to conducting even a census. See, e.g., E. H. Slade, *Census of Pakistan, 1951*, vol. 1 (Karachi, Pakistan: Manager of Publications, Government of Pakistan, 1951). "In this operation every enumerator made a thorough reconnaissance of his block and prepared a list of all the dwelling places in it, painting a number, corresponding with the list, on every building capable of being used for dwelling purposes" (4).

[51] The lack of order—i.e., order from the perspective of the modern bureaucratic system—may account for the significant undercount of nonwhite males in the United States Census. Conrad Taeuber and Morris H. Hansen, "A Preliminary Evaluation of the 1960 Censuses of Population and Housing" (Washington, D.C.: U.S. Department of Commerce, Bureau of the Census, n.d.), 6. It is estimated that there was an undercount of 16 percent of nonwhite males in the age group 25–44. In light of these data we can assume that a reliable probability sample of nonwhite males would be exceedingly difficult, if not impossible, to attain except at great expense.

[52] One has but to examine the Sudan Census (Henin, *op. cit., passim*) to recognize the impossibility of drawing a reliable probability sample of nomadic peoples.

[53] John Useem and Ruth Hill Useem, *The Western-Educated Man in India* (New York: Dryden, 1955), 18.

[54] Robert L. Thorndike and Elizabeth Hagen, *Ten Thousand Careers* (New York: Wiley, 1959), 13–15.

They sought to do a follow-up study of men who had taken a battery of tests during World War II. Out of the original universe of 17,000 persons, 10,000 or so were contacted during 1955 and 1956.[55] The authors concede that although additional funds would have increased this figure somewhat, the cost of finding even a few extra persons would have been considerable, and some individuals, because of death or spatial mobility, would never be uncovered.

Another reason for the failure to draw a random probability sample is the researcher's financial plight or lack of other resources. Many kinds of research, particularly those involving the selection of samples on a nationwide scale, cannot be realized without substantial monetary resources.

In some situations researchers, to gain financial support, must make compromises with the ideal research design. It appears that some grant-dispensing agencies by, for example, demanding "immediate" progress reports commit the researcher to sampling procedures that are less than the best. The researcher feels compelled to produce in a hurry.

Perhaps the main deterrent to random sampling is social resistance—in the form of values and power. For when the value system of a person or a group obviates the goals, or even the activity, of social research to the point that potential informants refuse to cooperate with interviewers, the barriers to achieving an ideal sample are formidable indeed. If a pervasive power structure inhibits social research, then we can dispense with probability sampling.

We need not look far afield to uncover examples of social resistance that preclude the use of simple random, or other forms of probability, sampling. A striking instance is the Harvard study of Russians who had migrated to the West after World War II. Social scientists—unable to carry out research in the Soviet Union and reluctant to rely merely upon published accounts in Russia about the operation of their own social system, or even upon accounts of Western correspondents in the Soviet Union—studied these *émigrés*.[56] But in no sense do these persons represent a random sample of the Russian society about which social scientists have sought to generalize.

Nor is the United States free of social values and power factors that make it necessary for researchers to compromise the ideal sampling design.[57] The research that led to the Kinsey report, acknowledged by its critics to embody numerous biases, nevertheless had to proceed more or less as it did, given the resistance at the time to questions concerning informants' sex behavior. The

[55] *Ibid.*

[56] Alex Inkeles and Raymond A. Bauer, *The Soviet Citizen* (Cambridge, Mass.: Harvard, 1959), chaps. 2 and 3.

[57] Researchers lack access to many realms of organizational life. See, e.g., William Delany, "Some Field Notes on the Problem of Access in Organizational Research," *Administrative Science Quarterly,* 5 (December, 1960), 448–457.

study's reliance upon voluntary informants suggests that the sample was not representative of American society—as indeed it was not. Such conservative elements as ruralites and Catholics were underrepresented in Kinsey's group of volunteers.[58]

An interesting sidelight to Stouffer's study of civil liberties in America was the relatively high nonresponse rate among newspaper publishers (compared to other leadership groups in the community).[59] Relatively speaking, the resistance to queries about civil liberties apparently came from the very group that has had as its major ideological commitment the free diffusion of information.

Nor should we overlook various mundane forms of resistance to the achievement of probability sampling. The kind of questionnaire, for example, can affect one's sampling design. Osgood seems to recognize that difficulties may arise in applying his semantic differential instrument,[60] for potential informants not only balk at long questionnaires but show little enthusiasm for questionnaires they do not understand. This may account for the popularity of using captive audiences, for example, college students, when applying certain instruments, for these informants not only may have some understanding of the goals of the research but they cannot afford to resist.

Circumventing the Barriers

Given these strictures on probability sampling, what are the alternative courses of action available to the researcher? A popular procedure within the sampling tradition is the quota sample. A nonprobability sampling device, its prime virtue has been to reduce cost, but it also provides a measure of representativeness in the face of social strictures. The quota sample involves deciding beforehand just what kinds of subjects one wishes to include: how many persons are to be men, how many women, how many should have particular levels of education, and so on. After establishing the quotas, one instructs field workers to locate and interview persons with the prescribed characteristics.

In addition to the fact that one cannot estimate sampling error via modern statistical tools for the quota sample, this type of sampling procedure leads to other difficulties. Because of the interviewer's freedom in selecting individuals who fit the specifications, certain biases seem likely to be present. The field worker may, for instance, interview persons he knows or persons who are easy

[58] For a critical evaluation of this study, see William G. Cochran *et al., Statistical Problems of the Kinsey Report* (Washington, D.C.: American Statistical Association, 1954).

[59] Stouffer, *op. cit.*

[60] Charles E. Osgood *et al., The Measurement of Meaning* (Urbana, Ill.: The University of Illinois Press, 1957), 32.

to interview. Nevertheless, the quota sample does tend to ensure the inclusion of persons who occupy diverse roles and statuses in the social order.[61]

A partial substitute for overall probability sampling is careful sampling of one sector of the special universe by means of a probability design. This procedure has been advocated by some critics of the first Kinsey report.[62] Even though an overall probability sample of, say, American society could not have been attained by Kinsey and his associates, they could have drawn probability samples from various subclasses of the broader society: college males, for example. They could then have compared the results of their probability sample with the group of college men who served as volunteers. Such a procedure would have exposed some of the biases in Kinsey's sample of volunteer informants.

Another realistic possibility involves replication: restudy of the special universe in question or of a similar one. In many respects this is the most effective and realistic alternative in situations where the social scientist can not draw random probability samples. In the replication process one is primarily interested, not in finding evidence that duplicates the precise statistical relationships among variables, but rather in discovering whether the *patterns* are similar to those yielded by previous research.

Sociologists can also state their hypotheses in terms of *form,* not content, and thus sidestep some of the dilemmas inherent in nonprobability samples. Thus one researcher studied the kinds of influences that operate to produce Jewish-Gentile marriages; he was concerned with their distribution in the universe of mixed couples.[63] In this situation the scientist must include cases that reflect the diversity within the working universe; adherence to the norms involved in drawing a quota sample appears to be an effective means for testing hypotheses regarding the form of social relationships.

Sampling and the Study of Social Norms

The study of form leads us to a discussion of social norms. It seems clear that probability sampling is not an effective mechanism for selecting informants in the study of social organization.[64] We have already commented upon the strictures that the social organization may impose upon probability sampling. But over and beyond these is the dilemma that lies at the core of much sociological enterprise. Although the primary goal of sociology is the formulation of

[61] Stephan and McCarthy, *op. cit.*

[62] Cochran, *op. cit.*

[63] John E. Mayer, *Jewish-Gentile Courtships* (New York: Free Press, 1961), 16.

[64] Cf. Morris Zelditch, Jr., "Some Methodological Problems of Field Studies," *American Journal of Sociology,* 67 (March, 1962), 566–576.

valid propositions concerning the nature of social organization, a sound method for selecting respondents (or the events to be observed) within the system under study has yet to be devised. Probability sampling, as presently constituted, contributes little to the resolution of this problem.

The classic studies of social organization, whether of large-scale bureaucratic structures or of communities, have placed little reliance on probability sampling.[65] True, researchers may employ random sampling for determining the characteristics of individuals in a system, but rarely can they do so for purposes of delineating the norms and processes of a system.

Thus Clark, conducting a study of junior colleges in California, leaned heavily upon indirect observation by nonscientists, specifically on records collated by the college itself.[66] But even when scholars take respondents as their prime data source, many make no use of probability designs. Blau, writing on informal organization within a bureaucracy, Dalton on business managers, and Gouldner on industrial organization, did not employ probability sampling.[67]

But why has probability sampling been accorded so little attention in studies of the normative order? Indeed the very persons who may study social organization without formal recourse to probability sampling (or even approximations to it) do an about-face in their opinion and attitude surveys, or in those surveys dealing with individual characteristics.

The paucity of probability sampling in research on social organization can be explained by the nature of the subject matter itself. We have here the age-old distinction between the parts and the whole: Simply adding up individual characteristics does not necessarily provide us with the desired knowledge of the collectivity.

Moreover, members of a social organization possess unequal amounts of knowledge about its operation. Large-scale governmental, business, education, and religious bureaucracies are after all nondemocratic. Some, to be sure, are more so than others. Nevertheless, the process of institutionalization within large-scale systems induces an unequal distribution of rights and privileges—and consequently of knowledge. And recall that one of the assumptions underlying probability sampling is that the units are equal. We can work on this assumption if we are concerned with the votes of individuals. In a democracy each person has one vote. But the very nature of social organization obviates against any

---

[65] For a broad-based discussion of research procedures (including sampling) in the study of organizations, see W. Richard Scott, "Field Methods in the Study of Organizations," in James G. March (ed.), *Handbook of Organizations* (Chicago: Rand McNally, 1965), chap. 6.

[66] Burton R. Clark, *The Open Door College* (New York: McGraw-Hill, 1960).

[67] Peter M. Blau, "The Research Process in the Study of *The Dynamics of Bureaucracy*," in Hammond, *op. cit.*, chap. 2; Melville Dalton, "Preconceptions and Methods in *Men Who Manage*," *ibid.*, chap. 3; Gouldner, *op. cit.*

assumption of the equality of units. Persons who carry out leadership roles, as well as specialized roles within the system, are expected to view the system as a whole, whereas other functionaries tend to view it from the vantage point of their own immediate concerns. A university president typically knows more about the system *in toto* than do individual members of his faculty. On the other hand, those in the lower echelons often have a fuller comprehension of the specific details of the day-by-day operation of the organization than do the topmost leaders.

Also, persons of supposedly equal rank may possess differential kinds and amounts of information. For example, all assistant professors at a large university do not have equally valid knowledge about the system's normative order. One person, as a result of an unusual combination of social contacts or perhaps due to his marginal position, may harbor information unknown to others of equal rank. Or, some persons come to occupy a variety of roles in the system, enabling them to perceive its operation through a variety of lenses, which provides them with a unique perspective on the social order.

Under these circumstances probability sampling of informants generally must be ruled out as inapplicable. As one of its most serious failings, it may exclude from the sample the strategic person (or persons) who knows most about the system or a particular facet of it. Given the presence in most social systems of informal structural arrangements functioning alongside the formal ones, even the most carefully devised stratified sample cannot ensure the selection of persons with special or strategic knowledge of the normative order.

Granted these limitations upon probability sampling in the study of social organization, just how do researchers select respondents? One approach is exemplified by certain studies of community structure, particularly those relating to social class and power.[68] A popular technique has been to select a number of "experts" as a board of judges to delineate their community's social organization. These persons are generally from the community's upper ranks and tend to have wide experience and contacts within this setting. The judges often form part of the old guard; they are the persons who are the most likely carriers of the kind of knowledge the researcher is seeking.

This sampling procedure has some obvious limitations. For one thing, it tends to impose upon the community the views of those persons who occupy the dominant positions. On the other hand, it conforms to the nature of social organization which, as we observed, is usually nondemocratic in orientation. Of more serious consequence, the selection of the judges in the manner noted above tends to stress tradition and omit change and disorder, for persons who reflect the latter patterns tend to lack knowledge about the system as a whole.

[68] Robert A. Ellis, "The Prestige-Rating Technique in Community Stratification Research," in Richard N. Adams and Jack J. Preiss (eds.), *Human Organization Research* (Homewood, Ill.: Dorsey, 1960), chap. 25.

This tendency to select upper-status judges who often have had long-standing contact with the community has led some students of social stratification to over-emphasize the rigidity of the American class structure.

Unquestionably we require many more detailed descriptions of the specific procedures researchers employ in their study of large-scale organizations if we are to formulate a more useful set of ideal norms. Even so, certain patterns emerge from the existing literature.

If the researcher proposes to study a complex organization, he often begins by observing or interviewing those persons who occupy formal roles within it. That is, the formal organization defines who is important and knowledgeable. Thus, few would consider studying any given university's social structure without interviewing the president, deans, departmental chairmen, and similar officials. After this, several alternatives are open to the scientist. He can check upon divergent formal roles that are known to him, beginning with instructors, retired professors, or other personnel who are not integrated into the system. Or he can in the process of interviewing the organization's officialdom inquire about the informal structure. Researchers frequently do this in a rather semiconscious manner. Informants are asked, "Who among the faculty do you believe possesses key information on the system?" Or at times an official will volunteer, "See so and so, he knows more about this than anyone else." In this fashion those who occupy the formal positions are used to identify strategic informants in informal positions. Or the researcher may follow a somewhat different course of action; he may seek out either the stable marginal type of informant or else the deviants or troublemakers, who usually have a distinct view of the system's functioning, especially concerning the informal structure. We shall examine the various kinds of informants in some detail in later chapters.

In any event, the researcher usually begins with some hypothetical model or image of the kind of social organization he is studying, and as he proceeds he checks this model with respondents, making various additions or deletions. Or he may check his original model against his observation of ongoing events. Ideally, the researcher proceeds until his key findings become repetitive and the inconsistencies either tend to disappear or can be accounted for.

CHAPTER 7

Direct

Observation

In direct observation the researcher witnesses or experiences events or phenomena firsthand, whereas in indirect observation he relies upon his interpretation of the sense impressions of informants. Although, on the empirical plane, the distinction between them is often blurred, certain analytical advantages accrue from treating these data-gathering procedures separately.

Ideally, one should be able to observe social reality in an objective manner, to "capture" the world about him as it "exists." Yet, nowhere in social research are sociologists so conscious of the persistent deviations from the ideal as in the realm of direct observation. Methodologists, therefore, are justifiably concerned with the reliability and the validity of the observations of both scientists and laymen. It is little wonder that some scientists have sought refuge in highly structured observation with built-in controls over both the observer and the observed that enable one to check for possible distortions in the observation process. Our analysis delves into some of the dilemmas inherent in this area.

Definition and Types of Direct Observation

Although social scientists might agree on what constitute the broader features of direct observation, consensus regarding certain aspects of this process is more difficult to achieve. Moreover, questions such as "Does one really hear Caruso when one listens to his records?" raise epistemological issues which, though pertinent to social research, cannot be explored herein.

We are concerned with direct observation: with the perception of human behavior or of objects in one's immediate environment, which perception has been conceptualized and is capable of being transmitted to others. As indicated earlier, only two kinds of behavior can be sensed "directly": linguistic signs and physical acts. Attitudes, mores, norms, and other concepts sociologists employ are imputations from, and in turn are used to interpret, direct observation of human behavior.

Analyzing direct observation, we can distinguish between the observations of scientists and those of laymen. The latter are nonscientists who not only systematize but formally report their observations to others (usually in the form of writing).

We can also distinguish between self-observation, or introspection, and observation of human behavior or objects external to oneself. Although introspection has fallen into disfavor in modern psychology and sociology, it cannot be summarily dismissed.[1] In the study of such "feeling-states" as motives or emotional tensions, self-observation has proven to be a useful device in generating new hypotheses.[2]

In turn, we can analytically separate controlled and noncontrolled observation. Controlled observation properly presumes external or independent checks upon one's findings. However, while chance or unsystematic observations can often be labeled "uncontrolled," it is debatable whether systematic observation by a single observer who takes careful and detailed notes can be so categorized. Empirically, then, there is a gradation in controls from the relatively rigid to the relatively loose.

Many methodologists draw a distinction between participant and nonparticipant observation. In the former the researcher engages in the activities of the persons he is studying; in the latter he remains aloof. But, as we indicate below, this classification is of doubtful utility and may actually lead the sociologist astray.

Limitations of Direct Observation

Whether one engages in casual observation of one's own group or functions as a participant observer in an alien group or employs some system of controlled observation of a group, certain limitations inhere in the method of direct observation.

First, this mode of research has only limited potential outside a relatively small group or subsystem. No scientist or layman can engage in direct observa-

[1] See, e.g., Peter McKellar, "The Method of Introspection," in Jordan M. Scher (ed.), *Theories of the Mind* (New York: Free Press, 1962), 619–644.

[2] Self-observation can prove useful in explicating issues relating to direct observation. See, e.g., George Orwell, *The Road to Wigan Pier* (New York: Berkeley Medallion Books, 1961). Orwell's reflections upon the problems he encountered in his observation of the miners of Wigan Pier point up issues that tend to be ignored by many social researchers. He indicates how difficult it is for a middle-class person to transcend his own status.

tion of huge collectivities such as nations or even large metropolitan centers.[3]

Second, direct observation must be supplemented by indirect observation, even within a small group setting. Although "Malinowski sometimes appeared to argue that no past event was of interest to anthropologists,"[4] nonetheless, he had to be concerned with people's traditions or history when carrying out his field work. The social scientist, if he is to gain a perspective on the present and judge whether the ongoing actions are typical or aberrant, must engage in observation of the indirect sort. And if he is to interpret the "meaning" of social actions, he must place these in terms of some broader whole, particularly in historical context. Even for the person being observed, the meaning of an act in which he engages is usually acquired through its relationship to a set of past actions or events. In traditional societies, especially, people reason: "Our ancestors did this, therefore we should do it too."

A third stricture upon direct observation stems from the society's power structure and value system. Every social order tends to consider certain spheres of social action to be sacred or private. In American society the act of voting is a private matter, and its sanctity is underwritten by the legal structure. In most societies sexual relations are regarded as private. To study such areas, one must employ some form of indirect observation.

Direct Observation by Laymen

Much of the material social scientists rely upon for their generalizations has been collected, analyzed, and written up by persons who do not define themselves as scientists nor are they labeled so by others. Such persons include newsmen, many free-lance writers, politicians, governmental bureaucrats, educators, and businessmen who record observations about their own experiences or the experiences of other persons.

That newsmen's observations of current events are an indispensable source for historians, sociologists, political scientists, economists, and even anthropologists is easily documented. In many societies newsmen are the eyes and ears of social scientists, for their special status and role permits them access to social activities often closed to social research. In certain countries, American foreign correspondents have been able to observe events (both directly and indirectly) far more readily than have American social scientists.

But it is not merely on the international scene that newsmen enjoy special

---

[3] A brief discussion of some of the difficulties encountered in direct observation of even a small sector of a large city can be found in Sheila Patterson, *Dark Strangers* (London: Tavistock, 1963), chap. 2.

[4] Lucy Mair, "Malinowski and the Study of Social Change," Raymond Firth (ed.), *Man and Culture* (New York: Harper & Row, Harper Torchbooks, 1964), 240–241.

privileges. In the United States, for example, their institutionalized status permits them to probe more deeply into sensitive political spheres than can most social scientists. The norm calling for "freedom of the press" is more compelling than any stressing "freedom to do social research." For this reason, also, in America newsmen can associate with and observe criminals and other "outcast elements" more easily than can social researchers who are connected with universities or governmental agencies.

But newsmen are only one of several types of observers upon whom social scientists rely. More than ever before in history, men of affairs, including politicians, military leaders, and business executives, are intent upon recording their experiences, personal as well as public, for posterity. In recent decades a number of American governmental leaders, including those in the military, have, after resigning from their official posts, published their memoirs or personal accounts in which they seek public support for causes that the bureaucracy may have rejected during their period in office.

Former government officials may in fact feel duty bound to record the "facts" and keep the historical record straight, although naturally they seek to enhance their role in history by casting themselves in the best possible light. Thus such World War II generals as Montgomery, Eisenhower, Bradley, and others have carried on running debates concerning the propriety of certain decisions that were made.[5] And publishing one's memoirs, as in the case of Eisenhower's *Crusade in Europe,* can be a highly profitable venture.

These kinds of data are often invaluable to social scientists, for given the relative scarcity of social researchers, many significant activities would otherwise remain unrecorded.[6] Most crucial of all, these records bear upon social actions the investigation of which often is closed to the social scientist. Much decision making in large-scale bureaucracies is simply not open to direct observation by outsiders, in part because of the fear that critical information might fall into the hands of the opposition, including one's chief competitors. Or, as we indicated in an earlier chapter, the heads of large-scale organizations may be wary of opening up their day-by-day operations to public scrutiny for fear that their public image will be damaged.[7]

[5] Bernard Law Montgomery, *The Memoirs of Field-Marshal the Viscount Montgomery of Alamein* (Cleveland: World Publishing, 1958); Dwight D. Eisenhower, *Crusade in Europe* (Garden City, N.Y.: Doubleday, 1948); and Omar Nelson Bradley, *A Soldier's Story* (New York: Holt, Rinehart and Winston, 1951).

[6] It is not just the military that poses this problem; large-scale corporate structures also do so. Thus, such a work as that by Alfred P. Sloan, Jr., *My Years with General Motors* (Garden City, N.Y.: Doubleday, 1963), is highly useful to social scientists.

[7] The gravest problems arise in organizations concerned with affairs of the nation-state. See, e.g., Herbert Feis, "The Shackled Historian," *Foreign Affairs,* 45 (January, 1967), 332–343. There are, of course, as Feis observes, other reasons for secrecy on the part of the nation-state.

An extreme case should clarify our argument. We lack data based on the direct observation by social scientists of the death camps operated by the Nazis in their efforts to destroy Europe's Jews during World War II. Obviously, the Nazis would never have permitted sociologists to wander about taking notes on the mechanics of their "final solution" to the Jewish question. In order to gain an understanding of this industrial-urban bureaucracy geared to mass murder and of the social-psychological makeup of its functionaries, we must of necessity rely upon the autobiographies of victims who escaped or who somehow miraculously survived until they were released and upon the writings of such functionaries as Hoess, the Commandant of Auschwitz, and the physician Nyiszli, who was notorious for his experiments upon human beings.[8]

Certainly the materials of nonscientists must be used with caution. For one thing, the writer does not always make it clear whether he viewed the action himself or whether he relied upon the observations of others. The records of newsmen often suffer from the failure to draw a distinction between direct and indirect observations. Then too, in many instances, as in memoirs or autobiographies, the data are set down years after the event, and the compiler may be dependent mainly upon his memory, which, as we know, can be highly unreliable.[9] The interpretation of events after a lapse of 5, 10, or 20 years is hazardous business. To be sure, some ex-officials have access to files or diaries which can serve as a significant check upon their memory of events as well as the interpretation of these.

More specifically, the social scientist must, when evaluating these data, ask himself: "Are the recorded events typical or divergent?" For so often it is the novel, the unique, that captures the attention of newsmen and autobiographers —and of course their readers. The daily routine is much less absorbing as a subject, and as a consequence aspects of it tend to go unobserved. The danger in this for the scientist is that deviant actions may be treated as if they were typical. But then this hazard is hardly unique to nonscientists, for sociologists, too, may lapse into viewing the unusual as commonplace.

Ultimately, the utility of direct observation on the part of lay observers depends upon the nature of the scientist's problem. If he desires data regarding the frequency of certain phenomena, the nonscientist's materials are often of little value to him. If on the other hand the sociologist concerns himself with social processes, the question of normality may be much less significant. For

[8] Rudolf Hoess, *Commandant of Auschwitz,* trans. by Constantine FitzGibbon (London: George Weidenfeld and Nicolson, 1959) ; Miklos Nyiszli, *Auschwitz, A Doctor's Eyewitness Account,* trans. by Tibère Kremer and Richard Seaver (New York: Frederick Fell, 1960).

[9] The research on memory is pertinent to any methodological inquiry. See, e.g., the summary by I. M. L. Hunter, *Memory,* rev. ed. (Baltimore: Penguin, 1964).

many social events are perceived most clearly when they appear in dramatic form: that is, as deviant cases.

Implicit in our discussion is another limitation of the direct observation of nonscientists. That is, the latter do not observe human behavior in terms of an explicit theory or set of hypotheses. Because of this, crucial materials may be omitted from the record, materials so strategic that if they were known they would force the scientist to revise his overall evaluation of the problem. But more generally, the data stemming from the direct observations of newsmen, autobiographers, and the like rarely are selected in terms of any strict canons of evidence. Thus, if the sociologist, say, uses these materials, he must some-how seek to assess the compiler's motives in writing up the data in the first instance.

But the scientist is often unable to assess accurately the writer's motives and thus the objectivity of the data. Newsmen often become captives of their news-papers and the group they observe.[10] And whether a man of affairs writes his memoirs in order to sway the course of present events or whether he does so to justify his actions to future generations bears upon the reliability and validity of the data. Historians frequently encounter this sort of methodological issue.[11] They are already beginning to grapple with the "rationalizations" of Churchill, Roosevelt, Truman, General Montgomery, General Eisenhower, and others who have sought to explicate the reasoning behind the Allied campaigns of World War II. One may infer motives from internal evidence (Is there consistency in the author's argument?) or often indirectly from other data, including the general value orientation of the period (Does it stress the recording of certain kinds of observations and the omission of others?).[12]

Although many lay observers present biased materials, others do attain a high degree of objectivity in their accounts. In certain instances the latter's subculture places a premium upon such objectivity. More challenging theoretically are the chronicles of those observers who have managed to sustain a high

---

[10] See, e.g., Dan D. Nimmo, *Newsgathering in Washington* (New York: Atherton, 1964). Also, the social critic Nat Hentoff's periodic column, "Review of the Press," which has appeared in the *Village Voice* in recent years, highlights some of the structural and ideological constraints upon newsmen and editors of leading New York dailies, particularly the *New York Times*.

[11] See, e.g., Louis Gottschalk, *Understanding History* (New York: Knopf, 1950), for an analysis of the problems of authenticity and credibility from the perspective of historical research.

[12] Feis, *op. cit.,* 333, observes:

Most valuable, in fact indispensable to the historian of recent times, are the memoirs by participants in, witnesses or auditors of momentous events. . . .
But what a tricky source of historical knowledge individual memoirs may be! The parentage and purpose of the documents themselves must be evaluated: who wrote them, why, and how good and fair a recorder was he?

degree of objectivity in the face of strong pressures to the contrary, pressures emanating from the broader social environment. Indeed, we can hypothesize that some persons utilize the "objectification process" as a means of sustaining personal stability in an otherwise chaotic world.[13] True, it has been averred that only the "true believer" can maintain stability under crisis conditions and that objectification, because of its secularizing effects, actually contributes to personal instability. Nevertheless, certain evidence seems to contravene this notion. Some persons clearly are able to maintain personal organization in the face of destruction of their normal surroundings and the mounting irrationality of their fellow men by observing and commenting upon these happenings in neutral terms.

We can cite the works of a number of nonscientists, who were able to objectify events while their former world of meaning crumbled about them during World War II. These include *A Woman in Berlin,* Nansen's *From Day to Day,* and Ringelblum's *Notes from the Warsaw Ghetto.*[14] If we can believe the statements of Ceram, who wrote the introduction to *A Woman in Berlin,*[15] here is a woman who underwent all manner of harrowing experiences as the Russian forces swept into the city but who nevertheless was able to write of her personal tragedy as a "detached observer" and at the same time display considerable understanding of why the events occurred as they did. Nansen, in his *From Day to Day,* notes that he recorded his matter-of-fact observations on scraps of toilet paper during his stay in a prisoner-of-war camp.[16] He observes that this activity helped to a degree to sustain him during this period of severe hardship.

Ringelblum's document, one of the most compelling of any written during World War II, details the experiences of the Jews in the Warsaw Ghetto and their relationships with the Nazis and the Poles. Although Ringelblum was a leader of the Jewish underground in Warsaw, he maintained a remarkably detached stance even toward those Jews who cooperated with the Nazis. Ringelblum's objectivity derived in part from his past formal education, in part from his passion for keeping detailed records through which future generations might evaluate this period of history, and in part from his own enormous efforts to sustain himself in a hostile environment.[17]

[13] This thesis is set forth by Bruno Bettelheim, *The Informed Heart* (New York: Free Press, 1960), 111.

[14] Odd Nansen, *From Day to Day,* trans. by Katherine John (New York: Putnam, 1949); Anon., *A Woman in Berlin,* trans. by James Stern (New York: Harcourt, Brace & World, 1954); Emmanuel Ringelblum, *Notes from the Warsaw Ghetto,* trans. by *Jacob Sloan* (New York: McGraw-Hill, 1958).

[15] *A Woman in Berlin, op. cit.* See the comments in the "Introduction" by C. W. Ceram, 8–10.

[16] Nansen, *op. cit.*

[17] Ringelblum, *op. cit.* See especially Jacob Sloan's "Introduction" (ix–xxvii).

Direct Observation by Scientists

Direct observation on the part of scientists differs from that by laymen not only in its overall purpose but also in the types of controls to which it is subject. Scientists strive to explicate their theory and to attain greater reliability and validity in their direct observation of events.

Social researchers employ direct observation in theory building, either as a test of existing theories or as a basis for discovery. A number of sociologists have relied upon crude observations for their theory building. Indeed, this tradition harks back to Georg Simmel and includes such well-known scholars as Cooley and, more recently, Goffman.[18] These sociologists have on occasion taken their immediate social environment as their laboratory so that their everyday life of work and play seemed to be their primary source of inspiration. Cooley, for instance, in building his theory about the formation of "self," used his children as subjects of observation.[19] Outside of sociology, such a figure as Freud relied heavily upon direct observation as a basis for developing a theory of human action. Not only did he observe his patients directly, but he even engaged in self-observation.[20]

In a sense, these social scientists have followed the procedure outlined by Mannheim and elaborated and documented by Garfinkel.[21] Mannheim and Garfinkel hold that the observer isolates identical and homologous patterns out of a mass of apparently divergent behavior patterns. These scientists apparently treat the direct observation of "behavioral events" as a kind of "document" (Mannheim's term) or "index" of some basic pattern. Garfinkel explicates the overall interrelationship between perception of events and conception of them as follows:

> Not only is the underlying pattern derived from its individual documentary evidences, but the individual documentary evidences, in their turn, are interpreted on the basis of "what is known" about the underlying pattern . . .

[18] See, e.g., *The Sociology of George Simmel,* trans. by Kurt H. Wolff (New York: Free Press, 1950); Charles Horton Cooley, *Sociological Theory and Social Research* (New York: Holt, Rinehart and Winston, 1930), chap. 5; and Erving Goffman, *The Presentation of Self in Everyday Life* (Garden City, N.Y.: Doubleday, Anchor Books, 1959).

[19] Cooley, *op. cit.*

[20] Ernest Jones, *The Life and Work of Sigmund Freud* (Garden City, N.Y.: Doubleday, Anchor Books, 1963), chap. 14.

[21] Karl Mannheim, *Essays on the Sociology of Knowledge,* trans. and ed. by Paul Kecskemeti (London: Routledge, 1952); and Harold Garfinkel, "Common-Sense Knowledge of Social Structures: The Documentary Method of Interpretation," in Scher, *op. cit.,* 689–712.

The method is recognizable for the everyday necessities of recognizing what a person is "talking about" given that he doesn't say exactly what he means, or in recognizing such common occurrences as mailmen, friendly gestures, and promises. It is recognizable as well in deciding the sociologically analyzed occurrence of events like Goffman's strategies for the management of impressions.[22]

We seem to have here, even in the formulation of certain concepts in one's everyday life, a process that Kepler utilized on a much more abstract level, that of moving from data back to theory and then checking the theory (or even isolated concepts) against the data until some usable set of concepts or categories is obtained.[23] This process of developing or utilizing concepts is an operational one in that particular physical movements or sounds are taken as indicators of underlying or unobservable patterns.

What made sociologists such as Cooley and Simmel so outstanding is that they were able to develop conceptual systems that ordered and made sense out of otherwise discrete observations. For it is not perception alone but perception combined with conceptualization that spells the difference between good and bad research. Original theory based on data secured via observation that is subject to few controls may be worth more than studies that are technically proficient but lacking in creativity.

At the same time, it is possible to objectify and standardize some of the procedures that occur in studies using direct observation (or so-called participant observation). For example, observers should be aware of the fact that they frequently think in quasi-numerical terms, using such categories as "sometimes," "often," and "almost always," to distinguish patterns of action within or among groups. Thus, Becker writes:

> The exigencies of the field usually prevent the collection of data in such a form as to meet the assumptions of statistical tests, so that the observer deals in what have been called "quasi-statistics." His conclusions, while implicitly numerical, do not require precise quantification. For instance, he may conclude that members of freshmen medical fraternities typically sit together during lectures, while other students sit in less stable smaller groupings. His observations may indicate such a wide disparity between the two groups in this respect that the inference is warranted without a standardized computing operation. Occasionally, the field situation may permit him to make similar observations

---

[22] Garfinkel, *op. cit.*, 691–692.

[23] See, e.g., Arthur Koestler, *The Watershed* (Garden City, N.J.: Doubleday, Anchor Books, 1960).

or ask similar questions of many people, systematically searching for quasi-statistical support for a conclusion about frequency or distribution.[24]

One of the problems in this situation is that observation and analysis of data often form part and parcel of the same overall process.

Impact of the Observer's Conceptual System

We have stressed that what the scientist observes is a function of several variables. In addition to the social world he studies, the scientist's scientific and personal conceptual systems (ideas, beliefs, values, and so on), as well as his status and role, structure his observations of social phenomena.

Some scholars enter the field with well-defined hypotheses which they propose to test. In such instances there is a danger that these hypotheses will become so fixed that they will deflect the observer from contradictory evidence. Actually, most social scientists who engage in direct observation tend to emphasize discovery rather than the formal testing of hypotheses. In this situation, the researcher begins with a broadly defined problem, or set of problems, which then may be radically revised during the observation process. Such a pattern has typified many investigations in social science.

But the scientist's observations are affected not only by his hypotheses or problems and theoretical assumptions but by also the ideas, beliefs, and values which he has acquired as a functioning member of society (or its subsystems). True, social scientists generally recognize the impact of ideas, beliefs, and values upon the manner in which preliterates observe their natural and social environment. Illustrative of this are the variations in the way different cultures may classify colors.[25] And anthropologists have detailed how particular preliterate groups believe that their members observe certain phenomena that are invisible to other peoples (especially to the empirically oriented scientist).[26] But it is much more difficult for the researcher to recognize the impact of the values and beliefs of his own social order upon his scientific observations.

Maquet has noted that anthropologists working in Africa have until recently tended to observe those actions that reflect order and adjustment, while over-

[24] Howard S. Becker, "Problems of Inference and Proof in Participant Observation," *American Sociological Review,* 23 (December, 1958), 656.

[25] See, e.g., Harold C. Conklin, "Hanunóo Color Categories," *Southwestern Journal of Anthropology,* 11 (Winter, 1955), 339–344.

[26] A. I. Hallowell, "Cultural Factors in the Structuralization of Perception," in John H. Rohrer and Muzafer Sherif (eds.), *Social Psychology at the Crossroads* (New York: Harper & Row, 1951), chap. 7, esp. 178–184.

looking those which reflect conflict.[27] This orientation suggests that many anthropologists have viewed African societies through the political values of the colonial system of which they have been a part.

The effects of the researcher's preconceptions upon his observations can be discerned in narrower contexts as well. The psychologist Robert Rosenthal and his associates have carried out some highly informative studies on observers under experimental conditions.[28] One group of studies dealt with the expectations of experimenters working with rats. Some persons were told that they had bright rats, others that their rats were dull. Rosenthal found that the experimenters who believed their rats were bright obtained better learning responses from these rats than did the experimenters who believed that their particular rats were bred for dullness.[29]

After completing certain experiments, Rosenthal discussed the project with the experimenters.

> There appeared to be great interest and animation on their part. One reaction, though, was surprising, and that was the sudden increase in sophistication about sampling theory in the experimenters who had been assigned "dull" rats. Many of these experimenters pointed out that, of course, by random sampling, the two groups of rats would not differ *on the average.* However, they continued, under random sampling, some of the "dull" rats would *really* be dull by chance and that *their* animal was a perfect example of such a phenomenon.[30]

Other research, for example in the field of hypnosis, confirms Rosenthal's findings that the investigator's own beliefs and concepts (of a rather nonscientific sort) can strongly influence an experiment.[31] And if the experiment is with humans rather than with rats, the possibility of distortion is still greater, for the subjects can, by their own reactions, reinforce the experimenter's biases.

When the value and belief system of the broader society is interwoven with a scientific theory, it becomes difficult to evaluate the reliability and validity of the researcher's observations. One of the most enlightening controversies in this

[27] Jacques Maquet, "Objectivity in Anthropology," *Current Anthropology,* 5 (February, 1964), 47–55.

[28] Robert Rosenthal, *Experimenter Effects in Behavioral Research* (New York: Appleton-Century-Crofts, 1966). Cf. Neil Friedman, *The Social Nature of Psychological Research* (New York: Basic Books, 1967).

[29] Rosenthal, *op. cit.,* chap. 10.

[30] *Ibid.,* 176.

[31] Martin T. Orne, "On the Social Psychology of the Psychological Experiment," *American Psychologist,* 17 (November, 1962), 776–783.

regard revolves about the works of Redfield and Lewis in the so-called village of Tepoztlán, Mexico (actually a small town with a large number of agriculturalists). In the 1920s Redfield, using both direct and indirect observation, studied the community's social-cultural patterns, and in 1943 Lewis undertook a restudy of it.[32] What is striking are the differences in the two authors' descriptions of this community. Redfield stressed the degree of integration, particularly that achieved through ceremonial activities, as well as the overall contentment of the people in Tepoztlán. Lewis, on the other hand, was impressed by the strains and conflicts, the personal disharmony among the inhabitants. These different emphases led to two divergent portraits of a single community.

We shall rely upon Paddock's discussion of anthropologists' efforts to account for the two divergent views of Tepoztlán.[33] Thus we can perhaps, as did Wolf, explain the divergencies by ascribing them to the many changes that had occurred in the period that intervened between Redfield's and Lewis' studies. Redfield (and Margaret Mead) attributed the differences in the findings to "the personal equation": to differences in temperament and in cultural orientation. In part Lewis agreed, but he also argued that Redfield perceived the patterns in Tepoztlán within too narrow a theoretical framework: Redfield's folk-urban continuum more or less assumed that the folk order (of which Tepoztlán is an example) is integrated and therefore characterized by harmonious relations. Redfield, for his part, contended that he formulated his folk-urban framework *after* he had entered the field.[34] Still, as a graduate student and as Robert E. Park's son-in-law, he must early have absorbed some of the theories of Maine and Tönnies, so crucial as a foundation for the folk-urban continuum.

Neither Redfield nor Lewis made his frame of reference sufficiently explicit before entering the field. Thus, the scientific framework through which each observed life in Tepoztlán was interwoven with the author's personal predilections. As Paddock observes, it is quite possible that both integrative and disjunctive processes were present in Tepoztlán during each period of study: "A single Tepoztecan might well be answering the questions of Lewis, Redfield, and others simultaneously."[35] Surely these townspeople are happy about some things and distressed about others. Thus, what the investigator extracts from the complex reality we term culture and society depends upon his personal beliefs, values,

---

[32] Robert Redfield, *Tepoztlan: A Mexican Village* (Chicago: University of Chicago Press, 1930); Oscar Lewis, *Life in a Mexican Village: Tepoztlán Restudied* (Urbana, Ill.: University of Illinois Press, 1951).

[33] John Paddock, "Oscar Lewis's Mexico," *Anthropological Quarterly, 34* (July, 1961), 129–149, and especially the longer English mimeographed version of this article, which was originally published in Spanish in *Boletín Bibliográfico de Antropología Americana,* part 2 (1960).

[34] *Ibid.*

[35] *Ibid.* This quote is drawn from the mimeographed version, p. 9.

and ideas,[36] as well as on his scientific theory and research procedures.

But the question arises: "How can the sociologist control for these hidden biases and bring his actual observations into line with ideal standards?" Self-criticism as well as a continuing dialogue among scholars are necessary, if not sufficient, conditions for sustaining objectivity. It is through this dialectic that scientists gain a conscious awareness of their theory, which in turn makes it possible to "hold constant" or to "suspend" one's personal ideas and values.

Certain recent works in psychology posit several levels of consciousness and/or awareness. Solley and Murphy, in their *Development of the Perceptual World,* speak of nonreflective and reflective consciousness; and whether or not one accepts this particular formulation, one must consider carefully the implications of their views for direct observation on the part of scientists. They contend that "there is nonreflective consciousness, as when you drive down a highway 'seeing' trees, signboards, cards, etc., experiencing the world immediately."[37] Here the observer is conscious of these stimuli as if they were part of him. "Man is *reflectively conscious;* he is conscious of being conscious. . . . It is at this level that a scientist operates; he is not merely nonreflectively conscious of a dial; he is reflectively conscious of his immediate consciousness in that he 'reads' the dial and it is his reflective-consciousness that he records, not 'immediate experience.' "[38]

But it is by no means easy to become reflectively conscious of one's actions and observations. In addition to carrying on some kind of critical dialogue, a researcher must often be able to remove himself intellectually and emotionally from the immediate social situation, to step back and examine his activities in broader perspective. It is through exposure to a variety of subgroups or cultures that one acquires sensitivity to the nuances of human experience, including one's own political and ethical commitments.

Moreover, the senior author of this book has, as one means of socializing students into the innuendoes and subtleties of gestures and the like, had them attend selected films. Movies or the theater are among the few situations wherein a variety of complex roles can be carried out within a short period of time and where these can be observed by a group of people. Many students with considerable formal sociological training are still quite unable to "read" cues— in either gestures or speech. And many of those who are able to note actions that escape most people cannot place these in any meaningful theoretical context, for they have not been taught to be reflectively conscious of what they observe.

[36] The role of the personal equation in observation and interpretation of the social world has also been noted by John W. Bennett, "The Interpretation of Pueblo Culture: A Question of Values," *Southwestern Journal of Anthropology,* 2 (Winter, 1946), 361–374.

[37] Charles M. Solley and Gardner Murphy, *Development of the Perceptual World* (New York: Basic Books, 1960), 292.

[38] *Ibid.,* 294.

Reflective consciousness is essential not only for identifying the normative order but for gaining an appreciation of the norms and values that shape the researcher's own actions.[39]

Impact of the Observer's Status and Role

Although one's conceptual system (both scientific and nonscientific) plays a crucial part in direct observation, the observer's own status and role affect the manner in which this conceptual system is applied. Earlier we mentioned that the researcher's social position influences the formulation of the research project. So also, one's status and role can hinder or facilitate entry into the field-work situation. Here, however, we hope to demonstrate how it can (1) shape the scientist's concepts and scientific theory and (2) influence the attitudes and responses of the persons being observed, which in turn affects what the researcher himself observes.

Within the limits imposed by such ascribed status characteristics as age and sex, researchers can and do modify their own status and role. Some sociologists and anthropologists, when carrying out research in the field, make it a practice to admit their identity, whereas others simply categorize themselves as social scientists; still others function under false colors. Some of the last-named may call themselves historians and say they are interested in delving into the community's history. This brings to mind a conversation with an anthropologist who had intended to study a small rural community in the United States in the guise of a "historian"—under the assumption that this role would facilitate his observation of community activities. But at one of his first stops, a small country store, he was asked who he was and what he planned to do. When he remarked that he was planning to study the historical background of the community, the woman questioning him remarked that her son was a graduate student in history at the very university where the anthropologist was teaching. It was immediately apparent to the researcher that he could not don his intended historian's guise but had to revert to his anthropologist's robes.

Related to the researcher's self-definition is the matter of sponsorship. If, say, the researcher enters a factory under the aegis of management, the reactions of the workers are likely to be quite different than if he enters under union auspices.

In practice the observer-scientist controls the definition of the situation only up to a point—then the system he studies takes over. For example, an anthropologist occasionally experiences difficulties where the preliterate group he is study-

[39] Fred H. Goldner, "Role Emergence and the Ethics of Ambiguity," in Gideon Sjoberg (ed.), *Ethics, Politics, and Social Research* (Cambridge, Mass.: Schenkman, 1967), chap. 11.

ing assigns him a specific status, such as in the kinship system; yet such a fixed position may be essential if he is to relate to his subjects in a way meaningful to them.[40]

One variant of this structuring of the scientist's position by the system under study has been discussed by Tugby:

> The fieldworker in a non-western culture enters the society then, as a stranger identified in terms of some stereotype of outside persons; he must subsequently take pains to change this identification or add additional roles to it. It is doubtful if he can ever completely overcome his initial handicap.[41]

Other dilemmas regarding status and role definitions emerge in modern complex industrial orders. One stems from the shifting status of the researcher over time. As social scientists have climbed the social ladder, they have gained easier access to such groups as business and corporate organizations that formerly were closed to direct observation.[42] Simultaneously, these upper-status groups have redefined the researcher's status and this redefinition affects what is being observed. Furthermore, as sociologists have experienced upward social mobility, their perception of the lower socioeconomic groups has shifted, with the result that the former may be less able to empathize with the latter's way of life.

More generally, the public (or elements thereof) in industrial societies appears to be developing stereotyped conceptions of sociologists and other observers. To the extent that this conception becomes solidified, what the researcher observes becomes rather standardized. Some of the persons being observed may even come to believe that they are supposed to act in a prescribed manner. The social researcher, then, may become a captive of the societal stereotype. This difficulty heightens whenever a marked status differential exists between the observer and the observed. The social distance inherent in this situation imposes limits upon the free flow of communication and encourages those being studied to restrict the observer's access to various "back regions."

---

[40] Ward Goodenough became a "brother" to a native informant and in the process discovered another type of kin. Ward Goodenough, *Property, Kin, and Community on Truk*, Yale University Publications in Anthropology, No. 46 (New Haven: Department of Anthropology, Yale University, 1951), 9.

[41] Donald J. Tugby, "Interview Technique or Conversational Gambit: Problems of Data-Gathering with an Example from Mandailing, Sumatra," *Australian Journal of Psychology, 10* (September, 1958), 221.

[42] Some relatively new problems have emerged as social scientists have assumed administrative posts and have reported upon certain activities after leaving these positions. See, e.g., Martin Meyerson and Edward C. Banfield, *Politics, Planning, and the Public Interest* (New York: Free Press, 1955), 14–15. Although these authors are at least aware that this kind of research reporting leads to special problems, no one seems to have analyzed the general methodological implications of this procedure.

Sociologists also must face up to the elusiveness of "objective data," for what they observe directly undergoes change as the researcher and the researched interact with one another. Berreman's *Behind Many Masks,* based on the author's experiences in a Himalayan village and utilizing the theoretical orientation of Goffman, examines some of the researcher's difficulties in capturing "social reality."[43] Although Berreman does not distinguish clearly between indirect and direct observation (actually he discusses both), his analysis is more relevant here than in the next chapter.

Berreman hypothesizes that field research involves some form of "impression management."[44] The observer is frequently called upon to manipulate the situation so that his subjects will expose the "back region" of their activities, for most in-groups keep certain secrets from the out-group.

Specifically, Berreman notes how the shift from one interpreter to another, each holding different positions in the overall Indian status system, permitted him access to data on different caste groups in the village he studied.[45] Yet Berreman's, as well as Goffman's, discussion leaves the impression that all reality is amorphous, that a person has no stable self-concept. While we would not quarrel with the proposition that one's status and role can greatly affect one's personality and actions, the distinction between "off-stage" and "on-stage" personalities suggests some inherent stability behind the many masks; for the off-stage personality implies something more basic, perhaps more enduring, than the on-stage one.

This line of reasoning brings to mind the question, "How deeply should the scientist become involved in the activities of the group under study?" If one accepts at face value the writings of some anthropologists, one gains the impression that the researcher should seek to become an integral part of the system he is observing. But if the scientist actually adopted such a course of action, he would lose his identity as a scientist and might never publish his findings.[46] A scientist, by his very commitment, must be marginal to any group he studies.

Nonetheless, a scientist is free to carry out a variety of roles when engaged in direct observation. These range from that of a detached observer peering at his subjects through a one-way mirror without the latter's knowledge to that of a participant observer within a system. Between these two roles we find various gradations, each with its particular advantages and liabilities.

We shall for purposes of analysis contrast the casual marginal observer with one who strives to maximize acceptance by the system he is studying. The former

[43] Gerald D. Berreman, *Behind Many Masks,* Monograph No. 4 (Ithaca, N.Y.: Society for Applied Anthropology, 1962).

[44] *Ibid.*

[45] *Ibid.*

[46] Benjamin D. Paul, "Interview Techniques and Field Relationships," in A. L. Kroeber (ed.), *Anthropology Today* (Chicago: University of Chicago Press, 1953), 435.

has the advantage of being able to maintain greater emotional detachment, and consequently to sustain a wider range of social contacts within the group under observation. As a result of his marginality, he is more likely to be acceptable to persons who are at odds with one another. Nonetheless, this type of observer sacrifices depth of insight for diversity of social contacts. He will experience difficulty in observing the off-stage activities within a social order.

As for the term "participant observer," it is a misnomer. The scientist (as we elaborate below) must always be able to take the role of his subjects, to participate symbolically, if he is to interpret or impute meaning to the actions of others. "Participant observation," as the term is usually employed by sociologists, simply means that the researcher engages in the activities of the group under study. He attends church, participates in festivals, drinks with the boys, or whatever.

The acting out of a role may take different forms. It may be rather perfunctory, often to gain acceptance by the group. One anthropologist notes that his crude efforts to hoe and to dance both amused and pleased the tribal group under study and led to greater rapport.[47] On the other hand, a person may be an "observer as participant" much as one can be both a patron at various bars (and indistinguishable from other patrons) and a social researcher.[48] In either case, the scientist is able to check some of his observations by acting out the role he is studying.

But there are liabilities to any effort to maximize one's immersion in a system. Aside from the danger of losing one's identity as a scientist, the researcher may become the captive of the group he is studying.[49] His observations may no longer represent his independent judgments or evaluations but may reflect the observer's definition of the situation. For there is more to observation than merely taking the role of the other: The scientist must remain free to make interpretative judgments. Although some studies of small groups warn against the distortions in the observer's perception that result from social pressures, few, if any, authors point to the misperception the scientist can experience in field-work situations, misperceptions that result from social controls exerted by the group under investigation.

Under special circumstances scientists can reduce, via experimental controls, their own impact upon the group under study and the group's impact upon their own observations. Lefkowitz, Blake, and Mouton, when investigating the effect of status symbols on social action, had observers, who were dressed differently

[47] Aidan W. Southall, *Alur Society* (Cambridge, England: Heffer, 1956), x.

[48] See, e.g., Sherri Cavan, *Liquor License: An Ethnography of Bar Behavior* (Chicago: Aldine, 1966). For a general discussion of the observer as participant in relationship to other research roles see Raymond L. Gold, "Roles in Sociological Field Observations," *Social Forces, 36* (March, 1958), 217–223.

[49] S. M. Miller, "The Participant Observer and 'Over-Rapport,'" *American Sociological Review, 17* (February, 1952), 97–99.

from one another carry out a variety of roles while crossing the street. Through this procedure, Lefkowitz *et al.* examined the influence of dress upon the reactions of other persons, without the latter's knowledge.[50] To a degree it would be possible to control for the observers' effect upon their subjects by having several researchers with different personalities carry out the same role and in the process record their own observations of the events.

Sherif has also striven to control for observer effect upon his subjects. In his study of juvenile gangs, for example, Sherif had a field worker appear more or less casually on a basketball court and eventually, by hanging around, come to know the gang without exposing his true identity. The goal was to observe the actions of gang members in their natural habitat.[51] Here, of course, the controls were by no means complete, for the gang might have functioned differently if another researcher of different age, personality, or social background had carried out the project.

Still other social scientists have utilized one-way mirrors or hidden tape recorders as a means of overcoming observer bias. But, as with Sherif's field worker among juveniles, the ethical dilemmas loom large when the researcher in effect functions as a kind of "spy."

THE ETHICS OF ROLE PLAYING IN DIRECT OBSERVATION

That the ethical commitment of the scientist is a major variable in the research design becomes transparent when one examines the role of the scientist in direct observation.[52] For the researcher is often faced with the question: "Just how much should I divulge about my activities in the process of observing an ongoing group?" The social scientist can hardly reveal *all* aspects of his role (and its implications) beforehand. Not only may his decision influence the kind of data he is gathering, but the researcher may simply fail to grasp the implications of his research design until after the fact. Nor do persons in most societies go about revealing everything about themselves to everyone.

However, extreme forms of duplicity or deliberate misrepresentation of one's identity poses serious ethical problems for social scientists.[53] This issue has been brought into sharp focus in a number of research projects in recent

[50] Monroe Lefkowitz, Robert R. Blake, and Jane S. Mouton, "Status Factors in Pedestrian Violation of Traffic Signals," *Journal of Abnormal and Social Psychology, 51* (November, 1955), 704–706.

[51] Muzafer Sherif and Carolyn W. Sherif, *Reference Groups* (New York: Harper & Row, 1964), appendix.

[52] Herbert C. Kelman, "Human Use of Human Subjects: The Problem of Deception in Social Psychological Experiments," *Psychological Bulletin*, 67 (1967), 1–11.

[53] See the discussion by Kai T. Erikson, "A Comment on Disguised Observation in Sociology," *Social Problems, 14* (Spring, 1967), 366–373. Erikson argues against the researcher's deliberate misrepresentation of his identity for purposes of entering private domains to which he is not otherwise eligible.

years. For instance, when Sullivan, Queen, and Patrick studied noncoms in the United States Army, they had one of their field workers undergo formal recruitment in order to acquire a proper cover.[54]

After these sociologists reported their findings in the *American Sociological Review,* Coser composed a brief, but harsh, note to the editor. He charged that his fellow sociologists were in effect employing the tactics of a garrison state.[55] This is a serious charge and one that merits a studied and reasoned reply. However, those associated with the study of noncoms do not seem to have grasped the implications of Coser's argument.[56] Their justifications rested upon the contention that they merely sought to get inside the military in order to collect scientific information that would help soldiers. In effect, they took the position that their data would be rationally and wisely employed by military leaders in an effort to assist the army personnel. Up to a point this is perhaps a defensible position. But it also requires some qualification. Totalitarian governments, after all, employ a similar line of reasoning: They too seek to assist their citizens. In more than one nondemocratic order, social research has been rationalized as a medium for gathering factual information that can be used to obliterate the traditional feudal traits that still stand in the way of a forthcoming utopia.

While we are not out to question the motives of Sullivan *et al.,* we must recognize that they were supplying a power group with potentially useful information, and the researchers could exert little if any control over the manner in which the data would be interpreted and utilized. Yet precautions are essential if the subjects of study are to be protected against misuse of data by agencies whose primary function is that of social control. Ideally, studies should be carried out openly so that the informants can protect themselves in advance by simply refusing to cooperate. How would sociologists react if agents of the federal government were sent out to study clandestinely the operations of sociology departments so that the latter might be improved—for the good of sociology and the broader society?

Another ethical dilemma surrounding direct observation involves the increased use of electronic devices as a substitute for the scientist's eyes and ears. These instruments permit "direct observation" without disturbing the system and without having the system affect the researcher. The advantages of such a procedure are apparent enough. Nevertheless, the use of such instruments has led to serious political and ethical conflicts. One of the most highly publicized

[54] Mortimer A. Sullivan, Jr., Stuart A. Queen, and Ralph C. Patrick, Jr., "Participant Observation as Employed in the Study of a Military Training Program," *American Sociological Review, 23* (December, 1958), 660–667.

[55] Lewis A. Coser, "A Question of Professional Ethics?" *American Sociological Review, 24* (June, 1959), 397–398.

[56] Mortimer A. Sullivan, Jr., "Ethics—and Difficulties: Replies to Coser and Roth," *ibid.,* 398–399; Stuart A. Queen, "No 'Garrison State'—Difficulties, Yes: Replies to Coser and Roth," *ibid.,* 399–400.

cases concerned the bugging of a federal jury trial in Wichita, Kansas, by a research team from the University of Chicago. Although this was accomplished with the permission of the presiding judge, and although precautions were taken to ensure the jury's privacy, public objections were so vociferous that the Senate of the United States passed a law making illegal the bugging of federal juries.[57]

In the long run, efforts by researchers to gain information under false pretenses are likely to undermine the public's confidence in research. The ideal norm, "open covenants openly arrived at," must remain the guide to action. Still, this norm collides with that which calls for the search for truth irrespective of social pressures. When a power group imposes serious strictures upon research, social scientists may be driven either to engage in open conflict with the system or to use image manipulation as a means of overcoming the restrictive norms. We believe that sociologists must be concerned about subject manipulation. However, sociologists must also be concerned with maintaining an open flow of information about organizations and persons within a society—with maintaining an open society. Otherwise, science itself cannot survive. Clearly researchers must become more consciously aware of the ethical decisions they make in designing their research projects, and they must seek to justify their actions in terms of broader ideals.

In addition, the scientist-observer often confronts the question, "To what extent should I intervene in the lives of those I am observing?" Anthropologists have long been plagued by this issue. The anthropologist moves into a small community and finds himself carrying out the role not only of a scientist but also of a counselor or mediator with an outside world that the group only vaguely understands. Although guide lines here are fuzzy, it is difficult to assume that the scientist, once having established close social ties with the individuals he is observing, should reject these persons when the latter ask for assistance. After all, the researcher by walking about observing, both directly and indirectly, intervenes in his subjects' private sphere. The anthropologist's very presence may intensify their desire to move into a larger social orbit. Reciprocity between observer and observed seems to be an essential part of social research. Nonetheless, the scientist-observer's role playing is likely to structure his perception of social events; thus his ethical decisions bear directly upon the end results of his observation.

The Sensitive Observer and Scientific Discovery

Most sociology departments assume that their students can be trained to carry out field work. At the same time, most sociologists and anthropologists

---

[57] Ted R. Vaughan, "Governmental Intervention in Social Research: Political and Ethical Dimensions in the Wichita Jury Recordings," in Sjoberg, *op. cit.*, chap. 3.

also recognize that field workers vary in their ability to observe and record, particularly in their ability to perceive the unusual in a familiar light or to set the familiar in new perspective. Certainly observers differ in their ability to discover new facets of social phenomena.

In light of our argument in Chapter 3, we would expect a marked difference in the patterning of observation among those scientists who emphasize discovery of or the search for new knowledge in contrast to those who emphasize the formal testing of theories or hypotheses. Thus the controlled observation of many small group researchers (discussed below) is neither congruent with nor conducive to discovery. It is the scientist-observer whose conceptual system (whose value, idea, or belief system) lacks closure who is most sensitive to new ideas or patterns of action. Such a conceptual system is a necessary, though not a sufficient, condition to creative observation.

The contradictions or ambiguities in the observer's value or idea system appear on one of two interrelated levels. The observer may experience a degree of disorganization as a scientist or as a private citizen. The scientist who struggles to resolve divergent theoretical perspectives, or the scientist-citizen who is concerned with certain personal dilemmas, is more likely to perceive new patterns and gain new insights than one who has a highly organized and rigid set of categories.

Regrettably we have little detailed knowledge about these patterns. Although analytically the personal and the scientific spheres can be separated, in actual practice scientists seldom compartmentalize their private and scientific sectors. Thus, more than one sociologist who has been viewed as maladjusted, according to broader societal standards, has used his sociological inquiry as a means for resolving his own personal dilemmas. Yet there are limits to the degree of personal disorganization that is beneficial to scientific inquiry, for if a scientist's ideas, values, or beliefs are too amorphous or in unmanageable conflict he may not even be able to function adequately as a member of a society.

Our argument rests on our earlier assertions: that perception is governed largely by conception. Therefore, an observer whose categories are more or less fixed takes the world about him for granted. If he is confronted with new or divergent data, his system of concepts denies existence of any incongruency— or, failing that, the phenomena are bent or reshaped to conform to the available categories. Rarely are new categories created to contain the deviant case materials. Indeed, only if the world external to this kind of actor changes drastically does he revise his categories to conform to the evidence. It follows that the scientist-observer with a rigid framework is necessarily nonreflective.

Support for our position can be adduced from the actions of true believers in the political and religious spheres. Though these men are not scientists, the principles regarding their patterns of observation are to a degree applicable to those of scientists as well. Among the most dramatic case studies is Arthur

Koestler's autobiographical account in *The God that Failed*.[58] Koestler details his conversion to Communism and his experiences while committed to this ideology. Time and again he and his friends were confronted with evidence that conflicted with their beliefs, but they rationalized this away by a set of techniques that were part and parcel of their ideological kit—one of the most effective being the logic of the dialectic. Commenting upon one of his visits to the Soviet Union, Koestler states: "My Party education had equipped my mind with such elaborate shock-absorbing buffers and elastic defenses that everything seen and heard became automatically transformed to fit the preconceived pattern."[59]

Although Koestler may be overstating his position in order to compensate for his later rejection of Communism, the writings of like-minded persons support his reasoning. And there is no empirical or theoretical evidence to suggest that scientist-observers who develop closed systems would act any differently from persons such as Koestler.

If we examine the problem in more positive terms we find that scientist-observers with conflicting belief, idea, or value systems usually have the ability to empathize with and understand the thought processes of other persons, including those with whom they may strongly disagree.

An inconsistent or conflicting set of concepts, moreover, motivates a researcher to seek to attain a new kind of order. One means of achieving this end is to *discover* patterns in the environment that will provide the basis for constructing more stable categories. Then too, a person who has ideas, beliefs, and values that are inconsistent with one another may be better able than one with a well-defined set of categories to compute, correlate, and compare divergent social phenomena and/or to abstract underlying patterns. Certainly scientists belonging to the first type are more likely to reflect upon their sense impressions.

Some evidence in support of our argument can be adduced from the autobiographical or biographical accounts of social scientists whose lives were filled with personal tensions and self-doubt. Max Weber could be placed in this group. And recent research studies on creativity among scientists suggest that creative persons are not those with the highest IQs but rather those who combine a better-than-average intelligence with drive and curiosity, that is, with an unstable set of categories.[60]

The contention that persons with conflicting values, ideas, or beliefs are more likely than others to be creative also finds support in the life histories

[58] Arthur Koestler in Richard Crossman (ed.), *The God that Failed* (New York: Harper & Row, 1949), 15–75.

[59] *Ibid.*, 60.

[60] See, e.g., Donald W. MacKinnon, "What Makes a Person Creative?" *Saturday Review*, 45 (Feb. 10, 1962), 15–17. For other views on scientific creativity see Calvin W. Taylor and Frank Barron (eds.), *Scientific Creativity* (New York: Wiley, Science Editions, 1966).

of playwrights, novelists, and actors. For example, Eugene O'Neill, Tennessee Williams, and Arthur Miller, who rank among the foremost American playwrights of the twentieth century, all have had a relatively unstable conceptual framework. Their lives and their perspectives have, by American middle-class standards, been quite unorthodox. Yet, as "alienated" members of modern society, they have struggled to establish an order for themselves and for others: They have abstracted a set of patterns from what has been for them a sea of confusion. These persons and a number of creative novelists have been able to observe the modern social order in a somewhat unique fashion and to arrange its parts into a new and comprehensible whole. For they have been exceedingly sensitive to the details and nuances of everyday living that tend to escape the observations of the average man.

So too, comedians and actors have at times been especially perceptive regarding the subtleties of human action. Charlie Chaplin, Alec Guinness, and Peter Sellers, among others, have been adept at grasping the salient aspects of divergent social roles. They have portrayed these on the stage and screen so convincingly that audiences have not only identified with the characters involved but have gained a better understanding of the differing societal roles. Significantly, all the aforementioned actors have, by their own admission, lacked any well-defined concept of themselves. Alec Guinness is one who lacks any real sense of identity, who apparently does not know who he is.[61] Such lack of a concept of self would account in large part for his sensitivity to the actions of others and for the fact that in playing out various roles he comes to "discover" himself.

Thus, the data on the lives of novelists, playwrights, and actors afford the methodologist certain clues regarding the nature of the sensitive observer. They point to a close interrelationship among conflicting values and beliefs, status instability, and sensitivity to cues and obscure patterns within one's social environment. We hope that social scientists will in time provide us with the data necessary for testing and elaborating upon this proposition.

Controlled Observation

Although one ideal norm in research calls for creativity (or discovery) through direct observation, another ideal norm emphasizes the need for control and standardization of the observation process. To some extent these norms conflict with one another. Yet it is apparent that creativity alone does not ensure advances in scientific knowledge; some standardization of observation also is required. Ideally sociologists should be able to agree upon what they observe. But because of the impact of various sociocultural factors upon the researcher, such consensus is often difficult to attain.

[61] "Least Likely To Succeed, *Time, 71* (Apr. 21, 1958), 52–54.

A number of suggestions have been advanced for controlling the effects of the field worker's own sociocultural background upon his observations. One is that a number of researchers, trained in the scientific method and selected from a variety of cultures, should study a single community. Then, by comparing the results, we could perhaps isolate the effects of the broader socialization process and thus provide a sounder basis for the achievement of consensus among scientists from divergent social systems.

Or, as has already been attempted, different researchers can be sensitized to similar categories prior to entering different field-work situations. By stabilizing the theoretical categories in this fashion, we can more readily evaluate the similarities and differences among observers in different sociocultural systems.

In addition to isolating the effects of the investigator's status and social background upon his scientific observations, we might, as has the social psychologist Sherif, strive to eliminate, or at least minimize, the scientist's impact upon the social group under study. Sherif took great pains to control for the observer's influence upon juvenile gangs (in the natural setting). But he never fully succeeded in this effort.[62] Nor would it be possible to introduce a new member into a group without affecting the structure of the group to some degree.

More elaborate controls have been instituted in the laboratory in an effort to eliminate the scientist as a variable in the research design. An early, but still informative, work of this type is that by Bales. Unlike many students in the area of small groups, Bales sought to relate theory to research in a rather systematic manner and to formalize the controls over direct observation. Here we review Bales's *Interaction Process Analysis* in some detail,[63] for it highlights the theoretical and practical difficulties of establishing effective checks upon direct observation and points up the need for the observer's participation, at least in symbolic form, in the activities he is observing.

Bales began by detailing a set of categories into which he could fit all the relevant actions of members of small groups. There are twelve in all. The actor (1) shows solidarity, (2) shows tension release, (3) agrees, (4) gives suggestion, (5) gives opinion, (6) gives orientation, (7) asks for orientation, (8) asks for opinion, (9) asks for suggestion, (10) disagrees, (11) shows tension, and (12) shows antagonism.[64] Concerning these, Bales writes:

> The set of categories is meant to be completely inclusive in the sense that every act which can be observed can be classified in one positively defined category. The method is continuous in that it requires

[62] Sherif and Sherif, *op. cit.*

[63] Robert F. Bales, *Interaction Process Analysis* (Reading, Mass.: Addison-Wesley, 1950).

[64] *Ibid.*, 9.

the observer to make a classification of every act he can observe, as it occurs in sequence, so that his work of classification and scoring for any given period of observation is continuous. No observed acts in a given period are omitted from classification except by error.[65]

Through use of a one-way mirror, Bales and his assistants observed small groups interacting. Prior to the study, the observers were instructed as to the kinds of acts that should be placed in the various categories. They also utilized an "interaction process recorder," a mechanical device that simplified the marking of the appropriate categories while the action was taking place.

While Bales has made progress in analyzing small group interaction, some of the dilemmas posed by aspects of his method are instructive for the methodologist. One of the difficulties Bales sought to overcome involved the establishment of proper "empirical indicators" for the various categories—an essential step in standardizing the observation process. He remarks upon his procedure as follows:

> Categories have been omitted which do not apply on the level of the single act, which require the observer to be evaluative in the moral, ethical sense, which require him to make judgments of logical relevance, validity, rigor, etc., or which are not readable in themselves in a minimum context.[66]

In the tradition of the extreme behaviorists, Bales is attempting to eliminate the errors in direct observation by removing the highly subjective or personalistic elements from this process. However, a few pages later, Bales writes:

> The observer attempts to take the "role of the generalized other" with regard to the actor at any given moment. That is, the observer tries to think of himself as a generalized group member, or, insofar as he can, as the specific other to whom the actor is talking, or toward whom the actor's behavior is directed, or by whom the actor's behavior is pereceived. The observer then endeavors to classify the act of the actor according to its instrumental or expressive significance to that other group member. . . .
>
> The observer carries the complication one step further by trying to empathize with the other or group member as the group member perceives the actor.[67]

[65] *Ibid.,* 35.
[66] *Ibid.,* 37.
[67] *Ibid.,* 39.

The above arguments are contradictory. For the notion of "taking the role of the other" involves logical relevance, validity, and so on. In effect, any effort to remove the interpretative (or conceptual) dimension from the direct observation of human action seems foredoomed. Although we admit the possibility of chance observation, perception remains private knowledge unless it is somehow conceptualized, and conceptualization involves some form of interpretation or the establishment of logical relevance.

Of course, the search for instruments to remove the subjective element from observation continues. It has reached its height in the lie detector: the "truth machine." However, the success or failure of this device rests upon the interpretation of the results.[68] Thus the ideal of the extreme behaviorists—to purge scientific inquiry of all human judgments—is still to be achieved. And rather than continue striving toward such an apparently unattainable goal, we must seek to improve our interpretative judgments of social reality.

Bales's study also brings to the fore a related methodological issue: the difficulty of distinguishing between participant and nonparticipant observation. Although Bales's observers did not interact in face-to-face relationships with their subjects of study, they nevertheless were part of the group in a symbolic sense. To interpret the actions of others, the observers had to act *as if* they were participating in the activities of the group they were watching, even though behind a one-way mirror. Otherwise, the researchers could not have "taken the role of the generalized other." True, one might profitably distinguish between researchers who act out physically the activities they are studying and those who merely engage in symbolic interaction. But participation there must be.

The need for interpretative understanding in direct observation raises theoretical and methodological issues that strike at the heart of the question concerning observer consensus. Laying aside the problems that result from Bales's particular statistical procedures, we find that Bales sought to increase the degree of consensus among observers not only by working out a set of explicit categories but by training observers to "see" certain phenomena in the same way.[69] In other words, observers were instructed that particular gestures were to be placed in given categories. But were not these observers in danger of becoming like Koestler vis-à-vis the Communist system: seeing what they wanted to see, believing what they wanted to believe? Or like the psychologists we alluded to earlier with their dull and bright rats? In other words, did Bales's observers read into the physical gestures or statements of various actors patterns that did really not exist, at least from the perspective of the persons being studied?

[68] See, e.g., Burke M. Smith, "The Polygraph," *Scientific American, 216* (January, 1967), 25–31.

[69] Bales, *op. cit.,* 100.

We can provide no ready answers to these questions. But one possible approach is to contrast the interpretations of persons who have been carefully trained to observe certain patterns with those of the recipients of less highly structured observation. If significant differences arise, we must seek to account for them. Then there is the question: What meaning do the conclusions of observers socialized to adhere to rigid categories have for the persons under study? Do these conclusions make sense to the latter? And why? It may be that sociologists may well have to accept more ambiguity than they would ideally champion; they may have to concede that discrepancies between the observations of the observer and of the observed are bound to appear under certain conditions.

Certainly when we seek to evaluate the reliability and validity of direct observations, we must take into account the goal of the scientific effort. We must ask ourselves: "Will these aid in prediction? Will they help the actors to better understand themselves?" We return to this issue in our discussion of reliability and validity.

CHAPTER 8

Indirect

Observation

Our attention now shifts from direct to indirect observation: that mode of observation wherein the observer does not actually perceive given social phenomena but rather depends upon persons who have directly observed or experienced these to reconstruct them for him.

Indirect observation is perhaps the most popular data-gathering procedure in contemporary sociology, if not in all of social science. The prime reason is the impossibility of researchers' observing directly certain kinds of behavior. For example, various socially sensitive spheres are regarded as off limits to sociologists. Indirect modes of observation, through the procurement of data from persons who do have access to these areas, are well-nigh indispensable here. In addition large-scale, highly complex systems can often be surveyed only through the eyes of members of the system who are functioning at the various levels therein. To carry out direct observation of the various subsystems within New York City or Chicago would perhaps require more sociologists than are currently available in the total society.

The social scientist is not alone in his reliance upon indirect observation for much of his data collection. Most persons in a society continually engage in questioning others, in collating data on their fellow man, so as to understand and predict the latter's actions. In the United States one who must interact with a stranger attempts to structure the new relationship according to information dredged up via such queries as: Where are you from? What do you do for a living? Are you married? Indeed, in the modern complex society a person depends upon this data-gathering procedure for his very survival.

Data Gathering by Lay Observers

Here, as in the previous chapter, we distinguish between information gathered by scientists and that collected by nonscientists. Although almost everyone in a society consciously or unconsciously absorbs data via indirect observation, we are, at this juncture, primarily concerned with those lay observers who purposively amass information on particular topics and write up their findings in ways that make their observations useful to scientists.

The materials lay observers collect via indirect observation vary widely. They include data gleaned on a more or less individual basis by newsmen, freelance writers, and by professional persons such as physicians who are not usually considered to be social scientists.

Newsmen are especially vital as observers in modern society. Without them, we would have much less information on the Hungarian Revolution, the Bay of Pigs invasion of Castro's Cuba,[1] and so on. Although ideally newsmen directly observe events as they occur, much significant news reporting has in fact been based upon indirect observation.

Quite in contrast to these individualized approaches are the highly formalized data-collecting techniques of bureaucracies. During much of recorded history, bureaucracies have been the prime data-gathering organizations;[2] however, it was the Industrial Revolution that led to the full flowering of this function. Today in industrial-urban orders almost every major bureaucratic apparatus amasses vast quantities of data, mainly through forms filled out by their employees and their clientele. The abundance of red tape that plagues even social scientists actually provides the latter with masses of useful data.

The data collected by bureaucracies are deemed essential for purposes of social control and for social planning, whether by the bureaucracies themselves or by elements of the broader society. In the United States, business corporations must collect an abundance of detailed information to satisfy the requirements of the Bureau of Internal Revenue and the Bureau of the Census. So it is with other bureaucracies. The federal government, of course, outdistances all other organizations in the amount of data it amasses as it collects taxes, dispenses welfare benefits, sustains the armed forces, or takes censuses.[3] Increasingly, however,

---

[1] See, e.g., Tad Szulc and Karl E. Meyer, *The Cuban Invasion: The Chronicle of a Disaster* (New York: Ballantine, 1962). This work on the ill-fated invasion of Cuba supported by the United States government relies to a large extent upon indirect observation.

[2] Various types of data were collected by preindustrial bureaucracies. In China, for example, data collection on the populace began centuries ago. See, e.g., Ping-ti Ho, *Studies on the Population of China, 1368–1953* (Cambridge, Mass.: Harvard, 1959). England had the Domesday Book of William I, compiled in 1086 on the basis of returns submitted at the King's request. Then too, such an organization as the Catholic Church amassed a great deal of information on the New World as its functionaries sent back detailed reports to Europe.

[3] Alvin Shuster, "Statistical State of the Union," *New York Times Magazine,* Nov. 16, 1958, 54 f. At the time this article was written there were "no fewer than 4,610 different kinds of questionnaires and report forms approved for use by some fifty Federal agencies" (65).

social scientists are supervising these data-collecting activities on the part of bureaucracies, with the result that the distinction between the lay observer and the social scientist is becoming blurred.

Social scientists can certainly profit from more adequate knowledge of the kinds of data bureaucracies collect as well as the means by which these are collected.[4] Many of the materials of interest to bureaucratic agencies are ignored by social researchers, frequently because the findings are never formally published.[5] The problem is a pressing one not only in industrial social orders but also in underdeveloped or modernizing societies. The observations of the economist Paauw are pertinent here.

> Whether or not the pace of effective empirical research can be stepped up until underdeveloped countries can supply more and better statistics is a valid question.
>
> In part, however, the problem may be one of the investigator's own making. Economists seem to be less disposed than other social scientists to collect and use data which does not already have the stamp (usually in the form of publication) of some respectable agency. There are some underdeveloped countries, if not many, where statistical reporting outpaces aggregation and publication. The data bottleneck, in other words, may in some instances lie in the shortage of competent personnel to compile and make available raw data which already exist in government files or other unobtrusive repositories. Indonesia is a case in point. . . . It is a rather amusing but depressing spectacle to see clerks solemnly file drawer after drawer with current statistical reports from outlying areas even though the accumulation is already so great that storage space has become a major problem.[6]

Data-collecting agencies in American society that tend to be overlooked by social scientists include the courts and the Congressional committees which collate specific data so as to facilitate the law-making process, and the courts which

---

[4] An important step has been taken in this direction by Harold L. Wilensky, *Organizational Intelligence* (New York: Basic Books, 1967).

[5] To be sure, Wilensky, *ibid.*, and others have emphasized the secrecy surrounding the data collected by bureaucracies. Even many governmental archives remain inaccessible to scholars for years after the actual occurrence of events. Herbert Feis, "The Shackled Historian," *Foreign Affairs, 45* (January, 1967), 332–343. The pattern of secrecy, moreover, varies from nation to nation. Cf. Feis's article with that of Krister Wahlbäck, "Sweden: Secrecy and Neutrality," *Journal of Contemporary History, 2* (January, 1967), 183–191.

[6] Douglas S. Paauw, "Some Frontiers of Empirical Research in Economic Development," *Economic Development and Cultural Change, 9* (January, 1961), 189–190.

amass data from litigating parties and witnesses as a guide to interpreting and preserving the laws. Significantly both kinds of agencies, backed as they are by police power, can secure information on large-scale power structures that are closed to the ordinary researcher. For example, the court case involving the price-fixing activities of executives of the General Electric Corporation laid bare information on the internal hierarchy, the communication patterns, and the ethical dilemmas in modern business bureaucracies that would otherwise be unavailable to sociologists.[7]

Not only can social scientists utilize the materials of nonscientists, they can also profit from investigating their data-gathering procedures.[8] A study of the manner in which newsmen collect information on large-scale organizations would be useful. Of major theoretical interest for the methodologist are the data-gathering *procedures* of such organizations as courts of law and governmental investigating committees. Certainly courts of law have faced many of the same problems that trouble social researchers. The chief difficulty the courts encounter is establishing the validity and reliability of the testimony of witnesses. In traditional preindustrial civilized societies "the truth" was often determined through magical practices, or via torture, or by the status of the accused. Today in British and American jurisprudence, courts of law check and cross-check witnesses' testimony according to prescribed "operational rules"; the judge and the jury become the final arbiters of what is "the truth."

Legal theorists have recognized that the validity and the reliability of the results vary (at least to a degree) with the procedures for obtaining and weighing evidence. Packer, for instance, has sought to examine the effectiveness of courtroom trials, Congressional investigations, and administrative hearings by gathering and evaluating the testimony made by ex-Communist witnesses in the late 1940s and early 1950s. Packer concluded that none of these organizational procedures was fully satisfactory.[9]

Consider Congressional committee hearings. Because their procedures were open-ended they could develop testimony into a coherent whole, and because

---

[7] See, e.g., Richard Austin Smith, "The Incredible Electrical Conspiracy," *Fortune, 63* (April, 1961), part 1, 132–137 f., and part 2, published in May, 1961, 161–164 f.

[8] Bear in mind that the data-collection procedures of formal organizations can be examined from two perspectives—one methodological, the other substantive. With respect to the latter, the data-collecting process casts light upon the nature of the social order itself. This becomes apparent if we compare the methods for determining public opinion in a totalitarian state such as Nazi Germany—see, e.g., Aryeh L. Unger, "The Public Opinion Reports of the Nazi Party," *Public Opinion Quarterly, 29* (Winter, 1965–1966), 565–582 —with those in a democratic order, where questionnaires and social surveys are common. Herein we are concerned with the methodological rather than the substantive dimensions.

[9] Herbert L. Packer, *Ex-Communist Witnesses* (Stanford, Cal.: Stanford, 1962), 227–231.

their procedures did not permit cross-examination through a battle between adversaries, witnesses were likely to speak relatively freely. However, these advantages were more than offset by certain crippling disadvantages, chief among which were the factors of politics and publicity attendant upon Congressional investigations. Moreover, the structure of the committees, with their often poor-quality staffs, intensified these difficulties.

Unlike Congressional committees, courts of law have the advantage of permitting some test of the credibility of witnesses. Yet the courts' heavy concentration on details, at least in the interrogation of ex-Communists, made it difficult to perceive the broad picture. Packer remarks, "The adversary process simply is not well adapted to the intelligible sequential ordering of complex factual data."[10] Other theorists have questioned the adversary procedure on the grounds that emotional appeals by lawyers may wring biased testimony from witnesses and clever cross-examination can confuse otherwise reliable witnesses.

Given the drawbacks in the procedures of Congressional committees or the law courts, the administrative inquiry has been proposed as an alternative. However, Packer stresses that administrative hearings generate problems of their own.[11] More broadly, some legal theorists have looked to the scientific method as one means of overcoming the deficiencies of the court system. Still, sociologists have much to learn from courts of law. Much could be gained from a cross-fertilization between the practices used by courts and administrative boards for establishing validity and the investigative procedures employed by social scientists.[12] The courts, after all, have for centuries been grappling with the general inability of witnesses to recall past events accurately, the tendency of some to purposively distort the facts, and the difficulties for judges and juries of adequately weighing this kind of testimony.

Although sociologists can profit from study of the data-collecting procedures of lay observers, the data themselves may have serious limitations. When scientists lack control over the actual observation process they are often unable, except through indirect means, to determine the reliability and validity of the findings. Particularly is this true today in many underdeveloped nations where administrative and field staffs of agencies have not yet internalized such ideals as the need for precision and accuracy.[13] Rational bureaucratic norms are one prerequisite

[10] *Ibid.,* 230.

[11] *Ibid.,* 230–231.

[12] Walter Firey and Ivan Belknap, "Social Operations for Standardizing the Imputation of Meaning," *Alpha Kappa Deltan, 30* (Spring, 1960), 18–24, have sought to cope with certain methodological problems in sociology, using the legal system as a point of departure for their analyses.

[13] See, e.g., Choh-Ming Li, *The Statistical System of Communist China* (Berkeley: University of California Press, 1962); and *Better Statistics in Korea* (Seoul, Korea: Surveys and Research Corporation, Statistical Advisory Group, 1960).

for amassing reliable information, and such norms are lacking in most developing societies.

Even in societies with rationally oriented bureaucracies, numerous difficulties arise in evaluating, for example, "official statistics." Jack Douglas, in a highly perceptive analysis of official suicide statistics which Durkheim and many American students of suicide have taken for granted, has come to grips with a fundamental problem. Douglas contends that the "operational definition" of what is a suicide (for example, should a suicide note exist before a person is classed as having committed suicide?) varies among societies and within them.[14] That is, bureaucratic officials define who commits suicide,[15] and they do so in different ways.

Douglas also believes that there are sound reasons for assuming that groups in a social order vary in both their efforts and their ability to conceal the existence of suicide among their members. Thus he suggests that these official suicide statistics may be biased in the direction of supporting, for instance, Durkheim's integration theory of suicide—that Durkheim's conclusions may be an artifact of the means by which the data were collected.[16]

Moreover, governmental agencies in advanced industrial orders are subject to political pressures calling for the inclusion or exclusion of questions on census, or other data-gathering, forms. Political pressures kept the question concerning religious affiliation out of the 1960 census in the United States. Shryock has demonstrated how various local communities in the United States aspired to the title of "standard metropolitan area" and have pressured the Bureau of the Census to accord them this classification—a status symbol.[17] On the other hand, the Census Bureau and other bureaucratic structures must struggle against forces that preserve particular data-collection procedures and classification schemes when these are no longer useful.

On a more general level, lay observers within all societies tend to focus upon specific, relatively culture-bound, or even organization-bound, problems: those of immediate concern to the general public, politicians, and bureaucrats.[18]

---

14 Jack D. Douglas, *The Social Meanings of Suicide* (Princeton, N.J.: Princeton, 1967), chap. 12.

15 The role of bureaucrats—examiners, court officials, and the like—in defining who is, for example, mentally ill is documented by Thomas J. Scheff, *Being Mentally Ill: A Sociological Theory* (Chicago: Aldine, 1966).

16 Douglas, *op. cit.*

17 Henry S. Shryock, Jr., "The Natural History of Standard Metropolitan Areas," *American Journal of Sociology, 63* (September, 1957), 163–170.

18 The struggle to initiate "uniformity" (in contrast to "flexibility") in financial accounting among organizations within a society is of considerable methodological import for social researchers. See the special issue on "Uniformity in Financial Accounting," *Law and Contemporary Problems, 30* (Autumn, 1965).

Pragmatic considerations loom large in determining the kinds of questions that are asked and the kinds of classification schemes that are employed. Governmental agencies, including census bureaus, generally collect data in terms of rather culture-bound categories. Consequently we need more crosscultural analysis of the relationships of bureaucratic structures and the validity and the reliability of data collected by lay observers.[19]

The Structured Interview

Having already drawn a distinction between the structured and the unstructured interview, we must now examine the functions of both in social research. The structured interview's prime function is standardization of the interviewing process by means of a questionnaire or schedule. Social scientists, particularly the logical empiricists, who are sensitive to the frequent charge that their techniques are lacking in rigor, commend this approach. Undeniably, it is in the data-collection process that the need for systematization and standardization is most imperative.

The structured interview is used primarily to verify existing theories and the hypotheses derived thereform. The scientist who employs this tool is usually intent upon testing an existing set of hypotheses; he is less concerned with discovery per se. And, of course, standardization greatly enhances reliability. Whether one investigator interviews ten respondents, or ten researchers each interview a dozen respondents, standardization of the interviewing procedures (including the methods of establishing rapport with respondents) is essential if all the answers are to be placed in the same hopper and treated as if of equal value.

The standardized interview also offers decided advantages in terms of efficiency: it affords savings in time, labor, and above all money. In theory at least the standardized interview helps to eliminate needless questions. Then too, the analysis can be formally built into the design of the questionnaire. And the more formalized the questions, the simpler the coding, computing, and tabulation processes.

These gains are functionally interrelated with the proliferation of large-scale research organizations in modern society. It is not just on the interviewing level but also on the level of collating and analyzing the data that these organiza-

---

[19] Of course, there have been efforts by international bodies to bring about some standardization in census categories. See, e.g., Population Division of the United Nations Department of Social Affairs and the Statistical Office of the United Nations Department of Economic Affairs, Population Studies, No. 9, *Application of International Standards to Census Data on the Economically Active Population* (New York: United Nations, 1951), *passim*.

tions seek to rationalize their internal operations. Without a high degree of standardization, there can be little cooperation among members of a research team.[20] Conversely, the project that emphasizes discovery calls for the lone researcher or at most small numbers of persons who can work intimately with one another and thus profit from any serendipitous findings that may emerge.

Yet, whatever the methodological and social advantages of the highly structured interview, it has certain drawbacks, not the least of which is the investigator's tendency to impose his own categories upon those of the informant. Thus social researchers often assume that when a person answers "Don't know" rather than simply "Yes" or "No," he is not neutral but actually leans more in one direction than in another. The respondent, it is argued, should be forced to make a choice. Some researchers go so far as to insist that questionnaires should be designed to uncover the interviewee's "true" feelings, motives, and values. Thus the questions should be those whose full significance is not likely to be understood by the respondent. Such thinking in fact underlies a number of measurement instruments employed by psychologists.

Most researchers who make this assumption believe that the informant's responses do not provide data about social reality per se, but rather serve as indexes to underlying patterns—to social phenomena that are not directly observable. In light of this belief, specific attitude questionnaires have been devised to uncover such latent attitude structures.

Other social scientists, however, take a dim view of the structured interview. To them, its strengths are inherently also weaknesses. They argue that the researcher cannot comprehend the complexities of social action or human motives merely by posing questions in a highly stylized, formal manner. Warner and Lunt remark concerning one aspect of this problem:

> The bias of the researcher is implicit within the framework and the detail of a questionnaire or schedule. The answers to the questionnaire are not answers to the questions asked but to what the subject thinks is being asked, and there is little or no opportunity for the fieldworker using such a technique to discover the difference. The same question or set of questions can elicit consistent misunderstandings which may indicate fictitious uniformities or differences.[21]

Although the opponents of the structured interview are by no means of one mind, they tend to perceive the standardized interview as oversimplifying or

[20] The need for formalization and standardization of research institutes has been noted by Peter H. Rossi, "Researchers, Scholars and Policy Makers: The Politics of Large Scale Research," *Daedalus, 93* (Fall, 1964), 1150–1151.

[21] W. Lloyd Warner and Paul S. Lunt, *The Social Life of a Modern Community* (New Haven: Yale, 1941), 56.

overstructuring reality: as imposing a spurious kind of order on the actor's "world of meaning."[22] Further, these scientists contend that to establish the reliability and validity of the informant's responses, researchers must employ depth interviewing, at times in an elliptical manner, in order to ferret out patterns of thought and action concerning which the interviewee may be especially sensitive or about which he lacks a conscious awareness until the scientist dredges them up. Many persons' actions and thought patterns, conscious or unconscious, evince internal contradictions. To understand, the researcher must be sensitive to the cues the informant may drop and able to turn them into meaningful questions. Because of these social patterns, many researchers advocate the use of the unstructured interview despite certain weaknesses which the structured interview is supposed to overcome.

Added to these more theoretical concerns are certain pragmatic problems the structured interview presents. Although this kind of procedure can reduce the time spent in interviewing, it creates practical difficulties of another sort. If, as commonly happens, the interviewee takes exception to the manner in which the questions are posed, the interviewer must either try to pass it off or else hastily revise his carefully planned procedure. A more informal approach, on the other hand, allows the interviewer greater flexibility in phrasing and rephrasing his queries; he can watch the informant's reactions—his hesitancy, irritation, or whatever—and word his questions accordingly. Informal or unstructured interviewing thus permits the researcher to approach the question-and-answer session much as one would an ordinary conversation.

Given the differing advantages and disadvantages of the structured and unstructured interviewing techniques, some researchers have sought to combine the two approaches. Each is best suited to different kinds of research, and each rests upon somewhat different assumptions concerning the nature of social reality as well as the best means of understanding the latter. The structured interview is more applicable to large-scale surveys and to the formal testing of hypotheses, whereas the unstructured type is most useful for studying the normative structure of organizations, for establishing classes, and for discovering the existence of possible social patterns (rather than the formal testing of propositions concerning the existence of given patterns).

Competent social researchers early become aware of the need for devising satisfactory questionnaires or schedules—the very basis of the structured interview. But they often overlook the fact that in addition to the ever-present ethical and political factors which cannot be ignored,[23] the researcher's own methodological

---

[22] Cf. Aaron V. Cicourel, *Method and Measurement in Sociology* (New York: Free Press, 1964), chap. 4.

[23] Certain questions may be excluded on the grounds that they represent an undue invasion of privacy, because they are politically sensitive, or for a number of other reasons.

and theoretical commitments structure the manner in which he designs his questionnaire. As indicated above, the social scientist who values the formal testing of hypotheses more than he does discovery is apt to devise rather rigid categories for his questions, to precode the latter, and to design dummy tables, all in the course of developing the questionnaire. Typically he then proceeds to collect the materials, summarizes them according to some prearranged plan, fits the data into the tables, and carries out the predetermined statistical analysis.

Furthermore, as Coombs has stressed, there is a close relationship between the scientist's measuring instrument and the particular way he words his questions.[24] That is, the specific kind of analysis one proposes to pursue (whether one utilizes, for example, a Bogardus-, Guttman-, or Thurstone-type of scale) will not only determine the nature of the queries but will strongly affect their phrasing as well. And each measuring instrument has various built-in theoretical and methodological assumptions.

Osgood's semantic differential illustrates the impact upon questionnaire construction of one's particular instrument, methodological orientation, and/or theoretical commitment.[25] Oversimplifying for purposes of exposition, we observe that Osgood's instrument involves constructing a multidimensional scale around certain concepts: for example, "mother," "father," "Texas." The instrument consists of a number of "polarized concepts," with the members of each pair standing at opposite extremes of a seven-point scale. The respondent's reaction

---

A Staff Study for the Research and Technical Programs Subcommittee of the Committee on Government Operations, *The Use of Social Research in Federal Domestic Programs,* Part 4 (Washington, D.C.: GPO, 1967). See, for instance, the discussion of the Budget Bureau's clearance of questionnaires, sec. E. Also, sec. D on the problem of privacy and questionnaires. The politics and ethics of questionnaire construction are encapsulated in the following quotation drawn from the comments of the Project Officer from the Office of Education to the Principal Investigator:

In conclusion, I told Prof. _____ (As I always tell all others) that we are extremely reluctant to require deletion or modification of any items; & that we do so only when it seems essential. Our function as we see it, is to protect research & OE against public attack—as well as against erosion of financial resources. We are working *with* and *for* our Principal Investigators: what could be more foolish than for us to do otherwise? But research supported by Federal funds is conducted in a public milieu, and by the grace of Congress. Purely scientific considerations, untempered by attention to mores and public sensitivities, cannot be allowed to exercise exclusive sway. I venture to boast as rigorous a scientific background, and as much appreciation of scientific considerations, as anyone; but ethics, and mores, and Congress—not to mention the *U.S. News & World Report!*—also require consideration. That's the kind of world it is (214).

[24] Clyde H. Coombs, "Theory and Methods of Social Measurement," in Leon Festinger and Daniel Katz (eds.), *Research Methods in the Behavioral Sciences* (New York: Holt, Rinehart and Winston, 1953), chap. 11.

[25] Charles E. Osgood *et al., The Measurement of Meaning* (Urbana, Ill.: University of Illinois Press, 1957).

to "mother," or "father," and the like is then gauged in terms of some point along each scale. For instance, we might construct a series of scales—for example, a seven-point scale along the "happy" and "sad" dimension—to measure the respondent's reactions to, say, "father."

happy —— : —— : —— : —— : —— : —— : ——sad

hard —— : —— : —— : —— : —— : —— : —— soft

slow —— : —— : —— : —— : —— : —— : ——fast

Here the instrument is associated with a particular type of question. Moreover, a number of assumptions (not always made explicit by Osgood) underlie the application of this instrument. One is that through this indirect approach the researcher is best able to capture a person's "basic,"or "true," attitudes toward his father, or mother, or whatever. For in this instance the respondent is reacting to an instrument the implications of which are beyond his grasp. Consequently, the respondent reveals his true attitudes and values, which normally would elude the researcher employing a more direct approach. In other words, Osgood seems to assume that underneath the confused surface of human actions lie certain stable attitudes and values.[26]

More broadly, the researcher's logical-theoretical constructs delimit, if indeed they do not actually determine, the kinds of questions he will ask. The objectification of one's own theoretical scheme is therefore a necessary condition for the construction of the appropriate kinds of questions.

Thus, the student of social stratification who assumes, for example, that social reality is understandable only from the actor's subjective perspective will pose a different set of questions than one who espouses a more materialistic, objective view of social phenomena. In the former instance the interviewee is asked to place himself, in one way or another, within one of several classes, whereas in the latter the researcher inquires about the respondent's income, education, and so on, and then from these infers the person's social class position.

Pursuing this reasoning a step further, we encounter still other complications. Researchers with a subjective view of reality (and of social class in particular) may, depending upon other assumptions they make, design their questionnaires differently. One could, as did Centers, utilize a set of prearranged class categories into which, it is assumed, the informant can correctly place himself.[27] On the other hand, this strikes some researchers as "overstructuring"; they prefer to have the informant place himself in a class category of his own making. In

[26] *Ibid.,* chap. 5.

[27] Richard Centers, *The Psychology of Social Classes* (Princeton, N.J.: Princeton, 1949).

any event, the scientist's theoretical constructs do much to determine not only the kinds of questions that are asked but also the way they are phrased; and they even shape the investigator's conclusions concerning his own findings.[28]

Implicit in the foregoing discussion is the premise that close familiarity with the subject matter under study is vital. Researchers cannot effectively design questionnaires without making full use of prior research, including the failures and successes of previous questionnaires. Where no such groundwork exists, intensive interviews, usually of a highly unstructured sort, are essential for indicating the range of issues one is likely to encounter. Or the researcher may utilize case studies to establish the limits of the class of data he is investigating.

But the researcher must do more than objectify his own theory and methodology and examine the implications of already completed research. As question maker he must, like Mead's actor, "take the role of the other" if he is to gain valid information from respondents. Even the "materialist" must adopt a subjective orientation when he engages in data collection. For the more one knows about one's potential informant—his values and the social structure within which he functions—the easier it is to devise meaningful questions. Sensitive issues in particular demand a rather full understanding of the actor's world of meaning. Only through this means can one be certain of what can be investigated with impunity and the best way to go about it. Of course, if one is to gauge correctly the degree of potential resistance and sensitivity to questioning on part of the interviewee, one must consider not only the informant's values and normative structure but also how these relate to the sponsoring agency, the orientation of interviewers in the field, and the investigator's own ethical commitments.

If, to elicit reliable and valid responses, the researcher must seek to understand the respondent's symbolic environment, it follows that the more homogeneous the working universe with respect to culture (including language) the simpler it is for the scientist to develop adequate questions. For here he need cope with only a limited number of symbols and concepts. On the other hand, in many underdeveloped countries today, where heterogeneity along class, ethnic, and linguistic lines is still marked, it may prove vastly more difficult to construct questionnaires that are equally applicable to all subgroups in question. Nor does this heterogeneity evanesce with industrialization. True, industrialization generally leads to increased homogeneity along, say, class, ethnic, and linguistic dimensions, but it also gives impetus to certain kinds of heterogeneity that stem from an increasingly complex division of labor. In any case, highly formalized questionnaires can be most effectively employed where interviewees exhibit a high degree of social and cultural uniformity.

At this point the question can be posed: Are there any norms to guide the

---

[28] See the discussion by Richard T. Morris, "Social Stratification," in Leonard Broom and Philip Selznick, *Sociology*, 3rd ed. (New York: Harper & Row, 1963), esp. 194–196.

researcher in selecting and phrasing his questions? Yes. But they must be phrased in rather abstract terms, and then they are generally not invariant. For every norm may on occasion be broken for various theoretical or practical reasons. This situation results in part from the differences among values and norms within and across sociocultural systems. As a result of this diversity, similar questions may evoke quite dissimilar responses. The indefiniteness of the norms regarding question phrasing also stems from the variety of methodological procedures social scientists employ, for, as we observed above, different measurement instruments call for different kinds of questions. Not surprisingly, then, questionnaire construction remains, in Payne's terms, largely an *art*.[29] Ultimately, however, the pragmatic test for the wording of questions must be applied: If a question elicits reliable and valid data, it must be considered satisfactorily phrased.

One assumption is universally accepted: The wording of questions is vital. The more structured the questionnaire the greater the need for precision in wording, for the interviewer has little freedom to clarify perplexing points for the interviewee.

The following are *some* of the norms that are most widely adhered to as the researcher selects and words his questions. First, one must not assume too much knowledge on the part of the respondent. Public opinion pollsters have learned that in the realm of current events, even in highly literate societies, the average person's ignorance (from the standpoint of the needs of the researcher) can be abysmal. The situation is worsened when one deals with persons having little formal education or little interest in the matters in question. Consequently, questions not only should be phrased in terms of the knowledge level of the interviewee but should have built-in face-saving devices to protect his ego. For instance, questions may be introduced by the phrase: "Do you happen to know . . . ?" or "You may not be familiar with this issue, but . . ." Actually, in order to evaluate the final results of one's opinion or attitude survey, it is essential to include questions especially designed to elicit information on the informant's education or "level of knowledge."

Second, the well-worded question employs a simple, straightforward vocabulary and style. The more complex and ambiguous the terminology and phraseology, the less reliable are the responses. Not only may informants misinterpret the question, but different interviewers, particularly in large-scale surveys, are likely to interpret the questions in varying ways, with consequent loss of reliability.

However, framing simple and unambiguous questions is far more difficult than the uninitiated might suppose. Even slight cultural differences among the subgroups within one's working universe can greatly intensify the problem. Simple words even in American society may take on varied pronunciations or

[29] Stanley L. Payne, *The Art of Asking Questions* (Princeton, N.J.: Princeton, 1951).

meanings in different regions. For example, "suite," as in "dining-room suite," is pronounced one way in the North and another way in much of the South. Indeed, even college students in the South may not recognize the term unless it is pronounced like "suit."

A third norm is: avoid emotionally tinged words. And these are many, notably in the realm of politics. "Conservative," "liberal," and "Socialist," for example, are labels that evoke strong feelings in many persons.

A fourth rule is that questions should be phrased so as to sustain the interviewee's interest. Apparently in some situations persons find it more interesting to rank occupations according to one procedure rather than another.[30] And one of the difficulties one would encounter in using the semantic differential is maintaining the respondents' interest.[31] Questions have been posed in a manner that most respondents cannot really comprehend, and this reduces their motivation to complete the questionnaire.

As for the order of questions, a widely accepted norm, or rule of thumb, is that sensitive questions should be placed in the middle or toward the end of questionnaires, to be raised only after some rapport has been established. Yet, a particular question's position in the series tends to affect the answers to other questions by introducing into the informant's stream of consciousness a certain range of associations. In the end much depends upon what the researcher is looking for and whether he is willing to sacrifice a degree of rapport in order to gain certain kinds of data. Such choices do in fact characterize the total question-making process. The researcher must balance off a variety of contradictory goals and requirements and thus seek a minimax solution.

More controversial are certain other norms. Some researchers believe that at least some questions should be drawn directly from other studies in order to provide one with an adequate base line for comparative analysis. For example, if a researcher studied political attitudes in France he could include questions from similar surveys in England, Japan, the United States, and other countries with which the patterns in France could be compared. To the extent that he strives to improve upon the questions that have been employed in other investigations, he loses a degree of comparability. Yet revisions may be essential to adjust the question to a new sociocultural situation.

Another norm concerns the utility of "why" questions.[32] Earlier we noted

[30] Cf. Kaare Svalastoga, *Prestige, Class and Mobility* (Copenhagen: Gylendal, 1959), 47.

[31] Osgood *et al., op. cit.,* seem to be vaguely aware of this problem. Speaking of the desirability of securing a cross-section of the general population, they write: "It is also hard to use subjects of this sort . . . and get across instructions for what seems superficially to be a trivial and repetitious task" (32).

[32] Paul F. Lazarsfeld has sought to close the gap between the open-ended interview (with, for example, the "why" question) and the more structured approach, in his "The

that some researchers doubt the reliability and validity of answers to such questions, for the interviewee may fail to mention some of the obvious reasons for his replies. He may take these for granted, so that they can be elicited only through structured questions that include the range of possible answers. That is, the question "Why?" assumes, often falsely, that the respondent will utilize the necessary set of categories when framing his reply.

Even so, the answers to "why" questions may serve as a crosscheck upon the adequacy of the categories employed in a questionnaire. Consider the sociologist who asks interviewees to place themselves in one of the following social classes: upper_____middle_____lower_____. If various subgroups differ as to the reasons for their self-placement or if some subgroups of respondents are more consistent than others in their answers to the "why" question, then we must at least exercise caution in evaluating the findings. Just because persons place themselves, say, in the lower class does not mean they necessarily define themselves in a similar fashion, for this category may have widely different meanings to the actors involved.

Of special theoretical import are the investigator's efforts to check upon the respondent's veracity and memory.[33] Some researchers purposively duplicate certain questions, presenting them in another guise: They may be phrased differently and/or set within a different context in some other part of the questionnaire. Here the assumption is that the degree of consistency in the informant's responses is a valid index to his honesty or to his accuracy of recall. But such a premise can be challenged. After all, the context within which a question is asked can shape the informant's response. Many persons in industrial-urban societies occupy multiple statuses and play multiple roles. To adjust to the divergent social pressures, they may compartmentalize their thought ways to such an extent that they are able to think and act in a variety of ways, depending upon the social situation. Thus a given question may invoke norms associated with one status and role, whereas a change in the context or phraseology of the question may suggest to the respondent quite another status and role, and thus prompt him to provide a different set of answers. And the respondent may not even be aware of the discrepancies in his replies.

The "consistency test" for determining "truth" is particularly of doubtful value in a complex industrial-urban order, wherein actors carry out many differing

---

Controversy over Detailed Interviews—An Offer for Negotiation," *Public Opinion Quarterly, 8* (Spring, 1944), 38–60. Yet the controversy persists because those who advocate open-ended questions and those who support the structured approach frequently hold different assumptions about social reality or, specifically, the motives and actions of persons in a system.

[33] For an informative—albeit divergent—interpretation of "faking" or "deception" in responses to tests, see Joseph Lyons, *Psychology and the Measure of Man: A Phenomenological Approach* (New York: Free Press, 1963), 226–239.

roles. Indeed, the more honest the individual attempts to be, the more he may have to respond to questions in a contradictory and inconsistent fashion. Only some kind of depth interviewing can come to grips with this problem.

The quality of an informant's memory is even more difficult to assess via formalized questionnaires. It has been amply demonstrated within courtrooms that the average person's memory can play tricks on him even when he is consciously seeking to tell the truth. His relationship to an event, particularly the degree of his involvement, can affect not only his perception of it but his retentive capacities as well. The latter are influenced also by the individual's social background, including his formal education, and the kind of social role (or roles) he plays. More generally, memory is a function of what the society deems significant and worthy of recall.

A related issue concerns the tendency of many interviewees to frame their answers in terms of ideal norms. The researcher may unwittingly phrase questions so that the respondent will answer the way he thinks he is supposed to. Thus for an opinion survey of graduate students' views concerning their professors, one could purposively devise a set of questions that would elicit such stereotypic answers as "Profs are essentially good guys, conscientious and scholarly, but absent-minded and a bit odd." Or, the question, "Are professors fair and honest?" would tend to yield affirmative replies. On the other hand, by phrasing questions so as to imply deviations from the ideal in concrete circumstances— for example, "Do you know of professors who treat graduate students unfairly? If yes, please specify." —the researcher may be able to bypass the ideal norms and acquire data that are closer reflections of reality.

Interviewer and Interviewee in the Structured Interview

The interview, we must remember, involves a complex set of interactions between persons who occupy particular statuses in the social order. Consequently, the reliability and validity of the data obtained depend not merely upon the merits of the questionnaire but also upon the degree of rapport, or trust, that develops in the interaction situation. Thus, if we are to understand the structured interview, we must analyze the status and roles of the principal parties concerned.

THE INTERVIEWER

Achievement of the goal of standardization presupposes the proper selection and training of interviewers. No simple task in the highly industrial urbanized order, it is a far more demanding one in still largely preindustrial societies, where the values that underlie the scientific method, the need for accuracy, objectivity, and the like, have so far made little impress. The kinds of obstacles social scientists encounter in their attempts to train field workers in nonindustrial orders derive mainly from the populace's (and even the educated elite's) unfamiliarity with, and lack of confidence in, the goals and methods of modern science. These facts, as we reiterate below, also affect the interviewee's capacity to provide the kinds of data social scientists want.

Even in the industrial-urban context, field workers require special training. Here too they must be indoctrinated into the norms of science, particularly those calling for accuracy and objectivity. The researcher who hires a large field staff must constantly guard against cheating, conscious or unconscious, and lack of attention to details. Untrained students carrying out field work for social scientists have in certain instances been known to fill out questionnaires themselves to avoid the bother of interviewing.

Perhaps the most effective means of overcoming these difficulties is to provide the interviewer with a clear understanding of the project's objectives. If the possible contributions of the project to science and to humanity are stressed, the interviewer can more readily be made to see why accuracy and detailed reporting are so essential. After all, job satisfaction involves more than functioning as a mere technician; it means being able to perceive the broader purpose of one's actions.

Efforts have been made to construct measurement devices to ferret out potentially skilled interviewers for large-scale surveys, but the results have not been fully satisfactory. For what constitutes skilled interviewing involves a variety of dimensions. Concerning his experiences in obtaining interviewers for a study of fertility patterns in Lebanon, Yaukey observed: "We are not prepared to give specific advice on the characteristics of good interviewers. Any generalization we might make would be contradicted by our own experience."[34]

This kind of view is unduly pessimistic. For certain general principles seem to emerge from the experiences of researchers, and these are reinforced by sociological theory.[35] One of the most important is that the most effective interviewers are those who have themselves played a variety of roles and have been exposed to a wide range of social experiences and are thus accustomed to tolerating and associating with persons holding quite divergent values and beliefs. Because of the need for individuals with diverse social experiences, capable interviewers are likely to differ considerably from one another in their personality characteristics. If our argument is correct, it explains why it is so difficult to design a unidimensional scale for determining which persons will make good interviewers. Also, it seems doubtful that good interviewers can be developed in only

[34] David Yaukey, *Fertility Differences in a Modernizing Country* (Princeton, N.J.: Princeton, 1961), 100.

[35] Compare the observations of Kurt W. Back and J. Mayone Stycos, *The Survey Under Unusual Conditions: Methodological Facets of the Jamaica Human Fertility Investigation,* Monograph No. 1 (Ithaca, N.Y.: Society for Applied Anthropology, 1959).

one or two courses on research methods. However, formal training can give focus to, and raise to the level of consciousness, certain latent abilities in individuals that are pertinent to effective interviewing.

Also crucial to the development of satisfactory interviewers is the individual's status and role in the social system and his commitment to the scientific method and the social order he is studying.

Although we lack data on many facets of these problems, we do know that the status and role of the scientist-interviewer varies among sociocultural systems and among subsystems of the latter. Hyman has examined the interviewer-respondent relationship at length.[36] But his focus appears to have been too narrow. He was concerned primarily with survey research and thus did not consider the kind of interview that is conducted for purposes of analyzing the structure of large-scale organizations. Moreover, he generally ignored the impact of social power considerations, in part because his work lacked a sound sociocultural orientation.[37]

It is clear that the status of the investigator is a significant variable affecting the quality of data that a respondent will provide. More generally, we advance the proposition that the potential impact of the interviewer on the interviewee, judged by the reliability and validity of the data collected, is greater in highly stratified social systems than in more loosely organized or relatively homogeneous ones.

The researcher's status and role in developing nations provides us with a valuable perspective for examining this proposition. In these societies there are persons, notably politicians, who are prepared to be interviewed at length by scholars from industrial orders.[38] Often they regard foreign scholars as more objective than local ones, and they recognize that the former's writings are likely to exert greater influence at home and abroad than the publications of their countrymen. Some politicians, therefore, view the foreign scholar as a means for advancing their own ends.[39]

The reverse is just as true: Potential informants will shy away from foreign scholars who seem to constitute a threat to their position or that of their nation.

---

[36] Herbert H. Hyman, *Interviewing in Social Research* (Chicago: University of Chicago Press, 1954).

[37] *Ibid.*

[38] Myron Weiner, "Political Interviewing," in Robert E. Ward *et al., Studying Politics Abroad* (Boston: Little, Brown, 1964), 123.

[39] *Ibid.* This problem also plagues American newsmen. Certain groups at home and abroad may protest the fact that a particular newsman has obtained and published material on a particular person or social movement—thereby legitimizing that person or movement. Recall the fate of Herbert Matthews' coverage of the Cuban Revolution. See, e.g., his *The Cuban Story* (New York: George Braziller, 1961). The charges against Matthews were not without some basis, for the diffusion of information has social consequences.

The controversy surrounding Project Camelot can be understood to a degree within this context.[40] One of the objections of American social scientists to this project—aside from the broader ethical and political dimensions—was that American social researchers working abroad might come to be identified as agents of the U.S. military or intelligence establishment, and this would result in adverse consequences for their research.[41]

The point is that when the status of the interviewer threatens the respondent, the validity of the latter's responses (if indeed these can be acquired at all) is open to question. In some developing nations the social researcher may be mistaken for a tax collector or other government agent and thus will be avoided.[42] This is hardly surprising, for the vast majority of persons in modernizing societies have no conception of the researcher's status and role. Yet, to the extent that interviewers are identified with officials of the government or other unwelcome outsiders, some kinds of information will be withheld. Secrecy traditionally has been a defense mechanism for the disadvantaged in their dealings with the power structure, particularly in an authoritarian state.

The impact of status relationships on the validity of interview data can be documented in somewhat more precise ways. In the Sudan, social researchers conducting a postenumeration survey on the census placed sole reliance upon female enumerators in order to counteract a suspected bias in the census data obtained by male interviewers who were not permitted to interview women, especially in Muslim households.[43] In a traditional Muslim social order, the typical housewife cannot be approached by a strange man.[44]

---

[40] For a good summary of this project, which had as one of its goals the collection of data that might be used to dampen revolutionary fervor in Latin America, see Irving Louis Horowitz, "The Life and Death of Project Camelot," *Trans-action, 3* (November–December, 1965), 3–7. Also Irving Louis Horowitz (ed.), *The Rise and Fall of Project Camelot* (Cambridge, Mass.: M.I.T., 1967).

[41] See, e.g., Munro S. Edmonson, David Felix, Daniel Goldrich, Joseph A. Kahl, and Henry A. Landsberger, "Letter to the Editor," *American Sociologist, 1* (August, 1966), 207–208.

[42] See, e.g., G. M. Culwick, "Some Problems of Social Survey in the Sudan," *Sudan Notes and Records, 35* (1954), 112, 114–115; Back and Stycos, *op. cit.;* J. E. Goldthorpe, "Attitudes to the Census and Vital Registration in East Africa," *Population Studies, 6* (November, 1952), 163–171; S. M. Hafeez Zaidi, "Social Research in Semi-literate Rural Society," in M. A. Salam Ansari (ed.), *Social Research in National Development* (Peshawar, Pakistan: Pakistan Academy for Rural Development, 1963), 144–151.

[43] Roushdi A. Henin, *First Population Census of Sudan 1955/56,* vol. 1 (Khartoum: Department of Statistics, Republic of the Sudan, 1960), 200.

[44] Frey confirms the fact that status is a crucial factor in the interviewer-interviewee relationship when he observes that in Turkey only women could interview women. Frederick W. Frey, "Surveying Peasant Attitudes in Turkey," *Public Opinion Quarterly, 27* (Fall, 1963), 349.

But status factors affect the course of research in advanced industrial orders as well. It is when status and power considerations loom large that the interviewer seems to experience some of his greatest difficulties in securing reliable and valid responses. This has been indicated, for example, in a study of the results of interviews of Negroes by whites.[45] Moreover, social scientists encounter problems in interviewing members of large-scale organizations,[46] particularly when the information being sought may expose the inner workings of the organization to public scrutiny.

Ethical and political factors also come to the fore when the status of the interviewer gives him possible control over the life chances of the respondent. The situation becomes acute if the researcher uses his links with the administrative hierarchy of an organization to collect from members of the system data which could be used against the respondent or which might at the very least be construed as an invasion of privacy.

Clearly we need more information about the impact of status and power considerations on the process of indirect observation, particularly on the way in which the professionalization of the scientist's role and his integration into the bureaucratic system in advanced industrial orders structure the collection of data from low-status individuals.

THE INTERVIEWEE

So vital for social research is the public's favorable conception of the interviewer that underdeveloped countries, and even industrial ones, engaging in nation-wide surveys such as census taking, expend much time and effort in educating the populace concerning the desirability (nay, the duty) of cooperating with the social researcher. For the degree of cooperation on the part of the informant is associated with prior knowledge and a favorable image of the status and role of the interviewer.

The status and role of the interviewer, however, more than that of the interviewer, varies among sociocultural systems and among subgroups within the latter. We find that the responses of interviewees are influenced in no small degree by the cultural definition of what can be discussed frankly and what should be avoided. Lerner, on the basis of his experience in France and the United States, concluded that Frenchmen tend to resist interviews more than Americans.[47] On the other hand, Bracey, drawing upon his experiences in urban-fringe neigh-

---

[45] J. Allen Williams, "Interviewer-Respondent Interaction: A Study of Bias in the Information Interview," *Sociometry*, 27 (September, 1964), 338–352.

[46] The efforts to avoid formal identification with the power structure of the prison and to sustain "objective neutrality" with respect to inmates, and thus to facilitate interviewing, have been noted in Rose Giallombardo, *Society of Women* (New York: Wiley, 1966), appendix A.

[47] Daniel Lerner, "Interviewing Frenchmen," *American Journal of Sociology*, 62 (September, 1956), 187–194.

borhoods in Bristol, England, and Columbus, Ohio, contends, "We found that most English householders are quite ready to talk about themselves and their neighbours—in fact, many appeared to gain some satisfaction in doing so. By contrast, American respondents were not especially forthcoming about themselves and showed a certain reluctance in talking about their neighbours."[48] It is unlikely that we can conclude that Englishmen are more open than Frenchmen. But these kinds of studies do raise a number of questions that require careful exploration. Undoubtedly the sociocultural setting of the interviewee affects the kinds of response categories that can effectively be employed.[49] The ability of the informant to express his opinions and the nature of his knowledge are products of his status and of his cultural values and belief system.

The subtle effect of cultural values upon the validity of response categories has been raised, at least indirectly, by Untereiner in his study of Puebloans and Homesteaders in New Mexico.[50] His data at least suggest some difference in the ability of persons in divergent cultures to rank order their preferences. We might expect that all cultures would force their members to engage in some rank ordering, but the Puebloans, more so than the Homesteaders, tend to place their preferences along a horizontal continuum rather than in any well-defined rank order. The implications of this phenomenon for the kinds of questions subjects are able to answer, and for instruments such as Guttman's scalogram, have not been explored by methodologists.

A striking instance of the effect of cultural values as well as status differentials upon interviewing can be observed in preindustrial orders, where, typically, many persons lack, or are unable or afraid to express, any individual opinion on a wide range of topics. Opinion-type questions may be of little utility under these circumstances. For example, the Rudolphs, on the basis of their research in India, conclude:

> The flaws in the assumption that most people hold opinions on a broad range of issues and are capable of articulating them became apparent as soon as field work began. To have an "opinion," for the purposes of the public opinion survey, is to be capable of articulating it. But articulation involves at least some degree of self-consciousness, sufficient to see that the dictates of custom are not the only source of beliefs and attitudes. Even if he clings to his customs and tradition, the person who has developed some self-awareness realizes, however dimly, that

[48] H. E. Bracey, *Neighbours* (Baton Rouge, La.: Louisiana State University Press, 1964), 1.

[49] See, e.g., Ezra Vogel, *Japan's New Middle Class* (Berkeley: University of California Press, 1963), 273–275.

[50] Wayne W. Untereiner, "Self and Society: Orientations in Two Cultural Value Systems," unpublished Ph.D. dissertation, Harvard University, 1952.

other ways of seeing the world exist. Only when this perception of alternatives arises does the individual appreciate that his views are in some sense peculiar to himself, that he *has* opinions.[51]

The authors go on to elaborate the often overlooked point that if the interviewer in a preindustrial order asks an illiterate his opinion on political matters, the latter is apt to refer him to a village elder or some other higher status person. If the informant is a married woman, she will probably say, "Ask my husband!"[52] A woman's husband is expected to think for her and speak for her on questions relating to matters outside the home.

Many persons in underdeveloped countries may find it difficult to answer even simple factual questions. Here is an instance where cooperation on the part of the interviewee is not enough. The lower-class person, long defined by those in positions of authority as ignorant, has accepted (at least in part) this definition of him. He is therefore indifferent and apathetic concerning many matters. Also, many uneducated and economically disadvantaged persons, especially in preindustrial orders, have little reason to absorb and remember the kinds of details that interest most social scientists, who usually reflect the concerns of industrial-urban societies. Thus, knowledge of one's date of birth, of certain kinds of economic data, even one's income or amount of property, tends to be blurred. The following remarks drawn from a census of the Philippines bear directly upon the issues at hand.

> Some people could not give their exact ages. Others gave vague answers to questions on employment. Due to lack of records, many heads of families could not give the exact areas of their agricultural, commercial, and residential lots. Some people believed that the census data were to be used for taxation purposes, and therefore, as a means of uncovering tax evaders. Other people had to depend solely upon their poor memory for the answers to some questions.[53]

These views are supported by Neale's observations regarding survey data from Indian villages:

> The shortcomings of Indian survey data are largely beyond the control of those who conduct the surveys. The causes of the shortcomings are inherent in the organization of Indian agriculture, in the knowledge

---

[51] Lloyd Rudolph and Susanne H. Rudolph, "Surveys in India: Field Experience in Madras State," *Public Opinion Quarterly,* 22 (Fall, 1958), 236.

[52] *Ibid.,* 238.

[53] Republic of the Philippines, Bureau of the Census and Statistics, *Summary and General Report on the 1948 Population and Agriculture, III, Population* (Manila: Bureau of Printing, 1954), part 1, ix.

of the cultivators, in their motivations, in the basic concepts of farm costs, and in the economics of village surveys.

Questions are asked of the cultivator to which he does not know the answer; sometimes because the questions are not asked in the cultivator's terminology, sometimes because the cultivator has no means of knowing the answers, sometimes because the questions are not ones to which the cultivator normally gives consideration. Thus "acres" and "guntas" are English revenue measures, not indigenous measures, while the cultivator cannot be expected to know yields by weight if there are no scales in the village. . . . The cultivator may not normally think about some of the questions in which agricultural economists are interested.[54]

Another factor militating against the effectiveness of the structured interview in nonindustrial societies is the interviewee's lack of prior experience with this kind of social relationship. Badenhorst and Unterhalter, authors of a careful study of a Native urban township in Johannesburg, South Africa, comment: "Controlled interviewing on the basis of a formal schedule is completely foreign to the culture of the group concerned, and many roundabout approaches had to be employed to obtain reliable answers to specific questions."[55]

It should not be inferred that social surveys in developing nations are of no value or that ingenious adjustments cannot be made to correct, or compensate for, some of the difficulties mentioned above. For example, researchers have utilized the notion of "event chronology."[56] Here, key events in the history of a group are listed on the questionnaire, and the interviewer asks the informant during which event he was born. In this manner he obtains the informant's approximate age.

---

[54] Walter C. Neale, "The Limitations of Indian Village Survey Data," *Journal of Asian Studies, 17* (May, 1958), 393–395.

[55] L. T. Badenhorst and B. Unterhalter, "A Study of Fertility in an Urban African Community," *Population Studies, 15* (July, 1961), 73. Cf. Karol J. Krotki and Sultan S. Hashmi, "Report on a Census Enumeration," *Pakistan Development Review, 2* (Autumn, 1962), 377–405. In this situation the interviewer's role in the face of the interviewee's lack of knowledge of interviewing procedures is of considerable methodological import. Krotki and Hashmi state:

Enumerators were encouraged in their instructions and during the training to assist respondents in formulating their answers to an extent which would be considered excessive and consequently distorting in conditions of higher interview sophistication. Though expectedly inevitable in the circumstances of the insufficient familiarity with interviewing techniques in Pakistan, it did produce some unexpected results. In East Pakistan it was noticed in three quarters of the cases that the religion was not being asked but assumed from the name (382).

[56] See, e.g., J. F. Holleman (ed.), *Experiment in Swaziland* (Cape Town: Oxford University Press, 1964), 64–66, 91–92.

At the same time, we can appreciate why some social scientists, especially anthropologists, who have studied preindustrial societies tend to doubt the validity of structured questionnaires. Our argument brings to the fore a proposition of major consequence for methodologists; namely, that a satisfactory response to formal interviewing procedures is itself a product of socialization. Furthermore, the special kinds of knowledge possessed by the preindustrialite are often not those that interest the social scientist. Whereas preindustrialites are not socialized into appreciating certain kinds of statistical data, many urbanites in the United States are expected to have at their command a staggering amount of this kind of information. The citizen must become "quantitatively oriented" in order to fill out his income tax and other forms—or even to have some understanding of batting averages in baseball.

Therefore, if social scientists are to maximize the results of social surveys and of the structured interview they should confine their research to societies, notably industrial-urban ones, that socialize their members into answering formalized questionnaires and that provide the vehicles (written records, computers, and so on) by which quantitative information can be stored. Thus, if informants are taught, or otherwise encouraged, to have at hand data of theoretical import to sociologists and to answer their questions carefully, the validity and reliability of the structured interview are enhanced.

We thus stress that it is essential not only to train scientists to construct carefully worded questions and draw representative samples but also to educate the public to respond to questions on matters of interest to scientists and to do so in a manner advantageous for scientific analysis. To the extent that such is achieved, a common bond is established between interviewer and interviewee. It is not enough for the scientist to understand the world of meaning of his informants; if he is to secure valid data via the structured interview, respondents must be socialized into answering questions in proper fashion.

In the United States, for instance, people are, from elementary school onward, taught to answer objective questions and otherwise to respond to the demands of a society which is quantitatively oriented. But, at least in social orders like the United States, certain counternorms also emerge. Books are even published in order to assist persons to "cheat on" or at least "beat" certain kinds of tests. Then too, serious ideological and ethical objections continue to be leveled against many testing devices. These criticisms have become so vociferous that some social scientists have called upon professional associations to educate the public and its leadership concerning the advantages of testing instruments.[57]

---

[57] See, e.g., Launor F. Carter, "Psychological Testing and Public Responsibility," *Science,* 146 (Dec. 25, 1964), 1697. Also the relevant essays in the *American Psychologist,* February, 1965.

This situation underscores the complex interaction that may prevail between social scientists and the society they study.

The Unstructured Interview

To overcome the limitations of the structured interview, the researcher must resort to the unstructured interview. Yet, the term "unstructured" is somewhat deceptive, for this type of interview is by no means lacking in structure. After all, if the researcher is to sustain his role as a social scientist, he must attempt to structure every interview. He must at a minimum clarify his goals, if only to himself.

The unstructured interview assumes a variety of forms, each of which tends to presuppose a different set of theoretical assumptions. But all offer, in contrast to the structured type, considerable freedom in the questioning procedure; at times the question-and-answer sessions approach the informality of ordinary conversations. Moreover, they emphasize the informant's world of meaning and utilize the informant's categories rather than the scientist's. After the scientist has collected his data, he can proceed to analyze them within his own frame of reference.

Unstructured interviews range, at least in terms of their underlying theory, from those utilizing rather crude common-sense approaches to highly conceptualized ones. Here we shall examine four of the more common types in present-day social research.

THE FREE-ASSOCIATION METHOD

Freudian psychoanalytic theory has had profound effects upon theorizing with respect to the unstructured interview. Freud's conception of the nature of man's mental processes, with its emphasis upon the role of the unconscious, and his method of free association have left an indelible mark upon modern social research. Today several schools, including the traditional Freudians and the Rogerians, take some form of free association as their primary point of departure. But the interview is seen more often as a therapeutic device rather than as a research tool.

Given the assumptions underlying the free-association method, the interviewer tends to view the actor's mental world as confused and difficult to grasp. Frequently the actor himself does not know what he believes; he may be so "irrational" that he cannot perceive or cope with his own subconscious thought patterns.

Because actors do not always think and act rationally, the interviewer must be prepared to follow the interviewee through a jungle of meandering thought ways if he is to arrive at the person's true self. To this end, the researcher (or therapist) utilizes the free-association method, wherein the informant (or patient) is permitted, even encouraged, to give free rein to his thoughts and in the process lay bare certain hidden, subconscious mental processes. Yet often it is the interviewer who must interpret for the interviewee the latter's own actions and statements.

Some of these patterns are dramatically illustrated in Lindner's popular account, *The Fifty-Minute Hour*.[58] One of Lindner's patients was a physicist whose case could be dealt with only after the psychoanalyst had taken it upon himself to study the complexities of the physical universe as perceived by the patient. The latter had constructed a rather bizarre and complex theory about the universe, and many of his actions were governed accordingly. Lindner was finally able to bring the patient "back to social reality" by exposing inconsistencies within the latter's frame of reference.[59]

Although the Freudian approach in its ideal form has been little used by social researchers, its theoretical implications for interviewing are many. It has, directly or indirectly, given rise to special forms of interviewing which are useful in collecting social data.[60] Among these is the nondirective method as formulated by Rogers. One of the admonitions of this approach is: Never provide the interviewee with any formal indication of the interviewer's beliefs and values. If the informant poses a question, the interviewer is expected to parry it. Thus if a person asks: "Is it significant that during the past thirty years I have never dreamt of a naked woman?" the interviewer might respond: "Was it significant?" or "It may or may not be significant. What do you think?" The interviewer thus encourages the interviewee to reflect upon his own observations. The social scientist who seeks to apply this mirrorlike procedure to data collection anticipates that the interviewee will pose some significant questions and seek to answer them himself.

Admittedly the foregoing is an oversimplification of a rather complicated process. But we trust that the principles of the method are clear. Of greater concern here are the advantages and disadvantages of the free association approach as a research tool.

First, to the degree that actors do not, or cannot, conceptualize or interpret the world about them in a "rational" manner, the free-association interview becomes almost indispensable for the researcher, particularly where he seeks case-study data. In other words, more than a few persons find it impossible to speak rationally about themselves or about the normative structure in which they are immersed; only through some indirect means of interviewing, such as the free-association method, can the scientist secure reliable and valid data from these

---

[58] Robert Lindner, *The Fifty-Minute Hour* (New York: Bantam, 1956).

[59] *Ibid.*, 156–207.

[60] Cf. Carl R. Rogers, "The Nondirective Method as a Technique for Social Research," *American Journal of Sociology*, 50 (January, 1945), 279–283.

individuals and ferret out some of their more complex thought patterns. Even applied to interviewing with so-called normal persons, the method can yield valuable kinds of social-psychological materials.

On the other hand, this instrument is unsuited to indirect observation in several respects. It is excessively time consuming and therefore often unusable as a means for interviewing many kinds of individuals. Psychoanalysts, after all, require months, even years, to probe a patient's subconscious. Moreover, their subjects generally are volunteers who pay for the opportunity to talk about themselves and their private world. Many informants would generally resist this kind of un-structured interview. Who wants to have his subconscious probed rather intensively at the whim of a stranger? Actually, there is reason to believe that psychoanalysts experience difficulty in interviewing some lower-class persons in the United States because the latter have not learned how to respond to the norms inherent in this interview situation. A third drawback of the free-association method is the fact that different persons interviewing the same individual would frequently obtain strikingly different findings.

THE FOCUSED INTERVIEW

Some sociologists have sought to formalize the unstructured interview in an effort to standardize the procedure and thus enhance its reliability. One result of their efforts is the "focused interview," a product of Merton and his associates at the Bureau of Applied Social Research at Columbia University. But Merton, Fiske, and Kendall speak for themselves quite effectively:

> First of all, the persons interviewed are known to have been in-volved in *a particular situation*: they have seen a film, heard a radio pro-gram. . . . Secondly, the hypothetically significant elements, patterns, processes, and total structure of this situation have been provisionally analyzed by the social scientist. Through this *content or situational analysis*, he has arrived at a set of hypotheses concerning the conse-quences of determinate aspects of the situation for those involved in it. On the basis of this analysis, he takes the third step of develop-ing an *interview guide*, setting forth the major areas of inquiry and the hypotheses which provide criteria of relevance for the data to be obtained in the interview. Fourth and finally, the interview is focused on the subjective experiences of persons exposed to the pre-analyzed stituation in an effort to ascertain *their definitions of the situation*.[61]

Thus, the focused interview presupposes the informant's involvement in the social situation being investigated. With knowledge of the social setting as a base, the scientist formulates certain general questions. Although the general

[61] Robert K. Merton *et al.*, *The Focused Interview* (New York: Free Press, 1956), 3.

questions are formalized, the question-asking process is unstructured.

The procedure outlined by Merton *et al.* has several decided advantages over the unstructured efforts of the Freudians. It comes to grips with the need for sustaining a degree of organization in the interviewing process, all the while permitting the interviewer considerable leeway in his questioning. In the words of its developers, the formulation allows for range, depth, and specificity. At the same time, this technique does not come to grips with the informant's subconscious as well as does the free-association method, nor is it as effective as the objectifying interview for studying problems in, say, social organization. The last-named technique makes use of the reflective capacities of the skilled, or expert, informant.

THE OBJECTIFYING INTERVIEW

This interviewing procedure, often employed but so far still unformalized, merits explication. Here is another instance that supports our theoretical orientation toward methodology: namely, that informal or actual norms in sociology can be used as the basis for formalizing ideal norms in social research.

The objectifying interview's fundamental premise diverges sharply from that which underlies the Freudian approach. The former gives relatively little heed to unconscious motivations and hidden meanings. Rather, the researcher informs the interviewee from the start, as well as at intervals during the questioning process, concerning the kinds of information he is seeking and why. The informant is apprised of his role in the scientific process and is encouraged to develop his skills in observation (and even in interpretation). This is not to say that the interviewee's "hidden self" is left unplumbed, but the emphasis is upon his role in the research process. Besides examining his own actions, the interviewee is encouraged to observe and interpret the behavior of his associates in his social group. Ideally, he becomes a peer with whom the scientist can objectively discuss the ongoing system, to the extent that he is encouraged to criticize the scientist's observations and interpretations.

In practice this ideal is difficult to achieve. Yet an examination of the literature indicates that the objectifying interview has been employed by a number of social scientists, notably as an adjunct to direct observation within a small community or an organization such as bureaucracy. Lessa, commenting upon his research on the Pacific atoll of Ulithi, remarks concerning his chief informant:

> Melchethal became something of a field worker in his own right. There were older natives who, while eager to help the *repsech,* or foreigner, were shy in his presence, or uncomfortable when seated for long, while others probably objected to working through a young interpreter. Melchethal would interview such men and women and report his findings. This technique, within its limitations, was remarkably

successful. It was in this way that the vast store of knowledge possessed by the old chief, Mälisou, was utilized. Almost daily, Melchethal would spend an hour or two with him. . . . Other men usually listened in on these discussions, and as the two thrashed out problems which had been raised by the anthropologist, they would join in with their own comments. Too much cannot be said for this way of augmenting the record. Not only did it save time, for it capsuled the conversations of experts, but it permitted informants to mull over problems leisurely and freely, without a feeling of being under pressure. . . . Fortunately, Melchethal had the respect and trust of everyone, and his friends took great delight in talking over matters af native culture with him. In turn, he loved the work he was doing, especially since he was partly paralyzed and limited in his economic usefulness. . . . Whenever Melchethal was present while others were being interviewed, he could bring his own experience to bear in facilitating questioning and answering, as well as in coördinating data. However, he was especially discreet and never interrupted an informant unless it was really necessary.[62]

A variant of the objectifying interview is described in Whyte's *Street Corner Society*.[63] In this study the author supplemented his own direct observations of a street-corner gang by encouraging certain members of it to become his "eyes and ears." Whyte, however, did not take notice of, or elaborate upon, the broader theoretical significance of working with these "lay observers."

Another sociologist who seems to have employed the objectifying interview was Lerner, who studied a segment of French society. At first his French informants were unenthusiastic about the whole interviewing process, in part because of their desire for privacy. Lerner was, however, able to overcome some of this resistance by casting his informants in the role of experts—by utilizing the objectifying interview.[64]

This kind of interviewing embodies some other distinct advantages over the usual methods. It eliminates or circumvents a number of thorny ethical dilemmas that confront the researcher. One of these has been pinpointed by Richard Colvard: namely, that frequently researchers, in the course of their in-

---

[62] W. A. Lessa, *The Ethnography of Ulithi Atoll,* Coordinated Investigation of Micronesian Anthropology, Report No. 28 (Washington, D.C.: Pacific Science Board, National Research Council, 1950), 3–4. Cf. Colin M. Turnbull, *The Forest People: A Study of the Pygmies of the Congo* (Garden City, N.Y.: Doubleday, Anchor Books, 1962). This kind of informant, judged by Turnbull's experience, is invaluable when the researcher seeks information on especially sensitive topics (21).

[63] William F. Whyte, *Street Corner Society,* 2nd ed. (Chicago: University of Chicago Press, 1955), appendix.

[64] Lerner, *op. cit.*

terviewing, establish rapport not as scientists but as human beings; yet they proceed to use this humanistically gained knowledge for scientific ends, usually without the informants' knowledge.[65] The rapport methodologists strive to establish is actually in the nature of a social bond betwen interviewer and interviewee, a bond that develops not because the former is working for the cause of science but because he is a friend, or at least an acquaintance, in need of information. Some researchers go to considerable lengths to prove they are friends with their informants. The objectifying interview, by clarifying the motives of the scientist, minimizes the possibility of exploitation, real or apparent, of the individual who cooperates with the researcher.

The objectifying interview has the further advantage of casting the informant in a favorable light both to himself and to his group. Rather than viewing himself merely as a tool, he can take pride in the fact that he is contributing to scientific knowledge. And to the extent that the interviewee develops a commitment to the research project he will strive to sustain objectivity and accuracy in the data he provides.

It has been the experience of the senior author that use of the objectifying interview reduces suspicion and hostility on the part of the respondent. Approaches like the free-association technique, on the other hand, can easily foster transference, on the part of the informant, followed by negation of the interviewer (as occurs so often in the case of psychoanalysis). Such reactions, of course, may have a certain therapeutic value, but they can be detrimental to social research, particularly if a rift develops therefrom between the interviewer-scientist and his sources of data.

The objectifying interview is less conductive to antagonism than most other methods mainly because the informant's own problems, beliefs, or attitudes are treated, in the ideal at least, as objective facts. For the researcher consciously seeks to place sensitive issues within the broader sociocultural context in order to demonstrate to the interviewee that his problems are not unique to himself but are experienced by many other people. Indeed, many individuals seem to enjoy talking about problems in the third person; they enjoy discussing issues as if they pertain to persons apart from themselves. It is in this attempt by the interviewer to impress upon his subjects the generality rather than the uniqueness of social problems that the objectifying interview diverges so markedly from, say, the Freudian orientation.

As might be expected, this interviewing procedure has pitfalls of its own. The first is the real possibility of the scientist's becoming a "captive" of the in-

[65] For Colvard's views on this complex issue, see his "Interaction and Identification in Reporting Field Research: A Critical Reconstruction of Protective Procedures," in Gideon Sjoberg (ed.), *Ethics, Politics, and Social Research* (Cambridge, Mass.: Schenkman, 1967), chap. 14.

formant. Consequently, he may be led astray by a person who, consciously or not, succeeds in turning the discussion in certain directions. A second danger, not to be underestimated, is that the interviewee, particularly if he occupies a lowly station, may be so anxious to please the sociologist that he will respond to questions with the answers that he thinks the interviewer wants or expects, whether these are accurate or not. If the data obtained via objectifying interviews are to be valid, the informant must exercise independent judgment, and the researcher must check the results against the observations of other members of the group under study. A third drawback of this approach is that one cannot always find highly intelligent informants who have the ability to observe and to reflect objectively upon their own situation.

But whatever the limitations of this interviewing technique, it offers social scientists certain unexplored opportunities in social research, notably in the thorniest area of all: the study of social organization, wherein the reflective capacities of the informant may be crucial.

THE GROUP INTERVIEW

Another basically unstructured kind of indirect observation is the group interview.[66] This device has for some time been popular among psychotherapists, who gather patients into discussion groups so that in the resultant personal interaction the individuals will help one another clarify their personal problems and perhaps even resolve them.

The group interview has proved useful for sociologists and anthropologists, some of whom have employed it informally at one time or another. Field workers, when interviewing persons about their own social system, may find themselves in a group situation, with the various members discussing the patterns among themselves and arguing over points. For all social systems display some areas of ambiguity and/or conflict with respect to norms and values; often these problems become clarified, or at least brought to the level of consciousness, only through group discussion, which in turn may depend for stimulation upon the questions of the researcher.

Social scientists have also set up semistructured group interviews in an effort to investigate, say, community organization. Here a number of persons are assembled and are asked questions. In the interchange some significant patterns may emerge that probably would not come to light if each person were interviewed in isolation.

The group interview, besides helping to clarify areas of ambiguity in the

---

[66] The military historian S. L. A. Marshall, *Pork Chop Hill* (New York: Morrow, 1956), has utilized group interviews with participants in battle as a basis for reconstructing the course of battle. However, he naïvely indicates that in these sessions the rank of the participants was put aside.

normative structure of social systems, has the added advantage of providing a check upon faulty memories or false replies resulting from misunderstanding or whatever. On the other hand, taking a cue from the small-group researchers, such as Asch and Sherif, we can readily perceive that group situations may encourage the rise of leaders who can influence the course of the interchange, perhaps by inducing individuals to take stands they would otherwise not espouse, or the reverse, stifling the expression of opinions by some persons.[67] Individuals who rank low in the group hierarchy are especially vulnerable to pressures from such "self-appointed" leaders. Obviously, the validity of the resulting data is jeopardized by these group pressures for conformity.

The Interviewee, the Unstructured Interview, and the Sociocultural System

So far we have said little about the informant's position in the sociocultural system and the implications of this for the unstructured type of interview. We have indicated that this kind of interviewing procedure does help the scientist hurdle certain cultural or social barriers. Yet, the researcher who seeks to apply it may encounter other barriers that are well-nigh insuperable. Some societies react against any kind of interviewing, even of the unstructured sort. Evans-Pritchard relates one of his experiences with the Nuer tribe of East Africa.

> Nuer are expert at sabotaging an inquiry and until one has resided with them for some weeks they steadfastly stultify all efforts to elicit the simplest facts and to elucidate the most innocent practices. I have obtained in Zandeland more information in a few days than I obtained in Nuerland in as many weeks. . . . Questions about customs were blocked by a technique I can commend to natives who are inconvenienced by the curiosity of ethnologists. The following specimen of Nuer methods is the commencement of a conversation on the Nyanding river, on a subject which admits of some obscurity but, with willingness to co-operate, can soon be elucidated.
>
> I: Who are you?
> Cuol: A man.
> I: What is your name?
> Cuol: Do you want to know my *name*?
> I: Yes.
> Cuol: You want to know *my* name?

[67] See, e.g., Solomon E. Asch, "Opinions and Social Pressure," *Scientific American*, 193 (November, 1955), 31–35; and Muzafer Sherif and Carolyn W. Sherif, *An Outline of Social Psychology*, rev. ed. (New York: Harper & Row, 1956).

I: Yes, you have come to visit me in my tent and I would like to know who you are.

Cuol: All right. I am Cuol. What is your name?

I: My name is Pritchard.

Cuol: What is your father's name?

I: My father's name is also Pritchard.

Cuol: No, that cannot be true. You cannot have the same name as your father.

I: It is the name of my lineage. What is the name of your lineage?

Cuol: Do you want to know the name of my lineage?

I: Yes.

Cuol: What will you do with it if I tell you? Will you take it to your country?

I: I don't want to do anything with it. I just want to know it since I am living in your camp.

Cuol: Oh well, we are Lou.

I: I did not ask you the name of your tribe. I know that. I am asking you the name of your lineage.

Cuol: Why do you want to know the name of my lineage?

I: I don't want to know it.

Cuol: Then why do you ask me for it? Give me some tobacco.

I defy the most patient ethnologist to make headway against this kind of opposition. One is just driven crazy by it. Indeed, after a few weeks of associating solely with Nuer one displays, if the pun be allowed, the most evident symptoms of "Nuerosis."[68]

A given sociocultural system not only may render ineffective any attempt to apply the unstructured interview, but it can influence the kinds of data that can be amassed. Edgar Snow, in his *Red Star over China,* observed that some of the Communist leaders he interviewed in the 1930s were reluctant to provide him with biographical data. Thus, even the close friends and wife of Mao Tse-tung did not know important details about his life before his Communist days.[69] The force of "collective consciousness" can be so overpowering and the individual so strongly identified with the group that he can purposively suppress his identity to a remarkable degree.

Margaret Lantis' work with the Nunivak Eskimos lends some support to this hypothesis. She indicates that those she studied lacked any basic conception of an autobiography and that this constituted a formidable barrier to the collection

---

E. E. Evans-Pritchard, *The Nuer* (Fair Lawn, N.J.: Oxford, 1940), 12–13.

Edgar Snow, *Red Star over China* (New York: Grove Press, Black Cat Books, 1961), 122, 148.

of personal data from individuals.[70] Compare this with the situation in American society: Here the high degree of individualization means that interviewees are ready and willing to provide the researcher with personal data about themselves. This may account in large measure for the popularity of the case study in American sociology.

WHO ARE THE STRATEGIC INFORMANTS?

In the chapter on direct observation, we considered the nature of the sensitive scientist-observer. We can now examine those informants who become the researcher's eyes and ears in indirect observation. One evidence suggests that the kinds of persons who can effectively carry out this role vary considerably not only among societies but often also within given sociocultural settings.

We begin with the proposition that persons who completely accept and identify with the ideal norms of their particular reference group are necessarily nonreflective. Asked for their views or opinions, they tend to parrot the ideal norms and to show unawareness of the existence of alternatives. Either that, or they are continually on guard lest they jeopardize their own status and that of their reference group. Such persons are the conformists in any social order.

Quite in contrast to the conformist is the "marginal man." This concept has been subject to considerable criticism in the sociological literature; nevertheless the idea is still useful for isolating certain persons who are likely to be of special value to the social researcher. We employ the term as follows: A marginal man is one who adheres only partially to the normative expectations of his reference group. In turn, there are two subcategories of marginal informants: (1) the "deviant" or "maladjusted" person who is either fully or partially rejected by (or partially or fully rejects) other members of the group and (2) the marginal but organized and stable individual. The latter, because he neither fully accepts nor entirely rejects certain roles that may accrue to him, is the ideal person to serve as a broker, or link, between systems or subsystems.

Deviant or maladjusted individuals (of whom there are a number of subtypes) have always been a focus of interest for social scientists. Much of American sociology has in fact been directed to studying persons in this category: the criminal, the prostitute, the dope addict, the alcoholic. Because of their outcast or highly disadvantaged status, sociologists can freely study them; moreover, such persons tend to talk uninhibitedly about themselves and their social experiences. They have much less to lose from speaking frankly than do higher status individuals, and they may actually have something to gain, if only in the form of catharsis or rationalization of their problems.

The deviant, often disgruntled, individual may be the sole source of information about a particular system or facets thereof.[71] Also, his unique perspective

[70] Margaret Lantis, *Eskimo Childhood and Interpersonal Relationships* (Seattle: University of Washington Press, 1960), vii–viii.
[71] See, e.g., Leslie A. White, *The Pueblo of Sia, New Mexico*, Smithsonian Institution,

provides the researcher with valuable clues for follow-up questioning of other members of the system. The utility of the deviant marginal informant is recognized by newsmen—persons who are frequently charged with the task of securing "restricted" or particularly sensitive data. James Reston, a leading reporter-commentator for the *New York Times*, is credited with the maxim: "You should always look around for the guys who are unhappy."[72]

Of course, that a respondent of this kind tends to be highly dissatisfied with his environment raises doubts about the validity of his observations. In so far as such a person uses the interview primarily to rationalize his own role to himself, certain distortions of reality may well result.[73] Moreover, this kind of informant may hamper the researcher who is carrying out field work within a particular community or organization; for association with the deviant individual makes the scientist suspect as well.

Another problem in the use of the deviant marginal informant is the ethical one. Researchers on occasion have relied upon this kind of person as a means of gaining entree into organizations otherwise closed to them. Dalton, for instance, gained some of his information about the managerial activities of certain businesses by just such a procedure.[74] However, if this practice became widespread, it could foster suspicion of social scientists by the citizenry at large.[75]

Bureau of American Ethnology, Bulletin 184 (Washington, D.C.: GPO, 1962). White takes note of the resistance to outside investigators, for members of the pueblo have been taught since childhood that their culture is sacred and information about it must not be divulged to outsiders. Although he does not make the point clearly, he seems to have relied upon "marginal individuals."

[72] "Man of Influence," *Time, 75* (Feb. 15, 1960), 78.

[73] Peter M. Blau, "The Research Process in the Study of *The Dynamics of Bureaucracy,*" in Phillip E. Hammond (ed.), *Sociologists at Work* (New York: Basic Books, 1964), 30–31. Blau writes:

It is my impression that the best informants in the early weeks tended to be officials who occupied marginal positions in the work group or the organization.

The marginal position of the observer in the bureaucratic field situation complements the marginal position of these informants, and this entails a danger. The observer may be tempted to rely too much on those officials who make themselves easily accessible to him. If he yields to this temptation, he will obtain a distorted picture of the organization and the group structure (30).

[74] Melville Dalton, "Preconceptions and Methods in *Men Who Manage,*" in Hammond, *op. cit.,* chap. 3.

[75] Researchers will find one subtype of marginal informant—the person who has retired or who has left the system—an invaluable source of data for the study of certain social organizations. John P. Lovell, *The Study of the Military in Developing Nations: Devising Meaningful and Manageable Research Strategies* (Bloomington, Ind.: Indiana University Department of Government, Carnegie Seminar on Political and Administrative Development, 1966), 8. Moreover, reliance upon this kind of informant bypasses some of the ethical and political dilemmas normally associated with the use of marginal members of ongoing systems.

Some of the disadvantages of the deviant marginal informant can be overcome by reliance upon the stable marginal man. In point of fact, the latter's utility is frequently ignored by scientists concerned with social organization, especially bureaucratic structures.

All social systems, or subsystems, seem to require some persons who function as mediators or go-betweens. In close contact with competing or antagonistic systems, they are prime sources of specialized information about the normative order. Industrial (or open) societies include persons occupying such a variety of roles. One is the professional politician. This kind of person, to be successful, must maintain working relationships with diverse and competing interest groups. But mediators are also active within more limited systems such as universities, churches, and business corporations.

What is significant about this kind of informant is that he has learned to subdue his personal prejudices and to sustain a high degree of objectivity. Without this orientation he could never have gained the confidence of disparate groups or antagonistic factions. Because of his links with divergent elements in a social order, he comes to acquire specialized knowledge that few other persons can obtain, information that in turn sustains his special role. For one thing, people must come to him for help in settling their differences. Moreover, since he is in a position to compare differing values and norms, the stable marginal informant becomes sensitized to the normative arrangements of the persons or groups with whom he deals. Social scientists studying social organizations should pay special heed to this kind of person—potentially a highly strategic informant. Then too, in most instances the stable marginal man is quite responsive to the objectifying interview. Some of these persons actually become "amateur scientists" who reflect upon the actions of others in an objective and universalistic manner, to the extent that people frequently single them out for the scientist who is searching for likely persons to interview.

CHAPTER 9

Theoretical
Analysis

In Chapters 2 and 3 we examined in general terms the nature of theory and logic of theory building and the role of theoretical assumptions in social research. Although we have throughout emphasized that theoretical analysis enters into every stage of the research process, we must now elaborate more fully upon certain aspects of theoretical analysis as they relate to the interpretation of the research results. Concrete illustrations concerning the application of the general principles discussed earlier seem in order. At this point we are especially concerned with the function of theoretical assumptions in the analysis of data, the variations in the kinds of inferences employed in research, and finally the construction and application of typological tools.

Theoretical Assumptions and Theory Building

It will be recalled that there are three dimensions to theory: the assumptions about social reality and method, the logical structure, and the substantive generalizations. Here we shall explore the implications of some of the premises enumerated in Chapter 3. But in order to limit the scope of the subject, which actually is deserving of book-length treatment, we must focus attention primarily upon the assumptions regarding the level and range of theory and the nature of social reality.

An understanding of these premises is a prerequisite to reasoned debate in sociology. Much of the drama in current sociology emanates from the ongoing dialectic whereby scientists belonging to different schools of thought become, in effect, pitted against one another. This debate confounds the novitiate and frustrates those who look to social science for the answers to modern-day problems. But the scientific method makes no claim that certainty can be achieved. It can only offer hope of advances in knowledge—advances that depend in large measure upon enlightened debate. The dialectic process, as Llewellyn Gross has observed, is especially useful in the social sciences, for here clear-cut testing of hypotheses is far more difficult than in the natural sciences.[1] Where empirical data are subject to diverse interpretations, argumentation based on reason can do much to clarify hidden issues. The dialectic process is perhaps the major means of objectifying the theoretical premises that guide social scientists in the collection and analysis of their data.[2] Unfortunately, much of the debate in sociology has remained sterile because the antagonists fail to grasp one another's theoretical premises.

LEVEL AND RANGE OF THEORY

Generalizations about substantive problems acquire meaning in terms of the scientist's premises, the level of analysis being one such premise. The level of theorizing in sociology is complicated by the presence of several dimensions, including the issue of reference points in analysis, the question of the merits of loose versus tight theorizing, the matter of methodological individualism, and the issue of whether the scientist, in analyzing his data, takes the viewpoint of the actor or whether he strives to impose his own theoretical framework upon reality. The arguments concerning methodological individualism and the scientist's versus the actor's frame of reference are in turn interwoven tightly with the scientist's other assumptions about the nature of social reality and the method to be adopted.

The reference points the scientist employs form a critical part of his statement of the problem. They assume special significance when it is realized that the scientific method involves the negation and reformulation of existing theories or hypotheses. When sociologists fail to make their reference points explicit, they neglect to make maximum use of their research findings and may be guilty of perpetuating spurious controversies.

In the field of social organization, Weber's analysis of bureaucracy has been widely debated. Many writers have objected to Weber's ideal-typical formulation, which, among other things, portrays the bureaucratic system as a formal hierarchy of statuses with marked impersonality among occupants of different positions. Some sociologists contend, on the basis of their field investigations, that bureau-

[1] Llewellyn Gross, "Preface to a Metatheoretical Framework for Sociology," *American Journal of Sociology*, 67 (September, 1961), 125–136, uses the term "neodialectic." See also Talcott Parsons' "Comment" on Gross's article (136–140) and Gross's "Rejoinder" (140–143). The article by Gross and the resultant debate are essential reading.

[2] This position is at least implicit in Nicholas Georgescu-Roegen, *Analytical Economics* (Cambridge, Mass.: Harvard, 1966), 22–29.

cratic practices in contemporary American society diverge in many respects from the Weberian model.[3] For one thing, informal groups within bureaucracies evince highly personal relationships. There is a tendency to assume that because of these divergencies and because of the data supporting the latter, Weber's formulation of bureaucracy has been more or less discredited.

But if we examine the statements of many of Weber's critics we discover that they frequently ignore his conception of bureaucracy, which was constructed in ideal-type terms. Weber's critics often fail to perceive the reference points of his formulation. Weber was, it seems, aware of divergencies from his ideal type in the Europe of his day, but he was intent upon contrasting the rational type of bureaucracy, which he felt characterized capitalistic societies, with its organizational counterpart in precapitalistic feudal orders, which he also saw in ideal-type terms. When sociologists contend that bureaucratic systems in contemporary America do not fit Weber's model, they are attacking a straw man, for Weber's concern was with contrasting the past with the present over a broad span of history, not with enumerating deviations from the ideal within the social orders of his time.[4]

We do not mean to imply that the observations of Weber's critics are without merit; rather we argue that any validity these observations may have rests upon grounds other than those that have been advanced. The various critiques of Weber reflect the marked differences in orientation between the old-line European sociologists—Weber, Sombart, Tönnies, and Troeltsch—and most contemporary American sociologists. The former were concerned with comparing capitalism with the medieval European order, whereas the latter are concerned with the differences between the ideal and the real (or actual) norms within modern societies. More adequate knowledge of the history of social thought would serve to eliminate some of these controversies, for if we are to evaluate and build upon the work of earlier sociologists, we must understand their problems as well as their intent.

But misinterpretation of the work of earlier scholars is not the only failing to which social scientists are susceptible. If we consider the Soviet class system as analyzed in the writings of Western social scientists during the past two decades, we discover that some scholars argue that the class system in the Soviet Union is becoming more rigid, while others believe the data point to increasing flexibility and fluidity. Still other writers claim they are unable to perceive any well-defined

---

[3] See, e.g., Roy G. Francis and Robert C. Stone, *Service and Procedure in Bureaucracy* (Minneapolis: University of Minnesota Press, 1956).

[4] *From Max Weber: Essays in Sociology,* trans. and ed. by H. H. Gerth and C. Wright Mills (Fair Lawn, N.J., Oxford, Galaxy Books, 1958) ; Max Weber, *The Theory of Social and Economic Organization,* trans. by A. M. Henderson and Talcott Parsons (New York: Free Press Paperback, 1964).

patterns over time.[5] Much of the confusion stems from a lack of clarity regarding reference points.

A probing of these controversies indicates that the antagonists are often talking past one another, for they are frequently not challenging specific findings as such. Those writers who contend that the Soviet system has rigidified seem to take as their base period the rather immediate post-Revolutionary era, one of considerable upheaval in the Soviet Union. On the other hand, those who argue for growing flexibility are prone to take pre-Revolutionary Czarist Russia as their point of departure.

Similar inconsistencies regarding the standards of comparison have plagued American students of their class system. Some scholars have taken the ideal of equalitarianism as the basis against which to contrast the existing order, others have taken some concrete historical era, and so on. All too often the reference points are only vaguely explicated.

The use of complex measurement devices in no way exempts the researcher from the need to specify his reference points. Many otherwise sound studies, utilizing various types of statistical analyses, have been seriously compromised by their neglect of appropriate standards of comparison. A case in point is Coleman's *The Adolescent Society*, a study of high school students and, among other matters, their motivations toward scholastic achievement.[6] Coleman took the Amish as his base, or standard, against which to interpret his findings about high school youth in industrial-urban America during the late 1950s.[7] However, the Amish are not representative of traditional rural society in America. Coleman compounds the confusion by his too adumbrated discussion of the Amish; in effect he expects the reader to intuit just what it is about this group that makes them significant for his comparisons.

Besides this frequent neglect of the matter of standards of comparison, sociologists differ considerably among themselves in their (often implicit) assumptions as to what constitutes the proper level of abstraction for social research in general or for any given study in particular.

The Parsons-Merton debate in sociology epitomizes one facet of this problem.[8] Although many of Parsons' critics contend that his theorizing consists more

---

[5] See, e.g., Claude S. Philips, Jr., "Class Stratification in Soviet Russia: A Bibliography Survey of Recent Literature," *Michigan Academy of Science, Arts, and Letters, 42* (1956), 195–216.

[6] James S. Coleman, *The Adolescent Society* (New York: Free Press, 1961).

[7] *Ibid.*, 1–2.

[8] Cf. Talcott Parsons, "The Position of Sociological Theory," *American Sociological Review, 13* (April, 1948), 156–164, and the "Discussion" by Robert K. Merton that follows, 164–168. Also note Merton's elaboration of his own remarks in his *Social Theory and Social Structure*, rev. ed. (New York: Free Press, 1957), 4 ff., as well as Talcott Parsons' "General Theory in Sociology," in Robert K. Merton *et al.* (eds.), *Sociology Today* (New York: Basic Books, 1959), chap. 1.

of constructing abstract classificatory schemes than of building logically deductive systems, Parsons has nonetheless been a leading exponent of grand theorizing in sociology. Parsons contends that if social scientists are to create theoretical systems that can be used to interpret a wide range of social phenomena, they must be willing to think in terms of high-level abstraction. They must be willing to take calculated risks. In this respect, Parsons is striving toward one of the time-honored goals of theory construction which is to gather under a single roof a host of variables and categories that will connect many seemingly disparate observations. As would be expected, Parsons has been frequently criticized on the ground that his work bears little relation to empirical reality, that it is difficult to establish reliable indexes for his concepts or to operationalize them. But Parsons is playing a loose strategy in which he is sacrificing reliability for generality, and in the process he admittedly resorts to loose theories.[9] Yet, synthesis is essential if social science is to rise above the level of common sense.

However, the concern with empirical validity and reliability has driven Merton, among others, to argue that sociology can best be served (at least for the present) by concentrating upon "middle-range" theory.[10] Merton, unlike some sociologists, is not opposed to grand theory per se, but he believes social research can be advanced most rapidly if sociologists work within the range of their capabilities. By utilizing middle-range theory, one can deal with fewer variables. And it is easier to derive testable hypotheses within this framework than via highly abstract systems. Thus Merton sees the criminologist and ecologist developing middle-range theories and testing them, leaving to future scientists the integration of these into some manageable whole.

In addition to Merton with his moderate criticism of broad generalizing theories, two other groups of writers stand opposed to grand theorizing. One group, which includes many symbolic interactionists and phenomenologists, would describe reality from the viewpoint of the actor and rely upon the actor's own categories to capture his world of meaning. Goffman in sociology and Oscar Lewis in anthropology are among those who study social reality through the eyes of the actor and who use the symbolism and richness of natural language in their description and analysis.[11] Of necessity these social scientists disavow abstract theorizing, something which, in their view, is not empirically realistic and fails to explain the way people really act.

A more extreme stance (that is, extreme relative to that of Parsons) is assumed by certain old-line positivists who argue that researchers should test

[9] Roger Nett, "System Building in Sociology—A Methodological Analysis," *Social Forces, 31* (October, 1952), 25–30.

[10] Merton, *Social Theory and Social Structure, op. cit.*

[11] Erving Goffman, *The Presentation of Self in Everyday Life* (Garden City, N.Y.: Doubleday, Anchor Books, 1959); and Oscar Lewis, *The Children of Sánchez* (New York: Random House, 1961).

specific, relatively limited hypotheses via statistical procedures. In their view middle-range theories merit little attention. Some within this group argue that ultimately all the significant findings will somehow coalesce. The notion that each scientist shapes one or more bricks of knowledge and that all of these ultimately fall together to form an imposing scientific edifice is one of the most compelling articles of faith in modern sociology. It serves to rationalize the high degree of piecemeal research one encounters in most journals. Yet if all the mud in the world were shaped into bricks, the result still would not be a house. So too in science. There must be persons who can fashion durable structures out of the building blocks others have created.

The point is that, ideally, the scientist who is concerned with testing limited hypotheses should be conversant with general theory. He can thereby put his findings to maximum use. Pertinent in this regard is the history of Sutherland's "differential association" construct, which sought to explain why some persons become criminals.[12] Sutherland contended, if we may oversimplify somewhat, that an individual becomes a criminal because of contacts with criminal patterns and because of isolation from anticriminal patterns. Numerous sociologists have adopted this theoretical orientation as a guide for their research. Yet, there has been little refinement or extension of Sutherland's construct since it was first advanced a few decades ago.[13]

Criminologists have in effect neglected to examine the logical and empirical connections between the notion of differential association and sociological theory and research in general. Not only have they failed to draw upon broader theoretical advances to clarify and elaborate upon the differential association construct, but they have failed to examine the utility of this notion in those realms of social deviation that are analogous to criminal action.[14]

Another facet of the debate between scientists intent upon testing low-level hypotheses and those interested in more sweeping generalizations emerges in the area of crosscultural analysis. In addition to the historicists, who deny the possibility of any form of crosscultural generalization, there are social scientists who argue that crosscultural research can be fruitfully undertaken only after a firm foundation of knowledge derived from specific societies has been laid. Only then should the sociologist venture onto the treacherous terrain of crosscultural inquiry. They contend that broad crosscultural research, if undertaken without such a

---

[12] See Albert Cohen *et al.* (eds.), *The Sutherland Papers,* Indiana University Publications, Social Science Series No. 15 (Bloomington, Ind.: Indiana University Press, 1956), part 1. The key section from the 1947 edition of Sutherland's *Principles of Criminology,* as well as other materials on differential association are reproduced therein.

[13] See, e.g., James F. Short, Jr., "Differential Association as a Hypothesis: Problems of Empirical Testing," *Social Problems,* 8 (Summer, 1960), 14–25. Note also the articles in this issue by Donald R. Cressey, Daniel Glaser, and Henry D. McKay.

[14] *Ibid.*

groundwork, involves merely high-level theorizing that has little connection with empirical data.

More relevant for crosscultural inquiry is the argument that revolves about whether it is feasible to analyze social patterns apart from their specific cultural setting. That is, should kinship, governmental, religious, and other structures be studied only in relation to a given cultural context? Jarvie and Popper dealt with one aspect of this problem when they compared the use of "situational logic" (the analysis of people's actions in terms of the specific social situation) with the use of more generalizing theories.[15]

The question of analysis of social phenomena in terms of the cultural context versus analysis in terms of some more general theory has, as we have already indicated, generated all manner of controversy.[16] A number of scholars have been committed, either in theory or in research, to the notion that one must deal with specific cultural contexts and one cannot hope to establish general principles.[17] Social scientists with historicist leanings thus reject the validity of Murdock's crosscultural files. In their view, such an approach treats social data out of context and thus seriously distorts reality.

Writers such as Marx and Weber, although they were interested in a broad comparative approach, nevertheless argued that social scientists must analyze social structures in relation to the particular sociocultural, and especially historical, context. Yet Marx utilized concepts displaying crosscultural utility and his "stages of evolution" were envisaged as having crosscultural applicability.[18]

The comparative method of Marx and, especially, Weber invites criticism. Weber, in particular, though generally regarded as a comparative sociologist extraordinary, nevertheless carried over many elements of the historicist tradition.[19] He was primarily concerned with explaining the uniqueness of the Western

[15] I. C. Jarvie, *The Revolution in Anthropology* (London: Routledge, 1964); and Karl R. Popper, *The Poverty of Historicism*, 3rd ed. (New York: Harper & Row, Harper Torchbooks, 1964), 147 ff., *passim.*

[16] Robert M. Marsh, *Comparative Sociology* (New York: Harcourt, Brace & World, 1967), chaps. 1 and 2, reviews some of the important issues.

[17] See the informative debate between F. G. Bailey, in "For a Sociology of India?" *Contributions to Indian Sociology,* No. 3 (July, 1959), 88–101, and the Editors in "For a Sociology of India: A Rejoinder to Dr. Bailey," *Contributions to Indian Sociology,* No. 4 (April, 1960), 82–89. Bailey argued (and we believe the evidence supports his case) that the Editors were committed to what we term an historicist position.

[18] See, e.g., Hyman Levy, "Marx as Scientist," *Centennial Review, 3* (Fall, 1959), 407–422.

[19] Reinhard Bendix, a contemporary who is committed to the heritage of Max Weber, encounters many of the same dilemmas as did his intellectual mentor. Bendix stresses differences without sufficient attention to the similarities. See, e.g., Reinhard Bendix, *Work and Authority in Industry* (New York: Harper & Row, Harper Torchbooks, 1963), and his *Nation-Building and Citizenship* (New York: Wiley, 1964). Another aspect of

World (notably the rise of capitalism) and he generally did this without first stating the points of similarity between it and societies in Asia.[20] Yet in science the unique is meaningful only when contrasted with the general.

It should be clear by now that we believe it is possible to transcend an historicist approach. In turn, as we discuss further in Chapter 11, one's generalizing concepts or propositions need not be equated with all the varieties of cultural representations. But they must be congruent with them. Thus crosscultural analysis, even of a broad sort, must proceed hand in hand with the study of individual societies. Of course, this also means that one must shift at times to a high level of abstraction in order to isolate regularities.

To merely study a sociocultural system other than one's own does not make one a comparative scientist. Social scientists who analyze other social systems may become as ethnocentric as those whose interests are confined to their own social order. Epstein's remarks are pertinent here:

> There are always certain dangers inherent, I think, in the approach of the anthropologist. Caught up in the minutiae of events which make up the social life of the community he is studying, he sometimes finds it difficult to avoid over-emphasizing the unique features of "his" community at the expense of features held in common with similar communities in less "exotic" regions.[21]

In other words, the scientist's immersion in a sociocultural system may lead him to exaggerate the uniqueness of particular patterns within that system, be these familial or friendship or other social phenomena. More specifically, one is left with the impression that a number of scholars writing on Mexican-Americans have exaggerated the uniqueness of the "Mexican" orientation toward time.[22] After all, many lower-class groups in American society (Negro or white) and

---

Bendix's work, one that emerges from his lack of attention to similarities, deserves special mention. He compares, for instance, two countries such as Germany and Japan. But without a sufficiently explicit or well-defined statement of the underlying similarities, it becomes difficult for other scholars to compare their nation (or nations) with those Bendix is studying—to determine whether they are similar or different. In the end each scholar has to use his own implicitly defined reference points, and thus much "comparative research" tends to be historicist in practice if not in theory.

[20] Cahnman, more than, say, Parsons sees Weber as part of the historicist tradition. Werner J. Cahnman, "Max Weber and the Methodological Controversy in the Social Sciences," in Werner J. Cahnman and Alvin Boskoff (eds.), *Sociology and History* (New York: Free Press, 1964), 103–127.

[21] A. L. Epstein, *Politics in an Urban African Community* (Manchester: Manchester University Press, 1958), 224.

[22] See, e.g., Lyle Saunders, *Cultural Difference and Medical Care* (New York: Russell Sage Foundation, 1954), 116–122.

peoples in other societies have viewed time in much the same manner as have the Spanish-speaking peoples of the Southwest.

Ultimately the most compelling case for placing one's own research findings within a crosscultural framework stems from the work of many American sociologists. Even today we can foresee considerable reformulation of concepts and hypotheses in the area of collective behavior when sociologists take it upon themselves to examine, for example, "controlled mobs" in some totalitarian countries or the dancing manias in medieval Europe.[23]

THE NATURE OF SOCIAL REALITY

Certain problems concerning the level of theory are intimately associated with the social scientist's conception of the nature of reality. One such issue is whether analysis should be in terms of the individual or the group.

The economist Von Mises, the sociologist Homans, and Popper, a philosopher of science, adhere to the principle of "methodological individualism."[24] These writers all assume that the individual is the basic unit of analysis. (There are social scientists who, by treating social systems as "individuals," practice a special form of methodological individualism.) Other scholars, including many nonpsychologically oriented sociologists, contend that the group is not reducible to individuals or "individual roles." To these scholars the system is more than the sum of its parts. In the next chapter we shall observe how recent methodological advances have served to clarify this controversy.

Whether one studies groups or individuals is related (though not in a one-to-one sense) to another issue: Should the scientist utilize the frame of reference of the actor or actors under study or should he employ the particular categories he or other scientists have formulated? The scientist's commitment in this area, as we have observed, structures the procedures used in gathering his data, and it greatly influences his analysis as well.

The divergence between Parsons and Lazarsfeld, mentioned in earlier chapters,[25] brings this issue to the fore. Parsons and students of his such as Smelser[26] more or less impose their framework (for instance, their system problems cate-

---

[23] See E. J. Backman, *Religious Dances*, trans. by E. Classen (London: G. Allen, 1952); and Norman Cohn, *The Pursuit of the Millennium* (London: Secker & Warburg, 1957).

[24] Ludwig von Mises, *Human Action* (New Haven: Yale, 1949), esp. 44 ff.; George C. Homans, *Social Behavior: Its Elementary Forms* (New York: Harcourt, Brace & World, 1961); and Popper, *op. cit.*

[25] Cf. Parsons, "General Theory in Sociology," *op. cit.;* and Paul F. Lazarsfeld and Allen H. Barton, "Some General Principles of Questionnaire Classification," in Paul F. Lazarsfeld and Morris Rosenberg (eds.), *The Language of Social Research* (New York: Free Press, 1955), 83–93.

[26] See, e.g., Neil J. Smelser, *Social Change in the Industrial Revolution* (Chicago: University of Chicago Press, 1959).

gories) upon the data, whereas Lazarsfeld sees the categories emerging out of the analysis of the research results. It is apparent that adherence to the actor's frame of reference can yield widely different results than adoption of the scientist's frame of reference.

Studies of American social stratification do in fact attest to this.[27] Those scientists who employ a subjective definition of class, who permit the actors in a class system to define the structure and the nature of that system, arrive at rather different conclusions than do sociologists who employ an "objective" definition of class, who use such indicators as the income, education, or occupational position of the informants. Interviewees usually do not perceive their own class system as being as well defined as the social scientist would. For one thing, the general populace has accepted to a considerable degree the American creed of a classless society.

More subtle interpretations arise in other realms of social research. Some sociologists, for example, consider myths to be those beliefs of ordinary men that scientists judge to be false but which nonetheless persist in the thought ways of the man in the street. Certainly the actor does not regard his own beliefs as myths: Myths are the beliefs of groups that are alien to him. The sociologist who labels the values or beliefs of, say, the Townsend Movement or the John Birch Society as myths would seem to be imposing his own out-group judgment and thus placing himself in the role of a "myth maker."[28]

Furthermore, the theorizing in the field of social control and deviant behavior indicates that one's level of theory and conception of the nature of social reality may have significant ideological consequences. There is a group of sociologists who consider the societal perspective to be the only valid one in the study of social control and social deviation. Durkheim adhered to this position in his early positivist writings, where he perceived of social control as "external to actors."[29] This societal orientation toward social control has its contemporary adherents.[30] A somewhat contrary position is espoused by those sociologists who are committed to the Mead tradition.[31] Although these scholars recognize the society's role in defining and controlling deviation, the consequences of adopting the actor's perspective are far-reaching. By striving to grasp the actor's rationale

---

[27] See, e.g., Richard T. Morris, "Social Stratification," in Leonard Broom and Philip Selznick, *Sociology,* 3rd ed. (New York: Harper & Row, 1963), chap. 6.

[28] Leonard D Cain, Jr., "The Role of Myth-Designation in Social Movements," unpublished Ph.D. dissertation, University of Texas, 1955.

[29] See Parsons' discussion of Durkheim's shifting orientation over time in Talcott Parsons, *The Structure of Social Action,* 2nd ed. (New York: Free Press, 1949), chap. 10.

[30] See, e.g., Alexander L. Clark and Jack P. Gibbs, "Social Control: A Reformulation," *Social Problems,* 12 (Spring, 1965), 398–415.

[31] Howard S. Becker, *Outsiders* (New York: Free Press, 1963). Becker contends that social researchers must take the viewpoint "either of those who are treated as deviant or of those who label others as deviant. . . . It is, of course, possible to see the situation

for deviating from established norms, the scientist to a degree legitimizes the deviant actor's definition of the situation and to a degree adopts an anti–status-quo position—a position that is at odds with the more conservative stance of Durkheim and his followers. In one sense the willingness to recognize the deviant's orientation relativizes the scientist's world view.

However, scientists who adopt the actor's view of reality differ among themselves, and these varying perspectives become crucial in the interpretations of empirical findings. We have only to contrast the action theories of Parsons in his *The Structure of Social Action* and of Znaniecki in his *Cultural Sciences* to realize this fact.[32] Although Parsons begins with the actor's orientation, he nevertheless places greater emphasis than Znaniecki upon the scientist's categories, even to the extent of imposing these upon social reality for purposes of analysis. Parsons' view is related to his greater insistence upon order and fixity in the social realm. Consequently, the researcher who utilizes Parsons' means-end schema takes the end as more or less fixed.[33] Znaniecki, on the other hand, contends that as actors strive to attain goals the latter change or become redefined.[34]

In turn the British economist Shackle begins, as does Znaniecki, with the assumption that the social world is not rigidly determined—that there is "bounded uncertainty." By implication the actor may remake his environment (at least to a degree) in the course of striving to attain certain goals. Yet, unlike Znaniecki, Shackle analyzes social action within an "uncertainty framework." At the same time, Shackle's formulation differs from the probability schemes employed by theorists within a more mechanistic tradition, whose deductive models are generally more elegant than Shackle's.[35] One consequence of both the Shackle and the Znaniecki positions is that they greatly complicate the task of analyzing human action within a group, for with these schema the scientist must see the social order as in a state of becoming.

Ideology and the Social Order

We have observed that the sociologist's theoretical assumptions structure his interpretation of the data. But these premises, we must recall, are also shaped

---

from both sides. But it cannot be done simultaneously. . . . We cannot describe a "higher reality" that makes sense of both sets of views" (172–173). While it is difficult to achieve a higher synthesis, and though such a synthesis is always a tenuous one, we can (and must) strive to achieve it. Becker's thesis commits him to a kind of historicism.

[32] Cf. Parsons, *The Structure of Social Action, op. cit.;* and Florian Znaniecki, *Cultural Sciences* (Urbana, Ill.: University of Illinois Press, 1952).

[33] Parsons, *The Structure of Social Action, op. cit., passim.*

[34] Znaniecki, *op. cit.*

[35] G. L. S. Shackle, *Decision, Order and Time in Human Affairs* (London: Cambridge, 1961), chaps. 9, 29, and *passim.*

by the researcher's ideology and group membership, including his status therein.

The variables of group membership and ideology operate on the international and national planes. One of the most all-pervasive influences upon the researcher, but difficult to evaluate, stems from his identification with a particular nation-state system. Max Weber, though he advanced the cause of social science considerably by his stress upon objectivity, failed to recognize the possible impact of nationalism upon his own writings and those of other scholars. For while Bendix, for instance, has admitted that Weber was committed to a "crude German nationalism,"[36] only a few commentators have considered the manner in which Weber's nationalistic leanings influenced his sociological analysis.[37] So too, it would be possible to show that Durkheim's emphasis upon the nation-state did much to structure aspects of his sociological thinking.[38]

In the United States similar patterns are observable. For this we need only examine the writings of Cooley and more recently Parsons and Lipset.[39] Lipset's *Political Man* is laden with nationalistic overtones. We offer the following quotation by way of evidence:

> The United States has not made a serious effort to overthrow Fidel Castro by force, to a considerable degree because the American political tradition finds such behavior so repugnant. It is, of course, true that certain groups in the military and the Central Intelligence Agency have engaged in secret operations which clearly violate these assumptions. But the very fact that these are done secretly pays tribute to the political

[36] Reinhard Bendix, *Max Weber: An Intellectual Portrait* (Garden City, N.Y.: Doubleday, Anchor Books, 1962), 10.

[37] See, e.g., Wolfgang Mommsen, "Max Weber's Political Sociology and His Philosophy of World History," *International Social Science Journal*, 17 (1965), 23–45.

[38] See, e.g., Emile Durkheim, *Moral Education,* trans. by Everett K. Wilson and Herman Schnurer (New York: Free Press, 1961), 74–76.

It is also of interest to recognize that Durkheim's sociology was a source of inspiration for the sociologist Ziya Gökalp, *Turkish Nationalism and Western Civilization*, trans. by Niyazi Berkes (London: G. Allen, 1959). Of course, Gökalp, who did much to lay the intellectual basis for contemporary Turkish nationalism, was influenced more generally by European nationalism. Cf. Uriel Heyd, *Foundations of Turkish Nationalism* (London: Luzac, 1950), 164–170.

[39] Charles Horton Cooley, *Social Process* (Carbondale, Ill.: Southern Illinois Press, 1966), 141, 147–148. Parsons' commitment to the nation-state as an ultimate source of moral authority is reflected—albeit in a subtle manner—in, for example, his analysis of the role of the American Sociological Association and of sociologists in general. He discusses these roles in terms of a societal (that is, national) framework. Certainly in his article, "Some Problems Confronting Sociology as a Profession," *American Sociological Review*, 24 (August, 1959), 547–559, Talcott Parsons fails explicitly to take into account the sociologist's necessary commitment to various broad transcultural or transnational values and beliefs.

morality of most Americans, and it should also be noted that, with the exception of Guatemala, accusations by foreign or domestic critics of such efforts have pointed to supposed American failures, as in Laos, rather than successes in affecting affairs abroad.[40]

This quotation from one of Lipset's works raises the following questions: Has intervention really been so repugnant to the American political tradition? What about the role of Americans from Theodore Roosevelt on through the 1950s and into the 1960s? And just how does Lipset *know* that the amount of secret intervention has necessarily been minimal?[41] It seems fair to assume that Lipset's reasoning is associated with an overidentification with his own country and his failure to "take the role of the other" and to ask, "How does the United States appear to other nations in this matter?"

Ideological factors also affect research on social patterns within nations. The studies of the French Revolution and the Industrial Revolution in England have all too often mirrored particular scholars' political identifications. Thus Palmer in his review of research on the French Revolution during the 1950s stressed the trend toward studying the revolution from the perspective of the *sans-culottes,* or the disadvantaged.

> This re-examination of the "lower" classes in France during the Revolution, based though it is on the most admirable and thorough archival researches, is closely identified with the European Left, and in the case of some writers with avowed Communism. The incentive, sympathy, and purpose sustaining the years of exacting work in difficult sources has been to a degree Marxist, and the cordial reception of the new writings in some quarters reflects the same affiliations.[42]

The various roles and ideological commitments of social scientists evince considerable complexity. The published statements of sociologists at the University of California (Berkeley) concerning the Free Speech Movement are a case in point.[43] While it is difficult to determine just what role these sociologists were

[40] Seymour M. Lipset, *Political Man* (Garden City, N.Y.: Doubleday, Anchor Books, 1963), xxx–xxxi.

[41] Since the publication of Lipset's book, his general proposition has been proven false. Not only has the CIA intervened more extensively than he thought possible in the affairs of other countries, but it has been infiltrated academic and scholarly activities in the United States and abroad. Christopher Lasch, a historian, has portrayed, in part at least, the intellectual climate of the 1950s out of which Lipset's work arose. Christopher Lasch, "The Cultural Cold War," *The Nation,* 205 (Sept. 11, 1967), 198–212.

[42] Robert R. Palmer, "Popular Democracy in the French Revolution," *French Historical Studies, 1* (Fall, 1960), 448.

[43] See some of the essays in Seymour M. Lipset and Sheldon S. Wolin (eds.), *The Berkeley Student Revolt* (Garden City, N.Y.: Doubleday, Anchor Books, 1965).

attempting to play in the matter—that of pure sociologist or that of moralizer—their statements clearly reflect varying political and ideological commitments. These range from those of Selznick, who defended the Free Speech Movement, to those of Petersen, who argued that the movement was at least in part "Communist inspired."[44] Then there was Lipset, who chastised the rebellious students for challenging the social order of the university. He was of course examining the movement from the standpoint of the system, not from the perspective of the students.[45] Lipset also criticized the students for being ideological at a time when, from the perspective of Lipset's own sociological theory, Americans should have reached "the end of ideology."[46]

American social scientists have, moreover, tended to examine their subjects through status-tinted glasses. Campbell and his associates argue as follows:

> Once again we see that the people who organize their political behavior in the manner often assumed by sophisticated investigators are those who are most similar to such analysts in political concept formation. The familiar picture of the democratic process as a clearing-house for conflicting class interest becomes increasingly inappropriate as we move to layers of the electorate more removed from the informed observer. If the role of social class in mass political behavior is less potent than we are frequently led to believe, these discrepancies in sophistication appear to be largely responsible. If we wish to deal with social class in its traditional garb in politics, we are dealing with a fairly restricted and sophisticated portion of the population.[47]

The implication is that the researcher tends to attribute to persons of lower status the particular view of social action that he himself has acquired as a citizen and as a member of a privileged group.

To compensate for these hidden biases, which lead to deviation from the ideal of objectivity, social scientists must engage in reasoned debate and criticism. They must encourage the writing up of self-examining accounts such as that of Homans, who admitted that one reason for his willingness to adopt Pareto's framework was his search for an answer to the arguments of the revolutionaries of the 1930s, especially the Marxists.[48] Self-criticism can also be advanced by comparing one's own work with that carried out in other cultural settings and by

---

[44] Cf. Philip Selznick, "Reply to Glazer," *ibid.*, 303–312; and William Petersen, "What is Left at Berkeley," *ibid.*, 367–385.

[45] Seymour M. Lipset and Paul Seabury, "The Lesson of Berkeley," *ibid.*, 340–349.

[46] Cf. Lipset, *op. cit.*

[47] Angus Campbell *et al.*, *The American Voter* (New York: Wiley, 1960), 353.

[48] George C. Homans, *Sentiments and Activities* (New York: Free Press, 1962), 4.

attempting to assess how future generations of sociologists may evaluate present-day research.

Diverse Logics of Theory Building

When the social scientist theorizes about substantive problems—be these in deviant behavior, formal organization, or the family—his own theoretical assumptions are everpresent to influence the final results. They provide the context within which the scientist formulates his deductive system or engages in discovery.

In Chapter 3 we outlined the general nature of the deductive model and the process of discovery. Some attention must now be given to the patterns and problems that emerge in actual practice. In point of fact, there exist modes of theory construction that do not fit into the categories of deduction and discovery as these have been employed by philosophers of science.

THE DEDUCTIVE ORIENTATION

We must distinguish between the *kinds* of deductive systems and the sources of such systems. In our discussion of logico-deductive theory in Chapter 3, our emphasis was upon the deterministic, or covering-law, or what Hempel has called the deductive-nomological, model. This kind of deductive system is to be distinguished from that variably referred to as the statistical, probability, or stochastic model.

The deterministic model, one that involves an *always* law statement, has been applied only infrequently in sociology. Firey, in his *Man, Mind, and Land,* cast his logico-deductive formulation into the deterministic mold.[49] But his theory emerged during the course of his research: he was not seeking to test an already existing theory.

Instead of employing the deterministic model, most sociologists have turned to statistical or stochastic models. Zetterberg's work, which has done much to popularize the use of deductive systems in sociology, is within this tradition. Zetterberg has set forth a number of postulates concerning the division of labor:

1. The greater the division of labor, the more the uniformity.
2. The greater the solidarity, the greater the number of members.
3. The greater the number of members, the less the deviation. And so on through 14 propositions in all.[50]

---

[49] Walter Firey, *Man, Mind and Land* (New York: Free Press, 1960).

[50] Hans L. Zetterberg, *On Theory and Verification in Sociology* (Stockholm: Almqvist & Wiksell, 1954), 18. Two of the 14 are identical, probably because of a typographical error.

Zetterberg proceeds to define such basic concepts as "uniformity," "deviation," and "deviate." He also indicates how his 14 propositions can be reduced to 4 and how, because of their logical interrelatedness, testing one of the postulates automatically involves testing the others as well (though this last point is, as we shall see, open to question).[51]

We must recognize that Zetterberg's axioms, stated as they are in relational form, must be tested via some measure of association. They could, of course, be recast into an *always* form: "If the division of labor within a group increases, the degree of uniformity always increases as well." As in all deterministic models, a single negative case would then suffice to falsify the hypothesis.

Zetterberg's use of the stochastic model poses special problems, for this system involves no strict implication. Thus, if one argues that *a* is correlated with *b* and *b* with *c*, it does not necessarily follow that *a* is correlated with *c*. Such would be true only where the correlations are high.

It seems clear that when strict implication is lacking, it is difficult to formulate models in social science that have their initial postulates on a high level of abstraction (and thus are not directly testable) and wherein one moves down deductively to testable hypotheses.[52] In sociology, where high correlations among variables are the exception rather than the rule, it is usually necessary to calculate the correlations for each postulate in order to ensure closure.

But the issues with respect to Zetterberg's formulation are even more complex than this. Zetterberg admits that he is dealing with statistical or stochastic or probability models, not deterministic ones.[53] However, he fails to explore the implications of this fact. For one thing, probability has a different connotation here than in the realm of inductive statistics. For the probability is associated not with the testing of the relationship of a sample to a working universe but with the phenomena themselves. Camilleri, for one, has recognized this distinction, and he and others contend that sociologists should emulate the natural scientists in constructing probability models.[54] Yet, these sociologists fail to recognize that natural scientists are able to utilize these models because their probabilities are so high; in effect they treat their logico-deductive systems *as if* they were deterministic. Therefore, if we had a chain of postulates concerning covariation between two variables, we would experience difficulty in deducing valid theorems unless we could assume the presence of high probabilities (as well

[51] *Ibid.*, 19 ff.

[52] One effort to bridge the gap between Zetterberg's form of model building and empirical research is found in Herbert L. Costner and Robert K. Leik, "Deductions from 'Axiomatic Theory,' " *American Sociological Review*, 29 (December, 1964), 819–835.

[53] This is true even of recent editions of his work: Hans L. Zetterberg, *On Theory and Verification in Sociology*, 3rd ed. (Totowa, N.J.: Bedminster, 1965).

[54] Santo F. Camilleri, "Theory, Probability, and Induction in Social Research," *American Sociological Review*, 27 (April, 1962), 170–178.

as high correlations) for each postulate. Thus Hempel writes concerning the probability or statistical model in the natural sciences:

> To account for the occurrence of a certain kind of event under specified (e.g., experimental) conditions, certain laws or theories of statistical form are adduced, and it is shown that as a consequence of these, the statistical probability for an outcome of the specified kind under circumstances of the specified kind is extremely high, so that that outcome may be expected with practical certainty in any one case where the specified conditions occur.[55]

This fact would seem to set significant limits upon the use of probability models in sociology.

Although we could pursue these issues at greater length, we must now turn to the *sources* of deductive systems in sociology. For the kinds of empirical materials used in building deductive schemes vary considerably.

The crudest and loosest form of the deductive model (one not usually signified by this label) results when researchers test an hypothesis or set of hypotheses and then seek to provide a theoretical framework embracing various postulates in order to explain these hypotheses. This is perhaps the most widely used procedure in sociology.

Sociologists also may test a particular hypothesis and then use that hypothesis as a basis for deducing certain consequences. Thus, if one were to confirm the hypothesis that more people in the United States migrate from the countryside to the city than the reverse, this hypothesis could then be turned into a postulate and, in conjunction with other postulates drawn from the confirmed hypotheses of other research studies, used as a basis for deriving a set of theorems (or what are often loosely termed "implications"). These are not tested but merely provide hypotheses for future research. We can also follow a method adhered to by some of Zetterberg's students. Hopkins, for example, combed the literature on small groups for various hypotheses and then knitted these together into a deductive system.[56]

Another mode of constructing deductive models from existing research has been demonstrated by Simon and Gross. Homans, after a careful investigation of a number of empirical studies, discovered a number of hypotheses concerning

---

[55] Carl G. Hempel, "Deductive-Nomological vs. Statistical Explanation," in Herbert Feigl and Grover Maxwell (eds.), *Minnesota Studies in the Philosophy of Science: III, Scientific Explanation, Space, and Time* (Minneapolis: University of Minnesota Press, 1962), 143.

[56] Terence Hopkins, *The Exercise of Influence in Small Groups* (Totowa, N.J.: Bedminster, 1964).

small-group activities.[57] Simon, in turn, translated a number of these hypotheses into the mathematical language of calculus and constructed a deductive system from which he derived certain theorems.[58] But, as Coleman suggests, the postulates themselves are weak (with the result that the deductions are not particularly novel).[59] This highlights a dilemma that faces sociologists who advocate the use of mathematical models. Where theorems display a high degree of novelty (and such is the ideal of deductive systems), then the postulates or axioms of the model tend to be so far removed from social reality as to be of little empirical relevance.

Gross, unlike Simon, used ordinary language rather than the language of mathematics to formalize Sutherland's theory of "differential association," a crude theory on the etiology of crime for which there is considerable empirical support. Gross's formulation was not especially rigorous, but it did permit him to retain considerable empirical content in his theory.[60]

The foregoing methods of constructing deductive systems rely heavily upon research in the social sciences. But others have been built upon "folk models."[61] For example, Von Neumann and Morgenstern's *Theory of Games and Economic Behavior* took the folk model of the game as the basis for their theorizing.[62] Specifically, the authors abstracted the key elements of the game and used these as the basis for developing a set of postulates from which in turn they derived some highly novel and useful theorems about social action in competitive situations.

The work of Von Neumann and Morgenstern has given rise to a variety of deductive models, so that by 1961 Shubik could state that some 20-odd models for *n*-person games were in existence.[63] There is a danger that deductive models are being spun simply for their own sake. Attention must also be given to determining when and where particular models are empirically valid.

Although ultimately we must assess the utility of these deductive systems in

[57] George Homans, *The Human Group* (New York: Harcourt, Brace & World, 1950).

[58] Herbert A. Simon, "A Formal Theory of Interaction in Small Groups," *American Sociological Review*, 17 (April, 1952), 202–211.

[59] James S. Coleman, "The Mathematical Study of Small Groups," in Herbert Solomon (ed.), *Mathematical Thinking in the Measurement of Behavior* (New York: Free Press, 1960), 28–38.

[60] Llewellyn Gross, "Theory Construction in Sociology: A Methodological Inquiry," in Llewellyn Gross (ed.), *Symposium on Sociological Theory* (New York: Harper & Row, 1959), chap. 17.

[61] Alan Ross Anderson and Omar Khayyam Moore, "Autotelic Folk Models," *Sociological Quarterly*, 1 (October, 1960), 203–216.

[62] John von Neumann and Oskar Morgenstern, *Theory of Games and Economic Behavior*, 2nd ed. (Princeton, N.J., Princeton, 1947).

[63] Martin Shubik, "Approaches to the Study of Decision-Making Relevant to the Firm," *Journal of Business*, 34 (April, 1961), 108.

light of empirical reality, we should not overlook some of the unique by-products of certain elegant deductive theories that have little or no direct empirical applicability. First, such theories tend to disclose the logical gaps and weaknesses in theories that involve only ordinary language. Second, by their very oversimplification of social reality they can serve in the social sciences as a partial substitute for the experimental method. Such theories as these indicate, for instance, the way individuals would act under ideal conditions and thereby provide a base (or reference point) against which to contrast human actions in the everyday world.[64] Third, it is possible to translate some of these mathematical models into ordinary language and to use the insights gained from the complex deductions in the mathematical models in the formulation of theories cast in ordinary language. Certainly, this has been true of game theory. Although the theory, translated into ordinary language, is loose and crude in many ways, it does represent an advance over formulations that have arisen out of the medium of ordinary language. To be sure, social scientists must continually guard against becoming so enamored of these abstract deductive systems that they lose sight of the ultimate goal of science, which is the explanation of empirical phenomena. Such apparently has occurred in some areas of economics.

The final source of theory building to be discussed is even farther removed from empirical research than is the folk model. Here one begins with certain primitive observations or "self-evident truths" concerning the social order and then proceeds to deduce theorems or hypotheses from them. Little or no attention is given to testing the theorems; they are presumed to be true because the postulates have been "verified."

The orientation that depends upon such self-evident truths has been most fully elaborated by certain economists, for whom Robbins has been an articulate spokesman:

> The propositions of economic theory, like all scientific theory, are obviously deductions from a series of postulates. And the chief of these postulates are all assumptions involving in some way simple and indisputable facts of experience relating to the way in which the scarcity of goods which is the subject-matter of our science actually shows itself in the world of reality. The main postulate of the theory of value is the fact that individuals can arrange their preferences in an order, and in fact do so. The main postulate of the theory of production is the fact that there are more than one factor of production. The main postulate of the theory of dynamics is the fact that we are not certain regarding future scarcities. These are not postulates the existence of whose counter-

---

[64] See, e.g., Kenneth J. Arrow, *Social Choice and Individual Values* (New York: Wiley, 1951).

part in reality admits of extensive dispute once their nature is fully realised. We do not need controlled experiments to establish their validity: they are so much the stuff of our everyday experience that they have only to be stated to be recognised as obvious. Indeed, the danger is that they may be thought to be so obvious that nothing significant can be derived from their future examination. Yet in fact it is on postulates of this sort that the complicated theorems of advanced analysis ultimately depend. And it is from the existence of the conditions they assume that the general applicability of the broader propositions of economic science is derived.[65]

Social scientists such as Robbins still walk among us. One is Firey, as exemplified in his *Law and Economy in Planning*.[66] However, unlike Robbins, Firey begins with postulates that stem from certain "categorical imperatives." For he is working here within the Kantian intellectual heritage. In any event, it is the form of theory building carried on by Robbins and Firey that led Northrop to differentiate between theories in the social sciences (notably economics) and those in the natural sciences.[67]

Of course, while this school of thought has developed some elegant theories, the limitations of the latter have become apparent as economists have attempted to apply them in non-Western societies. What seems self-evident in the West has proved not to be so everywhere.

DEDUCTIVE SYSTEMS AND THEORETICAL ASSUMPTIONS

Having discussed various kinds of deductive systems and the sources thereof, we can now return to the problem of the relationship of these to broader theoretical systems.

Broadly, the scientist's conception of the level of theory influences the level of abstraction of his postulates. That is, his theoretical assumptions more or less determine the manner in which he tests his hypotheses. Zetterberg's propositions concerning the division of labor (mentioned above) seem to have been formulated with an eye to testing these from the scientist's perspective, not from that of the actors within the social order being studied.[68]

On a more general level, the implications of a given hypothesis depend upon the scientist's understanding of his assumptions regarding the nature of social

[65] Lionel Robbins, *An Essay on the Nature and Significance of Economic Science*, 2nd ed. (London: Macmillan, 1935), 78–79.

[66] Walter Firey, *Law and Economy in Planning* (Austin: University of Texas Press, 1965).

[67] F. S. C. Northrop, *The Logic of the Sciences and the Humanities* (New York: Macmillan, 1947).

[68] Zetterberg, 1954, *op. cit.*

reality. For example, Gibbs and Martin set forth certain hypotheses or propositions concerning the interrelationships of urbanization, technology, and the division of labor. They link these propositions together into a "low-level" deductive model:

1A. The degree of urbanization in a society varies directly with the division of labor;

1B. The division of labor in a society varies directly with the dispersion of objects of consumption;

IIA. The degree of urbanization in a society varies directly with technological development;

IIB. Technological development in a society varies directly with the dispersion of objects of consumption.[69]

The authors' theoretical assumptions of a materialistic and mechanistic social order stand somewhat apart from the foregoing propositions. And because awareness of these is essential if one is to test and properly interpret the results of a study, Gibbs and Martin are led to discuss these assumptions.[70]

A somewhat similar pattern emerges in Homans' *Social Behavior: Its Elementary Forms* where Homans sets forth the following interrelated set of postulates:

1. If in the past the occurrence of a particular stimulus-situation has been the occasion on which a man's activity has been rewarded, then the more similar the present stimulus-situation is to the past one, the more likely he is to emit the activity, or some similar activity, now.[71]

2. The more often within a given period of time a man's activity rewards the activity of another, the more often the other will emit the activity.[72]

3. The more valuable to a man a unit of the activity another gives him, the more often he will emit activity rewarded by the activity of the other.[73]

4. The more often a man has in the recent past received a rewarding activity from another, the less valuable any further unit of that activity becomes to him.[74]

---

[69] Jack P. Gibbs and Walter T. Martin, "Urbanization, Technology, and the Division of Labor: International Patterns," *American Sociological Review*, 27 (October, 1962), 669.

[70] *Ibid.*, 676–677.

[71] George C. Homans, *Social Behavior, op. cit.*, 53.

[72] *Ibid.*, 54.

[73] *Ibid.*, 55.

[74] *Ibid.*, 55.

5. The more to a man's disadvantage the rule of distributive justice fails of realization, the more likely he is to display the emotional behavior we call anger.[75]

In this book Homans devotes most of his exposition to justifying his theoretical construct. Homans' framework includes an assumption of extreme reductionism and others regarding the nature of profit and exchange among individuals. Some of the assumptions (for example, that concerning the nature of reward) enter the deductive scheme implicitly via the definition of key terms, but the premise of reductionism clearly stands apart from the author's postulates.[76]

One of Blau's chief criticisms of Homans' work stems from the latter's failure to put together a set of postulates that are congruent with his broader theoretical assumptions.[77] Proposition 5, relating to the rule of distributive justice, implicitly introduces the concept of "norm." The use of this concept leads Homans to contravene his basic premise of reductionism: that one must concentrate solely on individuals and sentiments.

THE EMPHASIS UPON DISCOVERY

Discovery has been the basis for the development not only of isolated hypotheses but of theoretical systems. Thus one may uncover a set of findings and order these into some classificatory scheme or retroduce a deductive theory to account for them (a pattern apparently followed by Firey in his *Man, Mind and Land*).[78]

It is significant that a large number of sociologists begin with a problem or set of questions about the nature of a particular social pattern, not with certain well-defined hypotheses to be tested. This stress on discovery can be found in many highly respected studies, for example, *Boys in White* by Becker *et al.* They write:

> In one sense, our study had no design. That is, we had no well-worked-out set of hypotheses to be tested, no data-gathering instruments purposely designed to secure information relevant to these hypotheses, no set of analytic procedures specified in advance. Insofar as the term "design" implies these features of elaborate prior planning, our study had none.
>
> If we take the idea of design in a larger and looser sense, using it

---

[75] *Ibid.*, 75.

[76] *Ibid.*, *passim.*

[77] Peter M. Blau, "Justice in Social Exchange," *Sociological Inquiry*, 34 (Spring, 1964), 193–206. Cf. his *Exchange and Power in Social Life* (New York: Wiley, 1964).

[78] Firey, *Man, Mind and Land, op. cit.*

fication of actions, but to a causal explanation of their changes. This attempt was published under the title *The Laws of Social Psychology*. Since then I have tested many times the generalizations included in that book, and always found them true, when tested with the help of the heuristic concepts there employed. Unfortunately, these concepts were not sufficiently exact to permit decisive tests, for I had not yet gotten rid of the psychological idea that the tendency is an *element* of the action. Moreover, I had not yet separated strictly enough the problem of *qualitative laws expressing causal relationships* from that of *quantitative laws expressing functional relationships*.

Still I believe that was a good beginning. However, the task of mastering descriptively the concrete complexity of social actions by purely inductive methods, without the use of deduction from psychological premises accepted in advance, had all to be done. . . . To conclude briefly the story, I worked this book over three more times. Some of its parts have thus been written and rewritten as many as six times in the course of fifteen years.[81]

Znaniecki obviously began with a theoretical framework. But it is his procedure after he rejected his original frame of reference that is of interest to us here. For he seems to have immersed himself in his data to the point that he engaged in what Peirce termed "abduction."

We can probably assume that many other classificatory schemes in sociology emerged in a manner similar to this. Weber, for example, undoubtedly depended upon immersal in a vast amount of historical data for his development of the distinctions among charismatic, traditional, and legal-rational authority.

OTHER ORIENTATIONS

There are other "logical systems" widely employed by sociologists in theory building that deserve special treatment. Although these systems may be used in conjunction with discovery and classification, they stand apart from the tradition of deductive logic. One of these "logics" relates parts to a whole, another relates parts to parts to a whole (within the dialectic framework), and the third is based on analogy.

Structural-functional analysis consists in relating parts to wholes. Here sociologists are intent upon establishing the function of a structure in terms of the purposes and goals of some broader system. Implicit in this type of analysis is the premise that the whole is more than the sum of its parts.

This type of reasoning (which we consider at greater length in Chapter 11)

[81] Florian Znaniecki, *Social Actions* (New York: Holt, Rinehart and Winston, 1936), vii–viii.

to identify those elements of order, system, and consistency our pr
cedures did exhibit, our study had a design.[79]

Furthermore,

> We studied what was of interest to the people we were investigating
> because we felt that in this way we would uncover the basic dimensions
> of the school as a social organization and of the students' progress
> through it as a social-psychological phenomenon.[80]

Researchers committed to a *verstehen* orientation, to taking the viewpoint of
the actor, are much more likely to stress discovery than they are to stress the
testing of well-defined hypotheses. Then too, in this kind of situation the researcher must carry on his analysis in conjunction with his collection of the data
(a point made earlier). Often he does this through some modified form of
analytic induction that emphasizes discovery.

Also, many of the classification schemes, or taxonomies, in sociology find
their origin in the discovery process. Prominent among the efforts in this direction
is the work of Znaniecki. Beginning with the framework of the psychologists
McDougall and Ross, Znaniecki spent some 15 years isolating the fundamental
and elementary attitudes underlying social intercourse among people:

> When, after two years' work, the outline was practically finished,
> I found that something was wrong. My materials simply did not fit into
> the original framework. . . .
>
> I had to reorganize and rewrite the whole thing. . . . Meanwhile I
> still went on gathering and analyzing cases. And again most of the facts
> did not fit the theory.
>
> Only then I decided to change my whole approach. I tried to get
> rid of the assumption that the whole variety of the social actions of man
> has to be deduced from a few permanent and fundamental psychological
> forces—essential attitudes, wishes, desires, or what not. Why not take
> these actions in their empirical concreteness and variety, and try to order
> them *such as they are*, without any *a priori* assumptions concerning the
> psychological sources from which they spring?
>
> It was not easy, however . . . Old traditions and my own previous
> theoretic attempts kept obtruding themselves. I therefore applied this
> changed point of view at first not to a systematic description and classi-

---

[79] Howard S. Becker *et al., Boys in White* (Chicago: University of Chicago Press,
1961), 17.

[80] *Ibid.,* 20.

has been the prime basis for social systems analysis, particularly the study of formal or complex organizations. Numerous studies of hospitals, prisons, the military, and so on fall within this tradition. Indeed, unless one resorts to some form of reductionism, the structural-functional framework seems difficult to avoid in any theoretical analysis of social organizations.

If we consider a system in process, we can study the interaction of its parts and so ascertain how this affects the total system. It is possible, like Parsons, to envisage the parts as functioning in relative harmony.[82] On the other hand, if one conceives of social systems as embracing contradictory goals and purposes and as made up of contradictory elements, then one must turn to the logic of the dialectic as a mode of analysis. Here one takes one part (the thesis) and another part (the antithesis) and examines how the resultant conflict and tension between the two give rise to some kind of synthesis.

Writers such as Marx and Sorokin have utilized the logic of the dialectic to good advantage in their analysis of social phenomena. And this mode of reasoning continues to serve the cause of social science. Although the logic of the dialectic has been severely criticized, it seems to be an indispensable tool in theory construction. Georgescu-Roegen argues that although "we are apt to associate dialectical concepts with loose thinking . . . the highly significant fact is that no one has been able to present an argument against dialectical concepts without incessant recourse to them."[83]

Sociologists like Ossowski and Lenski have utilized the logic of the dialectic in developing new thories in the field of social stratification.[84] Lenski strives to synthesize what he regards as two contradictory intellectual heritages in social science. But then, after he has arrived at the synthesis, he attempts to state it in terms of certain formal propositions.[85]

In other words, Lenski does not appear to use the logic of the dialectic in his analysis of data—of power and privilege. On the other hand, Blau has applied the logic of the dialectic to the analysis of the social world.[86] It is noteworthy that Blau's assumption about reality seems to have influenced his choice of logic, for he writes: "There is a dialectic in social life, for it is governed by many contradictory forces. The dilemmas of social associations reflect this dialectic, and so does the character of social change."[87]

---

[82] See, e.g., Talcott Parsons, *The Social System* (New York: Free Press, 1951).

[83] Georgescu-Roegen, *op. cit.*, 27.

[84] Stanislaw Ossowski, *Class Structure in the Social Consciousness,* trans. by Sheila Patterson (New York: Free Press, 1963); and Gerhard E. Lenski, *Power and Privilege* (New York: McGraw-Hill, 1966).

[85] Lenski, *op. cit.*

[86] Blau, *Exchange and Power in Social Life, op. cit.*

[87] *Ibid.,* 336.

The use of analogy has also been of significance in the construction of social theory. By "analogy" we mean resemblances in the systems of relationship of two or more phenomena rather than resemblances among the phenomena themselves. Those who employ analogy are interested in abstract relationships, not in the relationships among concrete empirical phenomena.

The logic of analogy has been used by some structural-functionalists and by supporters of the logic of the dialectic in furthering their analyses. This sort of theory building continues to be employed. Goffman in his influential work has taken the theater as his vantage point for illumining aspects of human action and personality. He perceives an analogy here with the personality patterns of individuals in everyday life, for, like Shakespeare, he regards individuals as incessant performers upon life's stage.[88]

It is true that many theories constructed by the use of analogy have proved erroneous and have consequently been rejected. Social Darwinism, for example, has been largely discredited as a basis for interpreting human relationships. Nevertheless, reasoning by analogy continues to be employed in theory construction, for it does suggest hitherto unperceived or novel relationships.[89] This form of reasoning as such is not hazardous; rather the danger lies in applying it indiscriminately without checking into the validity of the theoretical formulations.

Typological Analysis

Typological analysis[90] deserves special attention. Although widely employed in social research, it is one of the least understood of the researcher's conceptual tools. Yet it has a long history of useful application: Weber, Tönnies, Sombart, and others used typologies in their historical studies. At the same time, certain typological formulations have been strongly criticized, especially by logical empiricists.

Many social researchers who are critical of typologies of any sort still employ

---

[88] Goffman, *op. cit.* To be sure, one of Goffman's main weaknesses is that he forgets at times that he is drawing an analogy and thus tends to make daily social life equivalent to the theater: Sheldon L. Messinger with Harold Sampson and Robert D. Towne, "Life as Theater: Some Notes on the Dramaturgic Approach to Social Reality," *Sociometry, 25* (March, 1962), 98–110.

[89] For a useful discussion of reasoning via analogies, see Herbert A. Simon and Allen Newell, "The Uses and Limitations of Models," in Melvin H. Marx (ed.), *Theories in Contemporary Psychology* (New York: Macmillan, 1963), chap. 4.

[90] Carl G. Hempel, *Aspects of Scientific Explanation* (New York: Free Press, 1965), chap. 7, considers typologies within a logical empiricist framework, whereas John C. McKinney, *Constructive Typology and Social Theory* (New York: Appleton-Century-Crofts, 1966), is much more within the interpretative sociology framework. In our own analysis we differ somewhat from both of these writers.

these tools in their analysis of social data. Thus Leach contends that he is skeptical of all typologies, yet proceeds to utilize them in ordering his materials.[91]

Some writers would see deductive systems, particularly mathematical ones, as permitting sociologists to dispense with the use of typologies. This we doubt. Firey, who used the covering-law model in his study of land use, still had to supplement this deductive scheme with typological constructs. The distinction among folk, feudal, and industrial types of societies is basic to his entire theoretical formulation.[92]

If we examine the issue pragmatically, we find that knowledge of a variety of typological tools is central to the development of classificatory schemes and to the understanding of conceptualization in social science more generally. Weber, who did so much to formalize the ideal type and its use, recognized that a number of types can be developed, a fact that some writers continue to overlook. Moreover, different types have different applications in social research.

THE IDEAL TYPE

Weber emphasized negative criteria in defining this conceptual tool, and most logicians recognize that defining any concept in negative terms leaves much to be desired. According to Weber, the ideal type was neither an average, nor a description of reality, nor a hypothesis.[93] The last-named negative criterion should be underscored; Weber, unlike some modern-day users of this tool was conscious that this ideal type was to be employed in testing hypotheses or, more generally, as a tool in constructing theories. It was not an end in itself.

Yet Weber did introduce certain positive criteria in his definition of the ideal type. He saw it as a "one-sided accentuation" of reality, as a magnification of certain crucial or unique features of the social phenomenon being investigated, as a utopia.[94] In practice Weber accentuated those characteristics that set off the phenomenon in question from those with which it was contrasted. The ideal type, as Weber saw it, also had to "make sense": it had to be logically consistent internally.[95]

Let us examine the way Weber applied this tool in his study of the relationship between religion and capitalism. One of Weber's prime goals was to attack Marxian doctrine, to show that the economic factor was not a necessary and sufficient condition for the emergence of capitalism. Weber nowhere insisted that

---

[91] E. R. Leach, *Pul Eliya: A Village in Ceylon* (London: Cambridge, 1961), 10, *passim.*

[92] Firey, *Man, Mind and Land, op. cit.*

[93] Max Weber, *The Methodology of the Social Sciences,* trans. and ed. by Edward A. Shils and Henry A. Finch (New York: Free Press, 1949), 90.

[94] *Ibid.*

[95] *Ibid.,* 90 ff.

religion was paramount; rather it was one among several factors, although one that could not be ignored in explaining the rise of capitalism in Europe.[96]

Weber began by constructing, through the use of historical data and the method of *verstehen*, an ideal typology for capitalism and another for Protestantism, Calvinism in particular.[97] In so doing he came to emphasize (or exaggerate) certain crucial features of capitalism and of Protestantism. Concerning the first, he stressed the role of acquisitiveness, or the search for profit. And in delineating the Calvinistic form of Protestantism he gave special attention to the notion of receiving a "calling." Indeed he exaggerated this trait, for this calling distinguished the Calvinists from other Protestant groups, and particularly from the Catholics.

Weber did not stop with the construction of his ideal type, which served to make sense of the reality he was studying. This simplification of reality having been accomplished, he went on to some rather complex mental experiments. One involved an attempt to show how the Battle of Marathon affected the course of Greek history. Weber apparently conducted a similar set of mental experiments when he sought to establish the relationships of Protestantism to capitalism. In these experiments he asked himself questions such as: What would have happened had Calvinism failed to appear on the scene in Europe? He then logically deduced the consequences of this hypothetical eventuality and "demonstrated" that Western society would have developed quite differently as a result. And from these mental gymnastics Weber claimed some significant conclusions.

But Weber went a step further. He sought to check his results on a broad comparative basis by studying the relationships of religion to economic organization in a number of socio-cultural systems.[98] His intent was to demonstrate that the religious system in China had quite a different impact on (or relationship to) the economic organization than did Calvinism in Europe. So too in India. Here Weber was employing the crosscultural setting as a kind of experimental laboratory. And although his research effort evinces major weaknesses—he did not, for instance, clarify the similarities among these societies and thus hold certain factors constant while permitting others to vary—the vision of enterprise is perhaps unparalleled in the annals of sociology. The point is that his typological formulations of the religious and economic systems in different social orders were an essential step in his analysis.

Ideal types have been used in other ways as well. They have been viewed as the extremes of a continuum against which social scientists have sought to establish empirical deviations. Recall the *gemeinschaft-gesellschaft* typology of

---

[96] Max Weber, *The Protestant Ethic and the Spirit of Capitalism,* trans. by Talcott Parsons (London: G. Allen, 1930).

[97] Parsons, *The Structure of Social Action, op. cit.,* 516–533.

[98] *Ibid.,* chap. 15.

Tönnies and the folk-urban one of Redfield. In recent decades such typologies have been formally linked to logical empiricists' interest in measurement, and researchers have employed the ordinal scale (for a discussion of measurement, see Chapter 10) as a means of determining whether communities are, for example, more or less folk (or more or less urban) in character.

The fact that the ideal type has been used in the measurement of social phenomena has stilled some of the criticisms of this notion by the logical empiricists. For many of the latter have felt that the ideal type is largely subjective and can be employed in a rather arbitrary fashion; there are no firm rules for its construction. Actually, the use of the ideal type has been criticized by scholars working within the *verstehen* framework. Parsons, relying upon Von Schelting, observes that Weber actually employed two kinds of ideal types and did not distinguish between them.[99] One was the individual historical type, the other the universal type. For example, Calvinistic Protestantism and even capitalism are ideal types that have a specific locus in time and space, whereas economic man as a type admits of no such barriers.

Other grounds for criticism of the ideal type include the question of "logical consistency." Weber seems to have aligned himself on the side of order and internal consistency with respect to social reality. On this matter, it is instructive to examine the way in which writers like Marx have applied their typologies, which many methodologists loosely refer to as "ideal types." What Marx did was to construct a "pure type" of capitalism, but one that, theoretically at least, could exist in reality. However, Marx permitted inconsistencies in his pure-type construct; indeed, the internal contradictions were the primary basis of his analysis employing the logic of the dialectic. He elaborated the essential contradictions of capitalism in its pure form—that is, as it would exist under perfect conditions. He assumed that even more so would capitalism find it impossible to survive in actual practice.

Here we are not concerned with the validity of Marx's conclusions. What is relevant is that Marx utilized this typology in a quite different manner than Weber used his. Marx apparently was considering a type that could, theoretically, operate in reality, and he was employing this type more or less as an end itself, not as a tool for testing hypotheses. Marx's typology more closely resembles that discussed by Becker than it does Weber's (although Becker, like Weber, did not allow contradictions to enter his formulation).

THE CONSTRUCTED TYPE

Becker's constructed type is an effort to bring typological analysis closer to empirical reality.[100] Eschewing the more utopian features of Weber's orientation,

[99] *Ibid.*, 601–610.

[100] Howard Becker, *Through Values to Social Interpretation* (Durham, N. C.: Duke, 1950), chap. 2, *passim*.

Becker saw constructed types as objectively probable, whereas Weber's ideal type, because of the way it was constructed, could never be achieved in reality.

In Becker's analysis, social scientists are analogous to judges at a dog show. In their mind's eye they have a conception of what an ideal collie (here we substitute social system X) or German shepherd (social system Y) should be like. This concept is an outgrowth of observation, but it is the social scientists, like the judges at the dog show, who round off the ragged edges, who remove the extraneous data, and thus create an image of what a particular system should be like. As with dogs, social orders never fit *all* the specifications, although under perfect conditions they would be expected to do so.

Now if we classify (or examine) dogs in ideal-type terms, we would stress those unique features of, say, the collie that demarcates it from other dogs.

To emphasize the differences between the ideal and the constructed type, we can consider Redfield's "folk society."[101] Redfield worked within the Weberian heritage when he developed his ideal type of the folk (or preliterate) order. He saw this as a small, isolated system, lacking any division of labor, possessing a sacred value system, and so on. Here Redfield exaggerated certain traits in order to set the folk order off from the urban community. And he recognized that no preliterate, or folk, order would ever fully correspond to his ideal type.

However, Redfield's ideal type might be reformulated along lines of a constructed type. To do this we would say that the folk order lacks any division of labor, except for the minimum imposed by age and sex differences, and that the folk society, although it tends toward isolation, sustains some external ties, at least in symbolic form. With these modifications the folk order becomes objectively probable, even though any given folk society would almost always deviate from this type in certain empirical details.

Although on the surface the constructed and the ideal types appear to be similar, upon closer scrutiny we see that the differences between them must be kept in mind by the researcher when he analyzes his data.

THE NORMATIVE TYPE

The ideal and the constructed types, though they take account of the actor's perception of the world, are typically products of the scientist's imagination. A preliterate confronted with Redfield's conception of the folk society would, we could safely predict, find it quite bewildering. And although Weber began with the actor's frame of reference, his conceptualizations of capitalism or of Calvinistic Protestantism were hardly those of the man in the street.

Yet actors in a society do employ typological formulations. These carry various labels, but we believe the term "normative type" best characterizes this

[101] Robert Redfield, "The Folk Society," *American Journal of Sociology*, 52 (January, 1947), 293–308.

variety. Ralph Turner, among others, has been conscious of this typology in social research.[102] Employing the term "folk type" he writes:

> But as organizing norms these principles are assumed to be present at least implicitly in people's thinking, guiding their judgments of what is appropriate on many specific matters. Such organizing norms do not correspond perfectly with the objective characteristics of the societies in which they exist, nor are they completely independent of them. From the complex interplay of social and economic conditions and ideologies people in a society develop a highly simplified conception of the way in which events take place. This conception of the "natural" is translated into a norm—the "natural" becomes what "ought" to be—and in turn imposes a strain toward consistency upon relevent aspects of the society. Thus the norm acts back upon the objective conditions to which it refers and has ramifying effects upon . . . related features of the society.[103]

As Turner recognizes, actors in a system use normative types, just as scientists resort to various typologies, in order to simplify the world with its many complexities.

But how are these normative types related to the scientist's ideal or constructed types? It would appear that from the point of view of the actor, there are two normative subtypes, one corresponding to the ideal type, the other to the constructed variety. Actors do exaggerate reality at times in an ideal-type manner (note the existence of stereotypes) whereas other formulations about the everyday world, perhaps the majority of those in a social order, are more in keeping with the constructed type.

There are, of course, complex interrelationships between the typologies of scientists and those of laymen in any social order. Not only do scientists use the nonscientist's world as a point of departure, but in time the former's conceptualizations, as with Weber's notion of the Protestant ethic, may be diffused to the latter. Laymen as a result may come to see social phenomena more clearly, or they also may come to misconstrue the scientist's concepts so that the latter may seek to avoid using his original formulations.

TYPOLOGICAL ANALYSIS AND PROPERTY SPACE

We come now to typological analysis as developed within a more empirical, positivist tradition. The outstanding example is that formulated by Lazarsfeld and

---

[102] Cf. Samuel M. Strong, "Social Types in a Minority Group: Formulation of a Method," *American Journal of Sociology*, 48 (March, 1943), 563–573.

[103] Ralph H. Turner, "Sponsored and Contest Mobility and the School System," *American Sociological Review*, 25 (December, 1960), 856.

his associates at Columbia University. Lazarsfeld, relying heavily upon the earlier work of Hempel and Oppenheim, has attempted to construct a bridge between the loose theorizers in sociology and those who stress the quantitative tradition.[104]

The various typologies employed by sociologists can be viewed as compounded of various attributes. Lazarsfeld's procedure, in the main, consists of identifying and measuring these attributes, making it possible to locate individuals or their characteristics in "property space"—somewhat as points in two-dimensional space are delineated by the Cartesian coordinates. The dimensions by which people or their characteristics are located in space are in terms of either continuous or dichotomous variables (attributes). We therefore could set up the following property space using as variables "income" and "voting behavior."

		Voting Behavior	
		Voter	Nonvoter
	High		
Income	Medium		
	Low		

Lazarsfeld and his associates have taken various typologies employed in sociology and, following the procedure (termed substruction), have broken these down into their component dimensions in order to facilitate measurement.[105] They have also utilized the procedure of reduction: the "construction" of broader categories (or types) out of smaller or more narrow ones.

Shevky and Bell have utilized the idea of "attribute" or property space in the measurement of various census tracts within a city.[106] They locate these tracts in terms of their social rank (along the X axis) and their degree of urbanization (along the Y axis). First, by working out an index for status (or rank) and an index for urbanization, Shevky and Bell are able to plot each tract in this particular social space. They can then proceed to contrast the tracts within a single city and also to contrast cities with one another in terms of the number of tracts (and groups of people) in different social statuses and in terms of the extent of urbanization of the various tracts. This of course assumes that comparable data are available.

---

[104] Paul F. Lazarsfeld's work in this area goes back at least to his "Some Remarks on the Typological Procedures in Social Research," *Zeitschrift für Sozialforschung*, 6 (1937), 119–139.

[105] See, e.g., Allen H. Barton, "The Concept of Property-Space in Social Research," in Paul F. Lazarsfeld and Morris Rosenberg (eds.), *The Language of Social Research* (New York: Free Press, 1955), 40–53.

[106] Eshref Shevky and Wendell Bell, *Social Area Analysis* (Stanford, Cal.: Stanford, 1955).

There have been many other applications of what might be called the Lazars-feld approach. Kornhauser's research is informative from several perspectives. Specifically, he classified societies in terms of certain political (or power) criteria:[107]

		Availability of Nonelites	
		Low	High
Accessibility of Elites	Low	communal society	totalitarian society
	High	pluralistic society	mass society

Kornhauser proceeds to develop various indicators for these societies and to make certain comparisons among them.

Kornhauser's work raises several questions which have been left unanswered in the literature. It is not clear just how he regards such concepts as "mass society." Is it as an ideal or as a constructed type? In practice, these appear to be more in line with Becker's constructed type than with Weber's ideal type, which ex-aggerates selected features of social reality. While sociologists within the Lazarsfeld circle may refer to ideal types, these are not of the same order as those Weber utilized when he discussed capitalism, the Protestant ethic, and so on.

WHY EMPLOY TYPOLOGICAL ANALYSIS?

Although we perceive a definite trend toward constructing typologies that relate more closely to the empirical data—particularly as a result of the positivist's objection to the impressionistic approaches social scientists traditionally employ—it is unlikely that we can dispense entirely with the ideal of the constructed or the normative type.

One is then faced with the query: Why, given the constant criticism and efforts to circumvent the difficulties involved, do social scientists continue to use these more impressionistic conceptual tools? Why have the positivists merely driven these so-called survivals of sociological mysticism underground rather than destroying them? One has simply to look at the writings of the proponents of the use of statistical tools at all cost to see that these studies rely heavily upon the kinds of typological procedures that are viewed as highly subjective.

Once again we resort to our sociology of knowledge perspective for an ex-plication of this apparent incongruity. Our contention is that typologies have been employed, and will continue to be employed, to order the complex data social scientists handle. The fact that so many empirical studies are not strictly comparable but can be related only in gross fashion commits one to some kind of methodology wherein conceptual modes of analysis, rather than strictly empirical procedures, serve to organize the available data.

[107] William Kornhauser, *The Politics of Mass Society* (New York: Free Press, 1959), 40.

Then there is the problem that while sociologists search for clear-cut differences or relationships, they often find only tendencies or barely perceptible patterns. What about the social scientists who are intent upon delineating social class patterns in America today? The published studies point to a good deal of inconsistency in the findings. Should scientists therefore abandon the class concept altogether? Perhaps. But this situation is typical of other kinds of studies as well. What happens is that social scientists continue to use the term "class," but they employ it in an ideal-type or constructed-type sense.

The very fact that sociologists do not find clear-cut patterns and are therefore forced to rely upon various kinds of typological formulations is itself an empirical fact that is almost totally disregarded. We suggest that this points up the inherently contradictory forces in social systems that lead to situations wherein few clear-cut patterns are discernible. An effort to construct a theory in keeping with the available evidence may in the long run prove more profitable than attempting to do something the data do not permit.

In the end, we favor any and all efforts to objectify and make more explicit one's actual research procedure—regardless of what it is.

CHAPTER 10

Analysis of Data:

Cases and Numbers

This chapter elaborates upon certain arguments in the preceding one on theoretical analysis. Here the emphasis is different, for we shall examine the utility and limitations of cases and numbers in the testing of hypotheses. We are primarily concerned with "induction" as defined in Chapter 3—induction as "the weight of evidence" that is brought to bear to disprove or prove either isolated hypotheses or hypotheses that form part of some broader theoretical scheme. Nevertheless, other relevant functions of cases and of numbers will also be considered in the context of our discussion.

Detailing the techniques or specific statistical procedures that are utilized in social research is not our goal; these tools have been ably discussed in other volumes. Instead, we strive to place the matter of cases and numbers into a broader frame of reference, including their relationship to the total research process. In addition, we seek to delineate the principal controversies concerning (or the norms with respect to) the use of cases and numbers in social research. The chapter immediately following will examine the reliability and validity of case materials and numerical data.

Case Analysis

Although the distinction between cases and numbers can be viewed as rather artificial, it is nonetheless useful analytically, for cases and numbers do often serve different methodological functions.

During the formative years of American sociology, the case-study approach was very popular. Thomas and Znaniecki's *The Polish Peasant in Europe and America*,[1] one of the first empirical studies of significance, utilized case materials,

[1] William I. Thomas and Florian Znaniecki, *The Polish Peasant in Europe and America* (Boston: Gorham, 1918–1920).

and this tradition was perpetuated by Park, Burgess, and other Chicago-trained sociologists during the 1920s and 1930s.[2] The analysis of data on individuals or subcommunities formed the basis of some of the most influential monographs to appear during this era in American sociology.[3] And while the case-study method has been strongly criticized, it continues to be widely employed in sociology and related disciplines more often than is generally acknowledged.[4] For one thing, what are aggregates on one level of analysis can become case studies on another level. Thus, the statistical analysis of a community's population is often treated as a case study on the national level.

THE NATURE AND USE OF CASES

It is possible to classify cases according to the substantive area being studied, be it individuals, families, communities, formal organizations, or total societies. Perhaps the most popular form of the case study since the 1930s has been the analysis of individual communities. From the time of the Lynds' sorties into Middletown (Muncie, Indiana), down to Warner's excursions into Yankee City (Newburyport, Connecticut) and Hollingshead's venture into New Haven, Connecticut, community studies have provided sociologists with a massive body of data.[5] Added to these are the investigations by anthropologists of villages in almost every part of the globe.[6] Also not to be overlooked is the crucial role of case studies, especially after World War II, in the analysis of formal organizations.[7]

But while the discussion of cases by substantive area might prove advantageous, it seems more profitable to analyze and classify them according to

[2] See, e.g., Ernest Burgess, "Research Methods in Sociology," in Georges Gurvitch and Wilbert E. Moore (eds.), *Twentieth Century Sociology* (New York: Philosophical Library, 1945), 20–41. Cf. John Dollard, *Criteria for the Life History* (New Haven: Yale, 1935) and Robert Angell, "A Critical Review of the Development of the Personal Document Method in Sociology, 1920–1940," in Louis Gottschalk *et al., The Use of Personal Documents in History, Anthropology, and Sociology* (New York: Social Science Research Council, 1947), 177–232.

[3] See, e.g., Clifford Shaw, *The Jack Roller: A Delinquent Boy's Own Story* (Chicago: University of Chicago Press, 1931).

[4] Cf. William F. Dukes, "$N=1$," *Psychological Bulletin,* 64 (July, 1965), 74–79.

[5] See, e.g., Robert S. Lynd and Helen M. Lynd, *Middletown* (New York: Harcourt, Brace & World, 1929); W. Lloyd Warner and Paul S. Lunt, *The Social Life of a Modern Community* (New Haven: Yale, 1941); and August B. Hollingshead, *Elmtown's Youth* (New York: Wiley, 1949).

[6] Clifford Geertz, "Studies in Peasant Life: Community and Society," in B. J. Siegel (ed.), *Biennial Review of Anthropology, 1961* (Stanford Cal.: Stanford, 1962), 1–41.

[7] For one perspective on the role of the case study method in research on formal organizations, see Peter M. Blau, "The Comparative Study of Organizations," *Industrial and Labor Relations Review,* 18 (April, 1965), 323–338.

their methodological functions. Here we shall examine the normal (or typical) case, the deviant (or negative) case, and the extreme case in relation to (1) the confirmation of hypotheses; (2) the clarification, falsification, and discovery of hypotheses; and (3) the question of "understanding." When considering the relationships of cases to the confirmation or to the clarification, falsification, or discovery of hypotheses, we must further distinguish between the relationship of cases to statistical hypotheses and their relation to universal hypotheses.

THE CONFIRMATION OF HYPOTHESES.   To confirm a hypothesis, the researcher must search for normal or typical cases, not deviant cases. But what is "normal" depends upon the particular kind of hypothesis to be tested—whether it is a universal or a statistical one.

With respect to universal hypotheses, "normal" refers to some relatively fixed standard. Take the hypothesis, "All societies have some kind of family system." Theoretically, any society should provide confirmatory evidence for this hypothesis. But when sociologists speak of the normal, or typical, case, they are usually reasoning not in terms of universal propositions but in terms of statistical hypotheses.[8] This actual norm, though it is adhered to by most researchers at one time or another, is seldom if ever objectified. Nevertheless, when sociologists generalize from, say, Yankee City or New Haven to the broader society, they generally postulate the existence of some statistical distribution of community patterns. Although this conception is vague and subjective, they often assume that the community they cite as typical, or normal, represents the modal category.

To generalize about a complex society from one or a few cases—be they individuals, communities, or organizations—is admittedly hazardous.[9] The researcher must select cases that reflect the diversity that arises as a result of differentials such as rural-urban, white-nonwhite, educated-uneducated, and others. It is especially difficult to confirm a statistical proposition about members of a complex society. For this reason many sociologists question the case-study approach as a valid sociological tool for testing hypotheses.

THE CLARIFICATION, FALSIFICATION, AND DISCOVERY OF HYPOTHESES.   Deviant (or negative) cases serve to clarify the relationships among variables in statistical hypotheses and to falsify universal hypotheses. But in both instances they may lead to the discovery of new relationships and thereby lay the basis for the formulation of new hypotheses.

---

[8] Cf. Howard S. Becker, "Problems of Inference and Proof in Participant Observation," *American Sociological Review*, 23 (December, 1958), 652–660.

[9] For instance, the findings of Norval D. Glenn and Ruth Hyland, "Religious Preference and Worldly Success: Some Evidence from National Surveys," *American Sociological Review*, 32 (February, 1967), 73–85, bring into question some of the findings of Gerhard Lenski, *The Religious Factor*, rev. ed. (Garden City, N.Y.: Doubleday, Anchor Books 1963), which was based upon the study of one city—Detroit.

One researcher who has examined negative cases as a means of clarifying his statistical hypotheses in Zelditch.[10] He tested hypotheses regarding role differentiation and role allocation or, more precisely, the existence of a differentiation between instrumental leaders and expressive leaders within families in societies around the world. Zelditch found that this differentiation held for 46 out of 56 societies. He then studied the 10 negative cases in order to determine whether, for example, an additional variable might account for the lack of differentiation— a variable that would suggest either a reformulation of the hypotheses or a more refined means of testing them. His procedure, then, was to utilize these deviant cases to clarify his hypotheses and set the stage for the discovery of new relationships.

Deviant, or negative, cases can be used to falsify universal propositions in instances where a logico-deductive system with a covering law is employed. Although the logico-deductive model is seldom utilized in sociology, this procedure, where applicable, could further sociological investigation. Here the case approach is indispensable, for one deviant case suffices to falsify the model.

Some sociologists have sought to formulate universal propositions concerning particular social systems or mankind as a whole with reference to the broader superstructure of the covering-law model.[11] Znaniecki and his followers have sought to attain this end through the use of analytic induction. Znaniecki argued that to construct universal generalizations we must search for deviant, or negative, cases and if these are found we must then reformulate our hypotheses, making them either more restrictive or more encompassing, in order to obtain propositions that are applicable to all cases.[12]

Among the sociological studies that have relied upon the method of analytic induction, two of the most widely cited are Lindesmith's on opiate addicts and Cressey's on embezzlers. Both utilized the negative-case approach in formulating their hypotheses. Lindesmith's hypothesis is as follows:

> Addiction occurs only when opiates are used to alleviate withdrawal distress, after this distress has been properly understood or interpreted, that is to say, after it has been represented to the individual in terms of the linguistic symbols and cultural patterns which have grown up around the opiate habit. If the individual fails to conceive of his distress as withdrawal distress brought about by the absence of opiates he can not

[10] Morris Zelditch, Jr., "Role Differentiation in the Nuclear Family: A Comparative Study," in Mathilda White Riley, *Sociological Research: 1. A Case Approach* (New York: Harcourt, Brace & World, 1963), 212–223. See also the commentary by Riley, 244–249.

[11] See, e.g., Walter Firey, *Man, Mind and Land* (New York: Free Press, 1960).

[12] Florian Znaniecki, *The Method of Sociology* (New York: Holt, Rinehart and Winston, 1934).

become addicted, but if he does, addiction is quickly and permanently established through the further use of the drug.[13]

Cressey's study led to the following hypothesis:

> Trusted persons become trust violators when they conceive of themselves as having a financial problem which is non-shareable, are aware that this problem can be secretly resolved by violation of the position of financial trust, and are able to apply to their own conduct in that situation verbalizations which enable them to adjust their conceptions of themselves as trusted persons with their conceptions of themselves as users of the entrusted funds or property.[14]

Both Lindesmith and Cressey, following the lead of Znaniecki, assume that we must accept their hypotheses as true until such time as a case may be discovered that will falsify them.

These studies have been attacked on several grounds. One of the most common objections, voiced by both Robinson and Turner, is that Lindesmith and Cressey failed to study nonusers of drugs and nonviolators of trust, with the result that they were unable to detail the conditions under which a particular phenomenon will occur.[15] Turner agreed that Cressey's formulation does not indicate who will have nonshareable problems, under what conditions a problem will be nonshareable, and in what circumstances a problem may cease to be nonshareable.[16]

Robinson and Turner seem to assume that only if we employ statistical hypotheses can we study both users and nonusers of drugs, for instance, and thereby delineate the conditions under which particular phenomena occur. But it is difficult to understand why the proponents of analytic induction could not study nonusers as well as users. Also, quite apart from their critique of analytic induction, Robinson and Turner's reasoning leads them, albeit unconsciously, to reject the covering-law model as a valid logical approach to empirical inquiry. For the covering-law model is built upon the falsification of hypotheses through the negative-case approach.

Turner's main conclusion, derived from his critique of the Lindesmith and

---

[13] Alfred R. Lindesmith, *Opiate Addiction* (Bloomington, Ind.: Principia Press, 1947), 165. Lindesmith refers to his final hypothesis as a theory.

[14] Donald R. Cressey, *Other People's Money* (New York: Free Press, 1953), 30.

[15] W. S. Robinson, "The Logical Structure of Analytic Induction," *American Sociological Review, 16* (December, 1951), 812–818; and Ralph H. Turner, "The Quest for Universals in Sociological Research," *American Sociological Review, 18* (December, 1953), 604–611.

[16] Turner, *op. cit.*

Cressey studies, is that analytic induction leads not to universal laws but to the formulation of definitions—a position closely related to the argument that analytic induction does not enable us to delineate the sufficient conditions under which social phenomena occur.[17] But this is a weakness common to all approaches in social science, not just to analytic induction.

Actually, Turner has in effect provided a rationale for the continued use of analytic induction. For definitions, broadly defined to include classification schemes, are still critical in social research. And negative cases are strategic for delineating the boundaries of classes. For example, to define the concept of marriage so that it has crosscultural validity, we must pay special attention to that among, say, the Nayars of India, whose marriage arrangements diverge markedly from those in other societies.[18]

More generally, Turner failed to grasp the critical role of analytic induction as a basis for discovery, as a means of uncovering new relationships and thus of generating new hypotheses. After all, Lipset and his associates used a typographical union as a negative case to question Michels' well-known proposition concerning the "iron law of oligarchy," and through this they were able to isolate certain forces that laid the foundation for a more adequate theory of formal organizations.[19]

Up to now we have focused upon the deviant, or negative, case as a means for clarifying, falsifying, and discovering hypotheses. But what about the extreme case, which we have distinguished from the deviant type? Extreme cases, as we have indicated, are those wherein a number of variables are "held constant."[20]

Inasmuch as political and ethical considerations greatly inhibit the scientist's purposive manipulation of his subjects, he must often rely upon the extreme case as a reasonable approximation to the laboratory experiment. For instance, much of the experimentation regarding the relative impact of biological and sociocultural factors upon the development of personality has had to be carried out mentally, with the scientist manipulating the variables in his mind and deriving his conclusions therefrom.

In this context Davis' analysis of Anna—a case of "extreme isolation"—takes on added significance.[21] Anna was an illegitimate child who had been deprived of normal contact and had received a minimum of human care for almost

[17] Ibid.

[18] Kathleen Gough, "The Nayars and the Definition of Marriage," Journal of the Royal Anthropological Institute of Great Britain and Ireland, 89 (1959), 23–34.

[19] Seymour M. Lipset et al., Union Democracy (Garden City, N.Y.: Doubleday, Anchor Books, 1962).

[20] Cf. Kurt Goldstein, Human Nature in the Light of Psychopathology (New York: Schocken Paperbacks, 1963).

[21] Kingsley Davis, "Final Note on a Case of Extreme Isolation," American Journal of Sociology, 52 (March, 1947), 432–437.

all her first six years of life. Eventually the situation came to the attention of doctors and social scientists. Davis used the reports on Anna to confirm the broad sociological proposition concerning the impact of socialization upon personality and to clarify other sociocultural processes relating to the acquisition of speech, maturation, etc.

In practice, extreme cases appear to be significant more for clarifying and falsifying than for confirming hypotheses, and as such they provide the basis for discovery. The example of the spy who is cut off from contact with his own social order is an extreme instance that would seem to challenge many of the propositions implicit in Goffman's *The Presentation of Self in Everyday Life*,[22] propositions which suggest, for instance, that the individual accept the values and beliefs of the group or groups with which he interacts on a daily basis.

Case materials are relevant for those social scientists who employ not only the logico-deductive method, discovery, and induction but also certain logical systems that do not fit into the traditional categories of scientific inquiry as formulated by philosophers of science. One of these logical systems involves relating parts to parts and parts to wholes. This process enables us to grasp the context within which social action occurs and thereby to understand that action.

Even social scientists committed to statistical hypotheses must rely upon case materials as a basis for understanding. One reason sociologists are so often unaware of the critical role of case materials for interpreting numerical data is that they tend to carry out research only within their own society and, moreover, to rely upon their own personal experiences as case data to provide the contextual basis for interpreting their findings. When social scientists study cultures divergent from their own, they become more aware of the role of case materials, whether normal, deviant, or extreme, in the interpretation of tabular data. The popular notion that cases serve primarily as illustrative materials misses the main point, for in actuality they are the chief bases for our understanding of the numerical information.

Cases are used not only for constructing typologies but for "testing" evolutionary and structural-functional theory. Although the scientist may utilize certain generalizing concepts in his analysis, the case (a society, social movement, or large-scale bureaucracy) is still the unit of analysis. Only through a study in depth are the relationships among parts of the system, and between the parts and the whole, explicated.

Sociologists who adopt an evolutionary frame of reference must demonstrate how and why certain elements (or parts) have emerged out of prior conditions and how elements of the past are integrated into the new order. The structural-functionalist is concerned with the interrelationships among structural elements

---

[22] Erving Goffman, *The Presentation of Self in Everyday Life* (Garden City, N.Y.: Doubleday, Anchor Books, 1959).

and especially with how these are necessary for the attainment of the goals of a given system—in other words, how the parts are related to the whole. For example, an effective military establishment (a part) is functionally required if the nation-state system (the whole) is to maintain its autonomy on the modern world scene.

Malinowski's works on the Trobriand Islanders are especially pertinent here. One of his lasting contributions was his "contextualizing of the facts," his description of human actions within their proper sociocultural context so as to demonstrate better the relationships of elements of the system to one another and to the broader whole.

> In demonstrating the interlocking of structural, technological and ritual aspects Malinowski does not stop short at integrative description; he uses it as a basis for the enunciation and clarification of sociological concepts. Thus the lively account of a feast at the ceremonial launching of a new canoe is made the occasion for an analysis of the rules governing the organization of labour and the distribution of wealth, and for the formulation of the principle of reciprocity and its importance in kinship, political relations, and law.[23]

Malinowski's writings suggest another use of case materials, for he relied upon dramatic, deviant cases to support his conclusions concerning the normative order.[24] Numerous social scientists have utilized such a procedure, but they have not generally been as aware of it as was Malinowski.

However, Malinowski apologies for being "lured by the dramatic, exceptional, and sensational."[25] He apparently did not recognize the role of these materials in the delineation of a normative order. After all, it was Durkheim who argued that we recognize what is a norm in terms of the deviations from it.[26]

Overall, sociologists depend upon case materials for interpreting the social order. Nevertheless, certain blind proponents of the case approach—those who see cases as ends in themselves—often lapse into a kind of historicism that denies the existence of a generalizing science of sociology. Because we ultimately use cases to generalize about social systems, we cannot avoid the question (even when we are concerned mainly with understanding): Are the cases we are studying normal, typical, or extreme?

[23] Phyllis Kaberry, "Malinowski's Contribution to Field-work Methods and the Writing of Ethnography," in Raymond Firth (ed.), *Man and Culture* (New York: Harper & Row, Harper Torchbooks, 1964), 84.

[24] *Ibid.*, 79, 85. Cf. Bronislaw Malinowski, *Coral Gardens and their Magic*, vol. 1 (London: G. Allen, 1935), 241, 462.

[25] Malinowski, *op. cit.*, 462.

[26] Emile Durkheim, *The Rules of Sociological Method*, trans. by Sarah A. Solovay and John H. Mueller, 8th ed. (New York: Free Press Paperback, 1964), 67 ff.

Numerical Analysis

Several interrelated factors have functioned to denigrate the case study as a tool in social research. That sociologists have been unable to adopt effectively the covering-law model, which can be falsified by a single negative case, has indirectly undermined the legitimacy of the case approach. A more direct and compelling factor has been the general awareness of the fact that certain case studies have proved misleading. Where social systems display considerable complexity and variability sociologists must exercise caution when they generalize from only a few cases to the working universe in question.

Besides these methodological factors, the movement toward numerical analysis has been hastened by the demands of the broader industrial-urban order. Modern bureaucratic structures—governmental, educational, business—are increasingly called upon to "quantify," or "measure," social phenomena. It is through quantification that these systems seek to determine the most efficient and rational means for attaining a given end.[27]

THE PRESENT STATUS OF STATISTICAL ANALYSIS

As a result of the aforementioned factors (along with others) the debate over whether social scientists can (or should) quantify social data has lessened, at least in many fields. Sociologists now generally accept the need for measurement, and the issues that held the attention of the leading figures of the 1920s and 1930s have largely been forgotten. Nevertheless, political scientists today are, like sociologists a few decades ago, still debating the relative merits of qualitative and quantitative analysis.

In the case of sociology, however, the debate has not been muted; rather its nature has shifted considerably. The argument now concerns the means rather than the ends, that is, the relative merits of particular statistical procedures. Although some writers apply statistical procedures unquestioningly, the more theoretically inclined are aware that many issues relating to the application of statistics to social data are still to be resolved. Thus Blalock writes:

> What is obviously needed at this stage is considerably more methodological research into the logic of causal inferences and into the nature of the methods that can be used to deal with specific types of complicating issues such as the existence of measurement error, multicollinearity, nonadditivity, and confounding influences.[28]

[27] See, e.g., Raymond A. Bauer (ed.), *Social Indicators* (Cambridge, Mass.: M.I.T., 1966). For a brief analysis of the social implications of this orientation, see Gideon Sjoberg, Richard A. Brymer, and Buford Farris, "Bureaucracy and the Lower Class," *Sociology and Social Research, 50* (April, 1966), 325–337.

[28] Hubert M. Blalock, Jr., *Causal Inferences in Nonexperimental Research* (Chapel Hill, N.C.: The University of North Carolina Press, 1964), 184.

We would suggest flexibility as the guiding theme. In our haste to become "scientific" we have perhaps overrigidly followed the few rules of inference which have been rigorously set forth. Thus many social scientists insist on proper sampling methods, significance tests that do not require normality assumptions, and statistical measures that do not violate the limitations of measurement procedures. This is all to the good, and we would certainly not suggest that these practices be abandoned. But there is a vast territory where explicit rules do not exist and where speculation has been allowed to roam freely. It is not entirely inconceivable that as rules are developed concerning this latter region these rules may be found to imply different decisions from those suggested by present knowledge.[29]

Blalock seems to be saying that the nature and mode of application of the existing norms (or rules) must be open to review, and that as new norms are developed in presently uncharted regions these new norms may well force revisions in the older.

NATURE OF STATISTICS AND MEASUREMENT: SOME ELEMENTARY CONSIDERATIONS

Terms such as "statistics" and "measurement" are not easy to define. The latter term has a much narrower connotation than the former. Measurement may be defined as the process of assigning numerals to "objects" or "events" according to specific rules.[30] Because these rules vary, we shall speak of different kinds of scales or measuring instruments.

Statistics is often defined in terms of its functions, be these descriptive or inductive. Descriptive statistics involves the summarizing of information about some working universe; inductive statistics involves generalizing from a sample to a working universe.[31] This distinction has found general acceptance. Less well understood, however, is the relationship between descriptive and inductive statistics and the logical structure of scientific inquiry discussed in earlier chapters.

Sociologists may utilize descriptive statistics as a means for either discovery or induction; induction here refers to the evidence brought to bear to test a hypothesis, either through confirmation or falsification. Simple measures of central tendency may serve as a basis for discovery or for testing hypotheses concerning the working universe. So does such a technique as factor analysis, with its complex correlation matrices; however, factor analysis has been employed by social

[29] *Ibid.*, 185.

[30] S. S. Stevens, "Mathematics, Measurement, and Psychophysics," in S. S. Stevens (ed.), *Handbook of Experimental Psychology* (New York: Wiley, 1951), chap. 1.

[31] Hubert M. Blalock, Jr., *Social Statistics* (New York: McGraw-Hill, 1960).

scientists primarily as a tool for discovery of possible relationships among variables in a particular working universe.

Inductive statistics, based on probability theory in mathematics is a deductive discipline which provides a rational basis for induction, for judging the weight of evidence used to test a particular kind of hypothesis—one stating a relationship between a sample and the working universe. Here the scientist is intent upon controlling for chance factors. At the same time inductive statistics, when used to infer (or to estimate) a population parameter from a sample, fulfills the function of discovery, or of the generation rather than the testing of hypotheses.

We have devoted some attention herein to the problem of terminology because the vocabulary of statisticians does not always correspond to that of philosophers of science.

THE NATURE OF VARIABLES AND INDICATORS

The process of measurement, or of statistical analysis of social data, involves some conception about the class of variables that is to be taken into account. Here we use the concept "variable" in a rather broad sense to encompass the idea of "attribute." Also, we recognize that variables can be continuous or discrete. The factor of age illustrates the former, sex the latter.

Kish has delineated the variables that the scientist must take into account. Although he focuses upon social surveys, his discussion has broader applicability. He contends that

    I. The *explanatory* variables, sometimes called the "experimental" variables, are the objects of the research. They are the variables among which the researcher wishes to find and to measure some specified relationships. They include both the "dependent" and the "independent" variables, that is, the "predictand" and "predictor" variables. With respect to the aims of the research all other variables, of which there are three classes, are extraneous.

    II. There are extraneous variables which are *controlled*. The control may be exercised in either or both the selection and the estimation procedures.

    III. There may exist extraneous uncontrolled variables which are *confounded* with the Class I variables.

    IV. There are extraneous uncontrolled variables which are treated as *randomized* errors. In "ideal" experiments . . . they are actually randomized; in surveys and investigations they are only assumed to be randomized. Randomization may be regarded as a substitute for experimental control or as a form of control.

    The aim of efficient design both in experiments and in surveys is to place as many of the extraneous variables as is feasible into the second class. The aim of randomization of experiments is to place all of the third class into the fourth class; in the 'ideal" experiment there are no variables in the third class. And it is the aim of controls of various kinds in surveys to separate variables of the third class from those of the first class; these controls may involve the use of repeated cross-tabulations, regression, standardization, matching of units, and so on.[32]

The determination of the independent, dependent, and extraneous variables in any research situation is a function of one's theoretical assumptions, the broader social order in which one works, the nature of the reality being studied, and the existing state of knowledge. Researchers find it especially difficult to isolate extraneous variables when the social reality is amorphous and complex.

But even after the sociologist has specified the variables that should be analyzed, he still faces the problem of formulating proper indicators for them. With respect to such variables or attributes as age and sex the issues are relatively simple. However, when a scientist seeks to measure, for instance, the impact of social class upon religious commitment, complications arise. The notion of "religious commitment" is not a unitary concept and is ambiguously defined by the society and the scientific community. But it is possible to use indicators such as church membership, church attendance, and belief in an afterlife in analyzing the idea of religious commitment. In turn we need to recognize that we must work out one or more indicators for the concept "belief in an afterlife," for example. The result is that the variable of religious commitment may be several levels removed from the direct observations a scientist or a respondent makes.

The selection of an indicator (or indicators) is of course intimately related to the issue of "operational definitions." The operationalizing of a concept or, more narrowly, the definition of the indicators to be employed in empirically defining a concept remains an area of controversy among sociologists. Just how are indicators selected? Primarily in terms of the availability of data, the researcher's theoretical assumptions, and the nature of social reality.

If the social scientist relies upon secondary analysis, the availability of data becomes a prime limiting factor in the choice of indicators. For example, census data confine the researcher to a rather restricted range of social phenomena in his attempt to clarify such concepts as industrialization or urbanization; in this instance, only certain kinds of data are available.[33]

[32] Leslie Kish, "Some Statistical Problems in Research Design," *American Sociological Review*, 24 (June, 1959), 329–330.

[33] Leo F. Schnore's mode of operationalizing certain concepts is a product of the data in, for example, his "The Statistical Measurement of Urbanization and Economic Development," *Land Economics*, 37 (August, 1961), 229–245.

In fact, it would profit sociologists to look at censuses as crude "indicators" of the kind of society one is studying. That certain data are omitted and others included provides us with clues as to the nature of the societal structure and value system,[34] which in turn might prove useful in interpreting specific census materials, especially in crosscultural perspective.

Another factor that operates in the selection of indicators is the sociologist's own theoretical framework.[35] The field of social stratification is an informative case study in this regard. If the sociologist assumes that social reality is defined by the actors within the system, then he will generally accept the actor's definition of the system as the most adequate indicator of social class. On the other hand, if the sociologist inclines to the notion that scientists are more capable of defining reality than the persons they study, he is likely to rely heavily upon such "objective" indicators as occupation, income, or formal education.

We should, however, recognize that sociologists who define class in "objective" terms cannot evade the broader social order's definition of the situation. They do in fact rely upon certain indicators and reject others (for example, the length of people's noses) according to whether these indicators make sense in terms of the cultural values of the society (or societies) in question. Criteria such as the length of people's noses are usually not meaningful either to the members of a system or to scientists who, as citizens, are concerned with the determinants of the class structure of their own social order.

It follows that if the values and goals of individuals or of the broader society are vague or ill-defined, scientists will experience difficulty in isolating agreed-upon indicators. This is particularly true when scientists seek to determine the most effective means for attaining a given end within formal organizations. Because what is efficient or rational can be judged only in terms of specific goals, the scientist, when he is faced with vague or contradictory ends, must either impose order upon his data or be satisfied with very crude indicators.

The efforts of Robert McNamara to measure the efficiency of the programs of the U.S. Department of Defense after 1960 are of considerable methodologi-

---

[34] For a discussion of some of these issues (though *not* within a crosscultural perspective), see John I. Kitsuse and Aaron V. Cicourel, "A Note on the Uses of Official Statistics," *Social Problems, 11* (Fall, 1963), 131–139. Through awareness of how official statistics emerge—that is, by knowing the process by which mental patients become statistics—we are able to understand a good deal about mental disorders, even within a single society: Thomas J. Scheff, *Being Mentally Ill* (Chicago: Aldine, 1966). See also the informative analysis on the use of official statistics in studying the economy of the Soviet Union by P. J. D. Wiles, *The Political Economy of Communism* (Cambridge, Mass.: Harvard, 1962), chap. 12. Wiles suggests various relationships between the kinds of data collected and the nature of the broader social structure.

[35] For a survey of differing orientations toward the study of social stratification, see Richard T. Morris, "Social Stratification," in Leonard Broom and Philip Selznick, *Sociology,* 3rd ed. (New York: Harper & Row, 1963), chap. 6.

cal importance. This case not only suggests the kinds of problems that can arise when the ends are inconsistent with one another but it underscores the intrinsic difficulty of establishing indicators for organizations whose success must be judged in "global terms"—that is without regard to the characteristics of the individuals involved.

Because McNamara relied heavily upon the work of Hitch and McKean in formulating this evaluative scheme, their procedures demand our attention. With respect to the formulation of criteria (or indicators) the authors state:

> Nobody knows precisely how satisfaction and military worth are related to the observable outcomes of various courses of action. We do not have the ability to translate outcomes into such terms. In practical problem-solving, therefore, we have to look at some "proximate" criterion which serves to reflect what is happening to satisfaction or military worth. Actual criteria are the practicable substitutes for the maximization of whatever we would ultimately like to maximize.
>
> In comparisons of military operations or equipment, what is desired is the course of action that would contribute most to "winning" or deterring some kind (or kinds) of war, or even more generally, to achieving national security. Since it will usually be impossible to measure achievement in any of these terms, it is necessary to adopt indirect but workable criteria that appear to be consistent with ultimate aims.[36]

Hitch and McKean argue that this "operationalizing process" must proceed on a piecemeal basis, for no single analysis can cover simultaneously all the problems of choice in all levels of a large organization.[37] Thus comparisons of alternative courses of action deal with problems in a particular sector of the organization, the others being temporarily shoved aside. Afterward, the scientist must strive to relate (albeit vaguely at times) the indicators employed to evaluate alternative courses of action in one part of the system with those used to evaluate, for example, by rank ordering, the relative effectiveness of alternatives in another part.

If the indicators of alternative means in different levels of the organization are to be explicit, the goals themselves must be clearly stated. It follows that broad and amorphous goals may come to be interpreted in terms of specific operational definitions provided by researchers. But to use concrete operations to define abstract goals raises a host of political and ethical issues. Thus, can universities, for example, judge (or rank order) their effectiveness in producing

36 Charles J. Hitch and Roland N. McKean, *The Economics of Defense in the Nuclear Age* (Cambridge, Mass.: Harvard, 1960), 160–161.
37 *Ibid.*, 161.

"educated men" according to such indicators as the ratings of their students on nationwide tests, the number of students who win special awards, and so on?

In any event, the methodology of Hitch and McKean is analogous to that of Lazarsfeld and his associates.[38] For the latter seek through the procedure of substruction to break down concepts into their basic dimensions in order to more readily establish empirical indicators and thereby measure social phenomena more effectively. But Lazarsfeld and his coworkers, unlike Hitch and McKean, tend to focus on individuals. Even where Lazarsfeld has studied the success of a group in attaining its goals, he has generally concentrated upon the characteristics of individuals within the system instead of taking a global or system perspective. Here the matter of reference points seems crucial. Formulating indicators for global characteristics (for example, the survival of a nation) is of a different order than formulating indicators for groups based on the characteristics of individuals (for example, satisfaction of individual clients with a particular agency's program).

THE NATURE AND LEVELS OF MEASUREMENT

Although the arguments continue over the nature of measurement, considerable progress has been made in the past few decades in clarifying some of the issues involved. Perhaps the most widely accepted definition of measurement has been that advanced by Stevens: "the assignment of numerals to objects or events according to rules." He has delineated four types of scales: the nominal, the ordinal, the interval, and the ratio.[39] But not all scholars accept this classification; Coombs, for example, has formulated a partially ordered scale type which stands between the nominal and the ordinal scales.[40] Others, such as Coleman, would exclude nominal scales as a form of measurement.[41] Nevertheless, several advantages accrue from including the nominal scale in our scheme; for one thing, this scale type provides us with some understanding of the link between qualitative and quantitative analysis.

NOMINAL SCALES. Here numerals are applied only as labels; words or letters would serve as well, and indeed are more frequently employed. Among the more commonly cited examples of nominal scales are the numbering of football players and the numbering of houses in a city block. Concerning the nominal

---

[38] Paul F. Lazarsfeld and Morris Rosenberg (eds.), *The Language of Social Research* (New York: Free Press, 1955).

[39] Stevens, *op. cit.*

[40] Clyde H. Coombs, "Theory and Methods of Social Measurement," in Leon Festinger and Daniel Katz (eds.), *Research Methods in the Behavioral Sciences* (New York: Dryden, 1953), chap. 11, and his *A Theory of Data* (New York: Wiley, 1964).

[41] James S. Coleman, *Introduction to Mathematical Sociology* (New York: Free Press, 1964), chap. 2.

scale, Senders writes: "Two classes which are different with respect to the variable or quality being 'measured' shall not bear the same name; two individual objects which are the same with respect to this quality shall not be placed in classes bearing different names."[42]

If we admit the nominal scale as a legitimate scale type, then all social scientists can be said to measure social phenomena. They all engage in classification according to the rules of the nominal scale. For example, they divide the attribute sex into male and female and classify each person according to the presence or absence of maleness or femaleness, and then count the number of cases that appear in the categories.

ORDINAL SCALES.   Here if $x>y$ and $y>z$, then $x>z$; the rule of transitivity applies. In modern society, this scale type is widely employed. Persons or objects are judged to be higher or lower than others in terms of prestige, skill, and so on. Grades given to students within a class are of this type. If one person receives an A, another a B, and another a C, we do not know whether the distance between A and B is the same as that between B and C. The Guttman scale, which received so much attention in sociology during the late 1940s and early 1950s, is an ordinal type of scale.[43]

INTERVAL SCALES.   This type of scale is quantitative in the ordinary sense of the term. Not only is there equivalence among, and rank ordering of, classes, but the distance between each class is the same. The Fahrenheit and centigrade thermometers are well-known illustrations of this scale type, for the distance between the units on the scale is the same. Within the social sciences, the Thurstone equal-appearing interval scale, used for measuring attitudes, has been viewed as a good approximation of this scale type.[44] The Thurstone scale rests upon a number of assumptions, including the notion of an underlying attitude continuum, say, with respect to attitudes toward race. Then we have a quite elaborate set of rules for constructing this scale and assigning numerical values to the questions asked of the respondents.

RATIO SCALES.   This type of scale has the characteristics of the interval scale and, in addition, includes a true zero point. The ratio scale, although widely employed in physics, has played an ambiguous role in social research. In recent years a number of psychologists have been attempting to apply this

[42] Virginia L. Senders, *Measurement and Statistics* (Fair Lawn, N.J.: Oxford, 1958), 52.

[43] Louis Guttman, "A Basis for Scaling Qualitative Data," *American Sociological Review,* 9 (April, 1944), 139–150.

[44] See, e.g., Allen L. Edwards, *Techniques of Attitude Scale Construction* (New York: Appleton-Century-Crofts, 1957), chap. 4.

scale type to a rather wide range of problems.[45] Further, we should recognize that certain kinds of demographic data in modern society—income, age, and education—come to us in ratio form, although, as we shall see, these data may not necessarily be meaningfully interpreted as a ratio scale.

APPLICATIONS OF MEASURING INSTRUMENTS

We have not discussed these scale types as ends in themselves; rather they are tools for analyzing empirical data. But to understand their utility we must place them in the context of the total research process and also consider some of the controversies revolving about their proper application.

We mentioned in Chapter 7 that the way questions are phrased in a questionnaire often reflects the kind of measurement instrument that the researcher plans to employ. We also discussed specific scales which belong in the various categories mentioned above.

What must be recognized in the use of scales is that the assignment of responses to their proper categories (or, from another perspective, the assignment of numerals to data) is itself a crucial aspect of the research process. This general problem leads us back to the nature of indicators of reality discussed above.

In developing a nominal scale, such as when we divide the category "sex" into male and female, few difficulties arise, for the interviewers and interviewees have a set of common understandings which make the assignment of responses to the proper category a simple one. For each respondent, the researcher can easily assign a 1 to the proper category and a 0 to the other class.

But if the social reality is rather ambiguous for members of the social order being studied and/or for the scientist, the assignment of responses to the proper class may prove difficult. Take the question "What is the relationship between science and religion?" Whether we employ a fixed set of responses or leave the question open-ended, a process of "data reduction," about which we know relatively little, must take place.

We might, for example, have a nominal scale with the following three categories: no significant relationship exists between science and religion; science and religion are in basic conflict; science and religion support one another. An interviewee who is confronted with a choice between these three categories must reduce what for him may be a complex set of beliefs concerning the relationship of science and religion into one category, which is then assigned a 1, with the other two categories implicitly being assigned 0s. We are not certain (in many situations) that different interviewers use the same set of "belief indicators" in assigning the verbal responses to their proper class. On

---

[45] See, e.g., Gösta Ekman and Lennart Sjöberg, "Scaling," in Paul R. Farnsworth *et al.* (eds), *Annual Review of Psychology,* 16 (Palo Alto, Cal.: Annual Reviews, 1965), 463–464.

the other hand, if coders are to assign open-ended responses to the proper class, they must not only understand what the respondents meant by the various responses but they must share a set of common understandings if the coding process is to be reliable and valid.[46]

Again, the reliability and validity of the coding operation depend upon a degree of consistency within the social world itself. If ambiguities or *contradictions* are present, even the scientist who seeks to employ nominal scales must impose a kind of "fictional" order upon the reality he is studying—a matter of serious concern to scholars who question the underlying assumptions of the measurement process.

Difficulties of assigning responses to the proper class arise on other levels of measurement as well. We might, for example, develop a simple reputational scale by asking judges to rank order members of a community in terms of their prestige position by assigning each person a numeral: for example, from 1 (the highest) through 5 (the lowest). But we still may not know whether one judge uses education as the key indicator of prestige, another uses income, and so on.[47] Unless the judges share some common understandings, certain persons may be grouped in the same class for particular reasons and placed in different classes for other reasons.

In ascertaining whether scale data support or disprove some particular hypothesis, we must not ignore the social factors that enter into the "data-reduction" process. In earlier chapters we noted the dangers of reifying official statistics. We should understand why statistics on juvenile delinquency, crime, suicide, and so on must be used with care. Within any community, official crime statistics, for instance, are the products of coding judgments by numerous people: police, court officials, and the like. But these persons may define the characteristics of criminals differently; consequently, a great deal of inconsistency can emerge in the coding operation, an inconsistency that is compounded when statistics are drawn from diverse communities and regions.[48]

In addition to the errors that arise from a lack of common understandings, there are those that result from carelessness, expediency, or the like. Julius Roth in his article "Hired Hand Research" suggests that both types of errors may emerge concurrently in large-scale research projects. Concerning one instance, he observed that "Various coders used various methods to determine

[46] Harold Garfinkel, "Remarks on Ethnomethodology," paper presented at the annual meeting of the American Sociological Association, Chicago, Ill., August, 1965.

[47] That persons in different social classes evaluate "status criteria" in different ways is indicated by William H. Form and Gregory P. Stone, "Urbanism, Anonymity, and Status Symbolism," *American Journal of Sociology*, 62 (March, 1957), 514.

[48] See, e.g., Nathan W. Goldman, "The Disposition of Juvenile Arrests by Urban Police," in Ernest W. Burgess and Donald J. Bogue (eds.), *Contributions to Urban Sociology* (Chicago: University of Chicago Press, 1964), chap. 37.

the code of an open-ended question. Toward the end of the coding process, expediency became the keynote, leading to gross inconsistency."[49] Given these situations, Roth entertains doubts as to the reliability and validity of many large-scale research enterprises.[50] Certainly, the researcher must have a clear comprehension of the overall coding operation if he is to properly evaluate scale data in testing hypotheses.

In addition to the problems associated with data reduction, or the assignment of responses to their proper category, one of the major areas of concern with respect to measurement involves the type of statistical rules (or norms) that one should adhere to when applying a given scale type. Hays remarks upon the controversy as follows:

> It is unfortunate but true that in their search for quantitative methods psychologists sometimes overlook the question of level of measurement and tend to read quite unjustified meanings into their results. This has brought about a reaction in some quarters, where people insist that psychologists are not justified in using most of the machinery of mathematics on their generally low-level measurements. Others have argued that psychologists are too concerned with level of measurement, and that ordinary mathematical techniques apply to virtually any numerical measurements.[51]

Siegel, for one, has argued that for each level of measurement only certain types of statistics apply. Thus, with nominal scales we can use, for instance, the mode and nonparametric tests; with ordinal scales the median, the percentile, Spearman's r, and nonparametric tests; with interval scales, the mean, standard deviation, Pearson's product moment correlation, and parametric and nonparametric tests, and so on. Statistics that are appropriate to nominal scales are appropriate to the ordinal, interval, and ratio; those appropriate to ordinal scales are appropriate to the interval and ratio; and those appropriate to interval scales are appropriate to ratio scales.[52]

One of the consequences of Siegel's argument is that only where one can employ interval or ratio scales do the most powerful mathematical or statistical tools become applicable. This logic leads McGinnis to reason as follows: "If the mathematical model is to be employed to any considerable effect in the social sciences, measurement functions with considerably more powerful properties

[49] Julius A. Roth, "Hired Hand Research," *American Sociologist, 1* (August, 1966), 190.

[50] *Ibid.,* 190–196.

[51] William L. Hays, *Statistics for Psychologists* (New York: Holt, Rinehart and Winston, 1963), 74.

[52] Sidney Siegel, *Nonparametric Statistics* (New York: McGraw-Hill, 1956).

than those of ordinality are needed."[53] The point is that nominal and ordinal scales are the most widely used scales in the social sciences, but they set limits upon the application of mathematical models.

At the same time, a number of writers have contended, as Hays suggests, that social scientists can employ any kind of statistical tool with any kind of scale type.[54] The assumptions underlying statistical measures per se do not limit the application of these tools to any particular scale. Rather the problems arise in the interpretation of the results.

The aforementioned disagreement among scientists arises in part from the divergent assumptions they make concerning social reality. Those who believe, as does Siegel, that given kinds of statistics are appropriate only to certain types of scales seem to assume a fundamental relationship between the numerals and the social objects or events they represent.[55] To manipulate nominal or ordinal data through the use of inappropriate statistics is to do violence to the nature of social reality. Coleman supports this line of reasoning when he states: "It is not up to the whim of the investigator to determine what operation is to be used to establish a definition; the operation must constitute action on the part of the objects of the theory, and it must be the same action that the theory is about."[56] Coleman, like his mentor Lazarsfeld, gives considerable weight to the nature of reality as the key determinant of the kind of measurement device to be employed. The opposing school of thought assumes (often implicitly) that the scientist can impose order through his measurement tools upon the social order.

One possible means of partially clarifying the problem of the relationship of levels of measurement and the utilization of statistical tools is to distinguish between semantic and scientific meaningfulness.[57] Scale results can be semantically meaningful but not scientifically meaningful. Thus, if we calculate standard deviations for ordinal data from a particular working universe and then rank order these standard deviations, the results can be viewed as semantically meaningful, but because the ranking of the standard deviations cannot be generalized inasmuch as they are not comparable with the rank orderings from another working universe, the results cannot be viewed as scientifically meaningful.

While we must recognize the problem raised by the application of powerful statistics to nominal and ordinal scales, we must also be somewhat cognizant of the situation in which we may be forced to throw away information because of the exigencies of the research design—as, for example, when we have a moderate-

[53] Robert McGinnis, *Mathematical Foundations for Social Analyses* (Indianapolis: Bobbs-Merrill, 1965), 289.

[54] Hays, *op. cit.*

[55] Siegel, *op. cit.*

[56] Coleman, *op. cit.*, 63.

[57] Cf. Ernest W. Adams, Robert F. Fagot, and Richard E. Robinson, "A Theory of Appropriate Statistics," *Psychometrika*, 30 (June, 1965), 99–127.

sized sample and the need to control for several variables. In this context, Blalock avers:

> Whenever crude categories must be used with either nominal or ordinal scales, a certain amount of information is usually lost. The seriousness of such measurement error depends, among other things, on the number of categories. Where there is an underlying continuous distribution, a simple dichotomy does more injustice to the data than would three or four ordered categories.[58]

Blalock, of course, appears to side with those who believe that one's measurement tools should be appropriate to the nature of the social data in question.

This discussion leads us to a position which is currently being developed by Lewis Carter.[59] Carter agrees, if we interpret him correctly, that the kind of scale one employs will vary with the society's or the organization's definition of reality. Indeed, this view may resolve some of the controversies in the field, particularly with respect to the application of measurement tools within a society.

We have already indicated that in the United States, much data, especially on age, income, and formal education, is ordered (on the surface at least) in the form of ratio scales. The data have equal-appearing intervals and a zero point exists. Although an economist may for certain purposes—say, to predict the absolute amount of purchasing power within a community—analyze income data as if these met the assumptions of a ratio scale, the society frequently analyzes income data as if they were ordinal in nature. The difference between $500 and $1,000 is not the same as that between $100,000 and $100,500 in terms of predicting psychic satisfaction, purchasing power for automobiles, or the amount of income tax that will be paid. Certainly, the U.S. Government, when working out income tax rules, categorizes the population in broad classes, which are then ranked according to the rules of the ordinal scale.

Or consider a hypothetical example of the manner in which a community planning agency may measure the relationship between age and certain community services or activities. For certain purposes, the agency might analyze the age data by use of a nominal scale; for other purposes, via an ordinal scale. In attempting to plan (or to predict) the kind of economic potential that might be required, the agency could resort to a nominal scale by dividing persons within the community into the categories "dependent" and "nondependent"—the former including the young and old, the latter the remainder. Or the agency could rank order certain broad categories of age groupings, or it could take a segment of the population (say aged 4 to 10) and use an interval scale in attempting to predict for future school needs.

[58] Blalock, *Causal Inferences, op. cit.,* 151.
[59] Personal conversations with Lewis Carter.

GENERALIZING FROM THE SAMPLE TO THE WORKING UNIVERSE

It is not enough to speak of measuring or statistical devices without considering the drawing of inferences from the sample to the working universe. Scholars (as well as laymen) were making these kinds of inferences long before the invention of modern statistics. Inductive statistics has, however, sought to formalize the process by assessing the role of chance factors therein.

Central to inductive statistics is the hypothesis concerning the relationship between the sample and the working universe. Some sociologists tend to assume that the way such a hypothesis is stated is not a matter of debate. But this is not correct.[60]

Fisher, a leading figure in the evolution of inductive statistics, set the tone in the field for a long period of time with his stress upon the "null hypothesis." This hypothesis (that there is no difference between the sample and the working universe) can never be *proved* by experimental data. It can only be rejected as highly improbable. And because an experimenter is rarely interested in merely "accepting" a null hypothesis, the statistician thus strives to reject it.

Fisher's conception of the statistical hypothesis has in recent decades largely been supplanted by the Neymann-Pearson perspective. This involves, among other things, the concept of type-I and type-II errors. The error of rejecting a hypothesis that is true is called a type-I error; a type-II error consists of accepting a hypothesis that is false. Without undue elaboration of the argument, we can say that Neymann and Pearson do not simply stress the rejection of hypotheses as did Fisher. Actually, for Neymann and Pearson the null hypothesis commands equal status with alternative hypotheses.

It is interesting, however, that in some respects Fisher's view is closer to Popper's conception of the scientific method than is the Neymann-Pearson stand. For Fisher, like Popper,[61] was intent upon rejecting hypotheses rather than accepting them. However, unlike Popper, Fisher did not emphasize the role of the logico-deductive method, and, as we have already remarked, Popper's conception of probability (relative to the covering-law model) is of a special type.

Still other views regarding the formulation of statistical hypotheses demand our attention. One of these, advanced by Tukey, distinguishes between con-

[60] Cherry Ann Clark, "Hypothesis Testing in Relation to Statistical Methodology," *Review of Educational Research, 33* (December, 1963), 455–473. Clark summarizes the major controversies in a useful manner and provides the reader with many of the basic references.

[61] Karl R. Popper, *The Logic of Scientific Discovery* (New York: Science Editions, Wiley, 1961). Cf. Ronald A. Fisher, *The Design of Experiments,* 7th ed. (London: Oliver and Boyd, 1960), 15–17.

clusions and decisions. According to Tukey, the pure scientist is concerned with conclusions.

> Conclusions are established with careful regard to evidence, but without regard to consequences of specific actions in specific circumstances. . . . Conclusions are withheld until adequate evidence has accumulated.
> A conclusion is a statement which is to be accepted as applicable to the conditions of an experiment or observation unless and until unusually strong evidence to the contrary arises.[62]

Conversely, according to Tukey, the applied scientist thinks in terms of decisions. Rather than adhere to the formula long conventional in decision theory, "we accept," the scientist reasons: "Let us decide to act for the present as if."[63] The practitioner then attempts to control at suitably low levels the error of either accepting a hypothesis that is false or of rejecting one that is true. In the end, the pure scientist exhibits greater caution than does his applied counterpart in both accepting and rejecting hypotheses, for the applied scientist makes decisions in the here and now. If Tukey's reasoning is sound, and it does have something to commend it, there is a degree of irony in the situation: the applied scientist, whose actual risks are greater than those of the purist, nevertheless cannot be as cautious as the latter in his orientation toward the scientific method.

Tukey's remarks carry overtones of another controversy in the field of statistics that bears directly upon hypothesis formation. This is the controversy between the Bayesians, who speak of "subjective probability" (and decision making), and the non-Bayesians, who reason in terms of "objective probability" (a concept more in line with positivistic thinking).

Roberts presents in capsule form the differences between these two approaches:

> A formal Bayesian analysis leads to probabilistic assessments of the object of uncertainty. For example, a Bayesian inference might be: "The probability is .95 that the mean of a normal distribution lies between 12.1 and 23.7." The number .95 represents a degree of belief, either in the sense of "subjective probability consistent" or "subjective probability rational" . . . .95 need not and typically does not correspond to any "objective long-run relative frequency. Very roughly, a degree of belief of .95 can be interpreted as betting odds of 95 to

---

[62] John W. Tukey, "Conclusions vs. Decisions," *Technometrics*, 2 (November, 1960), 425.

[63] *Ibid.*, 424.

5 or 19 to 1. A degree of belief is always potentially a basis for action . . .

By contrast the traditional or "classical" approach to inference leads to probabilistic statements about the method by which a particular inference is obtained. Thus a classical inference might be: "A .95 confidence interval for the mean of a normal distribution extends from 12.1 to 23.7." The number .95 here represents a long-run relative frequency . . . (It is not to be inferred from the fact that we used the same numbers, .95, 12.1, and 23.7, in both illustrations that there will necessarily be a numerical coincidence between the two approaches.)[64]

Roberts, however, indicates that the Bayesian and classical schools are closer to one another than each is to other viewpoints.

But just what are the implications of this debate for methodology? First, it suggests that different conceptions of the nature of reality lead to different conceptions of probability; for example, the classical school seems more inclined to accept a mechanistic view of social reality than does the Bayesian. Moreover, it appears that the use of these differing conceptions of probability will lead to somewhat different interpretations of research materials. Unfortunately, the specific implications of the foregoing debate for the practicing sociologist have been indicated only in rather broad terms.

This discussion of probability leads us to still another problem area: the different conceptions of "chance" that can be found in social science literature. The notion of chance, something one strives to control through inductive statistics, is itself a confusing concept. It should be recognized at least that statistical hypotheses generally refer to the chance factors that stem from probability sampling. This notion differs somewhat from the idea that chance influences human action. Thus, the probability that one third of all entering freshmen will fail sociology in a given set of colleges is of a different order from the hypothesis that a sample drawn from these colleges is representative thereof. Sociologists have formulated many hypotheses concerning the relation of samples to a working universe, but few concerning the probability that human action is patterned in a particular manner.

HYPOTHESIS TESTING

The specific mode of testing hypotheses regarding the relationship of a sample to a universe has also been a matter of disagreement in sociology. One method is applying the test of significance. In 1957 Hanan Selvin leveled a frontal

---

[64] Harry V. Roberts, "Bayesian Inference," *American Statistical Association Proceedings (Social Statistics Section), 1963* (Washington, D.C.: American Statistical Association, 1963), 76.

attack against the use of such tests in survey research.[65] On the other hand, a number of methodologists have come to the defense of this statistical tool.

In this connection Selvin considers two main problems: (1) the difficulty of designing procedures for testing hypotheses and (2) the problem of interpreting the results of tests of significance in survey (or nonexperimental) research. Concerning the question of the research design, Selvin reasons that

> *Only when all important correlated biases have been controlled is it legitimate to measure the possible influence of random errors by statistical tests of significance.* These tests must be the last step in statistical analysis, not the first.
>
> In principle, then, tests of significance have a place in nonexperimental research. But in practice conditions are rarely suitable for the tests. We can distinguish three factors that work against the complete removal of the correlated biases. 1) In few if any surveys is the number of cases large enough to control simultaneously all the important uncontrolled variables. . . . 2) All variables known to be relevant may not have been included in the design of the study. . . . 3) Some variables are so "confounded" with the variables whose relationship is being analyzed that they *cannot* be controlled.[66]

With respect to the meaning of tests of significance, Selvin argues that researchers have confused substantive with statistical significance. "A 1 per cent difference may be significant at the .001 level if the sample is large enough, yet such a small difference is essentially meaningless for sociology at present."[67] He also considers the matter of "random errors," which, theoretically, can be "controlled" via tests of significance. But random errors, he avers, occur in other instances than in the selection of cases, as in responses to interviewers, and in those situations they cannot be "controlled for" by tests of significance.[68] Selvin also

[65] Hanan C. Selvin, "A Critique of Tests of Significance in Survey Research," *American Sociological Review, 22* (October, 1957), 522–523. Although we refer to this article for purposes of discussion, it appears that Selvin has modified his position somewhat. "As nearly as I can tell now, the only significant mistake in the original article was the claim that all variables correlated with the independent variable must be held constant before the test can be properly interpreted." Hanan C. Selvin, "Durkheim's *Suicide*: Further Thoughts on a Methodological Classic," in Robert A. Nisbet, *Emile Durkheim* (Englewood Cliffs, N.J.: Prentice-Hall, Spectrum Books, 1965), 122, ftn. 24. For an extended discussion of many of the issues raised by Selvin as well as of other issues surrounding the use of tests of significance, see Johan Galtung, *Theory and Methods of Social Research* (New York: Columbia University Press, 1967), 358–388.

[66] Selvin, "A Critique of Tests of Significance in Survey Research," *op. cit.,* 522–523.

[67] *Ibid.,* 524.

[68] *Ibid.,* 524–525.

objects to "hypothesis hunting" in survey research—to the search for hypotheses that will prove to be statistically significant.[69] For the more hypotheses one searches for *after the fact,* the more likely one is to find hypotheses displaying significant differences. Yet, seeking hypotheses is legitimate enough, provided each of them is tested in a different setting.

Selvin's position reflects the methodological orientation of the Columbia School—of Paul Lazarsfeld and his students. These workers have applied multivariate analysis, rather than tests of significance, in their research efforts. Thus Lipset *et al., Union Democracy,* and Merton *et al., The Student-Physician,*[70] are both studies that shun tests of significance in favor of the multivariate approach. According to this approach, the researcher, after he crosstabulates his data to discern the effect of a third variable upon the interrelationships of two other variables, looks for the *patterning* of differences rather than the occurrence of absolute differences among social phenomena.

Just how sound is Selvin's position in judging the evidence needed to support or overthrow a hypothesis? McGinnis and Kish have challenged certain features of it, particularly the assumption that tests of significance are possible only after all important correlated biases have been controlled for. McGinnis' chief objection is that Selvin failed to recognize that there are three different kinds of statistical hypotheses.[71] Selvin considered only one type: that wherein all the variables are intended to be controlled. Kish, whose analytical distinctions among variables we cited above, contends that tests of significance are useful for isolating random variables (his Class-IV type above).[72] Selvin's premise that we cannot know the size and direction of uncontrolled variables and thus can only employ tests of significance leads, in Kish's view, to the rejection not only of statistical tests of significance but of the very ideal of delineating explanatory variables in survey data. Kish, therefore, regards Selvin's main criticism of tests of significance as highly unrealistic.[73]

The Selvin-Kish confrontation illustrates the conflict between the scientist (Selvin) who champions the ideal norm at all costs and the scientist (Kish) who holds that rigid adherence to the ideal would stifle social research. Selvin's solution is to develop a different set of normative rules (multivariate analysis), while Kish's solution is to refine current norms with respect to testing hypotheses and admit that one cannot always adhere to the ideal procedure. It seems to us that there is room for both approaches.

The disagreement between McGinnis and Selvin suggests the presence of

---

[69] *Ibid.,* 526.

[70] Lipset *et al., op. cit.,* appendix 1; Robert K. Merton *et al.* (eds.), *The Student-Physician* (Cambridge, Mass.: Harvard, 1957), appendix C.

[71] Robert McGinnis, "Randomization and Inference in Sociological Research," *American Sociological Review, 23* (August, 1958), 408–414.

[72] Kish, *op. cit.* 328–338.

[73] *Ibid.*

divergent theoretical assumptions. McGinnis, a positivist in his orientation, is less concerned with "causal analysis" than is Selvin, who seems to regard this perspective as basic to sociological inquiry. Put in other terms, researchers who hold to different theoretical assumptions often adhere to differing norms in the testing of statistical hypotheses.

The Selvin-Kish-McGinnis debate relates to still another question, albeit only implicitly or tangentially: "How should data be analyzed if probability sampling is lacking?" Many social scientists utilize tests of significance when, for example, no probability samples have been drawn. One position, taken by Lieberson in a book based on his Ph.D. dissertation at the University of Chicago, runs as follows:

> Turning to the question of tests of significance, we should first observe that in most instances in this study we cannot infer the probability of an association existing in either the larger universe of cities in the United States or in the larger universe of all the ethnic groups within a particular city.[74]

> Social scientists are not in full agreement concerning the applicability of significance tests, but we do not wish to go into that issue here. We may simply note that tests of significance cannot for the most part be used in this study to infer the probability of a given association in a large universe. That is, our concern with tests of significance is based on the necessity for the investigator and the reader to use some objective, if arbitrary, method for deciding whether or not an association between two variables does or does not exist for the groups or cities actually studied.[75]

One could argue, as does Lieberson, that his orientation provides him with a convenient device for distinguishing among significant associations within a single sample. But social scientists cannot take these results as a basis for comparison with those of other samples. The cutting points in determining significant associations simply are not comparable. We can, as we did earlier, argue that the tests of significance used by Lieberson provided him with semantic, but not scientific, meaningfulness.

Actually, some of the assumptions of sociologists regarding tests of significance and probability sampling should be examined carefully. McGinnis, for instance, has remarked that "most sociological research is nonexperimental and more often than not it involves probability sampling from some population.

[74] Stanley Lieberson, *Ethnic Patterns in American Cities* (New York: Free Press, 1963), 42.

[75] *Ibid.*, 43.

Thus, the door is opened to the possibility of making statistical inferences."[76] But is the initial assumption warranted? Even where probability samples are drawn, the response rate (due to refusals and the like) is usually less than 90 percent.[77] Researchers devote too little attention to such deviations from the ideal norm and to the question of how these deviations affect one's interpretation of, say, tests of significance. Certainly some doubt can be raised concerning their utility in circumstances where the response rate is only 85 to 90 percent.

Perhaps as a result of the difficulties of testing hypotheses via probability statistics, Blalock, among others, has suggested that we deemphasize our concern with relating samples to their working universe and focus instead upon the analysis of interrelationships among variables.[78] This emphasis upon multivariate analysis is of course in part Selvin's position. But in addition Blalock argues for simplified models in establishing these relationships. Clearly the use of simplified models has permitted Blalock to bring to light assumptions—overlooked, for instance, by the Columbia School—that scientists are forced to make when they utilize multivariate analysis. But Blalock encounters other difficulties. For just how useful are simplified tools for analyzing highly complex social data? The present state of knowledge suggests that their applicability will be limited to narrow empirical domains.

Analysis of Individuals and Collectivities

Much confusion in testing hypotheses, either by cases or by numbers, has been generated by the scientist's disregard of the individual-group dilemma. In the preceding chapter we indicated that conclusions based on individuals (typically, roles) and conclusions based on collectivities can differ considerably. We can now, on the basis of recent methodological advances, deal more adequately with the issues involved.

Robinson in his article "Ecological Correlations and the Behavior of Individuals" brought the problem to the attention of the sociological community when he demonstrated that correlations drawn from group data cannot be generalized to individuals.[79] (The reverse is also true.)

Robinson illustrated his argument by showing that the correlation between

[76] McGinnis, *op. cit.*, 408.

[77] Ronald Freedman *et al.*, *Family Planning, Sterility, and Population Growth* (New York: McGraw-Hill, 1959). With respect to national sample surveys, they write that an 85 percent response rate is often viewed as satisfactory, and an 87 percent response rate as typical (14).

[78] H. M. Blalock, "Some Important Methodological Problems for Sociology," *Sociology and Social Research*, 47 (July, 1963), 398–407; Blalock, *Causal Inferences in Nonexperimental Research, op. cit.*

[79] W. S. Robinson, "Ecological Correlations and the Behavior of Individuals," *Ameri-*

color and illiteracy for the Census Bureau's nine geographic divisions in 1930 yielded a Pearsonian correlation of 0.946, whereas the Pearsonian (fourfold-point) correlation for individuals—where color and illiteracy are viewed as properties of individuals rather than of geographic divisions—was 0.203. And when states (rather than regions) are treated as ecological areas, still another set of correlations can be derived.[80]

While Robinson's argument did much to undermine once highly regarded research efforts, his paper also set the stage for further clarification of this problem area. Menzel, for example, in his reply to Robinson defended the use of ecological correlations for certain purposes.[81] Then, some years later, Menzel along with Lazarsfeld provided us with perhaps the most useful scheme for coping with the study of individuals and collectivities. They classified various approaches to the study of individuals and groups according to the measurement operations performed.

Lazarsfeld and Menzel distinguish among three types of properties that describe collectivities:[82]

1. Analytical properties. These are obtained by performing a mathematical operation upon some property of each unit within the group. The average salary for all working wives in the United States compared with that for working wives in the Soviet Union is an analytical property of a collectivity of individuals.

2. Structural properties. These are obtained by performing an operation on the data about the relations of each member (or unit) to some or all other members. Studies of best-liked classmates, for example, can yield structural properties. Groups, then, can be described and compared as to the degree that such choices are concentrated or dispersed.

3. Global properties. Here collectivities are described in terms of some property that is not dependent upon information about the properties of individual members: for example, the presence or absence of atomic power among nations.

Lazarsfeld and Menzel describe four types of properties which are limited to describing individuals within groups:[83]

---

can Sociological Review, 15 (June, 1950), 351–357. Cf. Erwin K. Scheuch, "Cross-National Comparisons Using Aggregate Data: Some Substantive and Methodological Problems," in Richard L. Merritt and Stein Rokkan (eds.), *Comparing Nations* (New Haven: Yale, 1966), chap. 7, esp. 148 ff.

[80] Robinson, *op. cit.*

[81] Herbert Menzel, "Comment on Robinson's Ecological Correlations and the Behavior of Individuals," *American Sociological Review,* 15 (October, 1950), 674.

[82] Paul F. Lazarsfeld and Herbert Menzel, "On the Relation Between Individual and Collective Properties," in Amitai Etzioni (ed.), *Complex Organizations: A Sociological Reader* (New York: Holt, Rinehart and Winston, 1961), 422–440.

[83] *Ibid.*

1. *Absolute properties.*   These data are characteristics of members that are obtained without recourse to information about the collectivity or about the relationships of the member being described to other members. Examples are income, age, education, and other characteristics used to describe individuals.

2. *Relational properties.*   These are computed from information about substantive relationships between the member described and other members. Sociometric choice (number of choices received) is a relational property.

3. *Comparative properties.*   These characterize a member by comparison between his value with respect to some absolute or relational property and the distribution of this property over the entire collectivity of which he is a member. Sibling order, or the ranking from the first-born to the last-born in a family, is illustrative of this.

4. *Contextual properties.*   These describe a member by a property of his collective. Graduates of large law schools are more likely to earn high incomes at age 40 than graduates of small law schools. Being a member of a large (or small) law school is a contextual quality.

The classification scheme of Lazarsfeld and Menzel points up some of the problems relating to the study of groups and their members. It is not merely the theoreticians but also the research practitioners who must take account of the differences between the study of individuals and the study of collectivities. More pointedly, the notions of global property and of contextual property each in its own way reflects certain critical issues in the individual versus group controversy.

The idea of global properties, those where knowledge of the collectivity does not rest upon knowledge of its members, presents sociologists with some of their most difficult problems. It is in the study of normative or value orientations of groups that many significant controversies remain, for here the nonadditive principle comes to the fore. The fact that certain characteristics of collectivities cannot be determined by adding up the characteristics of individuals or individual roles is related to some of the major controversies in explanation (see next chapter).

The notion of contextual properties was taken into account by Durkheim in his study of suicide when he argued that rates, or kinds, of suicide vary among sociocultural contexts. Modern contextual analysis—termed the study of "compositional effects" by Davis[84] and "structural effects" by Blau[85]—has sharpened the logic which was inherent in the Durkheim perspective. Thus Blau was able to isolate six types of structural effects. Two of these are (1) direct structural effects of common values, where the individual's conduct is influenced not only by his own value orientation but also by the social pressures arising from shared

[84] James A. Davis, *Great Books and Small Groups* (New York: Free Press, 1961), chap. 1.

[85] Peter M. Blau, "Structural Effects," *American Sociological Review,* 25 (April, 1960), 178–193.

group values, and (2) inverse structural effects, where group values give rise to normative constraints that counteract an individual's psychological response to his own value orientation.[86] Here individual properties are seen in relation to collective ones: in this instance, global in nature. In the end, sociologists must continue to seek clarification of the individual versus the group issue on both the theoretical and the methodological planes.

[86] *Ibid.*

CHAPTER 11

The Nature and Adequacy of Explanation

Now that we have considered the relation of cases and numbers to the testing of hypotheses and to theoretical analysis more generally, we are in a position to discuss the nature of explanation. We seek answers to such questions as, "When can data be considered adequate to support a given theory or set of hypotheses?" In the course of our discussion, we pay special attention to the matters of causation, reliability and validity, and prediction and control in sociology.

Explanation: Some General Considerations

There is no firm consensus among methodologists as to the nature of theory or of explanation. Some writers, as we mentioned in an earlier chapter, would equate the two. Nagel, for example, lists the following types of explanation: the deductive model, the probabilistic explanation, the functional or teleological explanation, and the genetic explanation.[1] But he fails to differentiate clearly among the logical structure of theory, theoretical assumptions, explanation, and so on. For us, explanation relates to the purpose or function of a theory, or, more narrowly, to the criteria by which a scientist judges the adequacy, utility, and/or validity of the data used to support (or negate) a particular set of substantive generalizations. These criteria are, of course, a product of one's theoretical assumptions.

There appear to be two major types of explanation employed within the social sciences: *verstehen*, or understanding, and prediction. Those sociologists who align themselves with the positivist tradition contend that prediction is the key criterion for adequate explanation, that the adequacy of one's data relative to one's

---

[1] Ernest Nagel, *The Structure of Science* (New York: Harcourt, Brace & World, 1961), 20–26, *passim*.

hypotheses or theory lies in the resulting ability to predict patterns in a given realm. Opposed to this group are sociologists in the heritage of Dilthey, Windelband, and Weber who see understanding as the basis for adequate explanation.

Hempel, among other theorists, has contended that all social theory must be evaluated in terms of its predictive power. Although he recently modified this position, he still argues for use of the logico-deductive approach (as described in Chapter 3) in all social inquiry, including history. Thus, ideally, even historians have recourse to universal hypotheses (or covering laws).

> Consider, for example, the statement that the Dust Bowl farmers migrated to California "because" continual drought and sandstorms made their existence increasingly precarious, and because California seemed to them to offer so much better living conditions. This explanation rests on some such universal hypothesis as that populations will tend to migrate to regions which offer better living conditions. But it would obviously be difficult accurately to state this hypothesis in the form of a general law which is reasonably well confirmed by all the relevant evidence available.[2]

It is because of the difficulty of specifying the *conditions* under which these general laws hold that Hempel speaks of historical research as providing an "explanatory sketch" rather than a true explanation of social phenomena.[3]

The point is that certain logical empiricists would cast *all* social research into the logico-deductive mold, and they would speak of "retrodiction" rather than "prediction" in evaluating research of a historical nature.

Many social scientists (and philosophers of science) who equate explanation and prediction fail to appreciate the logical as well as the sociological issues this orientation involves. Not a few social scientists equate effective prediction with explanation without recognizing the need for a logico-deductive system permitting an explicit statement of the conditions under which generalizations hold. And we must also take cognizance of the writings of Scheffler and others who question the structural identity (in a logical sense) of explanation and prediction.[4]

Natural scientists, in contrast to social scientists, can more readily equate prediction with explanation, for they can more easily manipulate and control the

---

[2] Carl G. Hempel, *Aspects of Scientific Explanation* (New York: Free Press, 1965), 236. This passage is contained in chapter 9, "The Function of General Laws in History," which is a slightly modified version on an article published in 1942. For an exposition of his more recent views, see chapter 12.

[3] *Ibid.,* chap. 9.

[4] Israel Scheffler, *The Anatomy of Inquiry* (Cambridge, Mass.: Harvard, 1963). For a summary of the criticisms of the deductivist thesis of explanation, though not from a sympathetic viewpoint, see Merle B. Turner, *Philosophy and the Science of Behavior* (New York: Appleton-Century-Crofts, 1967), 276 ff.

variables via experimentation. And, historically at least, it is experimentation rather than prediction that distinguishes modern science from the intellectual endeavors of preindustrial civilized societies.[5] Prior to the modern scientific revolution, men were able to predict certain patterns of natural and social events, but the dominant value orientation negated any effort to manipulate the natural and the social orders. Thus, the Greeks advanced quite well in astronomy, where they did not have to tamper with the natural order when testing their predictions, but in those realms of natural science where experimentation was essential, they made much less progress.

If one is to control events, he must do more than predict: He must be able to isolate some of the strategic variables that determine events and to detail the conditions under which these events occur. There is a vast difference between predicting that certain bands of clouds will bring rain and preventing rain or bringing it about. Only the knowledge of the necessary and sufficient conditions (or "causative" factors) can enable one to manipulate natural forces effectively.

Many sociologists employ the notion of prediction in a special sense. They predict that certain hypotheses will be supported by data that are to be collected. Far more difficult is the shaping of events to produce predictable results.

Of course most social scientists recognize that they have attained only limited success in predicting, much less in controlling, the course of human events. Nevertheless, they would argue that more effective prediction (and control) will follow from more adequate theoretical formulations and research procedures. However, the nature of social reality, particularly the scientist's relationships to his data, imposes functional limits upon social prediction and control which can be circumvented only via novel, and perhaps heretical, theories.

But what are the alternatives to prediction as a form of explanation? One answer lies in the reasoning of those who, either directly or indirectly, associate themselves with the neo-idealistic tradition. From this perspective, the major function of social theory or social research is to promote understanding. To achieve this goal, sociologists rely heavily upon typological tools, classificatory schemes, and the analysis which calls for relating parts to wholes.

Admittedly, most *verstehen* sociologists profess little faith in most of the logic and techniques of the positivists. The former, as we have remarked at several junctures, diverge considerably from the logical empiricists in their conception of social reality. They reject the notion of predicting human action in strictly mechanistic terms. Because of man's active role in reshaping his environment, many of these sociologists reason that we must rely upon theories that stress understanding rather than those concerned with prediction per se.

However, those sociologists who equate understanding with scientific ex-

---

[5] For a popular account of man's efforts to cope with the future, an account that indicates some of the differences between preindustrial and industrial man, see Richard Lewinsohn, *Science, Prophecy and Prediction,* trans. by Arnold J. Pomerans (New York: Harper & Row, 1961).

planation use the term "understanding" in a number of ways, and these usages remain largely unexplicated in the literature. We shall elaborate upon a few of the more common ones.

One group of sociologists, although interested in predicting human action, remain unconvinced that the logical empiricist's position is fully applicable to the study of social reality and thus, by default, tend to align themselves with those who emphasize understanding as the goal of scientific inquiry. Outstanding within this group are persons who admit the legitimacy of "teleological analysis" on both the individual and the group levels (a point elaborated upon below). For those who study the group are often relating parts (or structures) to the broader whole (or system).

More generally, those writers who stress understanding as the key criterion of explanation often cling to a special type of "coherence theory of truth." Although a few are concerned primarily with the internal consistency of their theories and only incidentally with the relationship of their analyses to data, most sociologists of this persuasion hold that a conjunction of theory and of supporting data is necessary and that furthermore, to be adequate, this system must provide scientists and/or laymen with a more orderly and coherent interpretation of social events. The adherents of this view, who rely upon what some writers term "disciplined insight," construct a theory that coheres with, or makes sense out of, the ideology and social structure of a society or societies.

Certain social scientists have sought to attain such understanding by setting the social actions or events under study in historical perspective. This usually means comparing the present with the past or explaining certain patterns in terms of their social origins.

The historian Dray has formulated a more precise conception of understanding in historical research:

> The function of an explanation is to resolve puzzlement of some kind. When an historian sets out to explain an historical action, his problem is usually that he does not know what reason the agent had for doing it. To achieve understanding, what he seeks is information about what the agent believed to be the factors of his situation, including the likely results of taking various courses of action considered open to him, and what he wanted to accomplish: his purposes, goals, or motives. Understanding is achieved when the historian can see the reasonableness of a man's doing what this agent did . . .
>
> Explanation which tries to establish a connection between beliefs, motives, and actions of the indicated sort I shall call "rational explanation."[6]

---

[6] William Dray, "The Historical Explanation of Actions Reconsidered," in Sidney Hook (ed.), *Philosophy and History* (New York: New York University Press, 1963), 108. This volume provides a diversity of viewpoints regarding explanation.

Sociologists may, of course, elucidate or otherwise "make sense out of" the current scene without recourse to a historical perspective. Here they strive to objectify, or raise to the level of consciousness, informal or *sub rosa* norms that are taken for granted or are little understood either by their fellow scientists or by laymen. The adequacy of understanding or explanation in this instance is frequently judged according to whether the analysis coheres with the ideology and normative structure of the society.

Riesman's *The Lonely Crowd* and Goffman's *The Presentation of Self in Everyday Life* utilize understanding as a form of explanation.[7] The idea of "inner-directed" or "other-directed" man, as advanced by Riesman, seems to have caught the fancy of social scientists and laymen alike, for it has served to order, to objectify, and even to predict the actions of individuals in mid–twentieth-century America—actions that were only dimly perceived prior to Riesman's efforts.[8] Although Riesman's ideal-type constructs are, by the standards of logical empiricists, crudely formulated, they do represent an advance in rigor over prior conceptualizations and find support in a massive amount of illustrative material, as well as in certain specific research studies.[9]

Although Riesman's work is to some degree historical (he utilizes the demographic factor to account for the general change in the United States from an inner-directed to an other-directed personality type), Goffman's is clearly ahistorical. Yet Goffman, like Riesman, has gained an extensive following. By comparing and analyzing the patterning of people's "on-stage" versus "off-stage" personalities, he has brought to the level of consciousness a key facet of personality structure in modern society.

Psychoanalysis offers a more dramatic illustration of the relationship of understanding to explanation. Most methodologists would agree that psychoanalytic theory is difficult to test,[10] and where it has been subjected to empirical

[7] David Riesman, *The Lonely Crowd* (New Haven: Yale, 1950) ; and Erving Goffman, *The Presentation of Self in Everyday Life* (Garden City, N.Y.: Doubleday, Anchor Books, 1959).

[8] For a critical evaluation of Riesman's ideas, see various essays in Seymour M. Lipset and Leo Lowenthal (eds.), *Culture and Social Character* (New York: Free Press, 1961).

[9] See, e.g., Sanford M. Dornbusch and Laurel C. Hickman, "Other-Directedness in Consumer-Goods Advertising: A Test of Riesman's Historical Theory," *Social Forces, 38* (December, 1959), 99–102.

[10] For a highly critical review of the logic of explanation in psychoanalysis, see H. J. Eysenck, "Psychoanalysis—Myth or Science?" *Inquiry, 4* (Spring, 1961), 1–15. Cf. B. A. Farrell, "Can Psychoanalysis be Refuted?" *op. cit.,* 16–36 as well as various essays in Philipp G. Frank (ed.), *The Validation of Scientific Theories* (New York: Collier Books, 1961), chap. 3.

test, as in the work of Sewell, it has been found wanting.[11] Despite this, many social scientists either tolerate psychoanalysis or champion some form of it for the reason that it clarifies aspects of the personal maladjustments and inconsistencies of modern man. Further, psychoanalysis provides the laymen and the scientist alike with one means of understanding and coping with personal disorders.

Yet the aforementioned kinds of understanding have frequently led social scientists into a crude form of historicism, into becoming captives of their own national heritage. Social scientists must constantly strive to place their own society in some broader crosscultural context; they must seek to understand how their own social order is similar to, and different from, systems in other parts of the world. Ultimately social theories must "make sense" in terms of certain crossnational categories. Sociologists must therefore be constantly on guard against becoming so closely integrated into their own system (whether their nation or some subsystem thereof) that they take its premises for granted under the assumption that these are universal. As we have argued before, an ongoing dialogue within the scientific community is a minimal essential for the attainment of this objective.

As a matter of fact, the logical empiricists also employ some form of understanding when they evaluate their scientific theories. In a broad sense they explain the utility of the scientific method in terms of its logico-meaningful relationships to the society at large. Although most logical empiricists admit that prediction has met with only limited success in social science, they view current theory and research as eminently worthwhile and worthy of societal support, for this enterprise articulates with, and lends support to, the industrial-urban order. It is no accident that positivists have envisioned a utopia resting upon scientific endeavor.[12] Today this utopia includes bureaucratic systems that can readily control many aspects of the physical and social environments and that become more rational with the proliferation of social research. In fact, as we elaborate below, the very idea of prediction can be subsumed under the broader category of understanding.

The Nature of Social Causation

We have dealt with only one facet of the debate over the nature of explanation. We shall now set sail upon more perilous seas and examine the meaning and use of the concept of "cause" in science.

[11] William H. Sewell, "Infant Training and the Personality of the Child," *American Journal of Sociology*, 58 (September, 1952), 150–159.

[12] Cf. Robert Boguslaw, *The New Utopians* (Englewood Cliffs, N.J.: Prentice-Hall, 1965).

Logical empiricists often argue that "causal analysis" is inadequate as a form of explanation.[13] Indeed some would purge the very notion from the lexicon of science. For them the concept "cause" loses its utility wherever scientists can employ a deductive theory, wherever they can specify the conditions under which certain events or actions will occur and where theories can be tested via prediction. The idea of cause connotes some mystical thought process. It conjures up the notion of "ultimate causation"—of a universe controlled by a supreme being or beings—an idea against which the early scientists struggled so long and so hard. In the eyes of some logical empiricists, the use of causal analysis simply serves to undermine the naturalistic world view upon which the scientific method rests.

A second objection to the concept of cause stems from Hume's analysis. In the view of many scholars, Hume demolished once and for all the assumption that cause inheres in the nature of things. Scientists, the proponents of this tradition would aver, can observe that X is always associated with Y, but cannot observe what binds X and Y together. They therefore must be content with specifying the conditions under which certain correlations hold and must rely upon prediction to validate scientific theories. Inasmuch as the concept "cause" has no empirical referent, causal analysis is associated with a form of theorizing that borders on the mystical.

A third criticism of the idea of cause arises from its association with the notion of teleology. The logical basis of teleological theorizing has been sharply scored by scientists and logicians. Teleology, in this instance, refers to attempts by scientists to explain or to predict the future, not in terms of antecedent conditions but in terms of purpose or some future state of affairs. Criticisms have been leveled against various evolutionary theories in the social and the natural sciences on the grounds that their supporters seek to explain evolution in terms of some hidden purpose in the universe, some goal toward which mankind is consciously or unconsciously striving.

In light of these severe objections to the idea of cause, we may rightly wonder about the place of this concept in modern social science. But there are several reasons for the persistence of causal analysis in sociology.

One reason is the difficulty of establishing logico-deductive schemes that will explain many kinds of social action. For the conditions under which a particular generalization will hold in an "if X, then Y" scheme are difficult to isolate. Sociologists must deal with numerous variables as they attempt to isolate the necessary and sufficient conditions, and because they cannot readily manipulate social

[13] The literature on causal analysis is vast. For a brief survey of some of the issues, see Herbert Feigl, "Notes on Causality," in Herbert Feigl and May Brodbeck (eds.), *Readings in the Philosophy of Science* (New York: Appleton-Century-Crofts, 1953), 408–418. For an up-to-date discussion by a logical empiricist, one cast in a moderate tone, see Rudolf Carnap, *Philosophical Foundations of Physics* (New York: Basic Books, 1966), chap. 19.

systems in a laboratory, the "if-then" sequence, notably the sufficient conditions, of the formula often remains in doubt. Consequently, sociologists will continue to search for the precipitating factor or sufficient condition, which then will be viewed as the causal agent.

Then too, sociologists must employ some form of the logic of the dialectic to explain given social patterns. The idea of "circular causation," advanced by Myrdal for explaining the relations between whites and Negroes in the United States and certain patterns in underdeveloped nations, seems to be an outgrowth of dialectic thought. Thus, Myrdal writes:

> In its simplest form the explanatory model can be reduced to two factors: "white prejudice", causing discrimination against the Negroes in various respects, and the "low plane of living" of the Negro population. These two factors are mutually inter-related: the Negroes' low plane of living is kept down by discrimination from the whites while, on the other side, the Negroes' poverty, ignorance . . . stimulate and feed the antipathy of the whites for Negroes.
>
> White prejudice and low Negro standards thus mutually "cause" each other. If at a point of time things tend to remain about as they are, this means that the two forces balance each other. . . . Such a static "accommodation" is, however, entirely fortuitous and by no means a stable equilibrium position. If either of the two factors should change, this is bound to bring a change in the other factor, too, and start a cumulative process of mutual interaction in which the change in one factor would continuously be supported by the reaction of the other factor and so on in a circular way.[14]

If one accepts Myrdal's reasoning, then we see that all theory in social science cannot be cast in a formal deductive scheme and the idea of causation eliminated.

Furthermore, although Hume demonstrated to the satisfaction of many scholars that the idea of cause does not inhere in the nature of things, it is nevertheless quite true that sociologists must frequently act *as if* it does. The assumption of causal relationships is interwoven with the nature of validation in social science as well as with the need to utilize some form of teleological analysis on both the individual and the group levels.

Even many theorists who speak of teleology as "psychologically satisfying" but logically unsound lapse into teleological reasoning from time to time. Indeed,

[14] Gunnar Myrdal, *Economic Theory and Under-developed Regions* (London: Duckworth, 1957), 16. Cf. Gunnar Myrdal, *An American Dilemma,* vol. 2 (New York: McGraw-Hill paperback, 1964), appendix 3: "Methodological Note on the Principle of Cumulation."

we must recognize the ubiquity of this form of reasoning in most societies. Our hypothesis is that men must think in teleological terms if individuals or groups are to be held "responsible" for their actions. It would be impossible to sustain Western legal systems, for instance, without some form of teleological reasoning.[15] Consider the person who murders someone by hitting him over the head with a rock. We could construct a simple proposition: to wit, "If one hits a person over the head with a rock weighing N pounds with force V, the person will always be killed." But such would be of little practical value in a court of law. Social systems in one way or another must concern themselves with the "motivation," or the purpose, of the rock wielder. Did he do it in self-defense? to avenge another crime? and so on.

Although most sociologists and philosophers of science admit to the utility of teleology on the individual level, many strongly challenge its validity on the group level. However, motivation is considered in assessing not only individual responsibility but also collective responsibility. Whether Franklin D. Roosevelt purposely led America into World War II was a point of considerable interest to politicians in the postwar period. For had the American public concluded that Roosevelt did in fact do so, it would in all likelihood have held members of the Democratic Party responsible for this action as well. Another kind of situation arose when Israel chose to try Eichmann some 15 years after the end of the Nazi atrocities against the European Jews. Israel was intent upon calling to the attention of mankind the importance of "individual responsibility." At the same time, Israel sought in a symbolic fashion to punish one man for the actions of a group and to portray to its younger generation the suffering of the Jews under the Third Reich.[16]

The issue of group purpose comes to the fore in structural-functional theory. Hempel, a leading exponent of the logico-deductive system in scientific research, has criticized structural functionalists for their teleological orientation in the study of social groups.[17] Although we grant the logical problems involved in structural functionalism, sociologists will find it impossible to keep from relating parts (structures) to wholes (systems) and reasoning in modified teleological terms with respect to the goals of systems. Only in this manner is it possible at times to understand (and even to predict) collective action.

It is not unusual to find sociologists who are opposed to structural-functional theory actually using this mode of analysis when they discuss their own departments or the American Sociological Association. Politicians also must think—and

---

[15] See, e.g., H. L. A. Hart and A. M. Honoré, *Causation in the Law* (Fair Lawn, N.J. Oxford, 1959).

[16] Some of these arguments are at least implicit in Gideon Hausner, *Justice in Jerusalem* (New York: Harper & Row, 1966). Cf. Hannah Arendt, *Eichmann in Jerusalem*, rev. ed. (New York: Viking, Compass Books, 1965).

[17] Hempel, *op. cit.*, chap. 11.

act—in terms of structural-functional categories. Indeed, the political leadership, notably during time of war, reasons specifically in terms of the survival of the system.

To argue that the Soviet Union, or the United States, or Nazi Germany did not during World War II act in terms of survival and that the leadership did not attempt to create structures or organizations that would sustain the system (that is, that they did not seek to relate parts to the whole) would be to cling to an extreme form of methodological individualism. Yet such is the view of many philosophers of science and a number of sociologists. They would grant the legitimacy of interpreting an individual's action in teleological terms, for the scientist can, by inquiring into the actor's intent, ascertain the antecedent conditions that led the individual to pursue particular goals. But individual goals are themselves products of group interaction, not of individuals per se. And the goal or goals of the group are more than the sum of the goals of the actors (or their roles) within the group. Thus the intent of an actor may be a product of the goals and values of the group. This line of reasoning thus leads us back into some form of teleology on the group level.[18]

The analysis of parts to the whole, or of structures to the group's overall purpose, cannot be dealt with within the logico-deductive frame of reference. Hempel and Popper are necessarily methodological individualists;[19] they must either analyze individual actors (or roles) within or among systems or treat systems as individuals. This logical framework is limited to the analysis of certain problem areas. It is for this same reason that it is essential to think in terms of understanding, not merely in terms of prediction, when seeking to assess the worth of theoretical systems.

Sociologists will also find it difficult to avoid use of the term "cause" insofar as this concept is associated with the "logico-meaningful" method of Sorokin[20] or with some variant thereof. Although Sorokin did not employ the term "cause" with reference to the logico-meaningful method, it nevertheless seems useful to do so. Surely sociologists choose particular variables and reject others because they view the former as meaningful for human action. Even positivists indirectly validate their statistical generalizations through a form of logico-meaningful

[18] We are *not* committed to any literal form of teleological reasoning. At the same time, social scientists cannot ignore the "collective image" that men have of their society's future. See, e.g., Fred L. Polak, *The Image of the Future*, 2 vols., trans. by Elise Boulding (New York: Oceana, 1961).

[19] Cf. Sidney Morgenbesser, "Psychologism and Methodological Individualism," in Sidney Morgenbesser (ed.), *Philosophy of Science Today* (New York: Basic Books, 1967), chap. 15.

[20] Pitirim A. Sorokin, *Social and Cultural Dynamics*, vol. 1 (New York: American Book, 1937), 22–47. Cf. Ronald J. Silvers, "The Logic and Meaning of the Logico-Meaningful Method," *Canadian Review of Sociology and Anthropology*, 3 (February, 1966), 1–8.

analysis, for they implicitly accept or reject the variables they employ in terms of their broader sociocultural implications.

Few variables can long be viewed as significant by the scientific community unless they can be conceptualized as meaningful by some elements of the broader society or of the groups to which the sociologist belongs. Earlier we argued that as sociocultural systems change, sociologists come to reconceptualize the variables that they view as paramount. Even when scientists rely upon materialistic forces, as do some ecologist demographers, to account for particular social phenomena, there are at least some elements in the broader society who see these materialistic variables as the basis of their own actions.[21]

So too, prediction is useful for judging the validity of a theory if it is logically or causally meaningful to scientists or other members of the broader society. From this perspective, we can subsume under the category of understanding the notion of prediction as a criterion for judging the adequacy of data relative to a given set of hypotheses. If, for example, the researcher argues that status incongruity leads to juvenile delinquency or narcotics addiction, it is clear that he has chosen this variable and not, say, changes in the temperature of the earth, because the former makes sense, because it is meaningfully relevant to him, to other members of his society, or to members of other societies.

As the social scientist moves into crosscultural studies, his categories become more abstract. Even here, however, some links must exist between his theoretical system and data and the categories of the sociocultural system under study. At this point, the link may be quite indirect. Yet, the scientist must be prepared to translate his categories into terms that are at least congruent with those of the system he is studying.

The Reliability and Validity of Evidence

Against the backdrop of these general considerations regarding explanation, we can consider the matter of the reliability and validity of evidence. In general terms, reliability refers to the consistency among observers regarding a given set of data; validity refers to the adequacy of data relative to a given set of hypotheses. In turn, the adequacy of data is judged in terms of prediction and understanding.

We shall first of all examine the relationship between reliability and validity and qualitative case materials. A number of "legal cases" have pointed up the dangers of using the "logical-meaningful" method in evaluating the reliability and validity of data at any given moment within a particular social order. We must

[21] Sidney M. Willhelm and Gideon Sjoberg, "Economic vs. Protective Values in Urban Land Use Change," *American Journal of Economics and Sociology, 19* (January, 1960), 151–160.

judge the adequacy of evidence in terms of whether the data are logically meaningful over a period of time or in terms of some broader crosscultural perspective.

This principle was dramatically illustrated by the Dreyfus case in nineteenth-century France. Perhaps someday the Warren Commission Report on Lee Harvey Oswald, supposed slayer of President Kennedy, will be viewed in a totally different light than it was when the report was issued.

In the Dreyfus case, the Court ruled that Dreyfus, an officer in the French army, was guilty of treason. However, certain minorities ultimately brought pressure to bear to have the verdict reevaluated. In the ensuing review, it was discovered that one of the key witnesses had lied and that the great body of the French populace had been all too willing to believe what they wanted to believe.[22]

We can only speculate about the ultimate fate of the Warren Commission Report. Clearly, most elements of the American power structure, including the national press, have accepted the Commission's verdict unquestioningly. The decision that a mentally unstable man killed the President coheres with the values and structure of the system; another verdict, for example, that some conspiracy was responsible, challenges the basic premises of American society.

To be sure, the Warren Commission's verdict may well survive the test of time. But certain minority voices in America and Europe have raised grave doubts about it. The latter included the British historian Trevor Roper and the French journalist Sauvage.[23] A critical examination of the data collected by the Commission (and others) suggests the possibility that the inconsistencies within the Report stressed by the voices of dissent will loom larger with the passage of time, as societal values and the power structure undergo change.

The debate concerning the Warren Commission Report brings certain issues to the fore. Not only in the Kennedy assassination but in many social situations contradictory observations are the rule rather than the exception, leading to honest disagreements over the evidence. Moreover, it is hazardous to judge the reliability and validity of such data at any point in time. Because evidence regarding social events is frequently not clear-cut, there is always the danger that what will emerge will be "political" rather than scientific truth.

This leads us to another dilemma inherent in the scientific method. Observations are made by individuals, whereas knowledge is a product of interaction within a group. Therefore, only when some tension exists between individual observers and the group, only when deviation is countenanced, can there be a

---

[22] See, e.g., Guy Chapman, *The Dreyfus Case* (London: R. Hart-Davis, 1955); and Nicholas Halasz, *Captain Dreyfus: The Story of Mass Hysteria* (New York: Simon and Schuster, 1955).

[23] Léo Sauvage, *The Oswald Affair*, trans. by Charles Gaulkin (Cleveland: World Publishing, 1966); Edward Jay Epstein, *Inquest* (New York: Viking, 1966); and Mark Lane, *Rush to Judgment* (New York: Holt, Rinehart and Winston, 1966).

check upon the validation of data by the group, be this the Warren Commission, the broader society, or the scientific community. Reliance upon systematic numerical analysis does not overcome the problems of reliability and validity that inhere in the aforementioned dilemma.

NUMERICAL ANALYSIS: RELIABILITY

There have been various efforts to formalize specific procedures (or norms) for establishing reliability. In order to achieve reliability or consistency among observers, the scientist strives to attain consistency between two or more independent observers or two or more independently derived scores or measures. Here we shall touch upon some of the theoretical issues regarding the use of various techniques for establishing reliability.

One means for determining reliability has been the "test-retest" procedure. In this instance, the researcher administers an instrument, say, an IQ test, and later readministers it to a "similar universe" in order to check upon the consistency of the results. A second technique, termed "equivalent forms," involves constructing tests that for logical or theoretical reasons can be regarded as equivalent. These in turn are applied to a similar universe in order to ascertain, through the use of correlation analysis, whether the results of the tests are similar. A third mode of assessing an instrument's reliability is the "split-half" technique. The scientist in this instance may divide the items on his measuring instrument into two parts. For example, even-numbered items would appear in one scale, odd-numbered items in the other. After administering these two scales to similar working universes, the researcher attempts to assess whether the results are similar— whether the scale is reliable.

A number of modifications of the aforementioned procedures are possible. Instead of assessing the reliability of items on a scale, a sociologist could employ the test-retest or split-half technique to evaluate the reliability of a researcher's observations, to determine whether these are consistent over time with respect to the same universe.

Although the aforementioned techniques have been formalized on one level, their interpretation remains a source of considerable controversy. There is no definitive answer to the question: "When is an instrument reliable?" Reliability is a function of the scientist's theoretical system, the social order being studied, and the use to which the instrument is to be put, either by scientists or by the broader society.

In practice an instrument such as the Graduate Record Examination may be accepted as reliable by one university and rejected as unreliable by another simply because the latter's goals and values differ from those of the former. Or an instrument for predicting the success of, say, parolees may be accepted by one prison system as reliable enough but judged by another organization as unreliable. Or, hypothetically, an instrument with a modest reliability coefficient might be employed to evaluate potential parolees from among prisoners who have committed theft, whereas a similar instrument with a higher reliability coefficient might be rejected for evaluating the potential success of prisoners convicted of homicide, for the latter group is viewed by society as a greater social risk. This aspect of reliability overlaps with the matter of validity discussed below.

Reliability is also, as mentioned above, a product of one's theoretical system and of the social order being investigated. With respect, for example, to the test-retest procedure, the subjects themselves may become a variable in the measurement of reliability. For the knowledge they acquire as a result of taking the first test may well be reflected in the results of the second test. More significant in determining reliability is the scientist's capacity to isolate homogeneous classes of social phenomena. If a group shows marked deviations from the norms in terms of the attributes being measured, we can suspect that the reliability of the instrument employed is rather low. Conversely, if we are working with a stable and homogeneous group, we can expect the reliability of our instrument to be fairly high. Still, it is difficult to know, with respect to, say, the split-half technique, whether a low correlation coefficient between the two halves of the instrument is the result of poor design or whether it stems from social disarray and a high degree of variability within the group being studied.

The need for homogeneous and stable categories if one is to attain high reliability frequently leads sociologists to sacrifice generality for specificity. The old-line Chapin socioeconomic scale is a dramatic case in point. Through the use of this scale, interviewers rank people in a community according to, for instance, the type and condition of furnishings in their living rooms. In the 1952 revision of the scale, a softwood floor received 6 points; a hardwood floor 10; a fireplace with three or more utensils 8; couch pillows 2 each; a piano bench 4; an alarm clock −2; and so on.[24]

The greater the specificity of the items to be counted, as in the Chapin scale, the greater the degree of reliability among observers. Yet this added specificity also means that the instrument is not equally applicable in all parts of the society. Then too, technological innovation and shifts in fashion quickly modify the kinds of articles people display in their living rooms, thus reducing comparability of the results over time and necessitating changes in the scale itself.

The limitations of the Chapin scale are most apparent when we view it in crosscultural perspective: it then emerges as culture-bound par excellence. It simply could not be employed for contrasting the social status of, say, villagers in India or in Mexico with that of ruralites in the United States.

Somewhat similar problems arise when sociologists seek to rank order social classes across cultures according to the indicators formulated by Hollingshead

[24] F. Stuart Chapin, *Experimental Designs in Sociological Research,* rev. ed., (New York: Harper & Row, 1955), 273–274.

and Warner.[25] To be sure, it is possible to make modifications in these scales, but then the problem of comparability arises.

NUMERICAL ANALYSIS: VALIDITY

The nature of validity, or the adequacy of a measurement device or a set of statistical data relative to a given hypothesis, is not only more difficult to analyze than the matter of reliability, but it is inherently a more significant issue.

In the terminology of those who have devised validation procedures, we can distinguish between external and internal validity. Or we can speak of specific validation procedures, predictive and concurrent (generally viewed as external), and content validity (usually considered as internal). In recent years psychologists in particular have introduced into the literature the added notion of construct validity.

The logical empiricists not only consider numerical analysis to be fundamental to scientific endeavor but they fall back upon prediction as a means for validating their measurement instruments or statistical findings. These scientists would take the results of a particular measurement device and seek to predict thereby some independent attribute of the group being studied. For example, many educators rely upon IQ scores to predict a student's academic success in grade school or high school. One could also employ IQ scores to predict success in a given occupation. This line of reasoning suggests that more than one index of validity is possible: in this instance, one for success in grade school, another for success in high school, and so on.

In actual practice, the notions of reliability and validity merge when prediction is taken as the sole criterion of the validity of an instrument. Researchers tend to assume that if an instrument is reliable, it must measure something (an IQ test is what an IQ test measures), and if an instrument is reliable, it can be used to predict (that is, it is valid).

The second kind of validity, concurrent validity, can be taken as a variant of predictive validity. In this instance, the researcher compares the results of an instrument with other contemporaneously obtained data. For example, he may predict that one scale will provide the same information as another one. Sociologists, in applying the idea of concurrent validity, have correlated the results of various socioeconomic indexes (or scales) in order to determine whether they are measuring the same social phenomena. In most instances, the logical empiricist is satisfied with ending his inquiry at this point. He does not proceed to an analysis of the nature of the indexes themselves or of the items in a scale.

Up to this point we have focused upon prediction (or some variant thereof) as a means of validating measurement techniques. But the latter must be used in

[25] For a general discussion of the logic of stratification scales, see Milton M. Gordon, *Social Class in American Sociology* (Durham, N.C.: Duke, 1958), chap. 7.

conjunction with those procedures that utilize the logical-meaningful method or some form of understanding. For example, frequently the internal structure or logic of the scale or measuring instrument must be examined. For example, we might compare items, or attitude statements, on a Guttman scale[26] to determine whether they are logically or meaningfully related to one another. This is at times done more or less semiconsciously by the researcher when he is a member of the sociocultural order he is studying. In addition, the scientist must be concerned with the representativeness of the items in the scale relative to some broader universe of items.

But even when we begin to talk about the representativeness of items, we are in a sense utilizing one form of "construct validity." This notion, introduced into psychology within the last decade or so, has received little formal attention from sociologists.[27] Perhaps one reason for this is the ambiguity of the concept.

Construct validity involves relating one's measuring instrument to the overall theoretical structure in order to determine whether the instrument is logically tied to the concepts and theoretical assumptions that are employed. The psychologist Cronbach, an early proponent of construct validity, has observed, "Whenever a tester asks what a score means psychologically or what causes a person to get a certain test score, he is asking what concepts may properly be used to interpret the test performance."[28]

We shall illustrate the utility of construct validity by applying it to the widely cited and much discussed National Opinion Research Center (NORC) scale for measuring occupational prestige. Ninety different occupations were included in this scale. For each job mentioned, the respondent was asked to "pick out the statement that best gives *your own personal opinion* of the *general standing* that

[26] Louis Guttman, "A Basis for Scaling Qualitative Data," *American Sociological Review,* 9 (April, 1944), 139–150.

[27] Lee J. Cronbach and Paul E. Meehl, "Construct Validity in Psychological Tests," *Psychological Bulletin,* 52 (July, 1955), 281–302; Lee J. Cronbach, *Essentials of Psychological Testing,* 2nd ed. (New York: Harper & Row, 1960).

The idea of "construct validity" has been subjected to extended criticism. See, e.g., Harold P. Bechtoldt, "Construct Validity: A Critique," *American Psychologist, 14* (October, 1959), 619–629. And such a positivist as Paul Horst in his *Psychological Measurement and Prediction* (Belmont, Cal.: Wadsworth, 1966), 346–347, suggests that the use of construct validity is a "semantic recreation."

But the notion of construct validity has had its defenders. See, e.g., Donald T. Campbell, "Recommendations for APA Test Standards Regarding Construct, Trait, or Discriminant Validity," *American Psychologist, 15* (August, 1960), 546–553. Also, Lazarsfeld has intimated that some of his own work on measurement has much in common with that on construct validity. See Paul F. Lazarsfeld, "Concept Formation and Measurement in the Behavioral Sciences; Some Historical Observations," in Gordon J. DiRenzo (ed.), *Concepts, Theory, and Explanation in the Behavioral Sciences* (New York: Random House, 1966), 187.

[28] Cronbach, *op. cit.,* 104.

such a job has." 1. Excellent standing; 2. Good standing; 3. Average standing; 4. Somewhat below average standing; 5. Poor standing; X. I don't know where to place that one.[29] The evaluations for each occupation were then translated into a single score and rank ordered.

Gusfield and Schwartz have raised some serious questions as to just what is being measured. They argue that

> Rating scales, such as the NORC scale, can be focused upon at least four different dimensions of "occupational prestige." . . . rating scales have confounded these and have led to conclusions which assume that only one of the following dimensions has been used by the respondent.
>
> 1. The respondent's perception of social differentiation: Here the respondent is telling the investigator that some jobs are perceived as "better" than others, as he sees it. . . .
> 2. The respondent's perception of others: This is the posture of the natural sociologist. . . . He tells us that whatever his own views or judgments, this is how jobs are ranked in his society. . . .
>
> In both of the above cases the emphasis is on the perception of the factual order—this is how things happen here.[30]

The authors then proceed to delineate two other dimensions of occupational prestige.

> 3. The prestige dimension *per se:* Here we attempt to find out what relative amounts of honor and respect are bestowed by the respondents on occupations. . . .
> 4. The attribution of justice: . . . This would represent the evaluation the respondent has of the rightness of the factual order.[31]

In line with this reasoning, Gusfield and Schwartz indicate that attempts to synthesize crosscultural studies of occupational ratings, wherein questions have been phrased in different ways, can and do lead to questionable results.[32]

Other somewhat similar uses can be made of construct validity. In measuring occupational mobility, the kind of occupational categories employed structure one's entire analysis. For one thing, the narrower the occupational categories the

[29] Albert J. Reiss, Jr., *Occupations and Social Status* (New York: Free Press, 1961), 19.

[30] Joseph R. Gusfield and Michael Schwartz, "The Meanings of Occupational Prestige: Reconsideration of the NORC Scale," *American Sociological Review,* 28 (April, 1963), 266.

[31] *Ibid.*

[32] *Ibid.,* 267.

more mobility is possible, for the finer the divisions the greater the likelihood that a man in one occupation will later be found in a different one. Thus Lipset and Bendix's findings that occupational mobility patterns in the United States and Western Europe are similar may hold true only within their own conceptual and logical framework, one which studies mobility from manual to white-collar occupations.[33] Had Lipset and Bendix employed narrower categories (admittedly more difficult to do in a crossnational study), they might have arrived at different conclusions.[34]

Although it is necessary to relate the conceptual framework to the instrument, we must interpret the concept of construct validity more broadly. For unwittingly or no, many social scientists evaluate the validity of their instruments in terms of their respondent's frame of reference and/or the norms and the values of the broader society or its constituent power structures.[35]

A number of social scientists assume that their respondent's frame of reference is the "ultimate" or "basic" reality, and they validate their instruments accordingly. Warner, for example, worked on the premise that "social class" is fundamentally what people in the community say it is. More specifically, the class patterns are a product of how the members of a community rank one another. On this basis, Warner and his associates constructed what they termed an Evaluated Participation (E.P.) score which, in turn, becomes the basis of a person's assignment to a class position.[36] Warner, however, recognized that the application of the E.P. method is time-consuming even in a small community and difficult, if not impossible, in a large metropolis. He therefore constructed a simplified method for delineating the community's class system. A number of indicators, on occupation, source of income, house type, and dwelling area, the data for which can readily be collected via a social survey, were combined into an Index of Status Characteristics (I.S.C.).[37]

What is methodologically relevant for our purposes is that Warner tinkered with his I.S.C. until it more or less fitted his E.P. scheme. We use the term "tinker," because Warner originally included education and amount of income among the dimensions of social class. Later these were discarded. Furthermore,

---

[33] Seymour Martin Lipset and Reinhard Bendix, *Social Mobility in Industrial Society* (Berkeley: University of California Press, 1959).

[34] Cf. the discussion by Edward Gross, "The Occupational Variable as a Research Category," *American Sociological Review*, 24 (October, 1959), 640–649.

[35] That social survey data, for example, may be viewed as valid in one institutional setting and not in another (such as a court of law) within the same society is suggested by Hans Zeisel, "The Uniqueness of Survey Evidence," *Cornell Law Quarterly*, 45 (Winter, 1960), 322–346.

[36] W. Lloyd Warner, *Social Class in America* (New York: Harper & Row, Harper Torchbooks, 1960), 36–39.

[37] *Ibid.*, 39–42.

Warner seems to have assigned weights to the various dimensions of the I.S.C. as a means of equating the results with those acquired via the E.P. technique, which for him seems to have been founded on more basic social reality.[38]

Warner is by no means alone in utilizing the aforementioned type of validation. Many other researchers (implicitly or otherwise) accept the "definition of the situation" by the broader society as a basis for utilizing certain variables and indicators and rejecting others.

One common variant of the societal validation process is to accept the power structure's definition of the situation. Here the criteria employed are logically meaningful, or causally meaningful, in terms of what the power structure considers to be significant. Lazarsfeld and Thielens, in *The Academic Mind*, constructed various indexes; for instance, one to measure the productivity of professors and another to measure the quality of universities.[39] With respect to the latter, the authors selected certain indicators (later molded into one complex index) that would distinguish among universities in terms of their eminence. In addition they listed a number of alternative criteria that they could have employed. Some, for example, were found to be interrelated and thus were discarded, and so on. But the crucial question is nowhere made fully explicit: How did the authors arrive at the original set of indicators in the first instance? It appears that they chose such indicators as size of library, number of books per student, budget per student, proportion of Ph.D.s on the faculty, production of scholars, and tuition fees for two reasons. The first, which they concede, was the availability of data.[40] The second, about which they apparently were unaware, was the fact that educators have typically viewed these criteria as meaningfully related to the rank ordering of colleges and universities in American society. The definition of eminence by Lazarsfeld and Thielens was made from the vantage point of persons in positions of power and authority (and even from the particular vantage point of Columbia University where Lazarsfeld was employed) and not from the perspective of persons in colleges that the authors would rank lower on their scale. Quite possibly, a number of functionaries in colleges strongly committed to religous beliefs would take exception to various indexes in *The Academic Mind*.

Similar hazy assumptions, many with ideological and ethical overtones, underlie other instruments used by sociologists.[41] If, for instance, we were to construct

---

[38] *Ibid.*, chaps. 10 and 11.

[39] Paul F. Lazarsfeld and Wagner Thielens, Jr., *The Academic Mind* (New York: Free Press, 1958), 402–414.

[40] *Ibid.*, 411.

[41] George A. Lundberg, *Social Research*, 2nd ed. (New York: McKay, 1942), 51, argued that measuring instruments are a major objectifying tool for sociologists. More recently, James S. Coleman has stated that one important value of highly quantitative research is that "the researcher's own biases cannot allow him to ignore results quite so easily." See his correspondence published in: A Staff Study for the Research and Technical Programs Subcommittee of the Committee on Government Operations, U.S. House of

an examination for sociology students entering graduate school, we could draw a sample of all sociology courses taught in this country and then sample the content of these courses. We could, in other words, approach the problem in an egalitarian fashion. But graduate education is not viewed as an egalitarian enterprise. Therefore, the Graduate Record Examination as presently constituted reflects what the "influentials" in sociology regard as relevant. Consequently, as the opinions and beliefs regarding the nature of sociology shift, so does the content of the examination. The examination system is valid only within a particular structural framework. After all, the Graduate Record Examination seeks to predict the student's potential performance at high-status universities, not at Crossroads College.

The Lazarsfeld and Thielens' study and the Graduate Record Examination both suggest that the more homogeneous and stable the universe the greater the validity to be expected, in the sense that scientists, and the laymen most immediately concerned, would agree that the measurement tools measure the phenomena in question. To the extent that the goals of organizations such as universities are contradictory or ill-defined, controversy over what any index actually measures is inevitable. And as long as sociologists function in a highly pluralistic and fluid society, they cannot expect to achieve consensus over which indicators are most satisfactory for measuring social class, alienation, or other variables.

We can see that homogeneity and stability in one's conceptual system and in the social system being studied are essential for achieving both reproducibility and validity. Consequently we can better appreciate why so many logical empiricists, committed as they are to prediction as the basis of explanation, must frequently focus upon particular, narrowly defined social systems in order to enhance the reliability and validity of their measurement devices. Such holds especially for those social scientists who deal with practical, everyday problems and who are intent upon predicting the success of individuals in modern, complex societies. Still, it is ironic that some logical empiricists, who theoretically would eschew historicism, should in practice become committed to this orientation.

Because of the tendency of those concerned with measurement to focus upon particulars, there is a need (as we noted in a previous chapter) for typological analysis as a means of bridging the gap between data that do not appear to be comparable on a rather immediate empirical level.

Representatives, *The Use of Social Research in Federal Domestic Programs* (Washington, D.C.: GPO, 1967), part 3, 56. One can agree with these arguments up to a point. But the evidence also suggests that many social premises and ideological positions are obscured by the technical aspects of measuring instruments. How many methods books attempt to explore the relationship between measurement tools and the norms of the broader society? Just how often has anyone detailed the way in which the Graduate Record Examination, for example, articulates with, or is a product of, the "power structure" of higher education in American society?

The Nature of Prediction and Control

Although we have stressed the notion that prediction must be subsumed under the broader category of understanding or the logical-meaningful method, we do not intend to imply that prediction (and control) do not play a strategic role in the validation of social theories. But most sociologists speak of prediction in an ideal sense—of what ought to be. They have not examined the actual norms with respect to prediction in social science. When we do this, we find that prediction of social events is not a unidimensional phenomenon but one that has complex multidimensional aspects. In order to predict effectively, and to understand the role of prediction in the validation of social theories fully, we must move toward developing a sociology of prediction.[42]

At this point we reiterate that sociologists must rely upon a variety of theories and research methods, for some are more adequate than others for predicting particular social events. Indeed, sociologists must under certain conditions rely upon speculative thought in predicting social events or patterns.

Sociologists, of course, do predict social events more effectively in certain realms than is often recognized. Even descriptive data are used by sociologists and policy makers to predict the future. Here one simply assumes that the future will be like the present or the immediate past. And this kind of prediction (or what some demographers term "forecasting" rather than "prediction") is quite reliable and valid for many purposes. There must be an element of predictability with respect to social events for any social system to maintain itself.

Moreover, a case can be made for the existence of numerous sociological laws, if by this we mean a statement that details the necessary conditions for the occurrence of an event (or set of events). For instance, if societies are to persist through a number of generations there must be some institutionalized means for replenishing their numbers. Sociologists are also able to predict the limits to actions or patterns. Thus, if a society is to sustain a high degree of industrialization, the class system will neither be completely egalitarian nor completely rigid. Or if a high level of industrialization is to be sustained, the system cannot maintain a fully centralized or fully decentralized political and economic organization.

But these laws are cast in highly abstract terms, and they are phrased in terms of form, not content.[43] The politician or administrator would usually view these as of little practical worth. The practical man of affairs is concerned with specific answers to specific questions. He is concerned, for example, with obtain-

---

[42] There are some efforts along these lines, to judge by Daniel Bell, "Twelve Modes of Prediction—A Preliminary Sorting of Approaches in the Social Sciences," *Daedalus, 93* (Summer, 1964), 845–880. Cf. Roy G. Francis, *The Predictive Process* (Río Piedras, Puerto Rico: Social Science Research Center, 1960).

[43] Hans L. Zetterberg, *Social Theory and Social Practice* (Totowa, N.J.: Bedminster, 1962), has attempted to formulate "laws" in terms of form rather than content.

ing information about where the optimum balance lies between a centralized and a decentralized economy, not about the polar extremes. Nevertheless, these broad generalizations have practical utility, though often in an indirect fashion. Sociology would profit from a systematic formulation of these laws about the functioning of social systems.

However, it is prediction about the content, not the form, that raises problems for sociologists who are intent upon measuring social action. They must, in many instances, be satisfied with less than the best. For example, the correlation between most college entrance examinations and success in college (as measured by a student's grades) is 0.50 and 0.60 in the upper limits.[44] Here we are predicting (or explaining) between 25 and 36 percent of the student's success on the basis of his entrance examination.

Yet, in the face of this evidence such instruments continue to be employed.[45] One reason is that they find favor among modern bureaucrats because the instruments often are superior to common sense. Even where they demonstrate low predictability, they may continue to be employed because they articulate with the modern society's normative order. The bureaucratic norms, in particular, ideally demand universalism in the selection of applicants for job vacancies and in the promotion of personnel. That is, persons should be judged in terms of their qualifications rather than in terms of more particularistic criteria. Moreover, these instruments, because of their technical nature, serve to rationalize and justify the decision-making process within bureaucracies vis-à-vis the broader public. Because the public at large does not comprehend the meaning of these techniques, the decision makers can justify their actions as "scientific," without serious questions being raised by the public they serve. For what is scientific articulates with the value system of the broader social order.

The interrelationships of measurement, prediction, and the bureaucratic structure give rise to a variety of methodological dilemmas. One emerges from the proclivity of managers of bureaucracies to impose (under certain conditions) unidimensional scales upon multidimensional data in an effort to obtain some semblance of order. The issue of what constitutes good teaching and how it should be measured has been a recurrent topic of debate in American education for several decades. There are persons, administrators included, who would take the

[44] Benjamin S. Bloom and Frank R. Peters, *The Use of Academic Prediction Scales for Counseling and Selecting College Entrants* (New York: Free Press, 1961), chap. 1. More specifically, "After almost fifty years of research and development, the average correlation between scholastic aptitude tests and college achievement is of the order of +.50" (126). Bloom and Peters increased the predictability between high school and college grades by, as we indicated above, utilizing greater specificity—holding constant the kinds of high schools and colleges the students attended, thereby creating more homogeneous subuniverses.

[45] For a review of large-scale ability-testing programs in American society, see David A. Goslin, *The Search for Ability* (New York: Russell Sage Foundation, 1963).

criterion of popularity as the sole index of good teaching. Even though many administrators do not hold to such a simplistic view, they still often must reduce multiple criteria to a few manageable ones if they are to measure this kind of social activity.

More generally, the goals and values of modern bureaucracies tend to become narrowly circumscribed—in large part because this pattern facilitates measurement. Ideally, universities may wish to produce "men of creative ability" or "well-educated persons." But such a goal is vague at best. Yet, the very process of specifying the dimensions of this broad goal leads organizations to focus on very concrete and specific objectives. The operational indicators of success for a university thus become, for instance, national awards granted students, the number of undergraduate students who go on to obtain a Ph.D., and so on.

Implicit in the foregoing discussion is another proposition: that the validity of prediction instruments frequently presupposes acceptance, by the technicians who construct and apply these instruments, as well as by the general public, of a particular constellation of values and goals and a given power structure. The following pattern within the New York City schools is illustrative of this fact.[46] In 1964 these instruments, after having been employed for a number of years, were rather suddenly assumed to be invalid. And for several compelling reasons. Negroes and Puerto Ricans, whose power had risen within the city, began objecting to these tests, geared as they are to a traditional middle-class way of life, as discriminatory, and the educators, whose values reflected the changing social conditions, concurred.

Political and ethical factors become a variable in evaluating many prediction tools. Personality tests have been challenged on the grounds that these instruments require information whose acquisition represents an invasion of privacy.[47] One might also question the Glueck Prediction Scale developed by the New York City's Youth Board, not only because its predictive validity has not been established but because of its ethical and political implications.[48] If we predict that certain persons will become delinquents, this could accentuate the deviation process among certain elements of this population.

But why haven't social scientists achieved greater success in social prediction? One reason is that they are frequently unable to manipulate the social conditions in order to check their predictions; another is that the scientist's prediction may itself become a variable in the prediction process.

[46] Fred M. Hechinger, "I.Q. Test Ban," *New York Times,* March 8, 1964, sec. E, 7; Fred M. Hechinger, "Testing at Issue," *New York Times,* Nov. 1, 1964, sec. E, 9.

[47] See the special issue of the *American Psychologist, 20* (November, 1965), for a consideration of some of the issues relating to testing and the invasion of privacy.

[48] See, e.g., Alfred J. Kahn, "The Status of the New York City Youth Board's Delinquency Prediction," Report of Citizens' Committee for Children of New York, Inc., New York City, January, 1965.

Thus, a number of economists believe that they have devised effective measures for overcoming depressions in American society. However, some economists recognize that doubts must be maintained concerning these theories, for they have not been put to a critical test. It is hardly feasible to foster a depression in order to determine whether these theories work in practice.

As for the effect of the scientist's predictions upon the future, two patterns can be discerned. In one situation the scientist predicts certain changes within a social order, and the actors in question then seek to falsify the scientist's conclusion. Or the actors may act in accordance with the prediction.

The predictions of Karl Marx are instructive here.[49] His prediction that capitalism would eventually disappear as a result of its own built-in contradictions and that communism would eventually emerge set in motion countermovements whose goal has been the falsification of Marx's view of reality. These movements may partially account for the fact that no industrial order has thus far chosen to follow the communist path.

Contrariwise, Marx's prediction has served as a self-fulfilling prophecy in other settings. Khrushchev, when he was leader of the U.S.S.R., not only spoke of the inevitable decline of capitalist imperialism in underdeveloped countries but formulated programs for these nations which would ensure the fulfillment of this prediction.

But we need not look only at Marxist-inspired movements to appreciate the function of predictions as self-fulfilling prophecies. For example, graduate students not infrequently find their scores on graduate record examinations becoming a variable in the faculty's expectations and evaluation of their success.

When a student scores exceptionally high, some professors tend to assume that his performance in his courses will necessarily be of high quality. Consequently the student may receive special encouragement or "the benefit of the doubt" when his performance is difficult to assess, particularly in the social sciences where the criteria for success are ill-defined. This process of reifying examination scores generates ethical and political dilemmas for the entire educational system.

But let us reflect upon a more complex, and little studied, social pattern. We have observed that official statistics on crime, juvenile delinquency, mental illness, suicide, and the like are products of the normative structure of the police and judicial systems, the mental hospitals, and other organizations that collect them. Yet these statistics are often used (by social scientists or the officials themselves) to predict (or project) crime rates and other social patterns. In turn, these predictions may lay the basis for future actions by the system. Here there is a kind of self-fulfilling prophecy which may reinforce existing patterns or

[49] For a discussion of some of Marx's predictions, see Fred M. Gottheil, *Marx's Economic Predictions* (Evanston, Ill.: Northwestern University Press, 1966).

trends within the organization that collects the data on which the projections are based. Clearly we need solid research on the interrelationships among official statistics, prediction, and organizational norms.

But there are other aspects to prediction and social system analysis. For in some instances a high level of predictability by social scientists may disrupt the system which is being studied. The following comments seem pertinent here:

> [The] automated systems being developed to forecast the nation's economic future might turn out to be too accurate. . . . The reason . . . is that once an economic forecasting system gets a reputation for being very accurate, people start acting on the basis of the forecasts.
>
> "Their actions tend to change the outcome in an unpredictable manner," . . .
>
> The most effective forecaster . . . might be a man whose predictions were right 60 or 70 percent of the time. Then his forecasts probably wouldn't be affected by people acting upon them.[50]

If we carry this argument a step further, some interesting consequences can be discerned. If very high-level, say, perfect predictability were attained for stock market forecasts, then this social system, as we know it, would disappear. Such has occasionally occurred with respect to games of chance where a high degree of prediction has made it possible to beat the system.

Another variable affecting the validity of the sociologist's predictions concerning the actions of individuals or groups is the scientific method, broadly conceived. Social scientists are usually concerned with predicting patterns in industrial societies, but many of these patterns are associated with discoveries within the natural sciences. This being the case, we would, in order to detail the nature of future events, first have to predict the discoveries and innovations within the natural sciences and extrapolate from these to the future.

The impact of automation or cybernetics upon society provides social scientists with a special challenge. This process may possibly create a greater discontinuity between the present and the future industrial order than presently exists between modern systems and their preindustrial counterparts. In light of this, we find it noteworthy that most of the major projections of the possible impact of automation upon the society as a whole appeared outside the major sociological journals during the first half of the 1960s. And this at a time when sociologists were championing the use of prediction as a means for validating theories.

One reason for this may be the fact that predictions of the impact of automation on modern society demand reasoned speculation rather than fact-finding or the testing of narrow empirical hypotheses—reasoned speculation that attempts to formulate alternative "models" of what may result from social forces that presently do not exist.[51] And many sociologists view such speculative ventures as nonscientific. Yet, in the next decade cybernetics may well falsify traditional sociological hypotheses of the 1950s and early 1960s as rapidly as it eliminates many occupational groups from the industrial-urban scene.

Moreover, those social scientists or sociologists who are both willing and able to grapple with the cybernetics revolution appear to hold marginal positions in the society. They are not committed to the premises of the present system and thus can step back and analyze their own system in perspective.

We come now to an issue that has troubled various social scientists for decades: the relationship of determinism and prediction. Some sociologists have justly reasoned that if it were possible to obtain an exceedingly high level of predictability, if the leadership knew what events were to occur, if the populace could depend upon stable and well-defined norms over time, then social scientists would have no place in the modern world.

But a more immediate and compelling moral dilemma has been pointed up by Eric Hoffer, who argues that Hitler and Stalin (both leaders of totalitarian states) were highly effective as "applied social scientists," for they eliminated deviants and thereby attained predictability.[52] Indeed, Robert Nisbet has, in a provocative essay, set forth the thesis that many social scientists in present-day America have become disenchanted with pluralism and unstructured social relations and wish to impose greater order upon society.[53] But such a world view challenges certain values of the open society that makes possible social inquiry.

Our argument does not imply that sociologists should not strive to attain greater predictability. What it does imply is that we require a fuller grasp of the social conditions where prediction can and cannot be effectively employed—that we must be prepared to consider the ethical, political, and scientific consequences of prediction. We must recognize the tension between sociologists committed to the study of "order" and those committed to the study of human "freedom." We require, in other words, a sociology of prediction, one that studies both ideal and actual patterns.

[51] Reasoned speculation or the "mental experiment" for dealing with one phase of economic development has been employed by Albert O. Hirschman, *The Strategy of Economic Development* (New Haven: Yale, 1958), 104–109. Dialectic (or countersystem) reasoning may be especially useful under the circumstances. For an effort to formalize and utilize this procedure, see Gideon Sjoberg, M. Donald Hancock, and Orion White, Jr., *Politics in the Post-Welfare State: A Comparison of the United States and Sweden* (Bloomington, Ind.: Indiana University, Department of Government, Carnegie Seminar on Political and Administrative Development, 1967), and the manuscript by Gideon Sjoberg and Leonard D Cain, Jr., "Negative Values, Countersystem Models, and the Analysis of Social Systems."

[52] Eric Hoffer, *The Ordeal of Change* (New York: Harper & Row, 1963), 123.

[53] Robert A. Nisbet, "Power and the Intellectual," *Yale Review*, 53 (Spring, 1964), 321–341.

CHAPTER 12

The Dissemination
of Research Findings

Although all fields of knowledge depend upon communication for their survival, science, particularly, seeks to build upon its past achievements. Consequently, the rapid and widespread communication of scientific findings becomes a central methodological problem.

Researchers implicitly assume that in the scientific market place, good ideas drive out the bad, but they have devoted surprisingly little effort to determining to what extent this ideal is attained or even to examining the norms that govern the diffusion of knowledge within the social (and the natural) sciences. Our goal here is to objectify some of these norms and in the process demonstrate how the scientist's logical-theoretical constructs as well as the social context in which he functions, including his role commitment, structures the manner in which scientific materials are written and diffused. At the same time, many of the norms regarding the communication of scientific knowledge are vague and ill-defined, and we can only indicate some of the steps that might be taken in their formalization.

The Nature of Communication

Much information is passed among scientists through face-to-face communication—at conventions, faculty seminars, or during discussions with friends and colleagues—as well as via personal correspondence or informal mimeographed newsletters destined for a limited audience. These devices are most effective for transmitting ideas and data in the early stages of project formulation when the researcher's hypotheses are still only tentative and he is groping for direction in his research. Such informal media also offset to a degree the inevitable communication lag between the completion of a research project and the publication of the findings via more formal channels.

But face-to-face contacts and personal correspondence among scientists have decided limitations; the most obvious is their narrow spread over both time and space. For adequate diffusion of their findings and access to those of their colleagues, scientists still must rely mainly upon formal publishing media. Printed materials, in particular, permit extensive multiplication, ready accessibility to scientists in scattered regions, and storage over long periods of time. Science could not have reached its present stature had it lacked effective means for preserving the ideas and discoveries of the past and disseminating these beyond the local setting.

Moreover, the printed word conveys a sense of finality that demands that the scientist assume responsibility for his assertions. And a peripheral, but meaningful, by-product of publication is the psychological satisfaction it affords. The prospect of communicating with a wide unseen and, in a large part, unknown audience and of getting one's own writings diffused is a stimulus for many scientists.

Factors That Affect the Publication of Research Findings

An author, to maximize his effectiveness, must be aware of: (1) the nature of his audience or reference group, (2) the style he employs in his research reporting, (3) the pressures to publish research findings and, conversely, the strictures imposed upon such, and (4) the ethical norms that govern what should or should not be published.

THE AUDIENCE OR REFERENCE GROUP

The form in which the scientist publishes his findings is fashioned not merely by his original statement of the problem, method of data collection, and mode of analysis, but also by his prospective audience. It therefore behooves the scientist to look ahead, to concern himself in the initial stages of his research with the ultimate disposition of his findings. He must ask himself: "What kind of audience do I hope to reach?"

To a large extent the scientist's role commitment, whether he identifies with the scientific community or with the broader society, determines his public. Moreover, the scientific community and the broader society include certain subgroups whose members may become the scientist's main audience. For example, the technician, although he is committed more to the broader society than to the scientific community, may write solely for his particular organization. Then there are the moralizers, those who write to influence the nation's decision makers, and the marriage-and-family experts, who focus their attention upon the everyday problems of the common man.

Even those who write for their fellow scientists often address themselves to special subaudiences. Some scientists, especially those committed to highly technical problems, may attract an audience of only a dozen or so colleagues, while others, just as committed to pure science, may write for large numbers of their peers.

Despite these qualifications, a cleavage seems to exist between those social scientists who direct their statements to other scientists and those who write for the broader society or elements thereof. This cleavage is analogous to the "elite-mass" conflict that is so vehemently debated in the cultural arts.[1] In effect, the pure scientist, whose audience is a select few, assumes an elitist stance. On the other hand, the scientist who is oriented to the broader society, though he is not insensitive to the criticisms of his colleagues, ultimately is concerned with the judgment and adulation of a "mass audience."

Those social scientists of a more elitist hue are prone to argue that their position maximizes freedom to pursue and report upon scientific research. They assume that the mass-oriented writer permits his less sophisticated audience partially to influence his results and structure the course of scientific inquiry. The mass-oriented scholar is frequently charged with writing in a deliberately entertaining manner, with failing to report frankly for fear of offending his public, and with oversimplifying his theories and his findings so as to make them palatable and understandable to persons of diverse educational backgrounds.

This equating of popularization with looseness and undue simplification, although overdrawn by many critics, is not entirely without reason. Perhaps the most convincing criterion is the fact that the popularizer, to attract wide readership, must skirt many areas of controversy within the scientific discipline and thus cannot carefully qualify his remarks. Conversely, bold, dramatic statements possess greater popular appeal than do painful qualifications concerning the limitations of the sample design, the interviewing technique, and so on. Such qualifiers, however, are part of the dedicated scholar's kit of verbal tools with which he seeks to abide by the norms calling for tentativeness in all scientific generalization. But the average reader has little patience with hedging. In most cases he is searching for absolutes and is willing to accept on faith propositions that the scientist has been taught to question.

The purist also tends to object to the popularizer's frequent drawing of moral judgments as a means of appealing to the reader. The layman is more concerned with answers to problems that confront him in the workaday world than with raw data or abstract theorizing. C. Wright Mills owed much of his popularity to the fact that he had a message, aptly expressed in his essay, "A Pagan Sermon to the Christian Clergy."[2] Nor has Mills stood alone. Numerous prominent soci-

[1] See, e.g., Edward Shils, "Daydreams and Nightmares: Reflections on the Criticism of Mass Culture," *Sewanee Review, 65* (Autumn, 1957), 587–608.

[2] C. Wright Mills, "A Pagan Sermon to the Christian Clergy," *Nation, 186* (Mar. 8, 1958), 199–202.

ologists have moralized more openly in their popular writings[3] than in their technical essays; moral judgments in the latter have tended to be merely implied.

Ultimately, scholars who address an extrascientific audience must employ a different set of criteria for measuring success than scientists who direct themselves strictly to their peers. To the former, what is "good" science is partially dependent upon the judgment of the broader society. They tend to gauge the quality of a publication by the number of copies sold—by the dollar sign—although such may undermine the authority of the scientific community. Moreover, popularizers stand a good chance of gaining not only financial reward but immediate fame. These rewards are difficult for purists to accept, for these popularizers are seen as doing little more than rewriting, for a broader audience, the technical reports of specialists, with little credit given the major scientific innovators.

Intensifying the elitist-mass schism is the tendency for this division to coincide with certain methodological differences in social science. Researchers who are strongly committed to utilizing complex and refined research procedures are apt to be unwilling, even unable, to present their materials in a manner calculated to attract readers. Many logical empiricists, intent as they are on technical analysis and unwilling to use sensitizing concepts, may find it particularly difficult to popularize their reports. Nevertheless, recent trends are to a degree counteracting this traditional pattern. The heightened sophistication of an educated public is multiplying the demands for more detailed and careful analyses of data. Demographers like Philip Hauser[4] find that they can write for a lay audience, and even pollsters who publish in the mass media realize that they can no longer water down their reports but must include some technical details and analysis. Nonetheless, our overall generalization—that the technically oriented scholar finds his writings to have little popular appeal—is valid in the main.

Conversely, the particular methodological orientation of some scholars gives them a decided advantage when they want to appeal to the mass audience. Writers in the *verstehen* tradition, who are uncommitted to the rigid and careful testing of hypotheses and who are the most willing to utilize sensitizing concepts or loosely formulated typologies, are able to present sociological data in a persuasive manner without doing violence to their own standards of sound scholarship, for their methodology involves disciplined understanding of human action rather than formal measurement of the latter. The popularity of Goffman and Riesman is in part associated with their methodology.[5]

Some social scientists have searched for compromises as a means of circum-

---

[3] See the writings of sociologists in *Commentary, Dissent,* the *Nation,* the *Reporter,* and so on.

[4] Philip Hauser, *Population Perspectives* (New Brunswick, N.J.: Rutgers, 1960).

[5] Erving Goffman, *The Presentation of Self in Everyday Life* (Garden City, N.Y.: Doubleday, Anchor Books, 1959); David Riesman, *The Lonely Crowd* (New Haven: Yale, 1950).

venting this technical versus popular dilemma. A few write for both kinds of audience, although usually via separate publications. Such a course of action enables the scientist to seek greater methodological purity yet address himself to the broader social order where his findings may have some practical utility.[6]

Having approached the specialist versus the popularizer dilemma from an elitist standpoint, we must also recognize the unique contributions of those who write for a mass audience. For one thing, these persons can enter the traditional intellectual battlegrounds unencumbered by the heavy cloak of tradition; consequently they may score breakthroughs that more conservatively oriented scholars, highly sensitized to the judgments of their peers, cannot.[7] Mills or Riesman have jarred some traditionalists loose from their moorings, forcing them to embark upon rougher, more controversial seas, or to enter into argumentation if only in self-defense. By appealing to an audience that extends beyond their colleagues, the popularizers counteract the tendencies of scientists toward premature closure. So too, the popularizers may induce the elite-oriented specialist to focus upon critical societal issues that he might otherwise ignore.

Those who write for mass consumption play another, oft-slighted, role: They help to bridge the chasms that divide specialists within a particular discipline or in quite separate fields of social science. In addition the popularizer is at times able to span the hiatus between the "two cultures" of C. P. Snow.[8] Through their popular writings, Ruth Benedict and Margaret Mead have diffused much of what is valuable in anthropology into psychology, economics, sociology, history, and political science.[9] Although some readers may have gained thereby a false impression of anthropology, the credits that have accrued from these writings seem to outweigh the debits.

More than this, the popularizers link the intellectual disciplines to the broader society and its decision makers. Directly or indirectly, they help to justify the scholar's existence. By identifying with the broader social order, the popularizers impress upon the citizenry the fact that the efforts of the technical specialists are worthy of support. More generally, writers like William Whyte or Vance Packard have done more to legitimize social science than many purists are prepared to admit.[10] For through their publications they have introduced the edu-

[6] Cf. Neal Gross *et al., Explorations in Role Analysis* (New York: Wiley, 1958); Neal Gross, *Who Runs Our Schools?* (New York: Wiley, 1958).

[7] John Kenneth Galbraith's concept of his audience bears upon the issue at hand, though somewhat tangentially. By his own admission, he began to write for a wide reading public because he felt that his fellow economists were more or less ignoring him and the issues with which he was concerned. See Victor S. Navasky, "Galbraith on Galbraith," *New York Times Book Review* (June 25, 1957), 2-3 f.

[8] C. P. Snow, *Two Cultures: and A Second Look,* 2nd ed. (London: Cambridge, 1964).

[9] E.g., Ruth Benedict, *Patterns of Culture* (Boston: Houghton Mifflin, 1934); Margaret Mead, *And Keep Your Powder Dry* (New York: Morrow, 1943).

[10] William H. Whyte, Jr., *The Organization Man* (Garden City, N.Y.: Doubleday, Anchor Books, 1957); Vance Packard, *The Status Seekers* (New York: McKay, 1959).

cated layman to sociology. By reading popular sociology, the lay person has gained some understanding of the field and sees that it deals with meaningful and challenging issues. To be sure, popularizers on the order of Vance Packard have been sharply scored by some sociologists for misconstruing sociologists' findings with respect to the status system in the United States. To a degree this charge is valid. At the same time, one can make a strong case for the proposition that Packard was articulating the views of one school of thought in sociology, a school that includes W. Lloyd Warner, Hollingshead, and others. Through popularization the ideas of this group were cast into bold relief, with results that were disturbing to some sociologists—so much so that Packard's study was belittled in part because he was not a "formally trained" sociologist (a point that has no bearing upon the validity of Packard's argument).[11]

THE STYLE OF RESEARCH REPORTING

That different scientific disciplines (within the United States, for example) have developed common, relatively standard norms for reporting research findings, and that these norms change over time is suggested by a cursory examination of journals in sociology, political science, psychology, and anthropology. Moreover, the kind of audience, as we indicated above, has a definite impact on the style of writing employed. And scholars committed to particular logical-theoretical constructs tend to develop distinctive ways of reporting and analyzing their findings.

For instance, the logical empiricist generally relies upon well-defined hypotheses and tests these through rigorous procedures, usually statistical ones. He has, within the limits imposed by his methodology, relatively little freedom for stylistic maneuvering. He is committed to a style which stresses technical precision and reduces readability. There is, if one accepts the following remarks of Bressler in the spirit in which they are intended, a ritualized way of reporting one's research results.

> The most striking feature of empirical sociology is its dominant mood of self-abnegation. . . . The ritual requires the author to begin his article with the mandatory *mea culpa* paragraph. Here, in anguished prose reminiscent of a counterrevolutionary at a Soviet show trial, he abjectly confesses his transgressions against the logic of inquiry, acknowledges the disparity between the theoretical importance of his subject and the triviality of the data, and inserts the usual caveat against extending his findings to aught save white, middle-class, urban males of college age, and so on. Having purged himself through the ecstasy of catharsis, the scholar now self-administers the sacrament of Rejuvenation, preceded by the incantation of the "Unsupported but Nevertheless." He is, to be sure, unworthy—but, nevertheless, the social importance of the

[11] See, e.g., Seymour M. Lipset, "Vance Packard Discovers America," *Reporter* (July 9, 1959), 31–33.

issue . . . but, nevertheless, even poor data. . . . The penultimate phase, the Exposition, is, despite the advance apologia, a careful investigation exhibiting considerable ingenuity, thought, and industry which makes a limited contribution to a growing body of research findings. . . . If additional research devoted to the same tiny sector of experience should confirm these pygmy generalizations, then, ah, then, we shall be on the Threshold of Knowledge. Empirical sociologists may be accused of many things—but they are not arrogant in print.[12]

Of course, the empirical sociologist who employs this means of reporting his results cannot disregard the matter of readability altogether. Indeed, there are some sociologists who, though admired by their peers for their technical knowledge and ability, publish little because they find writing such a difficult chore.

As we turn from the logical empiricists to the *verstehen* sociologists—say, symbolic interactionists like Goffman—we find that in their absorption with uncovering sensitizing concepts they pay little homage to technical procedures calling for formal specification of the research design, including the limitations of the latter.[13] Rather the symbolic interactionists, because they convey meaning through sensitizing concepts, must be attuned to the innuendos of the words and phraseology they employ. They must paint a picture wherein the total effect is more significant than the details.

As we might expect, the *verstehen* sociologist pays a price for his theoretical orientation. If he is faithful to his fundamental premise, namely, that he should analyze the social order from the actor's viewpoint, he faces the almost herculean task of weaving together the various nuances of meaning as perceived by the actor who plays a variety of roles and interacts with other actors. Not only do the more successful practitioners of the *verstehen* approach write with a flair, but on occasion they employ a novelistic approach in scientific reporting. Oscar Lewis' *The Children of Sánchez* illustrates in dramatic and sophisticated form one author's ability to piece together into an integrated whole—into a work of art and science—the tape-recorded commentaries of lower-class residents in Mexico City.[14] Each person in this drama reflects upon himself and upon other members of his family.

Obviously the novelistic approach is ill-suited to journal articles, which must be short, succinct pieces. To overstate the case somewhat, the logical empiricist would present his entire argument within the space some *verstehen* scientists require simply for their introductory remarks.

As for other aspects of reporting research findings, social scientists are beset by vague and ambiguous, perhaps even contradictory norms in seeking to de-

[12] Marvin Bressler, "Some Selected Aspects of American Sociology, September 1959 to December 1960," *The Annals,* 337 (September, 1961), 156.

[13] Goffman, *op. cit.*

[14] Oscar Lewis, *The Children of Sánchez* (New York: Random House, 1961).

termine how sharply they can and should criticize other scholars in print. Pointed criticism may give focus to certain issues or uncover those that are merely implicit in an argument. Yet, criticism can easily become emotional and undermine rational and disinterested evaluation of theories and research findings.

The lack of consensus regarding the amount and nature of criticism that is to be permitted was brought to light in *Current Anthropology,* where the editor, Sol Tax, had attempted to tone down certain personal shafts made by a Polish anthropologist in his comments on a review article in that journal.[15] Tax later changed his mind and permitted the personal remarks to be presented, when the author contended that European scholars are typically more critical of one another than their American counterparts. Tax granted that his own view was possibly an ethnocentric one. However, he received a number of letters from readers expressing disagreement with the decision, and Tax, in turn, seems to have revised his position again somewhat.[16]

Actually our impression is that, at least in the United States, social scientists criticize one another less heatedly today than some decades ago. Though this pattern seems to be changing, we witnessed a "revolt of the moderates" during the 1950s and early 1960s. Ideological issues were less clearly drawn than they were some decades earlier, and social scientists have felt less constrained to choose sides. Also, many of them, integrated as they have been into large-scale bureaucracies, have found it politically expedient to avoid any frontal attack on their intellectual opponents.

Even so, we can expect a widening rift between social scientists in the United States and other Western industrialized countries and those in some of the have-not, or underdeveloped, countries.[17] We have only to look to China and examine what passes for social science writing, with its violent negation of any opposition to the status quo, to recognize the implications of revolutionary ideologies for social science.

A more specific issue that raises tempers is the matter of jargon. Few debates generate so much heat and emit so little light. The humanists have subjected sociologists in particular to an unremitting barrage of criticism for obfuscating their thinking in a welter of labored and muddled terminology.

But what is jargon? Broadly it denotes merely a specialized or technical terminology. More narrowly, it may refer to words that have been coined to describe special phenomena. Or to some persons jargon simply means those terms they find objectionable, confusing, or difficult to understand.

Admittedly, few sociologists are particularly skilled in wielding the pen. Most are unwilling to pay the price, in time and effort, to express themselves

[15] Sol Tax, "Arguments *ad hominem,*" *Current Anthropology,* 5 (April, 1964), 78 f.

[16] Sol Tax, "Letter to Associates," *ibid.,* 104A.

[17] For instance, Frantz Fanon's *The Wretched of the Earth* (New York: Grove Press, 1965) symbolizes one aspect of the rift between contemporary sociological theorizing and that of a revolutionary who is writing from the vantage point of the dispossessed.

clearly and succinctly. Little wonder, then, that when a sociologist who writes laboriously adds to the confusion by employing an aberrant terminology, the reader quickly becomes discouraged.

Unfortunately an excess of cumbersome writing, including a poor choice of terms, can obscure what may be first-class science. The works of Parsons and Levy are recognized even by some of their supporters as encumbered by a burdensome style.[18] Levy tries the patience of the reader by combining a complex and tedious terminology with questionable grammatical constructions. A "master of the indefinite antecedent," he obscures salient arguments by overloading his discussion with terms like "it," "this," "that," "they," and "those" whose identities become almost a guessing game.[19] Parsons, as Coleman has documented, confounds the reader by failing to organize some of his essays into a coherent logical structure and by occasionally using a given term in different ways within a single paragraph or page without due warning to the reader.[20]

Still, humanists, and some social scientists, err in objecting indiscriminately to the norm that calls for the use of technical or complex terminology. They fail to appreciate that the endless repetition of a standardized jargon may be required for precision and clarity of expression. Even sociologists like Blumer who contend that we are inevitably committed to using "sensitizing concepts," or terminology that is less than precise, would apparently concede that over the decades some advance in conceptual rigor has been achieved and that a certain amount of jargon is essential.[21] Moreover, with the burgeoning of formalization, including the use of symbolic logic, we can anticipate further strides toward conceptual precision.

The problem of terminology becomes more complex when we examine scientific reporting in relation to the broader sociocultural context. Often the concepts scholars employ (for example, "culture") have one meaning for them, another for the layman. This situation is complicated by the fact that phraseology introduced into a discipline during one era may take on different connotations in later decades as the scientist's terminology is diffused into, and is itself corrupted by the broader social order. To attain greater clarity and precision, scientists frequently coin new terms and redefine certain shopworn expressions in order to make their meaning more explicit, once more giving rise to the charge of "jargon."

[18] See, e.g., Talcott Parsons, *The Social System* (New York: Free Press, 1951); and Marion J. Levy, Jr., *The Structure of Society* (Princeton, N.J.: Princeton, 1952).

[19] Levy, *op. cit.*

[20] James S. Coleman, "Comment on 'On the Concept of Influence,'" *Public Opinion Quarterly*, 27 (Spring, 1963), 63–82. Cf. Talcott Parsons, "Rejoinder to Bauer and Coleman," *ibid.*, 87–92.

[21] Herbert Blumer, "What Is Wrong with Social Theory?" *American Sociological Review*, 19 (February, 1954), 3–10.

Ideological shifts within the discipline or the society, and ideological conflicts among societies, frequently affect the social scientist's use of concepts. The label "primitive" has recently come under heavy fire in anthropology.[22] The innuendoes conveyed by this term are those that anthropologists seek to avoid; indeed, one popular connotation of "primitive" is "quasi-human." Such contravenes not only the ideals of anthropologists but also the ideology of equality that is currently sweeping the world.

It is more difficult still to write in a neutral fashion about competing ideologies—for example, with respect to situations that have been associated with the Cold War between the United States and the Soviet Union in the post–World War II era.

Jargon, in the sense that it is associated with a technical vocabulary, may under special circumstances serve rather unique functions. One of these is helping the author, especially in totalitarian orders, to achieve a degree of immunity from governmental strictures. Although it is easy to overdramatize this pattern, it does play a role. Persons in positions of authority are more likely to permit the publication of controversial materials directed to a specialized audience than writings which, having a mass appeal, may spread discontent.

Other norms relate to when, where, what, and how to footnote. It is generally assumed that scientists should acknowledge their sources of ideas and data. There are several reasons for this aside from maintaining continuity within a discipline. Footnoting is a screening device whereby the author indicates for the benefit of the reader what he considers to be worthy of attention. A common criticism of the popularizer is that the latter tends to ignore the contributions of other persons, particularly specialists.

Proper footnoting is also a convenient shorthand device for noting important but peripheral arguments. Without it the author might have to digress from his central theme and consume precious space merely to mention the existence of alternative views. Moreover, footnotes provide a basis for evaluating the worth of the author's contribution. They reveal his tastes as well as the schools of thought upon which he relies and those that he ignores. Footnotes make the scholar the way clothes make the man.

Although sociologists may agree that footnoting is desirable, many of the norms connected with it are ill-defined. They vary among subfields within a discipline and perhaps from one sociocultural system to the next. For example, to what extent should one recognize writers who have shaped one's thinking? More concretely, should one cite the person who first formulated the idea or later ones who brought it to fruition? We are inclined to favor citing the

[22] See, e.g., Sol Tax, " 'Primitive' Peoples," *Current Anthropology, 1* (September–November, 1960), 441. Also Lois Mednick, "Memorandum on the Use of *Primitive*," *ibid.*, 441–444. Cf. Catherine A. Berndt, "The Concept of Primitive," *Sociologus, 10* (1960), 50–69.

scholar who first clearly developed an idea, theory, or problem—although, as indicated by our footnoting, we have deviated from this norm on a number of occasions.[23]

Moreover, there is some danger in citing data obtained from secondary sources. This is especially true when one is dealing with factual data. Seligman has documented the use of "unknowable" statistics in popular and semipopular literature. For example,

> An article in *Barron's* . . . quoted the Wurlitzer company as having announced that "While music is a great art, it is also a $2-billion-a-year industry." . . . I wrote to the Wurlitzer people and asked them, politely, what they were talking about. A vice president reported, after several exchanges, that he had been unable to find out who issued the statement and was, in general, baffled by it.[24]

Seligman proceeds to criticize such writers as Frank Gibney, *The Operators*,[25] for reporting as fact "unknowable" statistics on the amount of money Americans dribble away on home repairs, on mail-order robbery, and the like. One important function of footnoting original sources is to permit the reader to double-check specific facts.[26]

And just how much should one footnote? Social scientists express a variety of opinions on this score, although generally they would agree in censuring the lack of footnotes where these seem required or, at the other extreme, obvious padding with irrelevant sources. Indeed, one has cause to wonder whether certain writers ever check some of the sources they cite. There is the famous "ghost book," a book on world urbanization by Kingsley Davis and Hilda Hertz which was advertised as forthcoming but was not published.[27] This supposed publication has been cited by several sociologists—with the specific date of publication supplied.[28] More generally, the increasing pressures for space in many

[23] We have attempted to follow several general norms (or rules) in our footnoting procedures. For example, we have sought to provide supporting evidence for our main generalizations and to indicate the range of materials consulted, both within and outside the sociological mainstream.

[24] Daniel Seligman, "We're Drowning in Phony Statistics," *Fortune, 64* (November, 1961), 146.

[25] Frank Gibney, *The Operators* (New York: Harper & Row, 1960).

[26] Cf. Larry Reynolds, "A Note on the Perpetuation of a 'Scientific' Fiction," *Sociometry, 29* (March, 1966), 85–88.

[27] Note the advertisement for the "book" ("Ready 1955") by Kingsley Davis and Hilda Hertz, *Pattern of World Urbanization*, in the *American Sociological Review, 19* (December, 1954), inside back cover.

[28] See, e.g., Alvin Boskoff, "Social Change: Major Problems in the Emergence of Theoretical and Research Foci," in Howard Becker and Alvin Boskoff (eds.), *Modern Sociological Theory in Continuity and Change* (New York: Holt, Rinehart and Winston, 1957), 271, ftn. 19.

scholarly journals will force social scientists to reexamine the norms that govern present footnoting practices.

In the end, the issues of jargon and footnoting are intimately related to style. Ultimately their use must be judged in terms of their value in maximizing communication. Those who ignore the need for clarity of expression fail to realize that a cumbersome style (including the excessive use of jargon and footnotes) often reflects the author's muddled thinking.

SOCIAL STRICTURES UPON RESEARCH REPORTING

The ideal norms of science presume that the scientist can freely communicate his theories and his data. But every writer functions within a social environment that limits his freedom of expression.

Just as when he first selects his projects, so too when he writes up his results the researcher generally must be sensitive to some reference group within science.[29] And when he endeavors to please one school of thought, he may encounter opposition from competing ones. More compelling are the extra-scientific pressures upon the scientist. Friendship circles, which may provide structural support for the scientific reference group, are often a subtle form of social control. Some scholars write with the specific intent of pleasing certain of their personal acquaintances. On the other hand, there are those who, like art critics and news analysts,[30] become highly selective in their personal acquaintance-ship in order to free themselves from obligations to offer special encomiums or withhold criticisms.

Most powerful of the strictures upon the author are the political ones. Often these stem from agencies that have supplied money for the researcher's investigations. Especially significant are the controls emanating from the national political system. The effect of these controls even in the United States and most Western democracies cannot be ignored.[31] In more closed societies, the prohibitions upon research may preclude any thought of publication. However, some of these closed systems permit scholars to explore selected social issues and amass relevant data but inhibit the publication of certain types of findings.

[29] W. Richard Scott, "Review of Amitai Etzioni (ed.), *Complex Organizations: A Sociological Reader* (New York: Holt, Rinehart and Winston, 1961)," *American Journal of Sociology,* 67 (November, 1961), 354–355. Scott contends that "all the authors represented are now or have been closely associated with the editor's home institution" (355). Cf. the subsequent "Letter to the Editor" by Etzioni and "Rejoinder" by Scott, *American Journal of Sociology,* 67 (March, 1962), 579.

[30] In an interview with Andrew J. Glass, Walter Lippmann contended that cronyism was the bane of modern journalism: *Washington Post,* Dec. 30, 1966, 1 f.

[31] The closer scholars come to discussing major power issues of the day the more likely is the matter of censorship to be a variable. Consider the views of Bernard B. Fall, formerly a professor of government at Howard University, who, in the course of reviewing two books, commented upon the problems of censorship when writing about the Vietnam War. *New York Times Book Review,* May 16, 1965, 3 f.

This pattern was not unknown in Poland in the late 1950s, when, after the "thaw," some research was reported upon verbally but not in print.

In some relatively closed societies, the ruling element, by permitting researchers a degree of freedom, profits from information that it could not uncover by itself. What is here viewed as politically dangerous is the dissemination of certain kinds of knowledge to the mass public.

Still, even in these societies scholars may employ various techniques that permit them to circumvent the norms that limit publication. One is, as we earlier reported, the use of a jargon that can be understood only by a few experts. Another is the studied apologia. Such a device has a long history. Copernicus attempted to justify his work in terms of certain values held by the Church—he seems to have dedicated his famous study to the Pope in order to blunt any counterattack.[32] In recent decades Russian social scientists have often devoted considerable space to defending and elaborating upon the Marxist-Leninist line—and attacking the capitalist system. Then, having expressed their loyalty, they may continue in a more scientific vein. Some Russian works on archeology, for example, have presented, after the introductory affirmations of faith, rather objective accounts of the relevant data and analysis thereof.

What of the American scene? Social scientists, when reporting their findings, usually take cognizance of various formal and informal political strictures. The existence of legal norms inhibiting the scientist's actions, including libel laws, cannot be gainsaid.[33] However, the impact of these is relatively mild. Social scientists in the United States can, with considerable impunity, criticize and evaluate public functionaries.

It is the informal norms that generate more severe tensions for the writer. Those who comment on sensitive subjects tend to cast a wary eye at national, state, and local politicians. The McCarthy era, particularly, left a mark upon many American social scientists. They became more cautious, and as a result more frequently employed apologias or reassertions of allegiance to the system and its values.

Still more sensitive to these political pressures are university administrators, especially where faculty members' publications may undermine present or future financial support for the university. Although most researchers manage to weed out the "dangerous" topics in the early stages of project selection, and although controversial writings are not always censored, meaningful strictures are present in Western democracies (including the United States) and these need to be carefully investigated. Nor can we assume that censorship occurs only in the

[32] Angus Armitage, *The World of Copernicus* (New York: New American Library, Signet, 1951).

[33] See, e.g., Robert H. Phelps and E. Douglas Hamilton, *Libel: Rights, Risks, and Responsibilities* (New York: Macmillan, 1966). A crossnational study of the impact of the legal system upon research reporting is badly needed.

less prestigeful academic centers. Even at relatively high-status universities certain completed manuscripts (or sections thereof) by faculty members have never been published because the press, the author, or university were fearful of endangering public support. Thus one author we know was forced to delete an entire chapter from his manuscript because a certain power group (ironically, one avowedly committed to the ideal of freedom of expression) objected to his materials.

Of course, persons working for governmental or business bureaucracies are subject to potentially still greater sanctions. The federal government may simply "classify" data on certain subjects concerned with the "national interest"— notably military or security matters—and thereby remove materials from general circulation.

Yet we must not overemphasize the restrictions upon publishing in democratically oriented societies. A person can publish "radical" materials if he is willing to pay the "price"—if he is willing to accept severe criticism and possible diminution in social position or career opportunities. But if the truly controversial author achieves a degree of societal support, he may enjoy considerable immunity from pressures to conformity. Even in rather closed societies, some persons have gained a degree of freedom (relatively speaking) by acquiring an international reputation, as witness Milovan Djilas in Yugoslavia.

THE ETHICS OF RESEARCH REPORTING

Various ethical norms also structure the reporting of one's results. Three aspects of this issue command our attention: the scientist's commitments to his subjects of study, his commitments to the broader society, and his commitments to his fellow scientists.

He who wields the pen wields power in a social order, and power begets responsibility. Authors surely have an ethical responsibility to their informants. But here dilemmas emerge.[34] Should the anonymity of respondents always be maintained? If so, by what means? The answer to this, of course, seems to be "It all depends." At times protection of the informant's identity is mandatory; in other situations it is quite unnecessary; and in still other circumstances the scientist may never know what is fair and just.[35]

[34] For a highly perceptive analysis of the dilemmas involved in the identification of the researcher's informants, as well as useful data in the form of correspondence between author and editor, see Richard Colvard, "Interaction and Identification in Reporting Field Research: A Critical Reconsideration of Protective Procedures," in Gideon Sjoberg (ed.), *Ethics, Politics, and Social Research* (Cambridge, Mass.: Schenkman, 1967), chap. 14. Cf. Howard S. Becker, "Problems in the Publication of Field Studies," in Arthur Vidich *et al.* (eds.), *Reflections on Community Studies* (New York: Wiley, 1964), chap. 8.

[35] In the U.S.S.R. the persons interviewed in at least some social surveys have been identified. Surely this lack of anonymity is likely to inhibit certain kinds of social research efforts, for the information could be used against the informants by social control

In certain types of situations one need not concern himself with anonymity. One is obviously where informants willingly provide the scientist with data and *when they understand the consequences of their actions.* In modern democracies, scientists generally face few difficulties when writing about the public acts of public officials. Secrecy is not called for (except in extreme situations) when the information has already been diffused through the mass communication media or can be freely obtained from legislative hearings, court records, and so on. As a matter of fact, the social scientist is bound by the rules of the democratic order to treat openly what public officials say and do. Any effort to preserve the anonymity of those carrying out public functions may well run counter to the ideal norms of the society. Of course, materials gathered in informal, off-the-record conferences with public officials are usually treated confidentially.

Protecting one's key informants can be difficult. Nevertheless, when a researcher has promised to do so, he should strive to "cover up" the sources of his data. Otherwise, the legitimacy of scientific activity in the society could be impaired. Even when the scientist does not assure his informant of anonymity, he must consider the long-run, perhaps adverse, consequences of public exposure for persons who provide him with data. The informant with little education and with no knowledge of the nature and aims of social research may freely give his permission, yet have no inkling of the possible repercussions of his cooperating with the researcher.

Anthropologists when they study isolated preliterate tribes have been relatively free to provide specific details on persons who are identified explicitly. In so far as preliterates have little contact with literate orders, they are immune to the effects of diffusion of this knowledge. But once anthropologists come to examine tribal communities that are being integrated into industrializing societies or communities within modern societies, the ethical issues become more pronounced. Thus Pieris, a Ceylonese sociologist, has intimated that the disadvantaged peoples of the world should rise up against the intrusion of social scientists into their personal lives without proper protection for informants.[36]

There are, of course, several different ways of circumventing the strictures upon the reporting of research findings. One useful device is reporting one's results in statistical form. An informant's identity can readily be obscured unless

---

agencies. Social scientists thus find themselves in a situation where the right to privacy on the one hand inhibits social research yet on the other hand is a precondition for securing many kinds of valid data.

[36] Ralph Pieris, "A Sociologist's Reflections on an Anthropological Case Study," *Ceylon Journal of Historical and Social Studies,* 3 (July–December, 1960), 153. However, data from India indicate that Pieris' comments can not be accepted uncritically. A number of field workers have noted that Indian villagers generally do not want the name of their village disguised. See, e.g., T. N. Madan, "Political Pressures and Ethical Constraints upon Indian Sociologists," in Sjoberg, *op. cit.,* chap. 7.

very small groups are involved, and then special categories can be employed.

Still other kinds of compromise (or actual) norms have arisen as a result of the attempt to uphold two rather conflicting ideals: (1) reporting scientific data in detail and (2) protecting one's informants. The most widely accepted norm is: Be vague about where, when, and how a given event transpired and from whom information was obtained. Some sociologists and psychologists have gone so far as to endow persons with false identities. Hunter, for instance, gave fictitious names to all individuals and to all organizations in the community he studied.[37] Dollard "operated upon" some of his informants, turning men into women and vice versa.[38] So it has been with other researchers. The "composite case approach" is another technique for sustaining anonymity. Here the researcher throws together a number of cases and extracts what amounts to an ideal or constructed type.

Those who endow persons with false qualities, as did Hunter, justify this on the ground that they are interested in patterns or processes—not in specific content. And this is a rather persuasive argument. Yet it almost entirely obviates any direct replication of the findings.

Social scientists who study large-scale organizations at times find it extremely difficult to decide one way or another just what is the most adequate means of protecting their informants. Consider those cases where even considerable manipulation of the material fails to obscure the informant's identity, or where a slight tampering with the data may endanger the validity of one's analysis. For example, just how does one ensure the anonymity of the mayor of a community or the head of a bureaucratic agency? An author cannot examine the status and role of a prominent functionary without sooner or later revealing the latter's personal identity. One could refer to, say, "a leading city official," but this label would not confound those "in the know" who might wish to turn the published findings to their personal advantage.

Social scientists are not alone in facing dilemmas concerning the diffusion of information in an open society, and they can place themselves in better perspective by considering the experiences of others, particularly newsmen. The latter, at least in American society, are continually beset by contradictory demands relative to identification of their sources of information. As a result, special adjustments and compromises have been worked out. For example, although a reporter cannot directly utilize data obtained in off-the-record conferences with

---

[37] Floyd Hunter, *Community Power Structure* (Chapel Hill, N.C.: University of North Carolina Press, 1953), 11.

[38] John Dollard, *Caste and Class in a Southern Town,* 3rd ed. (Garden City, N.Y.: Doubleday, Anchor Books, 1957). "In reporting particular incidents the sex of the person giving a bit of information has been changed when this change was not important; marriage status and number of children and relatives have frequently been altered, always with care to preserve the correct impression." (30)

public officials, he can employ these materials as background for interpreting related matters. Similar procedures are at time followed, and could perhaps be more frequently employed, by students of large-scale organizations.

Prospective informants, of course, may too frequently attempt to keep interviews off the record. During the 1960 Presidential campaign in the United States, Nixon was taken to task by reporters for failing to take responsibility for his off-the-record comments. Social scientists, however, can hardly use such direct attacks against reluctant informants.

American newsmen, moreover, utilize *sub rosa* norms to circumvent non-quotable briefings. One approach has been to record the observations of those reporters who attended the interviews in question. Here there is no formal or direct violation of trust, but other ethical issues come to the fore.

Like newsmen, social scientists resort to various compromise norms to cope with the tensions between the norms of the scientific community calling for the dissemination of information and the norms of the broader society demanding protection of the individual and of his right to privacy. For example, in one case which came to our attention, the director of a research team apparently made an effort to prevent a certain publication from falling into the hands of members of the community under study. The implication was that the book contained data that would not only jeopardize further research in this community but also adversely affect some of the informants.

The aforementioned ethical problems inhere in the scientist's relationship with his informants and with the social system he is studying. However, the dissemination of data about a given subsystem may also have implications for elements within or outside the broader social order. Some social scientists have been so concerned about the possible impact of their research upon the broader social order that they have quailed at publishing their data. But nonaction also has ethical consequences. Reluctance to publish controversial data may place the social scientist alongside the defenders of the status quo.

One social scientist who studied land use in an underdeveloped country told us that he held back publication of his data because of the potential impact upon the governmental structure, which was avowedly conservative and closely aligned with the United States. But when the nation in question experienced a "revolution," the researcher felt free to publish his results, for their dissemination would no longer be "dangerous."

The practice of postponing publication finds its corollary among persons who have occupied governmental posts (especially in the United States). Some of these persons have specified that their papers are not to be made public until after their own death or after the key officeholders have retired. Immediate publication of highly controversial observations would lead to charges and countercharges. Thus, George C. Marshall, prior to his death, provided reporters and would-be historians with a mere sprinkling of data regarding his views on policy making during World War II. However, at least one person was favored with an off-the-record interview providing substantial information with the stipulation that this was not to be published while he, Marshall, was still alive.[39] The postponement of publication until officials (or former officials) could no longer be harmed is one means of ensuring the publication of materials, all the while protecting those most likely to be adversely affected by publicity.

A final ethical issue concerns the scientist's relationships, not merely with the broader society (including his informants) but also with his fellow scientists. Under this rubric we might include purposive misquotation of authors, questionable manipulation of data to meet heavy demands for publication, the omission of pertinent evidence, and so on. These are indeed highly delicate matters. Mere reference to them may be seen by some scholars as a threat to certain "sacred values" of the scientific enterprise. Nonetheless, the rumblings concerning the existence of such actions cannot be stilled.

Science has been the breeding ground for a few famous frauds that have long gone undetected. One reason for encouraging researchers to specify their procedures, open up their questionnaires for inspection by other qualified scientists, and so on, is to prevent just such unethical action.

Apart from outright fraud, which is rare, one hears of other questionable practices with respect to the writing up and publication of materials. One sociologist has indicated that ghost writers are at work, writing or rewriting books for "name" individuals.[40] Or, more frequently, it is alleged certain professors fail to credit their student assistants, who may have not only done the bulk of the research but also much of the actual writing up of the reports. Some sociologists, of course, argue that if the original idea is the scientist's, and he has the money to purchase students' time and skills, he is entitled to full credit for the results. But such a practice is highly questionable and perhaps should be censured. Although it does not involve distorting the data, it undermines confidence in scientific activity and creates a climate of distrust. Certainly as much creativity and skill may be required to work out the implications of an idea as to formulate it in the first instance.

Among the gravest ethical problems in publishing that the social scientist faces, arising from the complex international power struggles in the modern world, are the conflicting demands between one's political system and one's rela-

---

[39] See, e.g., John P. Sutherland, "The Story Gen. Marshall Told Me," *U.S. News and World Report,* 47 (Nov. 2, 1959), 50. Of course, the question of when an ex-government official should speak and how much he should reveal has been the subject of widespread discussion in the United States. See, e.g., Adolf A. Berle and Malcolm Moos, "The Need to Know and the Right to Tell: Emmet John Hughes, *The Ordeal of Power*—A Discussion," *Political Science Quarterly,* 79 (June, 1964), 161–183.

[40] See, e.g., Joseph S. Roucek, "13. Memoir of an Inveterate Writer," *Prod, 1* (March, 1958), 33–36. This account is admittedly written from a nonestablishment perspective.

tions with fellow scientists. One such challenging ethical dilemma was aired in the journal *Encounter*.[41] Robert Redfield and his wife had, just prior to the Communist victory in China during the late 1940s, spent some time there and had obtained from the anthropologist Fei a manuscript of what was later published as *China's Gentry*. This book consists of a number of earlier articles by Fei that Mrs. Redfield had translated into English with Fei's assistance. Upon her return to the United States she decided to publish these materials in book form under Fei's name, for this apparently was his wish at the time of the Redfields' visit to China. To avoid embarrassing Fei, who was then living under a Communist regime, Mrs. Redfield did not seek his formal permission for publication after their return to the United States. Later, however, strong objections were voiced by Fei, who insisted that he had in the meantime changed his views about many facets of the Chinese social order and that if he had been asked in 1953 he would not have acceded to publication of this work. This case, complicated as it is by shifting ideological tides of the most violent sort, illustrates a pattern that is likely to be oft repeated in the decades to come. The manner in which the individual scientist resolves this kind of ethical crisis will depend largely upon his role commitment—whether he is dedicated to science or to the broader society.

Publishing the Findings

Journals, book publishers, and other media that serve the scientific community usually have an editorial panel at the helm comprised, ideally, of prestigeful scholars whose task it is to judge manuscripts in terms of their contribution to knowledge or, as in the case of commercial publishers, in terms of their potential monetary return.

Formally printed materials are, on the whole, more meaningful, prestigeful, and more convenient than those in typescript or in mimeographed or microfilmed form. Still, certain status distinctions are to be found among printed works. Some journals have higher prestige than others, often being viewed as more useful to the discipline. Sociologists would probably agree that among journals the *American Sociological Review*, the *American Journal of Sociology*, and *Social Forces* have in the past few decades ranked highest in American sociology. Also, certain book publishers exhibit higher status than others in particular fields. The "charity publishers," those who leave it to the author to pay the publishing costs, stand

[41] The material came to light as a result of a critical review of Hsiao-t'ung Fei's *China's Century* (Chicago: University of Chicago Press, 1953) by Karl A. Wittfogel in *Encounter*, 4 (January, 1955), 78–80, and the comments by Cedric Dover, William Empson, Wittfogel, and Robert Redfield in *Encounter*, 5 (August, 1955), 73–75, as well as those by Dover, Fei, Mrs. Robert Redfield, and Wittfogel, in *Encounter*, 6 (February, 1956), 67–70.

far lower in the hierarchy than those who absorb the financial risk. But even the latter fall into a rough rank order in terms of the quality and kinds of materials they publish. Those who print scholarly monographs seem to enjoy greater prestige than those who concentrate on textbooks.

A scientist places himself within the hierarchy of his own discipline in part according to the media in which he publishes. This extends beyond the scientific community, for many university administrators are roughly aware of the ranking of publication media within a discipline. However, the surging tide of new journals and of scholarly output in general is admittedly blurring many of the traditional status lines, with consequences for methodologists, as well as for administrators whose task it is to judge scientists.

But just what is it that imparts prestige to a particular journal or publishing house? The ability to reach a strategic audience is one criterion of status. This is related to a journal's ability to command a powerful editorial staff with a reputation for competence in evaluating manuscripts. Also, the ability to attract articles by "established authorities" can be a decisive factor. Thus new journals aspiring to high status often solicit manuscripts from outstanding scholars or publish special symposia.

The actual contributions of editors and the effect of their policies upon the advancement of scientific knowledge are complex matters so far little understood. Certainly, scientific journals are a crucial link in the development and dissemination of knowledge. Above all, they are the prime screening mechanism through which the bulk of scientific writings must flow before they reach the consumer public. Theoretically, the editorial board's prime task is to sift out the dubious from the better-quality materials. The editor's impact is all the more potent when he seeks to further a given point of view—by, for example, inviting scholars with a given point of view to write special articles for the journal.

The editorial board, of course, functions in accordance with the norms, be they folkways or mores, of the scientific community and the broader society. Some of the informal norms are crucial for governing the kinds of articles that are accepted. For instance, it is generally not the practice to publish articles that report "failures" in social research or provide materials demonstrating that such and such hypotheses were not significant[42]—unless, of course, such negative findings disprove heretofore accepted hypotheses.

Unfortunately we know little or nothing about the long-range impact of the failure to publish findings upon social research. One wonders just how frequently researchers have repeated studies that others have discovered to be unfruitful. Some careful research on this methodological issue is sorely needed.

But to return to the editor. Ideally he removes the chaff, leaving the kernels

[42] See, e.g., Theodore D. Sterling, "Publication Decisions and their Possible Effects on Inferences Drawn from Tests of Significance—or Vice Versa," *Journal of the American Statistical Association, 54* (March, 1959), 30–34.

of knowledge for scholars to savor. The process is far from perfected, however. At times editors find themselves sitting in judgment upon highly specialized manuscripts they are simply not equipped to evaluate. In certain instances they find themselves with too few norms to guide them, or they may face the need to search for compromises between contradictory norms.

One of the ambiguities of the editor's role concerns his stands on matters of conservatism or deviation. Should he stress the sheer codification of current knowledge, or should he encourage instead more creative or highly speculative ventures? In practice, it is easier for editors to evaluate essentially conservative studies, for here the guide lines to what is "good" and "bad" in science are more clearly defined. Almost by definition, the deviant work is difficult to judge by current standards. Indeed, the author may be challenging these very standards. Under these circumstances, the best the editor can do is work out some reasonable compromise between the demand for conformity and that for creativity. Both are essential for the maintenance of a viable science.

The editor may also have to make some difficult decisions in the matter of style. Other things being equal, papers written in a clear and compelling style stand a better chance of publication than those that require extensive editing. But what if the argument is potentially important but poorly stated? How far should an editor go in rewriting or suggesting revisions? In certain extreme cases the author ends up as author in name only. On the other hand, if the ideal is the dissemination of knowledge, some compromise here seems in order.

Another question that emerges is whether the editor should impose his own viewpoint on the journal or accept a variety of articles, including those that run counter to his image of what is sound social science. There is a tendency, or so it would seem, for the first-named course to predominate. Thus the practices of such editors as Faris, Page, Smelser, and Ryder of the *American Sociological Review* seem, at least on an impressionistic basis, to reflect their differing sociological orientations. But we need some careful work in this area. For one thing, we do not know the kinds of articles that were turned down, nor do we know whether certain kinds of articles were submitted because at the time the editorial policy was slanted in their favor. For the aspiring author often takes editorial policy into account when deciding where to send a manuscript.

At times editors seem to bend universalistic criteria perceptibly in response to extrascientific pressures. In order to sustain their readership they must seek a balance in the kinds of articles they accept. This is a special source of concern for journals that attempt to cater to the needs of an entire discipline. One editor of the *American Anthropologist* stated that such fields as archeology, culture history, and linguistics were not being adequately represented in the manuscripts he received, whereas social anthropology was overrepresented.[43] In such a situation an

---

[43] "Official Reports . . . Remarks by the Incoming Editor, Edward H. Spicer," *American Anthropologist*, 62 (June, 1960), 519.

editor may have to accept lower quality manuscripts in a subfield in order to maintain a "balance." Still another factor that may sway the editor's judgment is the author's particular regional or university ties. Nevertheless, many editors seek contributions from more than a limited region or a restricted set of schools— in part to ensure a wider readership and thus financial solvency for the journal.

The aspiring author should recognize that the aforementioned extrascientific criteria do influence the acceptance of manuscripts and thus tend to distort the ideal norms. Moreover, authors, particularly those who are seeking to propagate "deviant" ideas, should bear in mind that a manuscript usually is evaluated by a board that includes at most three or four referees. These men are not likely to represent a cross-section of views within the author's field, nor, as we have implied above, do editors necessarily possess the detailed knowledge necessary for evaluating a manuscript and its possible import for a particular specialty.

The generally small size of the editorial board inevitably affects the acceptance or rejection of manuscripts. The experience of a professor of Romance languages is worth citing; it illumines some of the patterns that prevail and is instructive for all who aspire to publish. The professor in question sent a manuscript of a book to three publishers, all of whom rejected it. One of the editors even made somewhat sarcastic comments on the work. Discouraged by these failures, the writer shelved his would-be text. Some time afterward, a representative of a publishing house entered his office and asked whether he had a manuscript in process or was planning to write one. The professor dusted off the thrice-rejected manuscript and handed it over. And just as in a Hollywood movie, the company published it, and the book came to have a sizeable sale.[44] The moral: editors, like all human beings, are far from infallible in their judgments.

Despite the advice of some editors, the author should not necessarily take no for an answer or become unduly disheartened by a few rejection slips.

PUBLISHING TECHNICAL DATA

A special problem with methodological consequences for social science is the difficulty of getting published, especially in book form, highly technical scientific data. Granted, the author can distribute this kind of material through simple duplicating methods. However, the audience reached thereby tends to be small, and the researcher will attain little international recognition from such forms of publication. Mimeographed volumes, for example, are seldom if ever reviewed in the major journals.

Even university presses at least in the United States, as outlets for highly technical materials, find relatively little room for the manuscript of clearly scholarly merit that cannot count upon at least a modest sale. Here, then, is a social condition that discourages some researchers from reporting on highly

---

[44] L. Clark Keating, "Pitfalls of Publication," *AAUP Bulletin, 45* (June, 1959), 245–246.

specialized topics and makes even the specialist sensitive to the need for a broader audience.

The publication of technical information presents other problems. As financial and space restrictions force authors to summarize their findings in succinct fashion, not just in normal articles but also in books, the question arises: What happens to the raw data or the analyzed materials that formed the basis of the published conclusions? Some authors make an effort to duplicate the data for distribution to interested persons. Unfortunately, many informal materials are not deposited in libraries. On the other hand, efforts are underway to create repositories for these kinds of data, particularly for materials in the areas of public opinion polling, demography, and the like.[45]

The methodological implications of the inaccessibility of pertinent materials have been made clear by Hoselitz in his review of the published findings of certain social surveys of cities in India. His complaint was that each of the authors utilized somewhat different categories in analyzing their findings on housing conditions, migration patterns, and so on. Consequently Hoselitz could only make certain crude comparisons. Were the original data, or more breakdowns, available, it would be possible for scholars, through reanalysis, to achieve more satisfactory results.[46]

The Impact and Use of Published Materials

If the prepublication stage has pitfalls for authors, the postpublication period can present still greater difficulties. The work may be completely ignored; or if it is cited, the main points may be overlooked and insignificant findings stressed. Occasionally a publication becomes so controversial that the author feels compelled to write a defense of his own views. Some scholars spend most of their lives justifying their earlier efforts.

In the end, the process of social selection takes its toll. Relatively few works are salvaged as "true contributions to knowledge"—as having had a major impact upon the thinking of a discipline. Most authors can only take solace in the fact that they are at least shaping the bricks of knowledge with which future scholars can construct a lasting edifice.

A variety of factors within science and the broader society lead to a publication's apparent success or failure. Regrettably little research has gone into this

[45] See, e.g., Philip E. Converse, "The Availability and Quality of Sample Survey Data in Archives within the United States," in Richard L. Merritt and Stein Rokkan, *Comparing Nations* (New Haven: Yale, 1966), chap. 19, as well as certain other chapters in this volume.

[46] Bert F. Hoselitz, "Indian Cities: The Surveys of Calcutta, Kanpur and Jamshedpur," *Economic Weekly, 13* (July, 1961), 1071–1078.

matter, and at this stage we can offer only a few speculative hypotheses. If one checks, even superficially, through the history of science, he discovers that not all who receive acclaim during their lifetime withstand the sterner test of history. Contrariwise, some persons' efforts are ignored by their own generation, for political or other social reasons, only to be acclaimed in some later period. Actually, some sociologists who are widely acknowledged as leaders today will leave scarcely a mark upon the history of ideas, for their current prestige rests not upon their scholarly productivity but upon their formal bureaucratic roles.

Although it is difficult to isolate the variables that determine a particular study's reception, the following patterns can be discussed. First, an article published in a major journal is more likely to be cited and widely disseminated than one that appears in a small, off-beat publication or in some form privately distributed by the author. The same holds for books. Those published and distributed by prestige houses are more likely to be given a hearing than works sponsored by charity publishers. If nothing else, the high-status publishing houses are more likely to have their materials reviewed in leading scholarly and mass media publications, which in turn attract attention to a study. On occasion a review may in fact become crucial to the study's distribution. For example, Edmund Wilson's review of Nomad's book on revolution in the *New Yorker* undoubtedly led to the reprinting of this work.[47]

The controversial nature of a study, either in terms of its strategic role in science or in terms of the broader social order, can play a part in its success or failure. That controversy helps to popularize a study has been demonstrated by Hannah Arendt's book on Eichmann, which has been subjected to extreme praise and extreme condemnation.[48] Another work that gained an unusual degree of publicity because of its controversial nature is Gellner's *Words and Things*.[49] The author, a sociologist, wrote a highly critical account of the linguistic school of British philosophy, a piece of writing so personal that the editor of the journal *Mind* refused to permit the book to be reviewed therein. But the resultant publicity in the *Times*, which carried letters pro and con on this censorship, more than offset the efforts to suppress the review of this work.[50]

The impact of a publication is also related to the author's position within the associational system that supports scientific activity. A person who is a member of an influential "sociometric circle" is more likely to have his work read than

[47] Max Nomad, *Aspects of Revolt* (New York: Noonday Press, 1961). This edition includes the revised review essay by Edmund Wilson which originally appeared in the *New Yorker.*

[48] Hannah Arendt, *Eichmann in Jerusalem,* rev. ed. (New York: Viking, Compass Books, 1965).

[49] Ernest Gellner, *Words and Things* (London: Gollancz, 1959).

[50] An entertaining account of this intellectual controversy is provided by Ved Mehta, *Fly and the Fly-Bottle* (Boston: Little, Brown, 1962).

one who is not. We can hardly ignore the influence that a scholar's former students may exert in his behalf. An ex-student may require his students to read his former mentor's work, or, as has occurred, an ex-student will write a review of his mentor's work.

This is related to perhaps the most crucial variable of all in any assessment of the impact of a scientific study: the relationship of the study's theory and findings to the ideology and power structure of the scientific community and the broader society.[51] As mentioned earlier, the popularity of Riesman's *The Lonely Crowd* can be attributed to its link with the climate of the times. Such was the case with Sumner's writings in an earlier era: His stress upon Social Darwinism and competition fitted neatly into the prevailing societal ideology.

The suppression of social science writings by various governments has a rather long history. Less transparent has been the role of the power structure within science. Here we shall go outside social science for our illustrative material.

The *American Behavioral Scientist* published an informative special issue on the patterns of acceptance and rejection by natural scientists of Velikovsky's *Worlds in Collision*.[52] This work, published in 1950, brought on a heated reaction from natural scientists: "Newspapers around the country were barraged with abusive reviews contributed by big-name scientists; some of these writings were syndicated to ensure better coverage."[53] Some scientists, such as the astronomer H. Shapley, spoke of Velikovsky as a fraud. And a critical examination of a number of reviews indicates that most of them were less than fair.

More serious were the attempts to suppress Velikovsky's effort. De Grazia writes:

> The suppression or influencing of professional opinion in the Velikovsky case occurred in the following ways: . . . (C) By seeking recantations. Shapley asked his colleague at Harvard, Dr. Robert H. Pfeiffer, to confirm the genuineness of his statements supporting Velikovsky's *Ages in Chaos*: Pfeiffer, Lecturer in Semitic Languages, did so. Atwater was asked by Professor Otto Struve in a menacing letter to reconsider and perhaps clarify his favorable disposition toward Velikovsky.

---

[51] For material relevant to a study within contemporary sociology, see Leonard D Cain, Jr., "The AMA and the Gerontologists: Uses and Abuses of 'A Profile of the Aging: U.S.A.'" in Sjoberg, *op. cit.*, chap. 4. History is filled with many instances of ideology or power relationships within the scientific community which have played a role in the acceptance of a scholar's ideas. The case of Freud is a notable illustration. See, e.g., Marthe Robert, *The Psychoanalytic Revolution*, trans. by Kenneth Morgan (New York: Harcourt, Brace & World, 1966), chap. 12.

[52] *American Behavioral Scientist*, 7 (September, 1963).

[53] Ralph E. Juergens, "Minds in Chaos: A Recital of the Velikovsky Story," *op. cit.*, 9.

At an AAAS meeting called especially to deal with problems of publishing ethics growing out of the failure to suppress completely the Velikovsky book, the Macmillan company was permitted to recant and state a safe position. . . . (D) By depriving opposing persons of positions. Their support of Velikovsky's right to be heard and/or of his theories appears to have played a significant part in the forced resignation of Gordon Atwater, Chairman of the Astronomy Department of the American Museum of Natural History and Curator of the Hayden Planetarium, and of James Putnam, a Macmillan editor for 26 years. The converse, promoting the useful allies, is found in Lafleur, . . . [who] reported that he had been appointed to a new university and promoted to a departmental chairmanship following his article on Velikovsky.[54]

Fortunately a few natural scientists have given Velikovsky a hearing, and noted that his predictions have been surprisingly accurate (though he is not often given credit for his successes).

The marked deviation from the ideal norm of free and rational debate that characterizes the Velikovsky case invites certain theoretical conclusions. Certainly we must recognize that on occasion it is rather difficult to distinguish between the "crackpots" and the truly creative scientists. This situation highlights the need for pluralism, for some means of dealing with divergent and "heretical" ideas in a rational, unemotional, manner.

The Velikovsky case also brings us back to a theme that appears again and again in the present volume: the constant struggle to balance off the need for sound, tested knowledge against the need for new and "deviant" ideas in science. It may be, as Polanyi suggests, that in some respects science, like other social systems, must remain somewhat conservative and must force scientists who champion new ideas to prove their case.[55] At the same time, such a position should not become a bastion for the defense of orthodoxy.

The Burgeoning of Publications

Another variable to be taken into account by one who seeks to assess the impact of given research publications is the vast outpouring of materials from scientists throughout the world.

A few ultranationalistic sociologists in the United States still assume that all good scholarship ends at the American shoreline. They disregard the vast body of literature (some good, some mediocre) that is emerging in societies that only a

[54] Alfred de Grazia, "The Scientific Reception System and Dr. Velikovsky," *op. cit.*, 60.

[55] Michael Polanyi, *Personal Knowledge* (Chicago: University of Chicago Press, 1958).

few generations ago had few if any trained social scientists. As industrialization proceeds, publication of scientific materials not only is facilitated in both a technological and an economic sense but becomes mandatory as well.

Social scientists might consider the situation in the natural sciences for an indication of what lies ahead. For the field of biology, one writer estimated that in 1958 there were at least 30,000 journals publishing original biological research papers—1½ million articles per year.[56] Or reflect upon Oppenheimer's comments for the field of physics: "I have a friend who calculated of one journal, an American journal for fundamental physics, that if it continued to grow as rapidly as it has between 1945 and 1960, it would weigh more than the earth during the next century."[57] Or consider sociology. In 1920 there were three sociological (and allied) journals in the English language, in 1940 about 11; but by 1960 the number had risen to 34.[58] Even this understates the proliferation of sociological literature. Many articles of significance to sociologists appear in social science journals in a number of other fields, in magazines written for the general public, in newspapers, and so on.

Already libraries are awash with materials, and the worst is yet to come. Scientists are beginning to recognize the impossibility of keeping pace with the growing number of publications that are spewing forth. Still, some social scientists, sociologists especially, fail to appreciate, much less study, the impact of this mass production process for the normative structure of science, including the methodology of social research. We offer here a few tentative hypotheses.

One result will be, in Sorokin's terminology, more and more Columbuses rediscovering ideas put forth in some earlier era. And progress will be slowed in other ways.[59] Sociologists are particularly prone, when designing their research or drawing conclusions from their own data, to utilize the findings contained in only a few major journals. In human ecology, for instance, a vast outpouring of articles and books is occurring with few if any efforts to relate the findings to one another. In this area the European literature alone has already reached major proportions. Yet no single article or book has sought to synthesize these data on human ecology.

The tendency to overlook significant sources is revealed in still other ways.

---

[56] Charles P. Bourne, "The World's Technical Journal Literature: An Estimate of Volume, Origin, Language, Field, Indexing, and Abstracting," *American Documentation,* 13 (April, 1962), 165.

[57] J. Robert Oppenheimer, "Reflections on Science and Culture," *Colorado Quarterly, 10* (Autumn, 1961), 107.

[58] Leo P. Chall, "Documentation and Diffusion of Information in Sociology," *Proceedings of the Southwestern Sociological Association,* vol. 13, Apr. 11–13, 1963, San Antonio, Texas, 29–42.

[59] Pitirim A. Sorokin, *Fads and Foibles in Modern Sociology and Related Sciences* (Chicago: Regnery, 1956), chap. 1.

We have only to examine the writings of social scientists on India to observe how infrequently newspaper materials are cited. Admittedly these data, collected by nonscientists, are uneven in their reliability and validity; nevertheless the Indian newspapers, some of the most important of which are printed in English, carry factual accounts of Indian social life that appear nowhere else.[60]

Unfortunately some sociologists, especially certain staunch empiricists, define library research as nonresearch. But this view is self-defeating. It deprives the scientist of his audience and makes it impossible to build upon the past. More, rather than fewer, sociologists must utilize libraries if the mass of data being collected is to be put to use.

We also hypothesize that the publication revolution will result in more and more social scientists reading less and less outside their particular fields of specialization. Time itself is a factor here. And it is exceedingly difficult, if not impossible, for a specialist to evaluate publications appearing outside his area of competence, especially those in mimeograph and microfilm form that have not been subjected to prior editorial scrutiny.

A high degree of specialization both assists and hampers certain kinds of scientific progress. It does permit research in depth, but inasmuch as the social order cannot be neatly classified into discrete units, the tendency to overspecialize can hinder creative effort. The researcher is unable to see his technical area in perspective.

Then too, the mass production of literature is likely to intensify the existing strains between the generalizer and the specialist. We can expect more attention to be given to generalizing, or survey, articles. But in some cases the generalizer must rely upon summaries of data in specialized areas. Thus at the very time the generalist is needed to provide a synthesis, he has to cope with perhaps even sharper criticism by specialists because the generalist is further than ever removed from the primary sources.

This publication revolution, moreover, forces science (and scientists) to invest more current capital into sustaining links with past research than in supporting new research. This results in disagreement over the allocation of funds, over whether a sound body of knowledge or new ideas are to be given priority. Related to the problem of allocating funds is the burgeoning of new kinds of personnel who stand between the researcher and his public. These intermediaries include abstracters, translators, and certain types of librarians—all of whom help to disseminate the products of the scientist. Although the status and role of these persons within the scientific community is rather ambiguous, their impact upon science can be profound. Often they judge what is significant and what is not. For example, the abstracter, by selecting certain publications and ignoring others,

[60] For a critical evaluation of the materials available to the social scientist studying the bureaucratic system of a developing society, see Ralph Braibanti, *Research on the Bureaucracy of Pakistan* (Durham, N.C.: Duke, 1966).

wields certain controls over the diffusion of information. He may commit a scientist and his works to obscurity simply by failing to abstract the latter. Librarians also make decisions that directly affect social research. The larger libraries receive all maner of data, including offbeat magazines, mimeographed materials, and newspapers, and some of this must be discarded. It is the librarian, rather than the specialized scholar, who generally decides what will be kept and what will be thrown away.

As an instance, the current policies of librarians will affect future sociologists and historians interested in "popular culture," for librarians are prone to discard pulp magazines, although these are of strategic importance for analyzing certain cultural patterns. Writers of the future are likely to underestimate the role of popular culture in mid-twentieth–century America, simply because of particular views concerning what should be preserved. Of course, from the librarian's viewpoint, discarding such materials is understandable. They consume much space yet attract few readers.

Undoubtedly automation and bigger and better computers can resolve many problems of storage and information-retrieval. In time, census data from all societies will probably be easily stored and freely drawn upon by interested scholars. The same holds for the information gleaned in public opinion polls.

Yet, ironically, this kind of solution encourages publication on a much vaster scale. Already automation is making data more readily accessible to more scholars. But machines cannot as yet engage in discovery or form judgments. The ablest evaluator of publications for some time to come will be the scientist himself. Only he can select from given publications the "meaningful" data upon which scientific advance must rest. Often it is not what is included in a publication but rather what is omitted that may be theoretically significant. The inferences the scientist can draw from the lack of certain evidence may well outweigh the positive findings. No machine can fulfill this function.

Then too, who will decide what data are to be stored in computers?[61] Somewhere along the line, some persons must make critical evaluative judgments. Yet without question, machines, by taking over certain routine chores in research,

---

[61] Yet we must also be aware of the political and ethical implications of data storage. The idea of a data bank for the United States has generated heated controversy, for these materials could be used to control and manipulate people. See, e.g., Edgar S. Dunn, Jr., "The Idea of a National Data Center and the Issue of Personal Privacy," *American Statistician,* 21 (February, 1967) 21–27; *Computer Privacy,* Hearings Before the Subcommittee on Administrative Practice and Procedure of the Committee on the Judiciary, United States Senate, Mar. 14 and 15, 1967 (Washington, D.C.: GPO, 1967). For a discussion of the social and political issues regarding data storage on a more general level see Kenneth L. Karst, " 'The Files': Legal Controls over the Accuracy and Accessibility of Stored Personal Data," *Law and Contemporary Problems,* 31 (Spring, 1966), 342–376. Karst observes that almost every fact, however personal or sensitive, is known to someone else. Thus in discussing privacy, we must recognize that ordinarily we are interested not in total nondisclosure but in selective disclosure.

will enable scientists to concentrate upon the more challenging problems.

As one means of dealing with the avalanche of publications, scientists no doubt will delegate more responsibility for perusing publications to research assistants or secretaries. This may be a satisfactory arrangement where one's primary purpose is simply to collate information. But only the trained scientist has developed the sensitive feelers for spotting potentially significant information. Indeed, on a certain level of theory or when the data are presented in a jumbled manner, only a highly trained specialist may be able to interpret the material. Thus it requires a skilled Sinologist to abstract the key data on modern Chinese society from the mountain of propaganda being published by the Communists.

In the end the publication revolution will reshape the structure of scientific activity and the scientific community's very ideology. Although most of the pressures call for increasing the volume of publications, countervailing demands for more quality and less quantity are being felt. Editors in some quarters are being called upon to judge contributions more harshly. And a number of scientists have recently condemned the tendency of administrators to encourage publication for publication's sake and the multiplication in variant forms of the same idea.

More significantly, the rising flood of publications will have the effect of eroding certain features of the traditional ideology within science. Merton avers that for the scientist, making a name for himself has long been a prime motivation in the pursuit of knowledge. Yet in the sea of publications, the individual scientist's contribution tends to be obscured. Those who, like Lazarsfeld, justify modern public opinion polls on the grounds that the data collected thereby add to the fund of knowledge for the future must face up to the fact that tomorrow's historians and sociologists will simply be unable to utilize such an overwhelming mass of data. Then too, as space in journals becomes more acute, editors are likely to restrict the amount of footnoting, once again reducing the scientist's links with the past and, consequently, his commitment to the future. It will become increasingly difficult to sustain the view that today's accomplishments will be significant generations hence.

The publication revolution will likely reduce the stature of the individual social scientist, lending greater prestige to the bureaucratically oriented scientist whose status derives from his positions in the associations that support the scientific enterprise. Yet, scientific advance depends upon creative thought. Men with ideas will remain the fountainhead of the scientific movement—as the source of both controversy and inspiration.

Index of Names

Abegglen, James C., 105 n.
Abercrombie, M. L. Johnson, 35 n.
Abrams, Mark, 91 n.
Ackerman, Charles, 34 n., 63 n.
Adams, Ernest W., 276 n.
Adams, Richard N., 158 n.
Albert, Ethel M., 141 n.
Alcock, Norman Z., 114 n.
Allen, Ernest M., 109 n.
Alpert, Harry, 93 n.
Anderson, Alan Ross, 240 n.
Anderson, Henry, 119 n.
Angell, Robert, 258 n.
Ansari, M. A. Salam, 205 n.
Antoni, Carlo, 5 n.
Arendt, Hannah, 296 n., 337
Arensberg, Conrad M., 90 n.
Aristotle, 43, 49
Armitage, Angus, 326 n.
Aron, Raymond, 61 n., 134 n.
Arrow, Kenneth J., 241 n.
Asch, Solomon E., 218
Astin, Alexander W., 76 n.
Axelson, Leland J., 81 n.
Ayer, A. J., 7 n.

Back, Kurt W., 203 n., 205 n.
Backman, E. J., 231 n.
Bacon, Francis, 49, 54
Badenhorst, L. T., 209
Bailey, F. G., 229 n.
Bales, Robert F., 183–185
Banfield, Edward C., 174 n.
Banton, Michael, 31 n.
Barber, Bernard, 22 n., 78 n., 97 n.
Barron, Frank, 181 n.
Barton, Allen H., 34 n., 64 n., 231 n., 254 n.
Bates, Alan P., 101 n.
Bauer, Raymond A., 154 n., 265 n.
Beals, Ralph, 79 n.

Beasley, W. G., 19 n.
Bechtoldt, Harold P., 303 n.
Beck, Robert N., 6 n.
Becker, Howard, 98 n., 251–252, 324 n.
Becker, Howard S., 127 n., 168–169, 232 n., 244–245, 259 n., 305, 327 n.
Belknap, Ivan, 191 n.
Bell, Daniel, 308 n.
Bell, Wendell, 113, 254
Bello, Francis, 98 n.
Ben-David, Joseph, 21 n.
Bendix, Reinhard, 131 n., 132 n., 229 n., 234, 305
Benedict, Ruth, 318
Bennett, André, 82 n.
Bennett, John W., 172 n.
Bennigsen, A., 87 n.
Bensman, Joseph, 125–126
Benson, J. Kenneth, 117 n.
Berle, Adolf A., 331 n.
Berndt, Catherine A., 323 n.
Berreman, Gerald D., 175
Bettelheim, Bruno, 166 n.
Bierstedt, Robert, 102
Bjorksten, Johan, 111 n.
Black, Max, 60 n.
Blake, Robert R., 176–177
Blalock, Hubert M., Jr., 265–266, 277, 284
Blanché, Robert, 43 n., 48 n.
Blau, Peter M., 157, 221 n., 244, 247, 258 n., 286
Blood, Robert O., Jr., 149 n.
Bloom, Benjamin S., 308 n.
Blumer, Herbert, 6, 41, 59, 63, 322
Bocheński, I. M., 39–40, 46
Bogue, Donald J., 108 n., 274 n.
Boguslaw, Robert, 293 n.
Boole, G., 43
Boskoff, Alvin, 98 n., 230 n., 324 n.
Boulding, K. E., 114

Bourne, Charles P., 340 n.
Bracey, H. E., 206–207
Bradley, Omar Nelson, 163
Braibanti, Ralph, 341 n.
Braithwaite, R. B., 30 n.
Bramson, Leon, 9
Bressler, Marvin, 64 n., 319–320
Bridgman, P. W., 7, 68
Brodbeck, May, 31 n., 32, 294 n.
Bronfenbrenner, Urie, 125–128
Bronowski, J., 20 n.
Broom, Leonard, 198 n., 232 n., 269 n.
Brown, Bruce, 21 n.
Brown, Roger, 38 n.
Brown-Radcliffe, A. R., 105, 138
Bruner, J. S., 38
Bruyn, Severyn, 5 n.
Brymer, Richard A., 120 n., 265 n.
Bukharin, Nikolai, 60
Burgess, Ernest W., 108 n., 143, 258, 274 n.
Burke, Kenneth, 32–33
Butterfield, Herbert, 20 n.

Cahnman, Werner J., 230 n.
Cain, Leonard D, Jr., 232 n., 313 n., 338 n.
Camilleri, Santo F., 238
Campbell, Angus, 236
Campbell, Donald T., 141 n., 303 n.
Caplow, Theodore, 103 n.
Carnap, Rudolf, 294 n.
Carter, Launor F., 210 n.
Carter, Lewis, 277
Catton, William R., Jr., 9 n., 23 n., 59 n.
Cavan, Sherri, 176 n.
Centers, Richard, 197
Ceram, C. W., 166
Chall, Leo P., 340 n.
Chapin, F. Stuart, 301 n.
Chapman, Guy, 299 n.
Chisholm, Roderick M., 71 n.
Christensen, Harold T., 135 n.
Christie, George C., 40 n.
Churchman, C. West, 85 n.
Cicourel, Aaron V., 195 n., 269 n.
Clark, Alexander L., 232 n.
Clark, Burton R., 157
Clark, Cherry Ann, 278 n.
Classen, E., 231 n.
Cochran, William G., 155 n., 156 n.
Cohen, Albert, 228 n.
Cohen, Bernard C., 95 n.
Cohn, Bernard, 142
Cohn, Norman, 231 n.
Coleman, James S., 226, 240, 271, 276, 306 n., 322
Colvard, Richard, 109 n., 215–216, 326 n.

Comte, Auguste, 7, 85, 93
Conklin, Harold C., 169 n.
Converse, Philip E., 336 n.
Cook, Robert M., 106 n.
Cooley, Charles Horton, 5–6, 111, 167, 168, 234
Coombs, Clyde H., 196, 271
Coser, Lewis A., 88 n., 134 n., 178
Costner, Herbert L., 238 n.
Cressey, Donald R., 260, 228 n., 260–261
Crombie, A. C., 14 n.
Cronbach, Lee J., 303
Crossman, Richard, 181 n.
Culwick, G. M., 205 n.

Dalton, Melville, 119 n., 157, 221
D'Andrade, Roy Goodwin, 36 n.
Davis, James A., 107 n., 286
Davis, Kingsley, 136, 262–263, 324
Dean, Dwight G., 93 n.
Deininger, Whitaker T., 41 n.
Delany, William, 154 n.
De Morgan, A., 43
Descartes, R., 49
Deutsch, Karl W., 31 n.
Devons, Ely, 34 n.
Dewey, John, 6, 46
Diamond, Stanley, 61 n.
Dilthey, Wilhelm, 5, 6, 10, 289
DiRenzo, Gordon J., 34 n., 63 n., 303 n.
Djilas, Milovan, 327
Dollard, John, 258 n., 329
Dore, R. P., 139
Dornbusch, Sanford M., 292 n.
Douglas, Jack D., 192
Dray, William, 51 n., 291
Dukes, William F., 258 n.
Duncan, Otis Dudley, 33 n., 61, 68 n.
Dunn, Edgar S., Jr., 342 n.
Durkheim, Emile, 32, 76, 192, 232, 234, 264, 286

Edmonson, Munro, 205 n.
Edwards, Allen L., 272 n.
Eisenhower, Dwight D., 163
Ekman. Gösta, 273 n.
Ellis, Robert A., 158 n.
Epstein, A. L., 230
Epstein, Edward Jay, 299 n.
Erikson, Kai T., 177 n.
Etzioni, Amitai, 285 n., 325 n.
Evans–Pritchard, E. E., 218–219
Eysenck, H. J., 292 n.

Fagot, Robert F., 276 n.
Fall, Bernard B., 325 n.

Index of Subjects

Analogy, 246, 248
Analytic induction, 54, 67, 260–262
Associations, scientific, 76–80
Axiomatic method, 46–48, 67
    See also Deduction; Logico-deductive
    system

Bureaucracy, 86
  analysis of, 224–225
  and data collection, 188–189, 192–193
  departmental, 101–102
  difficulty of study, 119
  and direct observation, 163–164
  and measurement, 265, 309–310
  and research projects, 108–112
  and research reporting, 327
Bureaucratization of research, 92–95, 112

Cases: selection of, 144–145
  types and uses of, 259–264, 298
Causation, 27, 64, 295–298
  circular, 295
Coding, 274–275
Conceptualization in science, 35–38
Conclusions vs. decisions, 276–277
Construct validity, *see* Validity
Contextual analysis, *see* Properties
Creativity, 72, 82
  and observation, 180–182
  and project selection, 104, 106
Crosscultural analysis, 11, 71, 170–171, 228–231, 250, 298, 301–302, 331–332
  and project selection, 113–115
  and special universe, 134–135

Data, 32–33
  and theory, 33–38
Deduction, 49–52
  and induction, 50
  See also Axiomatic method; Logico-deductive system

Departments, academic, 98–103
Dialectic, logic of, 30, 44, 56, 172, 224, 247, 295, 313
  relation to formal logic, 44
Direct observation, 160–186
  and ethics, 177–179
  limitations of, 161–162
  types of, 160–161
Discovery, 35, 52–55
  and analytic induction, 262–263
  and induction, 54
  relation to logico-deductive system, 56–57
  and selection of special universe, 137
  and sensitive observer, 179–182
  and theory building, 244–246

Ecological correlation, 284–285
Editors, role of, 333–335
Ethics, 3, 74, 83
  and direct observation, 177–179
  and interviewing, 206, 210, 215–216, 221
  and prediction, 310–313
  and project selection, 120–128
  and research reporting, 327–332
  and sampling, 151
    See also Moralization and science
Event chronology, 209
Experimental design, 55, 141, 170–171, 278
  and observation, 176–177
Explanation, 31–32, 288–313
  and prediction, 289–290
  and understanding, 291–293
Exploratory research, 57
Extreme cases, 262–263

Fact, definition of, 32
Footnoting, 323–324
Freedom and social research, 117, 119–120

Group and individual, *see* Individual and group

353

6985 1

68   69   70   71   7   6   5   4   3   2